The Asbury Theological Seminary Series in Christian Revitalization

This volume is the first title in a new sub series of the Asbury Theological Seminary Series in Christian Revitalization, edited by Professor Laurence Wood. It joins five other sub series, and is published in collaboration with the Center for the Study of World Christian Revitalization Movements, a cooperative initiative of Asbury Theological Seminary faculty. Building on the work of the previous Wesleyan/Holiness Studies Center at the Seminary, the Center provides a focus for research in the Wesleyan Holiness and other related Christian renewal movements, including Pietism and Pentecostal movements, which have had a world impact. The research seeks to develop analytical models of these movements, including their biblical and theological assessment. Using an interdisciplinary approach, the Center bridges relevant discourses in several areas in order to gain insights for effective Christian mission globally. It recognizes the need for conducting research that combines insights from the history of evangelical renewal and revival movements with anthropological and religious studies literature on revitalization movements. It also networks with similar or related research and study centers around the world, in addition to sponsoring its own research projects.

Professor Edwards's study in "Spiritual Values and Evaluations" is offered as a superb treatment of spiritual values from an insightful theoretical perspective of how persons make decisions about the values they cherish. Being no moral reductionist, Edwards develops his discussion with a substantive engagement of core Christian beliefs, and the doctrines of the new birth and sanctification in Christ, in particular. His engagement of the theologies of Jonathan Edwards and John Wesley within this context opens the discussion of Christian revitalization – the focus of this study project – to a fresh engagement and meaningful reflection. As such, it is my privilege to commend this volume as the inaugural title in the new Revitalization Series in Systematic/Philosophical Studies.

J. Steven O'Malley, General Editor
The Asbury Theological Seminary Series in Christian Revitalization Studies

Sub-Series Foreword
Systematic/Philosophical Studies

This work is a remarkably clear presentation and lucid discussion of the relationship between the philosophical discipline of axiology and its religious significance. Without reducing religion to morals, Edwards employs the insights of Robert S. Hartman (his late colleague at the University of Tennessee) to explain the interaction between what we value and what we believe religiously. Axiology is the theory of understanding how people make decisions about the realities and values that they cherish. Usually these decisions are made more implicitly than explicitly. Edwards shows that developing a matured self-knowledge is vital for moral and spiritual growth. Edwards incorporates explicitly the spiritual dimensions of axiology, which has been treated inadequately or ignored by interpreters because they lacked the conceptual framework provided by Hartman. Focusing on what we value and coming to understand how we arrive at values form the essence of spirituality, which Edwards highlights throughout this highly readable and informed study. Typical of his insights is his carefully nuanced integration of rational impartiality and affective religious commitment. Edwards delineates the religious significance of distinguishing among extrinsic, systemic, and intrinsic values and shows that values cannot be dismissed as merely existential feelings or mere abstract notions. Rather, he relates this axiological study to the core beliefs of the Christian faith, highlighting that the new birth and sanctification move one from extrinsic to intrinsic values as we come to value everything and everyone as possessing intrinsic value. Drawing from the rich tradition of thinkers like Jonathan Edwards and John Wesley, the author develops an axiology of saintliness and its significance for our world today. The appendix in a book is often overlooked by most readers, but the appendix in this book is most interesting and informing. It provides an understanding of Robert S. Hartman's theory of value along with Edwards' clear explanation of the three kinds of value. This may well be the best and most comprehensive treatise on this subject ever written, and it has great relevance in today's world with its fact-value dichotomy where values and faith are often degraded as merely emotional.

Laurence W. Wood, PhD, Sub-series Editor
Frank Paul Morris Professor of Systematic Theology/Wesley Studies
Asbury Theological Seminary

SPIRITUAL VALUES AND EVALUATIONS

~ ~ ~ ~ ~

Rem B. Edwards

Asbury Theological Seminary Series:
The Study of World Christian Revitalization Movements in
Systematic/Philosophical Theology, No. 1

EMETH PRESS
www.emethpress.com

Spiritual Values and Evaluations

Copyright © 2012 Rem B. Edwards

Printed in the United States of America on acid-free paper
All rights reserved. No part of this book may be reproduced, or stored in a retrieval system or transmitted in any form or by any means, electronic, mechanical, photocopying, recording, scanning or otherwise, except as permitted by the 1976 United States Copyright Act, or with the prior written permission of Emeth Press. Requests for permission should be addressed to: Emeth Press, P. O. Box 23961, Lexington, KY 40523-3961.
http://www.emethpress.com.

Library of Congress Cataloging-in-Publication Data

Edwards, Rem Blanchard.
  Spiritual values and evaluations / Rem B. Edwards.
    p. cm. -- (The study of world Christian revitalization movements in systematic/philosophical theology ; no. 1)
  Includes bibliographical references (p.   ) and index.
  ISBN 978-1-60947-043-2 (alk. paper)
  1. Values. 2. Conduct of life. 3. Worldliness. 4. Ideology. 5. Spirituality. 6. Christian ethics. 7. Jewish ethics. I. Title.
  BJ1531.E38 2012
  204--dc23

2012026386

Front Cover

Dr. Rem B. Edwards grows cacti as a hobby and has one of the largest outdoor cactus gardens in the state of Tennessee. The photo on the front cover is of one of his favorites that bloomed recently. He believes the three blooms together might be viewed as having Trinitarian significance, but in this case they could stand for full spiritual maturation in all three value dimensions.

Dedication

To Louise

My dear wife, my guardian angel

Contents

Preface 11

Chapter One: Worldliness and Extrinsic/Worldly Religion 17
   Gaining the World, but Losing the Soul 19
   Defining Worldliness and Worldlings 20
      Worldliness as the "Natural Man and Woman" 25
      Worldly Values: Things 37
      Worldly Values: Other People and Social Status 40
      Society and Worldly Self-Knowledge 44
      Down to Earth Language 48
      The Cash Value of The Fine Arts 51
   Extrinsic/Worldly Religion 53
      Worldly Religion: Survival, Health, Prosperity, Social Position 54
      Worldly Religious Language and Concepts 61
         Worldly Other Worlds 66
         God and the Image of God 67
      Spiritual Strengths and Weaknesses of Religious Worldlings 71

Chapter Two: Ideology and Systemic/Ideological Religion 75
   Defining Ideology and Ideologists 76
      Ideological Language and Values: Conceptual Constructs 77
      Ideological Values: Ideas vs. Persons and Things 79
      Ideological Evaluation: Cognition, Feelings, and Actions 81
         Ideological Evaluation and Cognition 82
         Ideological Evaluation and Feelings 84
         Ideological Activity 85
      Confusing Ideology with Spirituality 91
   Systemic/Ideological Religion 95
      God and the Image of God 96

8   *Spiritual Values and Evaluations*

    All or Nothing Belief Systems 99
    Rules and Rituals 103
  Systemic, Extrinsic and Intrinsic Faith 105
    Systemic Faith and Belief 106
    Extrinsic Faith and Belief 108
    Intrinsic Faith and Belief 111
  Defining "Good Religion" 117
  Religious Concepts and Beliefs as Symbols 119

Chapter Three: Saintliness and Intrinsic/Saintly Religion 123
  Saintliness: Pure Intrinsic Evaluation, or Wholeness? 124
    Saintliness and Ideal Spiritual Self-realization 125
    A Critique of Purely Intrinsic Saintliness 128
  Defining Holistic Saintliness and Saints 134
    Saintly Values: Self and Others 136
    Saintly Evaluations: Feelings, Cognition, and Actions 141
    Saintly Values: Things and Status 144
      Our Natural Environment 147
      Renouncing It All 148
      Having It All 150
  The Scope of Saintly Evaluation 155
  The Language of Saintly Evaluation 161
    Saintly Spiritual Metaphors 165
    God and the Image of God 171
  Conclusion: Saintliness as Salvation 179

Chapter Four: Moving Up from the Dark Side 185
  Guilty Conscience 186
  Conversion and Self-reformation 192
  Deciding What Counts as Sinful 195
  New Birth and Sanctification 205
  Mixed Blessings 208
  Other-religious and Extra-religious Transformations 212
  Value Theory and Spiritual Personality Types 214

Appendix: Axiology, Self-knowledge, Values, and Evaluations 217
  Three Kinds of Value 218
    Extrinsic Values 219
    Systemic Values 221
    Intrinsic Values 222
  The Hierarchy of Value 224
  Three Kinds of Evaluation 231

    Extrinsic Evaluation 231
        Cognition and Extrinsic Evaluation 232
        Feelings and Extrinsic Evaluation 234
        Dynamics and Extrinsic Evaluation 236
    Systemic Evaluation 237
        Cognition and Systemic Evaluation 237
        Feelings and Systemic Evaluation 239
        Dynamics and Systemic Evaluation 241
    Intrinsic Evaluation 242
        Cognition and Intrinsic Evaluation 242
        Feelings and Intrinsic Evaluation 244
        Dynamics and Intrinsic Evaluation 246
    Systemic, Extrinsic, and Intrinsic Dimensions of Self 247
        The Systemic Self-dimension 248
        The Extrinsic Self-dimension 249
        The Intrinsic Inner Self-dimension 250
    Knowing and Valuing Our Uniqueness 253
    Knowing Our Limitations 255

Notes 259

Index 275

About the Author 283

Preface

In this book, "religious" and "spiritual" are treated as synonyms, as they often are in ordinary English. Some people restrict the meaning of "spiritual" to the realm of the highest religious values, but this book will show how every dimension of value and evaluation can be spiritualized. Others equate being spiritual with being moral, but this book rejects all attempts to reduce spirituality to morality. Not all moral people are spiritual. Moral values belong within spirituality, but that is not the whole of it. And spiritual values have real objects that are far more than our own valuing of them. Still others equate being spiritual with subscribing to an ideology or to some world view that will insure prosperity and success, but that doesn't quite get it either.

This book explores three easily recognized personality types of great spiritual significance, *worldliness, ideology, and saintliness*. These spiritual types are defined by the dominant values they manifest. The thoughts, experiences, actions, feelings, and overall characters and behaviors of people belonging to these types are shaped and expressed by what and how they value, as explained in the following chapters. A distinctive mode of spirituality is also correlated with each type, based on what and how religious people most value. What and how people value are the keys to everyone's personalities, whether spiritual or not. Real people do not fall neatly or completely into any one of these types, but in most of us some dimension of value is dominant over all others, and this has great spiritual significance.

Most religious thinkers have acknowledged through the ages that gaining self-knowledge is essential to anyone's spiritual quest. Learning to know ourselves involves getting to know what and how we value. Understanding the spirituality of others also involves learning what and how they value. This book shows how spirituality is structured by our values and evaluations, but it does not reduce religion to ethics or values alone.[1] It does not eliminate God or theology as such, and nothing said here should be so construed. Value theory should not block our path of inquiry or squelch our wonder and curiosity about God and divine things. This book does not illogically convert "God is love" into "Love is God." It takes the commandment to love God, which presupposes God's reality, with utmost seriousness. Love to God includes but is not identical with love to neighbors and cannot be reduced to it. In holistic saintly spirituality, loving and doing the works of love are paramount, and systemic doctrines are minimal but still very present and prominent. How do we grow spiritually and become saints, and what distorted values stand in the way? This book addresses such questions, along with many others.

Many philosophical and spiritual thinkers emphasized the importance of self-knowledge for moral and spiritual growth. Spiritual thinkers from St. Bonaventure, St. Ignatius Loyola, and Søren Kierkegaard to James W. Fowler have described various stages of ethico-religious growth and development, but they lacked a truly adequate systematic frame of reference for understanding and ordering their subject matter.

Values (what we value) and evaluations (how we value) constitute the hard core of religion or spirituality. We need a general frame of reference that orders and makes sense out of the things we value spiritually and out of how we evaluate them. For our purposes, Robert S. Hartman's theory of value, "Formal Axiology," will provide the previously missing valid systematic frame of reference. "Axiology" is "the general theory of value and evaluation." Hartman's extremely illuminating and helpful approach to it focuses on the general forms or patterns present in what and how we value. It identifies three kinds of goodness, intrinsic (good in itself), extrinsic (good as a means), and systemic (good as a symbol), and it ranks their relative goodness. Symbols are very good, real means to real ends are even better, and final ends are best.

This theory immensely illuminates the three abstract forms of personality and spirituality described in this book. When applied, the theory says that God and people (intrinsic goods) are more valuable than physical things, actions, and processes (extrinsic goods); and physical things are more valuable than the ideas and beliefs (systemic goods) that we have about them. Desirable realities are more valuable than our symbols for them. A good person is better than our idea of a good person. A good God is better than our idea of a good God. A good car is better than our idea of a good car. If you agree, then you will have no problem with the value theory employed in this book. This account of basic human values and their proper order or ranking seems so simple and obvious that it hardly deserves to be called a theory! Yet, if you take it to heart, it will both transform your life and help you to understand where you and other people are in your and their moral and spiritual development. Sometimes we can do quite amazing things with simple theories, as this book shows.

Of course, this theory can get a bit more complicated. Its bare essentials are explained at the beginning of Chapter One in a manner that is not difficult or burdensome. Then it is applied thereafter. The successful application of a theory is significant evidence of its validity, as any natural scientist will tell you. Hartman himself often said, "The proof of the pudding is in the eating."[2] Much later, in the Appendix at the end, the theory is explained and defended in much more depth; you may or may not want to read this Appendix. Logically, a detailed theoretical discussion should come first, but this is not always the best way to communicate effectively. Some readers might get so bogged down in the theory itself that they never get to the really good stuff—how it makes sense of different kinds of personality, their corresponding modes of spirituality, and their respective strengths and weaknesses.

Once you absorb this theory of value, you should be able to pick up any story with a plot, any theological or devotional publication, or any study in the psychology of religion, and be able to tell almost immediately what is going on, make sense of it, and assess its strengths and weaknesses. This axiological frame of reference makes literature, religion, spiritual writers, and studies in the psychology and philosophy of religion intelligible—as no other systematic frame of reference can.

The three personality types covered in the first three chapters are based on three dominant value orientations that spill over into spirituality. *Worldliness* (Chapter One) is a state of soul dominated by extrinsic values like material goods, possessions, physical activities, and social status. Worldly people identify most fully with doing, success, prosperity, and high social positions. They act accordingly and create prosperity gospels to support their reigning values. Systemic-minded *ideology* (Chapter Two) ranks mental, cognitive, or doctrinal values over all else. Ideologists identify themselves most fully with conceptual beliefs, doctrines, rules, symbols, and formalities. They think that true religion is believing the right doctrines, affirming the right words, and they condemn everyone who thinks or acts otherwise, everyone who does not agree with them. *Saintliness* (Chapter Three) is a state of soul in which devotion to intrinsic values (God and people) is supreme. Saints identify themselves with unique conscious beings, the more the better, all the way up to and including God. They evaluate them knowingly, lovingly, and compassionately, and they act and think accordingly. Their extrinsic and systemic values are subordinated to their intrinsic values. Worldly people overvalue mere things. Ideologists overvalue mere beliefs. Intrinsic saints may overvalue love and spiritual feelings, but holistic saints properly include and evaluate every kind of goodness. Chapter Four recognizes the dark, finite, and sinful side of all human beings and explores ways to move up or away from them with God's help.

All of us belong to the same species biologically, but we do not belong to the same species spiritually and morally. We differ greatly with respect to the kind, development, and intensification of our moral and spiritual consciousness. Through the centuries, spiritual thinkers made many fascinating and significant discoveries about our spiritual strengths and defects and our potentials for positive spiritual development. Value theory can make such claims much more orderly and intelligible.

Illustrative quotes from Christian and Jewish thinkers are presented at the beginning of each section and sub-section of this book. Editorial additions are indicated by brackets, [ ]. In addition to the Jewish and Christian writers of the Old and New

Testaments, relevant quotes are also given from St. Augustine, St. Thomas Aquinas, St. Anselm, Søren Kierkegaard, Jonathan Edwards, John Wesley, William James, Rabbi Harold S. Kushner, Rabbi Abraham J. Heschel, H. Richard Niebuhr, and many others. Robert S. Hartman's reflections on values are also well represented. Readers are encouraged to think carefully about the beginning quotes before moving on to the discussions that follow. Most illustrative materials are from Christian sources because the author is most familiar with that tradition. However, spirituality within any historical religion could be analyzed fruitfully in terms of the patterns of value and evaluation described in this book. You are encouraged to do this for your own, Christian or not; I have done it elsewhere for my own Wesleyan Christian tradition.[3]

This book also relates spiritual values to evolutionary psychology, sociobiology, attachment theory, and the psychology of religion. Evolutionary psychology and more recent work on brain imaging[4] make it academically respectable to talk and think again about our common and genetically transmitted *human nature* and the bearing that it has on both inhibiting and allowing for spiritual growth.

Our common human nature was formed during the hundred thousand or more years that our pre-historic ancestors lived and competed to survive and reproduce as hunter/gatherers. Their situation was the original "state of nature" or "Garden of Eden" dreamed of by philosophers and theologians. The character traits they evolved to survive, reproduce, and flourish in small social bands of hunter/gatherers persist in us today, but we struggle to adapt these to our strange urban, industrial, technological, modern world. Our hunter/gatherer ancestors most successfully developed the personality traits of worldliness, and their evolution best explains how and why most people are worldly even today. Yet, as often noted, evolution (and God) created an enormous surplus of human capacities that go far beyond anything essential for mere survival and reproduction. These include most of the systemic, extrinsic, and intrinsic evaluational and spiritual capacities explored in this book. We are just as much spiritual and intellectual beings as we are biological, social, and sexual beings. Curiosity has great survival and practical significance when focused on things essential for or threatening to ongoing life, but curiosity also leads to philosophy and theology, much of which has little or no survival or reproductive significance whatsoever! Philosophy begins and ends in wonder, but for the most part it is practically useless, just as Aristotle said. Such wonder is a wonderful thing, mainly because there is much more to life than mere survival and reproduction. This book explores the "much more."

Most of the short quotes in this book fall within "fair use," and other quoted material is in the public domain. I do thank each of the following publishers or authors for permission to reprint quoted material:

Abingdon Press, *The Works of John Wesley*, several volumes.
Leggett, Richard, unpublished "Essay on Value and Individuality."

Robert S. Hartman Institute for Formal and Applied Axiology, for use of the published and unpublished writings of Robert S. Hartman quoted in this work.

Rem B. Edwards
Lindsay Young Professor of Philosophy, Emeritus
The University of Tennessee, Knoxville, TN
E-mail: remb1@att.net

Chapter One

Worldliness and Extrinsic/Worldly Religion

> Socrates. *And can we ever know what art makes a man better, if we do not know what we are ourselves?*
> Alcibiades. *Impossible*
> Socrates. *And is self-knowledge such an easy thing, and was he to be lightly esteemed who inscribed the text ["Know Thyself"] on the temple at Delphi?*
> Alcibiades. *At times I fancy, Socrates, that anybody can know himself; at other times the task appears to be very difficult.*
> Socrates. *But whether easy or difficult, Alcibiades, still there is no other way; knowing what we are, we shall know how to take care of ourselves, and if we are ignorant, we shall not know.*
> Alcibiades. *That is true.*[1] Plato

Do we know who we are? Are we trying to find ourselves? Do we know what is best for ourselves. Do we value or disvalue ourselves? Do we value or disvalue others? Some things within us and in our broad intellectual, physical, social, moral, and spiritual environments are more valuable than others, but how can we, how should we, evaluate or prioritize them? Can we answer such questions rationally and spiritually? It has been said that "We are what we eat." This is not the whole truth; it oversimplifies immensely. "We are what and how we value" would be much closer to the whole truth. What we value and how we value are the real keys to our personalities, our spirituality, and our whole reality. Understanding these keys can unlock the doors to self-knowledge, self-appreciation, self-development, spiritual fulfillment, and abundant living.

Yes, we are largely what and how we value. The things we value and the way we value them make us who we are; they order our personalities for better or for worse. They order our moral and spiritual realities. But what are value-objects? In what different ways do we evaluate them? How do our values and evaluations make us into very different but still similar moral and spiritual beings? How can understanding values and evaluations help us to gain self-knowledge and knowledge of others? How can this understanding help us to grow spiritually and morally?

To use what and how we value in learning about ourselves and others, we must first grasp some key concepts. Values are connected to meanings, and everything of which we are conscious has some meaning. Value-objects are *what* we value or evaluate. Evaluation, how we attach value to them, is personal involvement with meanings or objects of value. Evaluation can be conscious or unconscious. Our focus here will be on conscious involvement with value-objects. Every moment of consciousness contains many values and evaluations. Every wakeful moment, by degrees we are valuing or disvaluing everything we experience. We are consciously involved positively or negatively with innumerable things in many ways. As we grow physically, socially, mentally, ethically, and spiritually, the things we value constantly change and increase, and how we value them may also change. To be alive and alert is to be saturated with value-objects and how we relate to them. Our values and evaluations can be very confused and disorderly, but we can bring order into this chaos if we learn some simple but important value concepts and distinctions and then put them to use.

Good things actually have the properties or traits that they ideally ought to have; they fulfill their norms and our expectations by degrees. Simply put, there are at least three kinds of value or goodness, and each can be fulfilled by degrees.

Intrinsic values are good to, for and in themselves. People, God, and all individual conscious beings are intrinsically valuable.

Extrinsic values are useful means to ends beyond themselves, instrumental goods. Physical objects, processes, and activities are extrinsically valuable.

Systemic values are mental or conceptual goods. Ideas, thoughts, beliefs, laws, rules, logic, mathematics, ritual forms, symbols, and formalities of every description are systemic goods.

There are also three ways in which we typically or naturally value each kind of goodness.

Intrinsically good things are typically and most appropriately evaluated in their uniqueness, distinctiveness, and completeness by passionately identifying with them through love, compassion, concentration, and loyalty. This is *intrinsic evaluation*.

Extrinsically good things are typically and most appropriately evaluated as good of their kind through ordinary but less intense practical desires, feelings, and interests. This is *extrinsic evaluation*.

Systemically good things are typically and most appropriately evaluated objectively, dispassionately, or disinterestedly (which is not the same as uninterestedly). This is *systemic evaluation.*

These three kinds of goodness fall into a *hierarchy of value* or worth. All are very good, but some good things are better than others, and one of the three is best of all. Any given thing is better than something else when it has more good-making properties, either quantitatively or qualitatively. It is best when it has the most good-making properties. Because they are richer in goodness, intrinsic values are better than extrinsic values, and extrinsic values are better than systemic values. Goods that actually exist are better than the signs that point to them. This means that *people and God are more valuable than merely mindless things, and desirable but merely mindless things are more valuable than the mere words or symbols that stand for them, or for people and God.*

This simple theory of value is more carefully explained and defended in the Appendix, but this much is sufficient for present purposes. Although simple and obvious, we can really do a lot with it. It can help us to understand ourselves, other people, and different types or kinds of spiritual development. Here is how this works.

Some people overvalue (or undervalue) the wrong kinds of good things and assign more (or less) worth to them than they really have. They evaluate them as if they were some other or higher kind of value-object. For example, some people love mere things but undervalue or fail to love real people as they should. They are the extrinsic worldly people discussed in this chapter. Some people overvalue mere beliefs, truths, doctrines, and formalities and may undervalue either things, or people, or both. They are the systemic ideologists, dogmatists, and authoritarians covered in the second chapter. Some saintly people may overvalue people while neglecting things and thoughts; they are purely intrinsic saints; but the best or most saintly people do not neglect anything of value; they are holistic saints. They do not overvalue or undervalue anything or anyone. They value as they should—in accord with the hierarchy of value.

Now, let's see how far these basic and intuitively obvious claims about what and how we value will take us. With them we can identify three prominent personality types, their strengths, their weaknesses and mistakes, and how they express themselves spiritually. For the moment, we will consider worldliness, but this is only an abstract personality type to which real people only approximate by degrees.

Gaining the World, but Losing the Soul

I do nothing but go about persuading you all, old and young alike, not to take thought for your persons or your properties, but first and chiefly to care about the greatest improvement of the soul. I tell you that virtue is not given by money, but that from virtue comes money and every other good of man, public as well as private.[2] Socrates

> *For what is a man profited, if he shall gain the whole world, and lose his soul? Or what shall a man give in exchange for his soul?* Jesus (Matthew 16:26)

Worldly people have existed from the beginning of humankind. Worldliness is recognized, discussed, and universally condemned by all the major world religions. The social anxiety and insecurity that Socrates and Jesus provoked in ancient Athens and Israel resulted partly from their rebellion against and threat to worldly values. Worldliness is not an exclusively modern phenomenon, but it was and is the most prevalent mode of evaluative consciousness in the world. Socrates, St. Augustine, Jonathan Edwards, John Wesley, Søren Kierkegaard, and many others were of that opinion. It has always been pervasive, despite all the warnings of both philosophical and religious critics of culture.

In their more reflective moments, most people in all cultures affirm the preceding hierarchy of values, as large data banks (of people who have taken the Hartman Value Profile) now show. When they really think about it, most people value people over mere things, and things over mere ideas of people and things. But in their less reflective moments, i.e., most of the time, people tend greatly to overvalue either extrinsic or systemic value-objects, the sensory things of the world, or belief systems of one kind or another. Most people greatly undervalue other people, intrinsic realities, precisely because they are so profoundly absorbed in and enthralled by extrinsic or "material" objects and events. Overvaluing systemic values is another way to fall short of spiritual maturity, but comparatively few intellectual-minded people make this mistake. Worldliness usually prevails in human practice, which is where our values really count. Most people live and act as if things (or thoughts) have more worth than people, especially things. Most of our moral and spiritual problems spring from these distorted values.

The de-humanizing, de-moralizing, de-spiritualizing features of modern science, technology, industrialization, urbanization, advertising, consumerism, and plastic mass culture express a civilization built primarily upon the values of worldliness. But how is worldliness to be defined? What are its strengths? Where does it fail?

Defining Worldliness and Worldlings

Worldlimindedness. How exceedingly are men blinded by their own interests. What is strong enough to overcome the prejudices of interest but God alone? What will not men believe if the thing believed makes for their worldly interest, and what will they not disbelieve when the belief makes against their interest?....To men to whom God has not given...largeness of heart, nothing seems real to them but what they see

> *with their eyes, and is the object of their bodily senses. The reason of this is a certain narrowness of soul, that has but a very scanty and confined knowledge, confined to the dust they tread on. This world appears great to them, and worthy to set their hearts upon....So they are of very narrow views and conceptions with respect to time. They can see no further than just before them....They...concern themselves only about sensible things, and...depend upon their senses only; and therefore nothing seems real to them but what is sensible. The business of their life has been about things that they can see and hear and feel and taste; their thoughts and designs and meditations have been confined to such things. They have tied down their minds to such objects of their senses....Men, if there are only dangers about their estates, and about their good names and about all their worldly interest, will bestir themselves.*[3] Jonathan Edwards

> *And thus it is precisely with the despair of finitude. In spite of the fact that a man is in despair he can perfectly well live on in the temporal, in fact all the better for it; he may be praised by men, be honored and esteemed, and pursue al the aims of temporal life. What is called worldliness is made up of just such men who (if one may use the expression) pawn themselves to the world. They use their talents, accumulate money, carry on worldly affairs, calculate shrewdly, etc., etc., are perhaps mentioned in history, but themselves they are not; spiritually understood, they have no self, no self for whose sake they could venture everything, no self before God—however selfish they may be for all that.*[4] Søren Kierkegaard

> *We think of what we love; but we do not love God; therefore, we think not of him. Or if we are now and then constrained to think of him for a time...we drive [such thoughts] out as soon as we can, and return to what we love to think of. So that the world, and the things of the world—what we shall eat, what we shall drink, what we shall put on; what we shall see, what we shall hear, what we shall gain; how we shall please our senses or our imagination—takes up all our time, and engrosses all our thoughts. So long, therefore as we love the world, that is so long as we are in our natural state, all our thoughts, from morning to evening, and from evening to morning, are no other than wandering thoughts.*[5] John Wesley

> *The mass of men lead lives of quiet desperation. What is called resignation is confirmed desperation. From the desperate city you go into the desperate country, and have to console yourself with the bravery of minks and muskrats. A stereotyped but unconscious despair is concealed even under what are called the games and amusements of mankind. There is no play in them, for this comes after work. But it is a characteristic of wisdom not to do desperate things.*[6] Henry David Thoreau

Worldliness must be defined in two complementary ways, psychologically and axiologically. *Psychologically defined,* worldliness is an aggressively self-interested absorption in the external world of sensory objects, actions, and stratified social relations. It is impelled by the drives to survive, acquire, dominate, copulate, indulge, compete, and seek revenge against all who jeopardize worldly instincts, attitudes, and values. Worldly people are lost in the external sensory world; they find and know themselves only through their body and its images. They cannot find or focus on their conscious inner moral and spiritual selves. Their absorption in the sensory world is not like that of Taoists, Buddhists, or those Western Mystics who, while knowing themselves internally, can also relate directly to the beauty and uniqueness of nature and existence as something valuable and satisfying just as it is, prior to human modification, ownership, improvement, and classification.

Worldly people are often conflicted about, alienated from, dissatisfied with, or ambivalent toward that in which they have lost themselves. The things of the world are only means to further worldly ends, which are in turn only means to even further worldly ends, but where are the final ends? Where does the buck stop? Where are the things that are good in themselves? Worldly people love mindless things with all their hearts, souls, minds, and strength; but mindless objects cannot reciprocate or love them back. They know, at least semi-consciously, that they seek ultimate satisfaction in things that really do not really satisfy (extrinsic values); and they only dimly envision the things that do satisfy, final ends, (intrinsic values).

Worldly people approach real existence mainly through the prosaic empirical class concept of ordinary language. They deal proficiently with practical or extrinsic values, but not so well with systemic and intrinsic values. Systemic deficiency makes them vulnerable to biases and to every form of ignorance, deception, superstition, error, and irrationality. Intrinsic deficiency makes them aesthetically, morally, and spiritually insensitive, boorish, snobby, inconsiderate, hard-hearted, and unresponsive or unfeeling.

Fortunately, psychological and axiological mind-sets seldom exist in pure form. Worldly individuals are *dominated* by extrinsic physical, material, behavioral, and social self-interests; but they also have *underdeveloped and undervalued* systemic and intrinsic values and evaluative capacities. Their limited affective intrinsic capacities for loving, caring, empathizing, and deep emotional involvement are focused primarily on extrinsic things, or on a small handful of people, those who directly affect their own physical and social well-being. As Jonathan Edwards expressed it:

> And yet how common it is among mankind, that their affections are much more exercised and engaged in other matters than in religion! In things which concern men's worldly interests, their outward delights, their honor and reputation, and their natural relations, they have their desires eager, their appetites vehement, their love warm and affectionate, their zeal ardent; in these things their hearts are tender and sensible, easily moved, deeply impressed, much concerned, very sensibly affected, and greatly engaged; much depressed with grief at worldly losses, and highly raised with joy at worldly success and prosperity. But how insensible and unmoved are most men, about the great things of another world! How dull their affections![7]

Not surprisingly, worldlings deeply love and identify themselves with the things of the world. They intrinsically value things that do not have intrinsic worth, things that cannot love them in return. Søren Kierkegaard remarked, "Worldliness means precisely attributing infinite value to the indifferent,"[8] (that is, to extrinsic values, as here understood). Worldlings are convinced that only objects of sense, physical actions, and exalted social rank are worth loving, having, experiencing, bringing into the world, acquiring, and preserving. The things of the world both serve and constitute their worldly self-interest. Their possessions and behaviors may also be useful to the very few others about whom they care and with whom they share, e.g., members of their immediate family and others of their kin and kind. Worldlings live and act as if things, deeds, and status are ends in themselves, but they may not think deeply enough to be fully conscious of this. Most philosophers pay too little attention to *how* we value, so they seldom realize that most people actually value extrinsic values as if they were intrinsic values. Worldly people tend to do just that.

Worldliness, like sinfulness, is an enduring condition or disposition of the soul, whether conscious or not; it is not a mere act or series of acts. Indeed, it is the most common form of innate sinfulness. It is largely identical with what the theologians have called "original sin," though it has nothing to do with Adam and Eve.

Axiologically defined, worldliness is overvaluing extrinsic value objects, the things of the world. It is an abiding attachment primarily to the extrinsic values of personal survival, sensory objects, social status, sexual indulgence and reproduction, broader libido gratification, pain avoidance, sweet revenge, and dominating-exploiting social subordinates. These are the supreme value-objects of worldly human existence. For worldly people, the "good life" consists largely in the competitive acquisition and possession of *material things, luxuries as well as necessities, exciting physical activities, high social status, power over others, sex objects,* and *success objects*. A "high standard of living" is a superabundance of such things. Evolutionary psychologists and sociobiologists study the sexual choices and reproductive strategies of individuals and groups. They underscore the reproductive advantages to both males and females of selecting sexual partners with ample material resources, physical prowess, and high social standing.

The worldly understanding of an "abundant life" is well expressed by, "He that dies with the most toys wins." Worldly abundant living involves mainly selfish self-fulfillment through extrinsic or so-called "temporal" goods; systemic and intrinsic values have a relatively low place in worldly souls. By contrast, a proper spiritual understanding of "abundant living" makes a significant place for values in all three dimensions. Its notion of "abundance" is much richer in kinds of value and evaluation, and in scope of things valued.

The supreme values of worldly persons are extrinsic sensory value-objects—physical things, processes, actions, and the marks or tokens of social status. All are vacuous, inanimate entities that have no consciousness of their own and can give nothing back intentionally, deliberately, or affectively. Devotion to them is ultimately unsatisfying because, as profoundly social beings, we deeply need reciprocated love and respect. The things of the world have no psychological properties;

they have no knowledge, feelings, or purposes; they are incapable of loving and respecting us back. Worldlings usually value extrinsic realities as if they were intrinsic realities, and they value intrinsic realities (for example, sexual partners and subordinates) as if they were extrinsic objects, mere means to their sordid ends. Some worldly people find little or nothing in life to be intrinsically worthwhile, so they value everything extrinsically, including people, as means to ends. Worldly John Dewey once suggested that everything is just a means to a means to a means to a means—indefinitely; and there are no intrinsic values, no final ends in themselves.[9] (In other writing, particularly those on aesthetics, Dewey was much more sensitive to intrinsic values and evaluations).

Although worldly people are dominated by extrinsic values, this does not mean that they do not have any systemic or intrinsic values. If we let "people," "things," and "beliefs" represent the three value dimensions, worldly people always value things the most; but they may still attach some value to some people and beliefs—sometimes valuing people more than beliefs, sometimes beliefs over people, and sometimes valuing people and beliefs equally. As for *evaluations*, their extrinsic valuational capacities for recognizing and manipulating means to ends are usually much better developed than either their intrinsic capacities for love and compassion or their systemic capacities for thinking. They tend to see almost all things as means to ends, not just things, but also people and ideas or beliefs.

To the extent that they can evaluate intrinsically, they usually love things the most and may continue to see people and conceptual knowledge as means to materialistic and social ends. They value extrinsic value-object as if they have intrinsic worth and intrinsic value-objects as if they have only extrinsic worth. They exploit and *use* social subordinates. They may go even further and disvalue or look down on them while taking advantage of them. They want both to treat people as inferiors and to make them actually feel as if they are inferior—to humiliate them. They may have contempt for others, not only because they are inferiors, but also because they resist and rebel against being exploited and humiliated. Worldly people may oppress, diminish, abase, and occasionally destroy "underdogs" just to get what they have. When "low down people" insist on more respect, they brand them as "uppity." Racists and snobs are experts in playing this game. Thus, worldlings extrinsically disvalue intrinsic value-objects.

When worldly people achieve position, prosperity, and coitus they discover that such worldly value-objects are not inherently or ultimately satisfying and meaningful; their lives are still empty and unfulfilled. Getting what you want is not always what you hoped for or expected. Be careful what you pray and strive for; you may get it! The net result of the worldly rat race, according to Kierkegaard and Thoreau, is despair. No matter how hard they try, worldly individuals cannot drown their sorrows, fill their emptiness, or give meaning to their meaningless lives. Greater power and more possessions, sex, alcohol, and other drugs do not work and do not fulfill.

Worldliness as the "Natural Man and Woman"

> *This form of despair (i.e. unconsciousness of it) is the commonest in the world—yes, in what people call the world, or, to define it more exactly, what Christianity calls "the world," i.e. paganism, and the natural man in Christendom.*[10] Søren Kierkegaard

Traditional theologians spoke of the "natural man" in depicting sinful human nature in its spiritually undeveloped and sinful state, but we will speak of the "natural man and woman." The portrayal of human nature in its original state, that of our hunter/gatherer ancestors, by contemporary evolutionary psychologists, coincides remarkably with worldliness as depicted by the classical theologians. Worldlings divide their time and energy by multiplying things, actions, and social rank. Such "resources" were (and still are) necessary for survival and reproduction. Our very early ancestors may have had little time or energy for much else. With more free time today, worldlings deliberately cultivate, exaggerate, and satiate their appetites for titillating sense objects, conspicuous deeds and displays, and exaggerated social power and positions. All of this is much encouraged by their worldly peers, consumerism, television, advertising, and the mass media. We live in a worldly cultural world.

The worldly or "temporal" quest for provisions, pretentiousness, prowess, and prestige is grounded in some of the most powerful basic instincts of all complex animal species, including our own. According to contemporary evolutionary psychologists, the basic drives of the "natural man and woman" are:

(1) the *survival* instinct, which is closely related to

(2) the *acquisitive* instinct;

(3) the drive for *social dominance* and its associated powers and privileges is closely related to

(4) the drives for *sexual and other libidinous or pleasurable indulgences* and

(5) for physical and psychological *pain avoidance*;

(6) the drive for *revenge* against actual or imagined threats to survival, possessions, accomplishments, dominance, sexual access and expression, and libido gratification. Social coalitions to counter such threats are closely aligned with:

(7) *nepotism and reciprocal altruism*, the propensity to encourage, praise, and reward those who contribute to our own worldly well-being, usually kin, clan, or allies within our social class, and

(8) *aggressiveness*, a disposition toward violence against and oppression of others who have what we want.[11]

Aggressive actions and threats are used to eliminate, control, degrade, or discriminate against rivals, members of the opposite sex (usually women), outsiders belonging to alien clans, villages, cultures, or lower-ranking sex, race, or inferior social classes within one's own larger social group. High status individuals endeavor aggressively to diminish the status, resources, and reproductive success of outsiders and of subordinate in-clan same-sex rivals. They may employ violence to appropriate or exploit the sexual partners (usually women), labor, talents, economic resources, and material possessions of inferior classes and out-groups. They take from those who have not and give to those who have, namely, themselves and others resembling themselves. Through tax codes, by buying politicians, and otherwise, they redistribute wealth to themselves—the rich and powerful, and they vehemently oppose redistributing wealth to lower social classes, the "least of these" as Jesus called them. Class warfare is very real, but it is often disguised and denied by accusing those who notice it of promoting class warfare!

Absent good mothering, synergistic culture, and the grace of God, these eight elemental drives are extremely powerful in both women and men, though not always equally so. Individuals vary even within each gender. These drives, heavily emphasized by evolutionary theorists, are the very essence of the theologians' "natural man" (and woman). Morality and spirituality do not aspire to eliminate all of them; but they try to tame them, prioritize them, and put those that ought to be saved into their proper place within a reasonable hierarchy of morally acceptable goods.

Additional elements of a broad hierarchy of values are connect in both sexes with needs that are also perfectly natural but significantly non-worldly:

(9) *systemic fulfillment* (curiosity, knowledge, truth, meaning) and

(10) *intrinsic fulfillment* (love and compassion for those who can love in return).

These non-worldly needs are, by degrees, underdeveloped and overwhelmed in most "natural men and women" by the first eight basic natural drives. Still, primitive human nature contains within itself the seeds of its own transformation. Systemics (e.g., curiosity and information) and intrinsics (e.g., love and compassion) are also adaptive! Yet, they are so much more than that!

By nature, Aristotle said, all people desire to know. Curiosity, the quest for abstract or conceptual meaning and truth, is also a powerful natural systemic drive. By nature, pervaded by common or prevenient grace, people want to live intrinsically meaningful lives, to find meaning in all of existence, to love and to be loved, to be respected and cherished as unique individuals, and so to relate to others. Worldly people constantly suppress, thwart, fail to activate, or otherwise defeat their own natural systemic and intrinsic non-worldly drives because they are so hung up on survival, security, sensations, acquisitiveness, social dominance, sexual gratification, libido indulgence, pain avoidance, revenge, rewards, and aggressive exploitation of so-called "inferiors." With dim self-awareness, they may not understand how much they are controlled by (in bondage to) primitive and largely unconscious drives inherited from their hunter/gatherer ancestors. Our worldly culture tells us that everyone is like that, so they must be OK. They may not realize that they can and should control, eliminate, or re-prioritized their appetites.

Domination, revenge, aggression, humiliation, violence, and oppression should be curtailed and replaced by cooperation, mutual respect, love, and rational persuasion. Nothing is inherently objectionable about our natural human needs to survive, to acquire adequate but not excessive resources, to indulge sexually and otherwise under appropriate conditions, to avoid unnecessary pains, and to reward others for their good and helpful deeds. Yet, these interests should be held in their proper place and not allowed to interfere with non-worldly human needs for knowledge, meaning, moral integrity, loving, and being loved. Usually, they do not stay in their proper place. Usually, extrinsic value-objects are over-valued. Human needs for and libidinous enjoyments of food, drink, shelter, comfort, and the necessities of life serve the drive to survive, the "will to live," as it is usually called. Sense objects, things, survival resources, are required for ongoing individual existence and sensory gratification as well as for the continuation of the species, so the acquisitive instinct is an integral part of the drive for survival, preservation, and perpetuation.

We inherited our appetites for and enjoyment of sweet, fatty, and salty foods from our hunter/gatherer progenitors, along with our aversions to bitter foods and snakes, and our aesthetic preferences for cooked as opposed to raw meat, and for certain kinds of landscapes. Our ancestors who ate the right stuff, avoided the wrong stuff, and lived in supportive environments, survived and reproduced; those with the wrong appetites and aversions did not survive, and they became no one's ancestors. In a competitive world where desirable resources are often scarce, acquisitiveness easily spills over into aggression. Elemental psychophysical drives bind worldlings to the sensory or physical world, from whence cometh our succor. Our most primitive instincts are naturally unbridled; they do not know when enough is enough. From the very outset they tend to be out of control, to run out of bounds. Worldly people, in bondage to these instincts, believe that and act as if greed is good, and the more the better. Their sense of insecurity knows no appeasement. They never seem to have enough worldly resources; they are never content, not even when "filthy rich."

Both women and men naturally strive for social dominance for themselves, value it highly in their mates, and want it for their offspring. Socially dominant individuals in every species get the best food, the best territories, the most attractive sexual partners, and incessant deference from their "low down" social inferiors. Of course, their dominance can be challenged. In our species, dominance is often euphemistically called "leadership," "command," "eminence," "distinction," "authority," being "number one," and so on. Kings, queens, chiefs, generals, admirals, CEOs, abbots, bishops, popes, presidents, senators, department heads, firstborns, males, champions, winners, and so on, are "top dogs." Their opposites are "underdogs." Note the sexuality inherent in this imagery, and that males usually are on top in worldly social hierarchies. Dominance often takes on snobbish, sexist, racial, and ethnic overtones.

We do not know how early our hunter/gather ancestors discerned the connection between having sex and offspring, but human sexuality did not evolve originally as a conscious desire to reproduce, much less as a desire to proliferate one's genes. Psycho-biological discussions of "propagating genes" and their "purposes" must be read with caution and can never be taken literally. The relation between wanting sex, wanting children, and wanting to spread our genes is very indirect at best. No sub-human animals, including intelligent chimpanzees, understand that sex results in reproduction,[12] and only in the 20th century have we human animals learned that genes exist. No one can consciously desire any x (e.g., to propagate genes) without a concept of "x". So, no pre-modern persons could have wanted to spread their genes, even when they consciously wanted to have children. Very few if any people today have such a conscious desire. The myth of "selfish genes" is just that—a systemic myth, a misleading theoretical explanatory construct, not a psychological description of anyone's actual values or motives in wanting sex, children, or anything else. It is not even a description of genes themselves, for genes have no minds, desires, or purposes. Closely related is the myth that reproduction, and only reproduction, is the only "natural purpose" of sexual intercourse. Since animals have no understanding of the connection between sex and reproduction, that can not be their natural purpose! They must do it just for the fun of it! That is its "natural purpose," not reproduction, since they do not grasp the connection. To understand such things more accurately and profoundly, a careful axiological analysis of concrete human values and evaluations, like that given in this book, is required. No doubt, people generally and naturally want the children that they raise to be their own, genes or no genes, but there is nothing inevitable about this; if there were there would be no such thing as adoptions.

Evolutionary psychologists note that reproductive success depends heavily on high social status, sexual access and fidelity, and possessing or promising material resources essential for survival and flourishing. When choosing permanent mates (as opposed to temporary sex partners), women everywhere try to "marry up" in social hierarchies. They strongly prefer males who both can and will invest heavily in them and their offspring with material resources, protection, parenting skills, time, strength, and effort. This is especially so because of their increased vulnerability during lengthy periods of pregnancy and child rearing. Both survival and long term reproductive success depend heavily upon material and economic resources as well as physical prowess. These and other assets correlate significantly with high social, occupational, and educational status, as well as with maturity, ambition, industriousness, emotional stability, courage, intelligence, good health, physical attractiveness, size, strength, capability, and pugnacity. In both human and non-human species, high status males are much more attractive to females and have many more choices of sexual partners than low status males.[13]

Because social dominance tends to ensure sexual access and reproductive success, men everywhere tend, by both nature and culture, to value it highly. David M.

Buss, a leading evolutionary psychologist, says, "Men are particularly concerned about status, reputation, and hierarchies because elevated rank has always been an important means of acquiring the resources that make men attractive to women."[14] Buss indicates that men seek physically attractive women, not merely because of their "reproductive value," but also because having an attractive wife, especially a "trophy wife," immensely enhances a man's social status and prestige.[15]

Feminists, reflecting on evolutionary psychology, acknowledge that the young, beautiful, fertile, and accomplished women who become trophy wives of older executives or other high status males are not merely passive victims of masculine dominance and manipulation. Trophy wives want trophy husbands! They are eager to "marry up." They deliberately choose and actively seek exactly what women "by nature" look for in men—socially dominant and mature husbands with exalted social status, abundant material resources, physical strength, and a willingness to provide for, share with, and invest in them.[16] To attract the most desirable mates, younger men must be regarded as likely to achieve such worldly success. Bachelors perceived to be otherwise are not deemed "eligible" or "promising" and are not likely to be selected as mates. At great risks to themselves, men participate eagerly in the worldly rat race, not just because they tend to be sensual, aggressive, greedy, clannish, and narcissistic, but because worldly success is exactly what worldly women want in their men!

We human beings are exactly like our primate cousins in naturally loving and striving for social dominance and hating subordination or inferiority. Like them also, when submissiveness is unavoidable, as it is for most people, we can learn to enjoy it, employ it as a survival strategy, internalize the values of those who dominate us, and even fight for our social masters against outside threats to the social structures that oppress us.[17] When we can't be "number one," we identify psychologically with those who are! Their superiority becomes our superiority. Dominant individuals always begin their lives as subordinates, continue with a lower status while they mature, and return to underdog positions after being deposed. The career of an alpha male (or female) is usually short. Like everyone else, top dogs know how to recognize and make submissive gestures, and, in our species, how to utter submissive words. Being "put in one's place" is often more ceremonial than lethal, and subordinates learn how to thrive submissively within stable hierarchical societies. They ingratiate themselves with dominant individuals, identify with them, secure their protection and favoritism, consummate their own agendas when dominant individuals are not looking, make alliances with other subordinates for mutual protection and profit, and lord it over those who are still lower on the social ladder.

Scrambling for social dominance occurs whenever any two living individuals, male or female, are placed together in the same environment, whether or not they belong to the same species. Friedrich Nietzsche made this "will to power" over others the paramount value and virtue of "master morality" and the "superman." Domineering is intimately intertwined with the drive for sexual access and gratification, but they are not identical, for it is present even where sex is not an immediate issue.

Fortunately, libido and sexuality can also find expression and fulfillment between *equals* who genuinely love, understand, respect, cooperate with, and are loyal to one another—as in good marriages and in other intrinsic human relationships.

The human quest for dominance over others is so conspicuous that a relatively new branch of social psychology called "social dominance theory" has come into being to study "social dominance orientation." Through extensive empirical studies, conducted and/or collated successfully by Felicia Pratto[18] and others, it finds that both sexes value status *very highly*; but they do not necessarily value it *equally*. Even within genders, significant individual variations exist. Social dominance is valued most highly by high status males and the upper class females who are associated intimately and profitably with them, those who already "have it made" and have the most to lose to social egalitarianism. Low status females aspire to be high status females because of the worldly advantages to be gained, and they compete vigorously with other females for status and for high class men. Low ranking males do not value high status for themselves quite so highly, but they still attach great importance to belonging to social groups or classes that are "better" than other "less desirable" groups or classes.

In the United States, poor white males who are exploited, undereducated, and greatly oppressed still take great pride in belonging to the "superior" white race, or to the class of heterosexuals, all members of which are, in their eyes, "better" than all other races and "queers." They may participate eagerly in oppressing blacks and/or homosexuals, e.g., by joining the Ku Klux Klan or other white supremacy groups and class-conscious organizations. Like high status white males, they can be deeply resentful when blacks, homosexuals, outsiders, illegal aliens, or potential rivals of any description do not "stay in their place." Persons at all social levels do not want their "inferiors" to get too "uppity," too competitive for higher socioeconomic status. They regularly humiliate their "inferiors," both publicly and in private. Men want social dominance directly for themselves, and they offer it to lower ranking females who will consort with them. Women want their long and short term sexual partners to have it; they also covet it for themselves and their offspring; and they endeavor to acquire it through their own accomplishments and through sexual, familial, or social alliances.

Available data show that a gender gap exists with respect to how highly women and men value social dominance, and with respect to the practical social-policy implications of pursuing it. Within each gender, individuals may differ immensely, and trends are affected by shifting political tides. Statistically, women are more likely than men to adopt egalitarian ideologies and to support social roles, positions, policies, political parties, and candidates that are "hierarchy attenuating"; and men are more likely to support the ones that are "hierarchy enhancing."[19] In the United States, women are significantly less racists than men and more inclined to vote

Democratic. They are more likely to support: (1) *racial equalization policies* such as quotas, affirmative action, school busing, civil rights, and helping minorities to get a better education and better housing, (2) *gay/lesbian rights* like the right to marry and share benefits with a same-sex partner, and (3) *social welfare programs* like government-sponsored health care, early education, help for the homeless, aid to poor children, benefits for the unemployed, low income housing, benefits for the elderly, and increased taxation for the rich. Women tend to oppose *military programs* like the Strategic Defense Initiative and the B2 Stealth Bomber that would increase defense spending.[20] Men are more inclined to support hierarchy-enhancing policies like enhanced military spending, providing arms to foreign countries, the death penalty, and to oppose gun control.[21] Guns symbolize power!

Today, natural human dispositions to oppress and exploit social inferiors are expressed in commonplace worldly biases, attitudes, and practices, including discrimination against and abuses of women and minorities and aggression against outsiders, strangers, and aliens. Snobbish worldlings find it difficult to accept a religion which affirms that we are all equally loved by God, and they abhor real democracy which, at its best, affirms and secures equal basic rights for all. They disvalue equal freedom of action for all, and equal basic human worth, because these ideals threaten the entrenched social hierarchies from which they so greatly benefit. They believe themselves to be better somehow than someone else, if not everyone else. They cannot control or overcome the ubiquitous human drive to "put down" those who resist or compete with them. Instead, they oppress them, bully them, discriminate against them, benefit unfairly from their labor, appropriate their meager belongings, and expropriate their attractive women and successful men. They find low status individuals to be unworthy and undeserving of all such worldly goods. Having over-inflated views of their own merit, they find human equality to be very "unnatural" precisely because it would transcend and depose their own primitive drive to dominance. Being just as good as everyone else isn't good enough for them; worldlings have to be better, even when they are worse.

Morally advanced societies make laws against excessive worldliness, laws that tend to equalize the playing field. They protect fundamental rights for all. They regulate free enterprise. They restrain the sinful unbridled dispositions of the "natural man and woman" toward domination, acquisition, aggression, and revenge. Every society restrains and regulates powerful primitive drives somehow and to some extent, and so does almost every individual a good bit of the time. Yet, no human being or society, not even those that are most saintly and egalitarian, can successfully eliminate all wanton worldly endeavor. Sin is very deeply entrenched!

People can be dangerous animals. Domination, acquisition, aggression, bullying, and revenge are in the genes that we inherited from our hunter/gatherer ancestors, but we are not inevitably controlled by them. As a descriptive science, evolutionary psychology repudiates genetic and sociobiological determinism and acknowledges that our natural drives and inclinations are pliable and somewhat susceptible to our control and choice.[22] It does not prescribe or sanction the domineering behavior that it describes; and it does not confuse what is "adaptive" for individuals or groups with what is moral or right, says Felicia Pratto.[23] Social Darwinism has no normative, moral, factual, or scientific basis. It is a sinful expression of natural selfishness.

Normative disciplines like axiology, ethics, and religion challenge our natural quest for superiority and its accouterments. This *ought* to be resolved, not to favor dominance and subordination, but by affirming equality of basic worth and rights. It is so resolved by morally and spiritually mature human beings. The saints do it best. Ethico-religious maturation liberates us *from* bondage to our most primitive but powerful extrinsic drives, and *for* intrinsic mutual acceptance, equality, understanding, affection, love, compassion, fidelity, respect, cooperation, and responsibility in interpersonal relations, including marriage, family, and religious organizations. Even from an evolutionary perspective, this is achievable, but not without understanding and overcoming the dark side of human nature bestowed upon us by our hunter/gatherer ancestors.[24] Adam and Eve could be our metaphor for them.

The passion for revenge against actual and perceived threats to self-preservation, acquisitiveness, social dominance, sexual indulgence, and broader libido gratification is at least as powerful as any other basic human instinct. Our close primate cousins seek and relish revenge just as much as we do.[25] Comparisons with chimpanzees are not inappropriate; over 98% of our genes are their genes! Over 98% of their genes are our genes! Passionate vengefulness for sexual infidelity and cuckolding is almost universally human. In primitive societies, only weakness inhibits revenge and violence against outsiders. Within most societies, revenge against offending social insiders is moralized, rationalized, and institutionalized as retributive justice.

Religion may project a powerful passion for vengeance onto, and reserve it for, Divinity (Deuteronomy 32:35; Romans 12:19). Much of historical religion was devoted to assuaging God's alleged passion for revenge against any and all challenges to *Ultimate Alpha Male Dominance*. Few things are as sweet as revenge, even to God, so many people believe, though others doubt that this was the Christian God. Our social existence actually would be much sweeter if we could restrict revenge to, and reserve it for, God alone. But to worldly religious people, "God loves everyone equally" and "Forgive seven times seventy times" just do not sound right. "A life for a life, and an eye for an eye" sound much better.

At their best, moral and spiritual maturity require us to constrain if not eliminate our powerful, elemental, natural, and universal drive for revenge. Spiritual advancement says that instead of an eye for an eye, we should turn the other cheek and forgive time and again. Individuals can do that; whole societies may find it more difficult but still greatly advantageous, far better than what we do now in international relations. The passion for revenge threatens societal preservation and cohesion with endless blood feuds and cycles of vengeance, so it is too dangerous to be left in the hands of individuals. Between states and social orders, it creates war, bloodshed, and destruction.

The systemic myth of the "social contract" says that to avoid endless cycles of revenge, members of society voluntarily transfer their natural right to revenge to civil governments and authorities. Some religions specify that this right belongs only to God (and, of course, to God's appointed magistrates). Actually, nothing like a contractual transfer of vengeance-rights has ever happened or ever will occur. Because unrestrained revenge threatens the very fabric of social existence both within and between social groups, enlightened societies and religions simply *take away* this "right," whether anyone wants to give it up voluntarily or not. For the sake of social stability and world peace, societal violence and Divine violence often take the place of individual and small group violence. Advanced spirituality offers more peaceful alternatives to such violence.

Associated with the passion for revenge is the typically weaker nepotistic propensity to reward those who are likely to contribute to our own welfare. Sociobiologists call nepotism and related behaviors "reciprocal altruism," the proclivity to scratch the backs of those most likely to return the scratch, usually mates, kin, and allies within one's own social class or kind. Philosophers call it enlightened or long range egoism. Worldly morality gets no further than this, if ever this far.

In its place, spiritual maturity offers genuinely unselfish altruism, compassion, love, forgiveness, and the social practices of encouraging, praising, and rewarding those who do unto others as they would be done unto, even if only in worldly ways. Some features of worldliness ought to be expanded in content and scope beyond their narrow self-serving and immediate-group-serving origins. Worldly expansions in scope and inclusiveness usually do not go far enough and are often made for the wrong reasons. Men often bond and collaborate with other men to control women, or to get others to do their dirty work for them, or to achieve more efficient fighting units, and to wage war on other societies. Women often ally with other women to protect or elevate themselves. Older, dominant, alpha human males with the collective power and will to do it send out younger subordinate males to wage war for them. On human warfare, Carl Sagan commented:

> The alphas—generally old men—sequester themselves in safety, often where the young women are, and dispatch the subordinates—generally young men—out to fight and die. In no other species have alpha males gotten away with such cushy arrangements for themselves....It [war] is an institution optimally configured to benefit the alphas.[26]

Thus, even bonding, cooperation, and the seeds of intrinsic relations are not always beneficial or admirable. In worldlings, intrinsic attachments may serve morally problematic objectives. Even very good things can be misused, abused, and loved inordinately!

Possibilities for abundant living not open at the "natural" or selfishly worldly stage of ethico-spiritual development are open at a higher stage, as the later chapter on saintliness will show. Human nature is exceedingly complex, and it has room to grow and to choose freely. It includes so much more than powerful elemental instincts for self-preservation, acquisition, dominance, sexual fulfillment, libido gratification, pain avoidance, revenge, rewards, and aggression. The psycho-spiritual development of worldlings is arrested at the most elemental "natural" stage. Far greater possibilities for abundant living are available at the saintly stage of spiritual development. Worldlings cannot appreciate or value mutual freedom and equality in society or in marital and familial contexts. Paternalistic dominance greatly appeals to male worldlings. Racial or ethic dominance greatly appeals to both male and female worldlings. Making unselfish sacrifices, carrying crosses for strangers and aliens, respecting everyone as an equal, forgiving offenders, and loving enemies are quite incomprehensible to them. They hear the words, and they may even pay lip service to them, but such things really do not register very deeply with them. By thoughts, words, and deeds, they try to sabotage reasonable restraints on self-gratification and glorification. They deeply resent and try to evade social and legal restrictions on greed, dominance, revenge, nepotism, oppression of subordinates, and aggression against those who have what they want. Political candidates, lobbyists, and parties take up their causes!

Worldlings cannot fathom the psychological, moral, and spiritual dimensions of many of the world's religions, especially their ascetic dimensions. One of Aldous Huxley's characters called Christianity "The ethics and philosophy of under-consumption."[27] Men and women of the world have only deaf ears for the Buddhist exhortation to abolish all desires for worldly things and social status. They are practical men and women of affairs who esteem and sometimes master applied systems and ideologies (systemic entities) because they are useful in acquiring, producing, increasing, and controlling things and for dominating and manipulating other people. They value systematically ordered and developed technologies for the same reasons. They value people, including themselves, (intrinsic entities) only to they extent that they have or can be used extrinsically to obtain for themselves such worldly goods as wealth and status, and the behaviors, powers, and privileges thereunto appertaining. They disvalue pure science, pure thought, and the liberal arts, especially the humanities, (systemic entities) having no immediate and obvious pragmatic application, and they devalue people (intrinsic entities) who lack status, influence, power, and worldly goods. Impoverished and socially insignificant people are "nobodies" whose well or ill being does not matter to them. Worldly language is ordinary literalistic prose, and its world view is common sense.

In sum, worldly people recognize as *objects of value* mainly physical things and social rank with all its amenities and prerogatives. Their capacities for *pragmatic extrinsic evaluation* are well developed, but not their capacities for *systemic and intrinsic evaluation*. Fortunately, no real people exist solely in a single axiological dimension. As Ralph Waldo Emerson remarked, "Man fallen into superstition, into sensuality, is never quite without the visions of the moral sentiment."[28] In real people, worldliness is always tempered by systemic and intrinsic capacities that transcend and mollify their powerful natural instincts for survival, acquisition, dominance, sexual gratification, libido satisfaction, pain avoidance, revenge, aggression, and nepotism. Worldly people always have some awareness that there is more to life than worldliness. Sinners are never *totally* depraved!

Is worldliness produced by nature or by nurture? Theologians who affirm that human nature is corrupt come down heavily on the side of nature, fallen nature. Very likely, nature and nurture are so intertwined in naturally social beings that they can never be cleanly separated and prioritized. We have genetic or natural capacities for worldliness, ideology, and saintliness—all three. The social, moral, and spiritual environments in which we grow up heavily influence how we develop and rank the three value dimensions. Human nature is very general and pliable, even if worldly values are naturally or at least typically dominant. Our genetic propensities are susceptible to activation, suppression, channeling, and modification by enzymal and hormonal reactions, social influences, individual decisions, and the grace of God. What we are now is not our inevitable norm or fate. Social support and personal decisions can modify our axiological orientation and thereby our whole outlook on all the problems of life. Value modifications, including those involved in spiritual conversions, can transform the ways we live.

Human nature has both a dark side and a bright side, even if theological pessimists think that darkness usually prevails. We are born and nurtured conflicted! Are we naturally good or naturally bad? Yes! Both!

Our value theory's hierarchy of values and evaluations may have some evolutionary significance. Evolutionary adaptive pressures may tend (weakly?) to weed out individuals who do not value people over things and things over ideas. Perhaps people who do not develop and exercise their innate capacities for intrinsic evaluation such as love, empathy, identification with others, kindness, and respect do not survive or reproduce their kind as well as those who do. In a relatively weak sense, this seems to be true, and evolutionary psychology may support this claim in the following way, and perhaps in other ways.

Evolutionary psychology indicates that both men and women must solve the problem of sexual fidelity, but for different reasons. Men are more inclined toward short term sexual affairs than women, but the difference is only one of degree, and individuals of either gender vary greatly. Without cooperative females, promiscuous males could not pass on their philandering genes, but we know that they did! We are full of them, but we can control them. In seeking long term mates, men desire and demand faithful wives because this is the only way to solve the problem of "paternal uncertainty" and avoid investing their resources and child-rearing efforts in other men's offspring. Even those who know nothing of genes want to do this! And genes themselves have no minds of their own, so calling them "selfish" is objectionably anthropomorphic, not scientific. Women also desire and require fidelity as the only way they can be assured that their sexual partners are not diverting material resources, time, talents, and efforts away from themselves to support mistresses and "bastard" progeny. Men and women who successfully resolve the problem of sexual fidelity may have distinct reproductive advantages over those who do not.

Evolutionary psychologists usually approach such problems extrinsically: men value sexual fidelity as a means to insuring paternity, and women value it as a means to securing adequate material resources over time, especially when pregnant, nursing infants, or otherwise vulnerable. To insure sexual fidelity, says Barbara Smuts, males often resort to such drastic extrinsic control strategies as: (1) constantly guarding women, or having it done by allies, friends, relatives, or eunuchs, (2) subjecting females to genital mutilation—clitoral excision, so-called "female circumcision"—so they cannot experience sexual pleasure, (3) beating and/or verbally and emotionally abusing unfaithful women or those suspected of being so, (4) keeping women locked up in harems or almost completely covered in public to avert tempting contacts with other men, and (5) thwarting women's economic self-reliance, making them economically dependent on men, so they can be intimidated by threats to withdraw support should they be unfaithful. In vulgar terms, worldly men try to control their women by keeping them "barefoot and pregnant." This list is suggestive but not exhaustive of extrinsic masculine efforts to insure feminine faithfulness.[29]

Yet, as evolutionary psychologists also indicate, (without using the technical terminology of value theory, or exploring the point in very much detail), *intrinsic strategies for insuring faithfulness* are also available and have been employed by both sexes from time immemorial. Women do not always have to be coerced into being faithful. Often they are faithful because they understand, respect, love, identify with, and do not want to hurt their husbands; and they seek and receive understanding, respect, love, trust, and intrinsic identification in return from husbands who do not want to hurt their wives. Husbands and wives can value one another for their own sakes and not merely as means to avoiding paternal uncertainty and maternal insecurity. This has evolutionary significance!

Many women do indeed desire worldly men with high status and ample material resources, but merely *having* such resources is not enough. Desirable males must be *willing* to share and invest their resources in a family over an extended period of time, and women need to *predict* which suitors are likely to do that and which ones are not. Males do indeed desire physically attractive females, but they need to distinguish between those likely to cuckold them and those likely to bear only children that they actually sire. Both masculine and feminine reproductive strategies are best served if individuals can find mates who are kind, respectful, empathetic, insightful, affectionate, intimate, and genuinely loving![30] Intrinsic attachment can be much more effective than extrinsic manipulation. Love insures faithfulness without coercion. Evolutionary psychologists recognize this, but interpersonal affection and commitment are also desirable for many other axiological and spiritual reasons. Both men and women would like to select mates capable of intrinsic evaluation to insure that their own intrinsic worth will be freely and willingly acknowledged in spirit and in practice. To this extent, evolutionary psychology supports the axiological hierarchy of value.

Our naturally evolved capacities for intrinsic evaluation tend to focus very narrowly on spouse, offspring, kin, and kind, but saintly love is not so circumscribed. It extends to everyone everywhere.

Worldly Values: Things

*Things are in the saddle,
And ride mankind.*[31] Ralph Waldo Emerson

The disastrous feature of our civilization is that it is far more developed materially than spiritually....A civilization which develops only on its material side, and not in corresponding measure in the sphere of the spirit, is like a ship with defective steering gear which gets out of control at a constantly accelerating pace, and thereby heads for catastrophe.[32] Albert Schweitzer

Some features of worldliness need to be explored in more depth. Worldliness is a definite type of consciousness having an identifiable psychological and axiological structure. In most people, worldliness may be even more unconscious than conscious. It is very natural statistically, but it is relatively undeveloped spiritually, and it is downright sinful. Worldly people are limited selves or souls, though they are in no position to know this in a very direct or conscious way. They have the ability to *attend* only or primarily to extrinsic value objects, external things, sense objects, including people regarded merely as sense objects. Like all the rest of us, worldlings value only what they are capable of noticing, but they notice so little. We perceive what we expect, want, hope, and are taught to perceive. Worldly societies produce worldly people, and vice versa.

Worldly persons perceive and most value the external world, the only reality they know, because it consists of processes, actions, and things that will increase or imperil their own prosperity, wealth, social and sexual well-being, and enjoyment. Because they are axiologically extroverted, things outside themselves catch their attention, interest them, and stir them affectively. From Plato and Aristotle to our own day, philosophers insist that human knowledge *begins* in sense experience; they disagree about whether or not it inevitably ends there. For worldlings, knowledge does end there, including self-knowledge. They relate to themselves and to the external world primarily through sensory experiences, ordered and informed by ordinary language and ordinary prose. Again, please keep in mind that most real people are not purely worldly and approximate worldliness only by degrees.

Worldliness is very natural, and, as Kierkegaard observed, the worldly man (or woman) is the paradigm "natural man" (or woman) of the theologians. Worldliness has immense utility in "temporal" struggles for survival, preservation, reproduction, gratification, and dominance. Human individuals and societies would not survive if not originally, predominately, and from an early age oriented primarily toward the external world of sense objects and sensed others. Sensory experiences (sight, hearing, taste, smell, and touch) naturally inform us about what is essential to survival and reproduction and filter out almost everything else.

Being able to relate differently to sensory experience—as, for example, through disinterested or impartial aesthetic sensitivity toward physical, moral, or spiritual beauty—requires significant self-development; so does experiencing in non-sensory, introspective, and highly reflective conscious modalities. Worldly people never quite outgrow or overcome their natural animal engrossment in sense objects, actions, and processes, and they have relatively little ability to attend to themselves, their inner self-conscious personalities, their own souls. They are conscious but only dimly self-conscious. They have little or no inwardness. They are predominantly egocentric or narcissistic; yet they are not pure egoists because by nature all real human beings have at least a touch of genuine altruism or unselfishness, moral conscience, and an objective or relatively disinterested sense of beauty and truth.

Worldlings usually think of themselves and others as mere things among things. Every thing and every person lies "ready to hand," to borrow an expression from Martin Heidegger, for their use. They have not transcended the "natural man and woman," never trans-valued their values or been born again axiologically, morally, or spiritually. For them, knowledge *begins and ends* in sensation. Since this is almost all they know, this is almost all they value. They are imprisoned by their own limited moral and spiritual self-development. Being "in bondage" to sin is a familiar spiritual theme. We now understand that to which worldlings are in bondage.

Since worldly people live and move and have their being primarily in the world of physical actions, things, objects, and processes encountered through the external senses of touch, taste, vision, and hearing, they are *materialistic*. They may be materialistic in the metaphysical sense—believing that only spatiotemporal sense objects and processes are real. Manifestly, they are materialistic in the axiological sense—primarily valuing *things* and the material symbols of social power and prestige. Properly understood, these are only extrinsic means to deeper inner and intrinsic ends that worldlings cannot fathom. Eventually, they may reach a point where the worldly rat race seems pointless and ceases to be meaningful. Internally, they always exist in at least semi-conscious despair, dimly aware that their lives are meaningless, that something important is missing. They are confused about what and how to value.

Without knowing anything about evolutionary psychology, St. Augustine affirmed that human interests, loves, and concerns are originally and naturally directed outwardly toward external objects of sense. Most people, he thought, are so absorbed in sense objects that they are virtually incapable of taking an interest in anything else. For everyone, the struggle to turn inwardly and overcome this natural orientation toward and love for externalities is difficult and prolonged. Worldlings either never overcome the world, or, knowing better, they deliberately choose to conform to the world. St. Augustine also believed that despair and other pains of soul accompany worldliness; all forms of separation from God are divinely ordained to make us miserable; God makes us restless until we find rest in Him.

Besides inner discomfort and psychic impoverishment, worldliness also has undesirable external effects, for example, environmental desecration and social alienation. In theory, a prosperous technological society might pay its own way, not pollute the air and water, not create global warming, not destroy wildlife, not fill the air with insufferable dust, chemicals, and noise, not congest the highways, not overpopulate itself, not produce global warming, etc. In practice, however, it has not worked out that way, largely because worldlings tend to be so extremely short-sighted. Kierkegaard affirmed repeatedly that most people live in immediacy and lack continuity and perseverance in their lives. Short-sightedness also has evolutionary origins. As David M. Buss indicates,

> Our cognitive and perceptual mechanisms have been designed by natural selection to perceive and think about events that occur in a relatively limited time-span—over seconds, minutes, hours, days, sometimes months, and occasionally years. Ancestral humans spent most of their time solving immediate problems such as finding food, maintaining a shelter, keeping warm, selecting and competing for partners, protecting children, forming alliances, striving for status, and defending against marauders, so there was pressure to think in the short term.[33]

Today we hear that "Instant gratification takes too long,"[34] and for worldlings, this is true. Natural short-sightedness partly explains why worldlings tend to be so self-and-other-destructive, why they so often choose immediate pleasures, profits, or objectives over long run health and rational self-realization for themselves, others, posterity, and the environment. When a choice must be made between short-term pleasure or profits and long-term health, clean air, water, trees, wildlife, and future generations, immediate pleasure/profit motives usually win. Short-sighted hedonistic profiteering causes long run medical, ecological, and economic catastrophes. Unbridled worldly yearnings for *growth* culminate in genocidal environmental pollution and desecration. But who cares? Not worldlings! The word "sustainability" is not in their vocabulary; they can't see that far into the future. They lack truly long-range plans of life, as we all do by degrees.

Worldliness generates and perpetuates worldliness. Worldlings love growth and bigness in power, possessions, prestige, population, entertainment, and business. They cannot comprehend that small is beautiful. *Growth* in business, technology, entertainment, and population is both a condition and a consequence of worldliness.

More stuff is always better, they assume uncritically. On the surface, unbridled growth appears to be a benevolent extension of our power over things, over nature. Eventually, we discover that we cannot control growth; it controls and overwhelms us. Technology makes more gadgets available to more people, who consume more and more of the earth's limited supplies of energy and other finite resources and who require more and more money with which to buy them. Worldlings never seem to have enough! Advertising produces artificial desires for more and more *things*. It insinuates that it is our moral duty to consume more and more. Sadly, these aspects of worldliness result in greater and greater global warming, environmental devastation, pernicious class consciousness, and impoverishment and deprivation for future generations.

Worldlings who control modern corporations and technology evaluate both nature and people extrinsically. They believe that nature exists only to be exploited for economic purposes, certainly not for its own glorious sake, or for God's sake. The quest for more and more *things* underlies both "man's inhumanity to man" and to our "bestiality to the beasts." Worldly evaluative consciousness views both people and animals as material resources to be exploited in producing more and more things, for the sake of even more things, indefinitely.

Modern technological worldliness may even try to desensitize our natural responsiveness to, love for, and sense of communion with nature, our inbred (but weak) *biophilia*[35]—our natural affinity and concern for non-human living things. To forestall opposition, sensitive people must be desensitized to the value of what is being destroyed. Respecting and enjoying nature do very little to keep the wheels of industry turning, and this may become a rationale for systematic and ruthless environmental desecration and destruction. In *Brave New World*, Aldous Huxley's worldly, technological, and crudely hedonistic Utopia, children are thoroughly conditioned to dislike nature and to enjoy only the plastic products of industry and technology because "A love of nature keeps no factories busy."[36] How far removed from this are we now?

Worldly Values: Other People and Social Status

> *Treat men as pawns and ninepins and you shall suffer as well as they. If you leave out their heart, you shall lose your own. The senses would make things of all persons; of women, of children, of the poor.*[37] Ralph Waldo Emerson

In one sense, social status, social roles, and public functions are intangible systemic values; they involve conceptual social constructs produced by human thoughts and beliefs about how and where persons fit into humanly contrived social systems and hierarchies. A clear awareness of this might save worldly people from being all out materialists, but they are typically not that reflective or thoughtful. Social status is a systemic social construct, but worldlings lean heavily on extrinsic "status symbols." Social superiority manifests itself in so many tangible ways: fat bank accounts, fine houses, ostentatious luxury, stylish clothes, fashionable cars, powerful computers, the very latest electronic communication devices, big trophies, shiny medals, trophy mates, unceasing deference from subordinates, etc. Behaviorally, social roles or functions are observable patterns of physical movements and acquisitions played out in public spacetime.

Worldliness has a price, now being paid by our secular civilization. Its competitive, acquisitive, exploitive, spiteful, self-centered way of life inevitably results in alienation and estrangement between human beings, environmental desecration, social disintegration, and ultimate economic collapse. Things and status are zero sum competitive goods which, unlike love, ideas, music, and other non-competitive goods, cannot be possessed by oneself and simultaneously shared with others. Teachers can give away every important idea they have without losing a single one of them, but if they give away all their *things*, they no longer have them. Christianity teaches that we can have love only by giving it away, and that it is better to give than to receive. By contrast, *status* is lost when abdicated to others. So is wealth.

Worldly people play zero-sum games; they compete for and identify themselves with value-objects that cannot be shared without loss to themselves. They even try to turn non-competitive goods into profit by buying and selling works of art, performers, copyrights, music, records, tapes, books, and the physical media in which they are embodied. If anything can be converted into a possession, worldly people will do so. They can't just let things be; they must be cashed in, owned, processed, improved, and flaunted. Worldly people are egoistic, grasping, envious, acquisitive, aggressive, pushy, snobby, vain, envious, and intensely competitive. They organize their educational systems to bring up their children that way. They willingly invest in and pay taxes to support *things*, and the math, science, and engineering that will produce them, but not *people*, not morality and spirituality, or liberal education, or the arts and humanities, or universal health care. But they will support religion when it promises to pay off.

After Charles Darwin, many worldly people rationalize their survival, prosperity, aggressiveness, and conceit by extolling their own merits, degrading the merits of others, and calling themselves "rugged individualists" and "the fittest." Social Darwinians believe that people (especially themselves) should get it and flaunt it, and the devil take the hindmost. They measure their own social worth by how much they are served and serviced by submissive others over whom they have power and control, and by how much these subordinates flatter, admire, obey, honor, and respect them for doing so. Yet, these are not easily reconciled objectives. People tend to resent their chains, even when they admire and identify with their oppressors.

"Making good" the worldly way can involve deceiving, discriminating against, and exploiting other people. None of these are promising strategies for achieving moral, spiritual, social, or self esteem. What worldly businessmen and politicians *say* for purposes of public consumption may not be what they really *do* behind the scenes. They pay lip service to moral and spiritual ideals, including the Ten Commandments, but they really just want *others* to be moral, not themselves, so they can take advantage of them. Worldly anxiety, cynicism, mistrust, and resentment result from serious discrepancies between preaching and practice. Worldly people put up a front, keep up appearances, save face, espouse noble principles like sexual fidelity and human rights, while constantly violating their public pronouncements. "Hypocrisy" is the word for it.

The highest price paid for worldliness is human alienation. Worldly competition, class-consciousness, condescension, snobbery, bullying, discrimination, deception, oppression, and violence make enemies. Constant conniving and striving for competitive values make almost everyone an enemy. One person's success always depends on another's failure when both are competing for the same worldly possessions, positions, or sexual partners. In classical Christian theology, greed or avarice is the basic sin of worldliness. It is sustained by envy of or covetousness toward those who have what we want, and by anger and hatred towards those who threaten our worldly success. The love of money, (and the things, prestige, and sexual access it can buy), says the Bible, is the root of all evils. (Well, maybe not literally all.) The fruits of this tree are environmental desecration, global warming, economic inflation, interpersonal alienation, social isolation, anxiety, despair, ulcers, heart failure, hostility, resentment, envy, vanity, sexual conflict, sham, hypocrisy, despair, and endless wars. The excessive pursuit of worldly values can turn violent and be downright illegal. The only honor remaining to extreme worldlings is that among thieves, con men, and hit men. Worldliness has an exceedingly high moral and spiritual price.

Worldly people tend to be philosophically shallow, confused, undeveloped, uncritical, and unreflective. Worldlings weak in systemic development do not become metaphysical or moral philosophers, but a few with well developed systemic and extrinsic capacities have produced worldly materialistic philosophies. In some people, both the extrinsic and systemic value dimensions can be almost equally well developed but with little intrinsic capacity. Psychologically if not logically, the step is short between "Only *things* are real" and "Only *things* are valuable."

Metaphysical materialism, naturalism, and positivism express the worldly philosophical conviction that only sensory things and process are real. Metaphysical (as opposed to methodological) behaviorism, positivism, and naturalism characteristically express and rationalize worldliness, not simply because they reject other-worldliness, but because they identify reality and value with sensory objects and processes. Worldly ideologists with well developed systemic and extrinsic capacities conceptualize and systematize worldliness. Typical worldlings who are not philosophers or psychologists are pragmatic men and women of affairs (in more than one sense). They are wary and suspicious of people who think too much, especially with non-empirical concepts and constructs. When they do philosophize, worldlings illustrate the claim that the kind of philosophy we adopt depends upon the kind of persons that we are, the kind of values that we have. So does the kind of theology that we adopt.

Lacking critical reflectiveness, most worldly people are not metaphysical or philosophical materialists, naturalists, or positivists. Yet, these metaphysical philosophies express and nurture worldly values, and they have helped create the axiological emptiness and perversity of today's secular societies. Gabriel Marcel claimed that historical materialists and naturalists were able to adopt idealistic and humanistic ethical positions only because they did not fully understand all the practical ramifications of their materialistic metaphysics; they continue to capitalized unknowingly on spiritual and moral legacies inherited from earlier non-materialistic eras. Evaluational materialism, according to Marcel, contends that only sense objects are real, that only the real has value, that people are merely physical objects on the model of machines, and that, given these "truths," it is ethically permissible to treat persons as mere things whose output is all that matters.[38] Worldlings are largely out of touch with intrinsic conscience and other features of intrinsic inwardness, including consciousness itself. They do not easily hear the still small voice of conscience within.

Worldlings who take axiological materialism to its logical, psychological, and practical conclusions regard and treat persons merely as physical objects having only the same sort of finite, expendable, and extrinsic utility-value that other sensory objects have. Considered only materialistically and behavioristically, no one has any "inwardness," to use Kierkegaard's word for it. No one has any inner or direct self-awareness, self-initiative, creativity, rationality, conscience, self-control, autonomy, capacity for choice, emotions, desires, or feelings. Reduced to mere things, mere machines, people can be manipulated, controlled, bullied, and exploited sexually and otherwise without having to consider, respect, and positively acknowledge their inner feelings, thoughts, beliefs, interests, or desires. They may pretend and profess otherwise, but worldlings are very inconsiderate, vain, snobby, envious, and contemptuous, even when not physically vicious and violent.

Human rights and moral duties to self and others presuppose intrinsic consciousness or inwardness in everyone; without it, moral rights and duties have no point. For worldlings, extrinsic values reign supreme in interpersonal relations—transmuted into inter-thing or "thing-thing" relations. People may be "worth a million dollars" (or more, or less); they can be bought and sold, as women and children are in many places today. The value of human beings is purely economic or crassly utilitarian. Jobs paying good wages to adults are shipped to other countries where people are cheap, especially minors.

For many worldlings, even children are mere things to be exploited. In many parts of the world today, parents sell their children to be slave laborers and/or prostitutes. Buyers, equally to blame, are abundant. In more "civilized" societies like our own, children are educated to be little more than producers and consumers of worldly goods. About us Americans, Kenneth Keniston wrote some time ago:

> More than most nations, we have defined children as future producers and have valued or disvalued them accordingly. The qualities that we have tried to implant in them have been the traits thought necessary for power and status in our economic system. The question that we confront today is whether it is possible for our society to begin to define children in some other way, a way that emphasizes the fulfillment of their potential, not merely as future producers but as unique individuals with a diversity of talents.[39]

Every man has his price, and so does every woman and child, worldlings believe. Sexually exploitable females, whatever their age, are expected to "submit," and "produce" for their male companions. For worldly men, women are just sex objects. Males too can be sex objects. Worldly women are more likely to regard men as "success objects,"[40] yet, as objects all the same. To worldlings, everyone is just an object, a thing, of one kind or another; no one is a conscious, sensitive, creative inner subject. On and off the job, worldlings expect other men, women, and children to "function" and "produce." Their human worth is reduced to their extrinsic value, their productivity. Businesses relocate to places where people are cheap, but they expect to sell their products to people who no longer have the jobs they took away. Worldlings assume that the obsequious words and slavish gestures of their social "inferiors" show that they love their chains and do not mind being reduced to mere objects. How little do they understand!

Society and Worldly Self-knowledge

> *It seems amazing,....when it is clear that God is so near to our minds, that there are so few who see the First Principle in themselves. But the reason is close at hand. For the human mind, distracted by cares, does not enter into itself through memory; obscured by phantasms [sensations], it does not return into itself through intelligence; allured by concupiscence [sensuous desires] it never returns to itself through the desire for inner sweetness and spiritual gladness. Thus, lying totally in this sensible world, it cannot return to itself as to the image of God.*[41] St Bonaventure

> Their sensuous nature is generally predominant over their intellectuality....They prefer to live ... in the determinants of sensuousness.[42] Søren Kierkegaard

> *Oh God, if there is a God, have mercy on my soul, if I have a soul.* A psychologist's prayer.

> *The majority of men live without being thoroughly aware that they are spiritual beings—and to this is referable all the security, contentment with life, etc., etc., which precisely is despair.*[43] Søren Kierkegaard

> It may sound surprising when I say, on the basis of my own clinical practice as well as that of my psychological and psychiatric colleagues, that the chief problem of people in the middle decade of the twentieth century is emptiness. *By that I mean not only that many people do not know what they want: they often do not have any clear idea of what they feel. Thus they feel swayed this way and that, with painful feelings of powerlessness, because they feel vacuous, empty....They generally can talk fluently about what they* should *want, to complete their college degrees successfully, to get a job, to fall in love and marry and raise a family, but it is soon evident that they are describing what others, parents, professors, employers, expect of them rather than what they themselves want.*[44] Rollo May

> We live in the world of the senses. This is the world of space and time, our social world....Ninety-five percent of the people in the developed countries, both in the West and in the East, both in capitalist and communist countries, live in this world, the world of extrinsic value. The vast majority of them believe this is the only world there is, and they neglect their inner being.[45] Robert S. Hartman

Logically, it seems, worldly people could not be self-centered or selfish if they have no direct self-awareness, so their selfishness must involve some other kind of self-awareness. What kind? They are keenly aware of their external, public, outer selves, their bodies, their physical deeds, and the roles their bodies play in public spacetime. They have a great deal of outer or external self-awareness; but they are deficient in inner self-awareness, though every real person has some small degree of it. Worldlings do, too, but only because their values are never purely or completely extrinsic or worldly. Axiological personality types are only abstractions to which living individuals only approximate. The three value dimensions have a place in everyone. The crucial consideration is, which one dominates the others?

Completely extrinsic worldlings would know themselves only in the manner of strictly consistent behavioristic psychologists. Directly, in mirrors, or through the eyes of others, they would know and perceive only their bodies and physical activities.[46] They would have no direct conscious awareness, no inner selfhood, because the very concept of such is empirically (sensorially) meaningless. They could not be introspective or self-reflective. They would have no second-order self-awareness. They would think but not be directly aware of their thinking. They would feel but could not attend directly to their feelings. They would choose but notice only things chosen and their own to and fro bodily motions, not their inner acts of choice. They would play social roles, especially status-enhancing roles, but not really understand their motives for doing so. They would attend to things but could not attend to their own attending. They would feel desires, pleasures, and pains but be deprived of their full exhilaration because they focus only on their external sources and manifestations, not on these inner feelings themselves. They cannot distinguish clearly between inner and outer and tend to conflate them. Conscience may be there in the depth of their souls, but they would have little awareness of it. Their meager sense of right and wrong is externally oriented and engendered; they are other-directed, not self-directed, for they have no self. They are worldly because their parents, friends, and societies are worldly. They do not *know* themselves inwardly, directly, and intrinsically, and in that sense they would not *have* or *be* a self. Their knowledge of others would be as superficial as their knowledge of themselves—something purely external, physical, material.

Worldly people are to themselves merely what they see with their own eyes and through the eyes of other worldlings—another thing in the mindless, spiritless, world of things. According to Kierkegaard, in his (or her) "immediacy" or undeveloped selfhood, a worldly person "recognizes himself only by his dress; ... he recognizes that he has a self only by externals."[47] To Kierkegaard, this lack of inward self-knowledge is a condition of despair, the worst form of despair, the kind that does not know itself to be in despair because it does not know itself at all.

"I" and "self" are familiar words in ordinary language, but they are systematically ambiguous with respect to their referent. In the depth of their hearts, worldly people accept, if only semi-consciously, the behavioristic identification of "I" or "myself" with "my body" and "the social roles I play out in the public spacetime world." Not given to philosophizing, most worldlings do not consciously hold this theory. They simply identify themselves with their body and its functions by default because they lack self-conscious reality, inwardness, and independence. They know themselves primarily as objects, not as subjects. They are self-less, not in the spiritual sense of deliberately surrendering, overcoming, or sacrificing ego-self, but in the more elemental sense of never finding themselves at all. The truly alarming and appalling thing about philosophical behaviorists and positivists is this: suppose that they are absolutely sincere! Suppose they really do lack all immediate self-awareness whatsoever! Kierkegaard would not be surprised.

With diminished inwardness, but not totally devoid of it, real worldlings are insensitive, callous, inconsiderate, spiritless, prosaic, boring, bored. With only dim reflective awareness, (unconscious despair, as Kierkegaard saw it),[48] their lives are empty, shallow, superficial, meaningless, a wasteland. Even to themselves, they are hollow men (and women), empty shells. They may live superficially at the emotional level of everyday interestedness, but they tend to lack deep feelings and profound intrinsic involvements. When they do get deeply involved, their passions center on things, status, sensuality, revenge, exploitation, and nepotism. This is the story of their lives. They despair, at least semi-consciously, over their emptiness, the ultimate meaninglessness of the things they cherish, and the shallow lives they lead. They try to overcome emptiness, boredom, anxiety, and despair through perpetual business and endless insatiable quests for more and more possessions, gadgets, things, and for higher and higher social caste. They love to "shop 'til they drop." Despite surface appearances to the contrary, they live in "quiet desperation," just as Thoreau said.

Non-worldly modes of conformity may exist, but worldly people are pressured to conform, despite their competitive self-centeredness. Their norms come from outside themselves. Social status is parasitic upon society, that is, upon the conventions, traditions, expectations, values, and attitudes of other people. Status seekers, like fame seekers, are at the mercy of others far more than they realize. Their social conformity and worldly conservatism are closely related to the way they know and evaluate themselves—mainly as they appear in mirrors and in the eyes of others, in the faces of the crowd. Despite their vaunted practical shrewdness, worldlings with weak systemic critical capacities are quite gullible and vulnerable to the fickle winds of fashion, popularity, social trends, and public opinion. If their systemic capacities for thinking abstractly and critically are weak, they cannot conceive of alternatives to the problematic values, conventions, traditions, fashions, and trends of their own limited caste, time, and place. They lack vision. Social conflicts can immobilized them, for they have no historical or rational depth of perspective on values, and they are disposed to view transient fads and local customs as timeless norms. Their self-expectations are mostly uncritical internalizations of the expectations of others who are equally worldly. When they live up to their own self-expectations, they either just do what others expect of them, or they follow the bent of their own natural self-centeredness, but these are often in conflict. They discriminate between right and wrong, not by consulting conscience, but by asking "What will it profit me?" and "What will the neighbors think?" They are greedy because almost everyone else is greedy; they are worldly because almost everyone else is worldly. They like to do what everyone else is doing.

To gain social status, worldlings must be what others want and expect them to be, for social status equates with what others think of us. This may be out of sync with what they think of themselves. Their self-knowledge mirrors what they think that others think of them, but they may have little awareness or understanding of how others really see them. According to R. D. Alexander, "The concept of status simply implies that an individual's privileges, or its access to resources, are controlled in part by how others collectively think of him as a result of past interactions."[49] Their quest for dominant social standing means that life is worthwhile for them only if they satisfy group expectations well enough to achieve exalted group rankings. Their self-acceptance depends heavily on being socially accepted, at least within their own worldly sub-culture, clique, class, or caste. They identify themselves with their images, honors, and reputations. They constantly strive to make a good impression as they vie for dominance, superiority, distinction, honor, and fame. They envy and identify with those who have such things. When their rebellious children or unfaithful spouses do something to mar their *image*, they lament, "Why did you have to do this *to me?*" They identify with their social images and damaged reputations, more so than with their children or spouses as unique individuals. They also identify intensely with their possessions. When their cars and/or other belongings are stolen or damaged, they experience this not simply as a property loss but as a personal affront.

Their egoistic quest for prosperity often conflicts with their quest for exalted social respect and position. Many of the inconsiderate, dishonest, abusive, exploitive, and violent things that worldlings do to prosper evoke keen social and moral disapproval; but worldlings may not respond by making constructive changes. Broad social disfavor may make them withdraw into grossly immoral sub-cultures where honor exists only among thieves. Some cultures and sub-cultures really are predominantly immoral. Worldlings want and try to control and exploit others, but they are also extremely anxious about social demotion, disapproval, denigration, slander, dishonor, disgrace, or ostracism. Their basic worldly values—things and status—often conflict with one another. Losing status is almost like ceasing to exist. Despite their other-disregarding materialistic self-centeredness, worldly people are in bondage to public opinion, group thinking, mass conformity, or what Kierkegaard called "the crowd." "Losing face" in the Orient is so horrible that it may call for self-immolation. In many parts of America and elsewhere, worldlings will kill you for impugning their honor. So will the Klingons!

Down to Earth Language

Language is fossil poetry.[50] Ralph Waldo Emerson

Conventional English is the twin sister to barren thought. Plato had recourse to myth.[51] Alfred North Whitehead

Everyday language is a forgotten and used up poem.[52] Martin Heidegger

"Rapid reading"—However useful it may be for certain practical purposes—represents the final corruption of language. Poetry—all imaginative literature of any quality—resists "rapid reading"....We have forfeited a language [poetry] that would nourish the relations that we now complain of having lost—to nature, to others and to ourselves.[53] Robert Penn Warren

When it comes to atoms, language can be used only as in poetry.[54] Niels Bohr

The constriction, confusion, cramped options, and value conflicts of the worldly life style result partly from linguistic and conceptual limitations. Extremely worldly people have little or no poetry or metaphors in their vocabularies or in their souls. Their natural language is ordinary language, ordinary prose, reduced to its most elemental literal or sensory significance. Their natural physics is Newtonian, not quantum or relativity. Philosophical worldliness, as expressed in the infamous logical empiricist Principle of Verification, contends that words are meaningful only to the extent that they have sensory import or reference; and systemic language is nothing more than empty tautologies constructed by self or society. If they were right, even the most basic concepts of today's natural science would be meaningless, as the above quote about atoms from Niels Bohr indicates. Without direct sensory import, words and sentences that seem to describe are actually meaningless, from this philosophical perspective. Worldlings accept such an outlook, at least by default, because they lack the wisdom and imagination to suppose otherwise.

A purely worldly language would lack: (1) "empty" formalities like logic and mathematics, (2) the abstract technical constructs of philosophy and natural science, (3) words having affective, introspective, and intrinsic referents or significance, (4) normative as opposed to purely descriptive words, and (5) poetic, metaphorical, figurative, and mythical imagery or symbolism. Most real people are not totally worldly, but linguistic impoverishment correlates with degrees of worldliness.

The highly prosaic language to which they are limited gives conceptual form to what worldlings are capable of experiencing, knowing, and valuing. Social expectations are deeply embedded in ordinary language, where the normal or typical is the norm. Most worldly Westerners know and define themselves largely through their social roles as businessmen, salesmen, associate professors, executives, engineers, producers, consumers, suburbanites, commuters, homeowners, housewives, parents, athletic supporters, Rotarians, Baptists, Episcopalians, Republicans, and the like. Worldlings seek high status roles for themselves. Hierarchical role-concepts like president, vice-president, treasurer, general, corporal, private, chief executive officer, middle-level manager, department head, policeman, and so on, contain their own normative expectations. So do non-hierarchical social roles like friend, teacher, and social worker. Every social station has its duties; social role concepts include duties within stations. Accepting a social role means embracing what society expects of those who play it. In learning *what each of our social roles means,* we discover ways to measure our own worth, extrinsically understood. Social measures of self-worth domineer worldly consciousness. If good is concept or standard fulfillment, worldlings are good, as they see it, to the extent that they measure up to the norms inherent in prosperous and prestigious social roles, functions, positions, and public images. As Kierkegaard said, "A self is qualitatively what its measure is."[55]

Worldly people measure their own worth and the worth of others largely by conventional social expectations embedded in ordinary language. The worth of their own spouse and children is gauged by the meaning of "normal" wife, husband, or child. The normal child is typically one who "makes good," that is, is ambitious, industrious, successful, becomes a wealthy "top dog," isn't queer, and stays out of trouble. The normatively normal husband is the faithful good provider and dominant member of the household. The normatively normal wife is the faithful and submissive housewife. Societies change, and new worldly roles are constantly being created for both women and men, but being too unique, unusual, or unconventional is anathema to them because social status depends on what other people think of us.

Freedom is gained by overcoming the world, by being liberated from bondage to the excessively finitistic and worldly standards of goodness that are embedded in ordinary prose, where every "is" contains a hidden "ought." Worldlings find it difficult to recognize and appreciate the uniqueness and intrinsic worth of those closest to themselves. They cannot respect their right to be just as they are and to pursue their own private interests and personal projects, despite what local conventions or caste customs dictate. They cannot recognize, relate to, or find satisfaction in persons as unique, conscious, ensouled realities. They even lack a suitable vocabulary for it. Unique conscious individuals are valuable in, of, and for themselves, but worldlings don't quite get it. They deal with people mainly as useful members of sensory and social classes. They inordinately restrict the value significance of others by appraising their worth in terms of whether or not they fulfill the extrinsic class concepts applied to them.

St. Paul and others writers of the New Testament repudiated the denigration and vilification involved in treating people as mere members of abstract extrinsic classes, and not as unique individuals living out their lives before God. St. Paul condemned the disdainful worldly practice of "writing people off" as *merely* Greeks, Jews, circumcised, uncircumcised, barbarians, Scythians, slaves, freemen, males, females, etc. The same inordinate, uninformed, contemptuous, arrogant, and excessive finitizing of human worth is involved in treating people as *mere* employees, employers, businessmen, salesmen, consumers, producers, customers, Holy Rollers, rednecks, foreigners, and members of one race or another.

Many worldly words and phrases reflect and express blatant worldly prejudices. Prejudicial, demeaning, and stereotyping words finitize human significance inordinately and systemically. They reduce human significance to the defining characteristics of pejorative words. Ordinary language abounds with them! Consider demeaning prejudicial labels like "gook," "nigger," "whitey," "oreo," "communist," "capitalist," "hippie," "skinhead," "liberal," "conservative," "effete intellectual," "redneck," "egghead," "hardhat," "nerd," "queer," "straight," "vermin," "weeds," and the like. The "best" worldly "WASP" neighborhoods are severely restricted to keep out "riffraff"—inferior human beings who are different—Blacks, Hispanics, Jews, Moslems, hippies, liberals, radicals, non-conformists, eggheads, the mentally ill and retarded, homosexuals, the poor, the "least of these." Prejudice (pre-judgment), a commonplace moral defect, results when worldliness unites with systemic ideologies. Some worldly/ideological communities contain only two mutually contemptuous classes of people, "local yokels" and "outside agitators."

Prejudicial labels reduce people either to merely extrinsic things or to mere instances of systemic stereotypes and constructs. Sometimes the two are combined. Worldlings exploit and deliberately perpetuate stereotypes, images, and language forms that favor themselves and disparage their competition, their "inferiors." Whoever controls the language of society can manipulate its members. Worldly individuals constantly try to have "I-it" relations, or more exactly, "it-it" relations, with other people because they regard people, themselves included, as "hollow men"—to use T. S. Eliot's somewhat sexist expression for it.

We live in our languages, as Heidegger, Whitehead, Wittgenstein and others stressed in their own respective ways. Language is a conspicuous but not a distinctly or exclusively human mode of being. The great apes can be taught to use sign languages within limits, and some may teach them to their offspring. A grey parrot named "Alex" learned to use elemental spoken language, not just repetitiously, but very meaningfully.[56] Even without formal languages, animals use images to represent things to themselves and to reflect on them. We should not be so vain as to think that we are the only rational creatures of God who understand! The language we speak in-forms (gives form to) our lives, experiences, activities, expectations, and how we measure worth. Systemic-minded intellectuals are both masters and slaves of technical languages. Worldlings are both masters and slaves of ordinary empirical prose. Saints strive to master but can be enslaved, confused, or deceived by metaphors, poetry, and myths. Whole persons, holistic saints, master all three languages and are slaves to none.

Worldlings are *prosaic*. They are masters of ordinary prose, ordinary language, literalistic sensory language, but they are also limited, dominated, or mastered by it with respect to what there is and to what there ought to be. Each kind of language serves as a measuring rod for the value and disvalue of things, ideas, people, events, and experiences. Each kind of language possesses its own distinctive concepts, thus its own peculiar measuring units. Linguistic limitations greatly restrict a person's capacity to evaluate. Worldly people all "talk the same language," a "down to earth" language. Language gives power, but it also subjugates. The limits of our languages are the limits of our world and of our power to evaluate. Teaching others, especially children, how to speak and how to develop and diversify their linguistic capacities empowers them as evaluators. The liberal arts, especially the humanities, give powers that merely empirical worldlings do not have. They do not even want "the soft stuff."

Replying to "What is this or that?" provides children and adults with criteria by which they can both identify and judge the goodness or badness of that kind of thing. Consider teaching a child the meaning of "screwdriver," "book," "person," "animal," "brother," "sister," "parent," or "race." We learn how to value them while learning how to conceive of them. In learning what these words mean, we inevitably learn also how to tell the good ones from the not-so-good ones. Criteria for *learning* meanings tend to be behavioral, so deeds are usually more powerful than words. But every "is" contains a hidden "ought."

The Cash Value of The Fine Arts

> The philistine's objection to art is that it is useless. And if we only knew what was really useful, this would be a damning indictment. But, not being much given to abstract reflection, the philistine is usually at a loss to inform us. However, by talking with him, we can eventually divine what they think the useful to be. Useful is what contributes to the procurement of those things which they value—material

> *wealth, power, and sensual enjoyment. Art is useless because it will not prepare a banquet, build a bridge, or help to run a business corporation. The artist is a contemptible fellow because they care more for their art than for the things of the world; for whatever the worldling values they think every one else should value.*[57]
> DeWitt H. Parker

Purely worldly people are prosaic both in the language they speak and in how they relate to and appreciate (or fail to appreciate) the "fine arts." Having little imagination, they cannot warm up to it in others. Lacking a profound sense of and respect for their own individuality, they cannot understand art when it expresses and celebrates uniqueness. Being mastered by and limited to literalistic prose, they are excluded from metaphorical and symbolical meanings that are conceptually and emotionally rich, complex, and deeply engaging. They are both morally and aesthetically insensitive. They see little or no value in the liberal arts, especially the humanities, the "soft subjects." They see works of art but not their beauty and uniqueness. They fail to comprehend the intrinsic standards and concepts of creative artists and writers. They are insensitive to and unappreciative of the intense identification of artists with their art during the creative process.

Works of art come alive to worldlings when measured by their own extrinsic worldly standards. A painting with little aesthetic significance for them is suddenly transvalued when it sells for thirty million dollars. Money talks! If well-to-do, as they aspire to be, worldlings buy works of art by noted artists as "good investments," or because they have "snob appeal," or just to display or flaunt their affluence. They attend operas and concerts of classical music for similar reasons, but not because they really appreciate them. They really prefer music about cigarettes, whiskey, wild wild women, hound dogs, and pickup trucks, though country and western music often ranges well beyond the narrow confines of worldliness. Worldly people are interested only in the economic or status-conferring significance of the fine arts, liberal arts, and performing arts. Apart from these, art is worthless, meaningless, and irrelevant to them.

DeWitt Parker put it bluntly; worldly people are Philistines. Poetry, literature, painting, classical music, sculpture, drama, opera, and other arts are not valued as such. They have little worth apart from their economic value and as emblems of conspicuous consumption, exalted status, and "high class." Philistines reassess their attitudes towards artists and authors who acquire fame and wealth through their arts and writings. Because of artists' fame or affluence, wealthy Philistines may decide to be their patrons—in a patronizing way. When artists get what Philistines value, they are then esteemed and rewarded. If art becomes fashionable, Philistines are won over because everyone else wants it, and because art has significant cash value.

Works of art can be regarded and valued as mere *things*, as extrinsic entities, as localized, finite, spatiotemporal objects having a price, and the pricier the better. So regarded, works of art are competitive goods ownable by only one person, gallery, or institution at a time. So regarded, art is valued economically, not aesthetically.

The aesthetic value of a work of art is a non-competitive good that anyone can enjoy and share, and price and ownership are irrelevant. Good teachers can give away their thoughts, musicians can share their music, painters or sculptors can share their visions, and dramatists, poets, and novelists can offer their creations to others without being in the least impoverished aesthetically. Worldlings play zero sum games where one person can win only if someone else loses.

Worldly persons are blind to aesthetic values as such, in part because they are non-competitive goods. If it has no price and can't even in principle be mine alone, they assume, art can't be any good. Properly understood, for a work of art to have intrinsic aesthetic value, that is, to be valued intrinsically, art only has to be; but it need not be mine alone or have great cash value. Without such aesthetic disinterestedness or impartiality, there can be no intrinsic aesthetic interestedness.

Extrinsic/Worldly Religion

> *'Tis not a good objection against any kind of preaching, that some men abuse it greatly to their hurt. It has been acknowledged by all divines, as a thing common in all ages, and all Christian countries, that a very great part of those that sit under the Gospel, do so abuse it that it only proves an occasion of their far more aggravated damnation, and so of men's eternally murdering their souls; which is an effect infinitely more terrible than the murder of their bodies.*[58] Jonathan Edwards

> *Beware of quenching that blessed hunger and thirst, by which the world calls 'religion'—a religion of form, of outside show, which leaves the heart as earthly and sensual as ever. Let nothing satisfy thee but the power of godliness, but a religion that is spirit and life; the dwelling in God and God in thee. The religion of the world implies three things, first, abstaining from scandalous outward sins like stealing, swearing, and drunkenness; second, doing good by giving to the poor; third, going to church and using the conventional means of grace like the Lord's supper. But it requires no inward change of heart.*[59] John Wesley

Worldly people are not necessarily irreligious; indeed, they may be very religious in their own worldly way. Worldly spirituality is adapted to and expressive of their peculiar worldly mode of evaluative consciousness. *Worldly religion offers extrinsic value-objects to people as ultimate goods in the name of God.* Having them *sanctioned by Divinity* insulates and shields worldly values against serious challenges from non-worldly values. The external forms and practices of religion are often employed in the service of worldly values and evaluations.

According to John Wesley (above), worldlings go through the motions of religion but miss its heart and soul. Worldly religious institutions exist to minister to the religious needs of worldlings, but just as no real people are purely worldly, so no religious institutions are purely worldly. It's just a matter of dominance. Where the heart is subordinated to the world, there is always hope that the world will become subordinated to the heart.

Worldly Religion: Survival, Health, Prosperity, Social Position

> *There is such an abundance of the here and now, such plenitude of the given and the conceived that our mind has lost itself in the world. All we can trust in is the work of our hands, the product of our minds, and what lies beyond it is considered an illegitimate fancy. The world to us consists of instruments, of tools, and the supreme ideas are symbols only.* God is a name but no reality. *The standard of action is expediency, and God, too, is for the sake of our satisfaction.*[60] Rabbi Abraham J. Heschel

> *But seek ye first the kingdom of God, and his righteousness, and all these things shall be added unto you.* Jesus (Matthew 6:33)

At its worst, worldly religion offers Divine confirmation and sponsorship of the worldly values of self-preservation, material prosperity, social superiority, power over others, sexual gratification, reproduction, revenge against enemies (conveniently classified as God's enemies), rewards to allies, and aggressive exploitation, damnation, and humiliation of inferiors and outsiders, especially those who subscribe to an "inferior" religion or to no religion at all. It *uses* religion to sanction and support the values of worldly health, survival, reproduction, prosperity, success, status, sex, or whatever "things" worldlings prize, and to gain more and more of the world. Its good news is a prosperity gospel. God wants us to be rich and successful and will make it so if we will only pay up.

In its *survival-confirming function*, worldly religion emphasizes the now well-confirmed fact that religious people are generally much healthier and more disease resistant, both physically and psychologically, than non-religious people.[61] Spirituality helps people to prosper and to live longer and healthier lives in this world. This is a very good thing, no doubt, but is it the end of the road? People stuck at the stage of worldly religion are like those who came to Jesus, as he recognized, only because he gave them extrinsic physical bread, not because he could offer them the eternal spiritual bread of intrinsic love and life (John 6: 26-27). They are the "Rice Christians" who affiliate with missionaries only because they provide them with food.

In its *prosperity-confirming functions*, worldly religion treats the kingdom of God and his righteousness as mere means to the "things" that they supposedly procure. The worldly gospel is *a gospel of prosperity*. God assures and insures that people who do his will are duly rewarded both now and later. God wants us to be rich and famous. Being an active member of a prestigious religious congregation is simply good business. Giving to religious projects, causes, institutions, and televangelists is a sound investment, good insurance, for God himself will repay those who do so manyfold. Sabbath or Sunday services are splendid occasions for displaying affluence, prestige, and pretentiousness. Being good Christians, Jews, or what have you, makes you more popular, more successful, and helps you to grow better crops, sell more products, and win more wars and football games, all of which enhance sexual access. This prosperity gospel is preached by many television evangelists and in many local congregations. Highly successful clergy at or near the top, especially rich and famous televangelists, are greatly prone to stray sexually. When they become top dogs for God, they feel that they deserve it!

Worldly religion proclaims that the competitive, avaricious, and aggressive worldly way of life expresses and fulfills the will of God. It is a magical religion that tries to get worldly effects, material goods, from immaterial causes, from unperceived spiritual Powers. Ceremonies, prayers, and incantations work external magic, not internal magic, worldlings assume. The main purpose of the earliest primitive religions was to insure that the gods would guarantee sexual fertility, favor tribal warriors in battle, and enable them to loot the worldly possessions of their neighbors in the name of God (or the gods). According to Karen Armstrong, the goal of the earliest known religious rites was "the achievement of material goods—cattle, wealth, and status."[62]

Much worldly religion can be found in the Bible. God sanctioned the genocide and territorial conquest of the "promised land" by the Israelites after their long homeless wandering in the wilderness. Love and kindness to strangers, commanded in the Old Testament, were not extended to the Canaanites! In the spirit of Job's comforters, much of the Old Testament portrays the Israelites as prospering in worldly ways when doing God's will and languishing when they lapsed. A precise correlation between obedience and prosperity was often proclaimed, but Job himself and Jeremiah knew better. So did Jesus (Luke 13:1–5 and John 9:1–2).

More recently, the "Protestant work ethic" expresses the prosperity-confirming function of worldly religion. Protestant prosperity is a sure sign or criterion of salvation. Actually, prosperity (here and hereafter) *is* salvation for men and women of the world. Godliness consists in being well to do, and poverty reliably indicates godlessness. In theory, godliness involves industry, hard work, and thrift; but if in practice prosperity can be had effortlessly through inheritance or by winning the lottery (a certain mark of God's favor!), godliness is still intact. The poor, who by definition do not work hard and are not thrifty, are the godless, and that is precisely why they are poor. Anyone who fails in the competition for wealth and status is godless, for godliness consists in worldly success. Greed, envy, rage, aggression, and deceit are the prevailing cardinal sins or vices of pursuing prosperity at almost any cost; but they are exalted as virtues in worldly religion.

In its *status-conferring function*, worldly religion proclaims that existing social and political hierarchies are divinely appointed, sponsored, established, and confirmed. Kings, rulers, and magistrates have divine rights; they are authorized by God. God established the establishment. God authenticates the social *status quo*.

This consoles those who have already "have it made," but not the "have-nots," not "the least of these." Worldly religion is found in those parts of the Bible where whole peoples are repeatedly given over into slavery with Divine approval, where men are authorized to dominate women, where only the Israelites or Christians are God's chosen people, and where earthly humanity is God's chosen dominant species, ranked only slightly below the angels in the total scheme of things. Vanity, conceit, and pride are the prevailing sins of obsession with social domination.

Though it should not be, the Bible can be read and understood in the worldly way. In the first chapter of Genesis, God gives human beings "dominion," that is, dominance or control over all other species of living things (Genesis 1:28). This is extended to cover killing and eating animals only after Noah's flood (Genesis 9:3). Divinely ordained dominion is susceptible to several interpretations, however, as is so much of biblical religion. According to the prevailing worldly interpretation, "dominion" means that all other living things were created by God for us to use as purely extrinsic goods; all other living things exist by Divine decree merely as means to human ends. St. Thomas Aquinas offered this worldly perspective as both a divinely revealed and a philosophically justified truth: God ordains and blesses our totally extrinsic evaluation and exploitation of sub-human animals. As St. Thomas put it:

> Hereby is refuted the error of those who said it is sinful for a man to kill dumb animals: for by divine providence they are intended for use in the natural order. Hence it is no wrong for man to make use of them either by killing or in any other way whatever. For this reason the Lord said to Noe (Gen. ix. 3): *As the green herbs I have delivered all flesh to you.*...There is no sin in using a thing for the purpose for which it is. Now the order of things is such that the imperfect are for the perfect...so...things, like plants, which merely have life, are all alike for animals, and all animals are for man. Wherefore it is not unlawful if man use plants for the good of animals, and animals for the good of man, as [Aristotle] the Philosopher states (*Polit.* I. 3).[63]

Other than God's creating them for us, the main thing here that justifies our exploitation of animals is that they are "dumb." That is, they are not rational, whereas we are. God is a purely impassive rational being, St. Thomas thought. (See the quotes on p. 96.) We exist in that rational image, but animals don't, so it is OK to kill them because they are "dumb."

A non-Thomistic, less systemic, and more saintly and intrinsic interpretation of Genesis shared by many theologians says that "dominion" authorizes us to be good stewards or caretakers of the earth and its creatures, but not to exploit them.[64] From this perspective, most if not all non-human species were also created as intrinsic goods having value in, of, for, and to themselves, and we should treat them with great respect. God pronounced all of non-human creation to be good even before human beings were made (Genesis 1:21), and God made animals to exist for their own sakes. Vegetarianism was originally the divinely prescribed diet for Adam and Eve (Genesis 1:29-30), so the "dominion" given to them in the first chapter of Genesis did not authorize killing and eating animals; that came later, after sin, and then only after the flood (Genesis 9:3). Good stewards respect, protect, preserve, and cherish the natural existence and ecology of living things. They live as harmoniously and non-destructively as possible, but this is not the worldly way. By nature, we are a predatory species with eyes on the front of our heads, not on the sides like prey species, but we do not have to be vicious. By nature or prevenient grace, we can also freely decide not to be the sinners against creation that we are and have been. We can commit ourselves to creation care.

Worldly people expect to be at an elevated rank in some prevailing social hierarchy. Today they reaffirm the extrinsic worldly parts of biblical religion, but they have almost deaf ears to the intrinsic saintly parts. They affiliate socially with religious groups that promise prosperity, both here and hereafter. They want both heavenly *and* earthly mansions, terrestrial *and* starry crowns, special divine favors now and later, anointed prestige, species dominance, confident living, peace of mind, eternal security, social acceptance, and social exaltation both in this world and the next. In heaven, some people will have more stars in their crowns than others, and worldlings expect to be at or near the top of the celestial pecking order. Jonathan Edwards, by contrast, wrote with disdain of those who believe themselves to be "some of the highest favorites of heaven"; he insisted that if they really got to know themselves as the prideful sinners they really are, "Self-knowledge would destroy them."[65]

Religious requirements of repentance, contrition, humility, forgiveness, equality among ourselves, and submission to God are in conflict with our powerful natural drive to dominance. This may be why worldlings and the rest of us have so much difficulty with genuine spiritual conversion, humility, and abasement before God. The difficulty is especially great for married males accustomed to the feminine passiveness and submissiveness championed by St. Paul. However, as Abraham Maslow indicated, a human male may regard religious deference as much less of a threat to domineering masculinity "if he can surrender to a God, to some omnipotent, omniscient figure, where rivalry is out of the question. Kneeling before a God is less an unmanly act than kneeling before a human rival, competitor, or peer."[66] Of course, domineering is not just a masculine vice; the drive is naturally powerful in both females and males; and spiritual contrition can be difficult for members of both sexes. Worldly women who are totally submissive to their husbands, as St. Paul required, can at least lord it over their servants, or slaves, or other "low down" women. Words and gestures of dominance and submissiveness pervade human religious orders, organizations, and devotional practices; but, for worldlings, humility goes against the grain, even when they pay lip service to it.

Worldly religion requires worldlings to be thoroughly regular and respected people, foursquare in conforming to the expectations of their religious traditions, subcultures, and congregations, conspicuous successes in the rat race for prosperity and prestige, and generous contributors to just the right (usually right wing) religious causes and institutions. It sets them up for conflicting values, frustration, and despair. It promises prosperity and prominence to highly self-centered and domineering people in exchange for unselfishness and submission, obedience, conformity to others, e.g., the clergy, or the top dogs in the world. Godlessness, to worldlings, consists in being an odd individualist, a humble saint, a non-conformist, a liberal, a rebel, an outsider, an illegal alien, and/or a pauper, a failure in the scramble for power, revenue, and social honor and respect. Religious worldlings have not been born again into the realm of intrinsic values and evaluations.

Religious institutions may be taken over by worldlings and manipulated to secure and display their affluence and high social status. A pecking order exists within and between religious groups, even within monasteries. Worldlings graduate from less prestigious to more prestigious denominations as they move up the ladder of success. Even within particular denominations, some local congregations are more prestigious than others, and successful social climbing worldly individuals move up through them. I once heard another college professor say, "I joined [denomination X] so I could get into high society."

Worldlings may begin in small struggling congregations in the country or the suburbs and end up as members of big and prosperous congregations downtown, or in their prestigious suburban relocations. What Jesus called "the least of these," Blacks, Indians, Hispanics, "poor white trash," and other "inferiors," may not be welcomed in class-conscious white churches. On Sunday morning, the most segregated hour of the week, the glad hand is extended to those who already have status and wealth; but "the least of these," receive no warm welcome. To those who have much, the glad hand will be given. From those who have not, the little that they have will be taken away. Jesus was right about that!

In worldly Christian churches, the sacraments, ordinances, and practices of religion are co-opted and transformed into expressions of worldliness. This is a perversion, to be sure; but in worldly religion, Christian service may involve "money-changing in the temple." Baptism symbolizes admission into the worldly establishment and readiness to enter the struggle for prestige and prosperity. Prayer is believed to have a direct cause/effect relation with superiority, security, wealth, prestige, health, and happiness. Ask and ye shall receive. The Eucharist or Lord's Supper affords forgiveness for shady business deals, illicit sexual conquests, and acts of vengeance; it renews the soul for further competition, aggression, and success in the worldly "rat race." Confession, formal or informal, wipes clean the slate of worldly sins so the whole process can start afresh with renewed vigor on Monday morning. Religious assemblies are splendid opportunities for business networking. Marriage symbolizes a willingness to conform (somewhat loosely?) to the sexual mores of one's religious sub-culture and to procreate new generations of worldly producers and consumers. Funerals celebrate lifetimes of worldly achievement that merit even "greater rewards" in the world to come. The distinctive beliefs, ceremonies, feelings, and practices of non-Christian religions are also often exploited for worldly gains. No religion has a monopoly on worldliness, but there is a more excellent way (I. Corinthians 13).

Worldly religion confuses and identifies current social norms and conventions with timeless religious ideals. According to H. Richard Niebuhr, in the New Testament, "the world" refers primarily to "the whole society outside the church"; and repudiating the world meant repudiating cultural norms and practices.[67] Worldly religion, by contrast, brings the world back into the churches and identifies Christ with culture. By confusing Christ with culture it idolatrously identifies that which is less than ultimate with the Ultimate itself.

What counts as "traditional religion" is relative to particular individuals and religious or social groups. Worldlings readily embrace any local version of "that old time religion" that promises worldly prosperity and elevated social standing. Christ and culture are confused when Christianity is identified with worldly ideals of masculine bravado, patriotism, honor, manliness, paternalism, and domineering, as well as with corresponding norms of femininity—subordination and submissiveness.

During and even after the Civil War, worldly Southerners identified Christianity with the slave-holding Confederacy, which explicitly claimed in its Constitution to be a "Christian nation," (as the U.S. Constitution does not). They believed on biblical grounds that slavery was God's ordained and preferred way to order social relations in general, and capital and labor relations in particular. Do we today exhibit similar confusions of Christ with culture, of church with state? How so?

Identifying spirituality with prevailing worldly religious and social beliefs, attitudes, practices, and standards definitely has a dark side. God approves of devotees only as long as they conform to the *status quo* requirements of some local worldly religious culture or sub-culture. The people that worldlings love to hate—protesters, innovators, reformers, liberals, abolitionists, deviants, competitors, inferiors, outsiders, illegal aliens, non-conformists—must be on guard because religious worldlings will really "Sock it to you in the name of the Lord." Through the centuries, worldly religion has repeatedly afforded and sanctioned revenge, oppression, nepotism, aggression, conformity, crusades, and holy wars.

Religious worldlings become ardent defenders of the *status quo* when they identify the essence of Christianity, Judaism, or whatever, with current worldly social conventions, expectations, and practices. Worldly social norms may also be projected into some past "golden age," as when Southerners yearned long after the Civil War for the "Lost Cause" of the Confederacy and for the glorious God-ordained racial superiority of whites over blacks. For religious worldlings, their own wealth and status is secure only as long as some established status-and-wealth-conferring religion-backed social system is preserved and used to reenforce favorable-to-them social and political orders, principalities, powers, and institutions, i.e., the world.

Recent work in the psychology of religion says that the positive correlation of extrinsic religion's quest for social gains with prejudice and discrimination, "might be explained by the same kind of boundary-maintenance function often ascribed to fundamentalist beliefs. Individuals who are primarily interested in the social rewards offered by religious involvement may be those most likely to view outsiders with alternative life-styles, belief systems, or ethnic backgrounds as competitors for social resources and thus as targets of discrimination."[68]

More positively, religious socialization, the extrinsic communion of the saints, can serve as a means or bridge to something intrinsic like loving interpersonal relations that are self-fulfilling and others-fulfilling. Religious socialization, as W. Larry Ventis indicated, can help people escape from loneliness because, "Religious involvement and the church community offer one prominent source of company, social support, and friendship with people of similar values and generally prosocial goals."[69] Nothing is wrong if and when religious socialization and institutions are used as means to mutual or complementary intrinsic self-fulfillment for both self and others. Even holistic saints highly value such a communion of the saints.

Different kinds of value can be *combined* into intricate organic valuational wholes. These new combinations can be valued as wholes in many different ways. Psychologists of religion influenced by Gordon Allport were puzzled that people often score highly on both extrinsic and intrinsic scales. This is due partly to Allport's confused and poorly differentiated notions of "extrinsic religion" versus "intrinsic religion," but this puzzle stems largely from not understanding and appreciating how different elements of religion can be taken up into larger wholes and assigned different positions in hierarchies of value and evaluation. Instead of being excluded, some elements can just be subordinated to others while still being fairly well developed. *How* values and evaluations are combined and ranked hierarchically makes all the difference. Real people are complex and can have both extrinsic and intrinsic values at the same time. Everything depends on how they are prioritized. The value dimensions do not necessarily exclude one another, for some good things may be equally valued, while others are valued subordinately.

Worldly religion *ranks* things higher than people, so its priorities are all wrong. People and social relations are valued as mere means to worldly goods. People were made for things, not things for people. Since they conserve wealth, status, and self-serving social hierarchies, religious establishments can be bulwarks of resistance to reforms—economic, political, social, moral, doctrinal, and otherwise. So can all conservatives, religious or not. Conservatives conserve, especially for themselves.

Insightful ministers who are aware of all of this cannot afford (financially, morally, and spiritually) just to give up on parishioners who are still at the worldly stage of psycho-spiritual development. They know that no real people are absolutely worldly, and there is always hope for everyone. Spiritual transformations (conversions) are possible. And before God, all of us are equally valuable and equally loved, even sinners, even worldlings.

Worldly Religious Language and Concepts

God himself does not speak prose, but communicates with us by hints, omen, inference and dark resemblances in objects lying all around us.[70] Ralph Waldo Emerson

This parable of the sower and the seed is one of the most noble of Christ's parables that we have account of: and it being so, 'twill not be improper in this place to inquire why Christ so commonly taught in this way. The following reasons may be given:
In the first place, 'tis an engaging way of instructing. It engages thee attention of the hearers, when any doctrine is taught in an allegory and by way of story. It is a most familiar way, as a parent would instruct a child. Christ condescended to the weakness and childishness of the people, and instructed by easy and familiar comparisons and similitudes.
And then it is a very instructive way. The reason of the thing many times will be presently seen by an apt comparison, that otherwise is difficultly explained.
And another reason why we are so often instructed in Scriptures in an allegorical way, in Christ's parables and elsewhere, is that we might have some exercise for our understanding to find out the truth contained in them. Our understandings were given us to be used, and above all to be exercised in divine things. Therefore God teaches us in such a way that we shall have some exercise of meditation and study. God gives us the gold, but he gives it to us in a mine that we might dig for it and get in a way of our own industry.
And then, when the truth is found out, it makes a greater impression, is much more pleasing. If truth was revealed in such a way that we could understand it as well without study or diligence as with, and fools could understand as much as wise men, truth would be despised. If gold were thrown plentifully before every man's face, and everyone could have it without any labor or industry, it would not be prized as now it is. But God gives it to us in mines; we must dig for it, if we get it, and that makes it precious. So God gives us divine truth as it were in mines—in allegories and parables and types—where we must dig for it to come at it.
'Tis for the same reasons that abundance of the Scripture is obscure and difficult to be understood.[71] Jonathan Edwards

Because worldlings are constrained by ordinary literalistic prose, they are incapable of recognizing the metaphorical and broader symbolical nature of the language of the scriptures and the saints. Since they take all language literally, they take religious language literally. Biblical literalism is an expression of worldliness.

Twentieth Century fundamentalistic Christianity exemplifies this aspect of worldly religion in one important respect. Fundamentalists profess to "take every word of the Bible literally," but it is very doubtful that they do. The word "day" in the creation story may be the only word in the Bible that they really want to take literally. Roman Catholics, who are generally very alert and sensitive to the symbolic, nevertheless insist officially on taking "body" and "blood" literally, even though the elements in the mass look, smell, taste, and feel exactly like bread and wine.

One problem with fundamentalism is that the distinction or contrast between "literal" and "non-literal" has many meanings and can be understood in many different ways. As Hans Frei indicated, "literal" can mean (1) the true and accurate sense (in which case all committed interpreters are literalists and just disagree about which religious beliefs are true and accurate); or it can mean (2) the most generally agreed-upon sense, or (3) what the original authors meant or intended, or (4) the meaning that best harmonizes with its hermeneutic context.[72]

One important aspect of worldly hermeneutics was well explained by the philosopher, G. W. F. Hegel, who identified the mythical or metaphorical meaning of a word not with error but with (5) "figurative meaning," that is, with sensory images employed to express non-sensory religious and philosophical truths or beliefs. Literal meaning, by contrast, just consists of sensory words and images as such taken at face value rather than symbolically or metaphorically—and this is what worldlings and fundamentalists seem inclined to do. The theologian Carl Michalson invoked this sense of religious myth/metaphor when he wrote, "Myth is a way of speaking about God as if his activity in the world were like any other object in the world, subject to touch and sight."[73] Michalson explained that much of the language of the New Testament is mythical in this sense.

> A great spiritual event occurred in the ministry of Jesus of Nazareth. When the apostles looked around for a language in which to express this spiritual reality, they found only the language of things. They made that compromise. They expressed this spiritual reality in the language of things. Subsequently, however, the church has forgotten that compromise and has treated its spiritual reality as if it were a thing. That is the meaning of mythologizing. We are now required to come clean and reappropriate the Christian message in the dimension of reality appropriate to it.[74]

In matters of religion, and wherever metaphors are used, worldlings are reluctant to "come clean." For them, the literal meaning of any word is its hard-core, face value, sensory import in ordinary English (or whatever) prose. Like the Logical Positivists, that is how they want to understand the import of *all* meaningful language, religious or not. Language has no other meaning; everything else makes no sense. Worldly individuals construe meaning as sensory reference, even though ordinary language is rich in words that have no obvious literal sensory reference—numbers, symbols, metaphors, myths, analogies, allegories, linguistic, social, and ethical rules, inner psychological concepts, abstruse philosophical and theological ideas, and even the most abstract and formal elements of scientific theories. The Bible is also full of many such non-literal, non-sensory, linguistic forms.

No sharp line exists between ordinary and extraordinary language. Ordinary language exists and develops in time. The unusual often becomes usual, and the usual becomes unusual. What, for example, are the sensory referents of words in everyday speech like "one," "godlike," the "Golden Rule," "soul," "consciousness," "ideas," "memory," "intention," "ought," "potential," "singularity," and "God"? Like sense-bound positivists and behaviorists, worldlings either dismiss such words as nonsense, or they try to construct some sensory import for them, or they just fail to comprehend them. We may *learn* the meaning of *psychological* concepts by employing behavioral criteria, as Ludwig Wittgenstein contended; but, once learned, the realities to which they point may lie deeper than sensory observation. So it is with most philosophical and theological concepts and judgments.

For worldlings and logical positivists, metaphors are construed as literally as possible, as having some marginal sensory import such as the "mouth" of a river and the "father" or our country. Otherwise, words are altogether nonsense (non-sensory thus non-literal), for example, the not-so-obviously-sensory words in the previous paragraph for which worldlings can make no literal or sensory sense.

Many categories of non-literal speech are recognized by linguists, theologians, and biblical scholars: metaphors, similes, myths, parables, allegories, analogies, poetry, and so on. Traditional religious thinkers always recognized the presence of these non-literal language forms in the Bible; see, for example, the quote from Jonathan Edwards that begins this section. Modern fundamentalism's insistence on biblical literalism is a Twentieth Century heresy. No great intellect is required to realize that much biblical language is not literal, that is, strictly sensory in import, as worldlings require. For example:

The Lord is my shepherd. (Psalms 23:1)

He [God] is my rock, and there is no unrighteousness in him. (Psalms 92:15)

The Lord is my rock, and my fortress, and my deliverer. (Psalms 18:2)

It is he [God] that sitteth upon the circle of the earth, and the inhabitants thereof are as grasshoppers. (Isaiah 40:22)

To the King of ages, immortal, invisible, the only God. (I. Timothy 1:17)

Jesus said to them, 'I am the bread of life'. (John 6:35)

Jesus said,...'I am the vine, you are the branches'. (John 15:5)

And looking upon Jesus as he walked, he saith, 'Behold the Lamb of God!'. John 1:36

He that descended is the same also that ascended up far above all heavens, that he might fill all things. (Ephesians 4:10)

Jesus Christ, who is gone into heaven, and is on the right hand of God. (I. Peter 3:21-22)

Only very dull wits would insist that God is literally a shepherd with a rod and a staff, a rock, a fortress, or an invisible King, that people are grasshoppers, or that Jesus was literally bread, a vine, or a lamb, or that Jesus literally came down from and ascended back to heaven above in a three storied universe, or that Jesus literally sits at God's right hand (because an omnipresent God has no finite humanoid body).

Without much difficulty, we can usually re-express such obviously metaphorical thoughts in less figurative speech. Other instances of biblical imagery are more difficult to decipher. All biblical figures of speech are mines, Jonathan Edwards suggested, and we must dig for their meaning. Is God literally (biologically) a father, as in "Our Father who art in heaven..."? (Matthew 6:9) Is heaven literally a place containing a finite, perceivable God having a symmetrically developed humanoid body with right and left sides and male genitals? Traditional theologians insisted that God is a pure spirit having no body at all. The one, perhaps the only, word in the Bible that fundamentalists want to interpret literally is the word "day" in the first chapter of Genesis and other biblical affirmations of divine creation like "In six days the Lord made heaven and earth, the sea, and all that is in them" (Exodus 20:11).

To us, a literal day is a clockable twenty four hour time period, the amount of time required for planet earth to rotate completely on its axis. But biblical authors knew nothing about clocks or the rotation of the earth on its axis. They did not even know that the earth is a planet among planets. They counted full days from sunup to sundown. Biblical authors had some ability to keep time and to contrast days (periods of light) with nights (periods of darkness). A literalistic interpretation of "day" in biblical accounts of creation rules out evolution, which took far longer than longer than six sunups to sundowns, or even six 24 hour days—144 total hours, as we would count them. For that reason, to rule out evolution, and perhaps only for that reason, fundamentalists claim to be biblical literalists; but clearly they cannot take every scriptural word literally, that is, empirically and non-metaphorically, even when they profess to do so. James Barr, one of the best experts on fundamentalism, says that today's fundamentalists do not even take "day" literally.[75] According to Barr,

> The point of conflict between fundamentalists and others is not over *literality* but over *inerrancy*. Even if fundamentalists do sometimes say that they take the Bible literally, the facts of fundamentalist interpretation show that this is not so. What fundamentalists insist is not that the Bible must be taken literally but that it must be so interpreted as to avoid any admission that it contains any kind of *error*. In order to avoid imputing error to the Bible, fundamentalists twist and turn back

and forward between literal and non-literal interpretation....In order to expound the Bible as thus inerrant, the fundamentalist interpretation varies back and forward between literal and non-literal understandings, indeed he has to do so in order to obtain a Bible that is error-free.[76]

Barr adds that even when a fundamentalist does take the Bible literally, he (or she) still has a serious problem, namely, "deciding which elements in passages, he will take literally and which he will not."[77] Fundamentalists actually take the Bible literally only "at those points at which the structure of fundamentalist religion requires that it should do so," that is, only to make their interpretations consistent with certain fundamental doctrinal "truths" like creation, the trinity, the virgin birth, the substitutionary blood atonement, the resurrection, the second coming, heaven and hell, and scriptural inerrancy. For thoughtful fundamentalists, literal interpretations are simply those that agree with certain antecedently selected doctrines; interpretations that undermine those doctrines are "non-literal." Fundamentalists claim to be literalists in the worldly or at least in some conventionalist sense. At times they are, but not consistently. The final question for them is, "What is true?" not, "What is literal?" In that respect they belong to a long and quite respectable hermeneutic tradition.

But what religious beliefs are true? Fundamentalist hermeneutics requires that we first know the truth as a pre-condition for interpreting the language of the scriptures correctly. If so, its fundamental "truths" cannot simply be read off of or derived from the scriptures, for no one knows what the scriptures mean until their antecedently selected fundamental doctrines are first accepted, then used to distinguish between true and false interpretations. For fundamentalists, their doctrinal selections come first, even though they claim that the scriptures come first.

Every interpretation of revealed scripture pushes some philosophical, spiritual, cultural, or personal agenda and should be proffered and accepted only with great humility. The scriptures may be of divine origin, but their interpretation and application are always human. God may be on the "sending end," but fallible human beings are always on the "receiving end" of every reveled proposition.

Consider one example of how non-scriptural presuppositions enter into human hermeneutics. Classical theologians like Augustine, Aquinas, and Anselm all dismissed as misleading non-literal metaphors the vast number of biblical statements that attribute temporality and spatiality to God because they accepted as literal the Greek philosophical view that God is absolutely timeless and spaceless.[78] But why should Greek philosophical discourse be construed as literal, and biblical discourse be construed non-literally, rather than vice versa? Why play the game of the Classical Theologians instead of the game of Process Theologians, who attribute literal temporality and spatiality to God for philosophical as well as scriptural reasons. For Process Theists, God really interacts with creatures in time and history, just as the Bible says, not in some absolutely changeless and timeless Greek philosophical eternity; and God as omnipresent has a body, a non-humanoid body—the spatiotemporal universe itself, for the universe is the body of God. If we believe that God has spatiotemporal properties, we will side with biblical discourse in taking scriptural language about God's acting in history more literally than figuratively. To side with the Greek philosophers, we must self-consciously take most of the Bible very figuratively. Of course, the universe as God's body is not a strictly literalistic rendition of the humanoid physical imagery often applied to God in the Bible, but it is literally compatible with biblical affirmations that God is everywhere, that God fills the heavens and the earth, that there is no place that we can go to escape from God, that we live and move and have our being within God, and that God interacts with people in time and history.

Fundamentalism is extrinsically worldly and empirically positivistic when it insists too much on sensory literality. When it turns to inerrancy, it becomes systemically ideological, as explained in the next chapter; and that is probably its deepest problem.

Whether fundamentalists or not, innumerable spiritual-minded people really do play worldly language games when they construe many important religious concepts and doctrines in merely or mainly literalistic physical and social terms, as next explained.

Worldly Other Worlds

> *If God were not to be enjoyed in heaven, but only vast wealth, immense treasures of silver and gold, great honor of such kind as men obtain in this world, and a fulness of the greatest sensual delights and pleasures; all these things would not make up for the want of God and Christ, and the enjoyment of them there. If it were empty of God, it would indeed be an empty melancholy place....The Godly have been made sensible, as to all creature-enjoyments, that they cannot satisfy the soul; and therefore nothing will content them but God.*[79] Jonathan Edwards

Worldliness, valuing primarily security, success, things, possessions, positions, and the like, is the opposite of *non-worldliness*, primarily valuing something else besides security, things, possessions, and positions. Non-worldliness should not be confused with *other-worldliness*, believing that other worlds or universes are real in addition to our own system of nature or spacetime, even if this is true. Worldliness and non-worldliness are mutually exclusive. Both are often confused with other-worldliness, but they do not have to be, even when other-worldliness is affirmed.

Both fundamentalists and worldly people tend to conceive of other worlds, for example, heaven and hell, in sensory/literal terms. Atheists do too, which is why they find the "other world" so easy to ridicule and reject. Worldly religion manifests its survival, prosperity, and status-confirming functions in unimaginative, prosaic, literal-minded concepts or pictures of heaven and hell. Worldly Christians require streets of literal gold in heaven, and literal fire and brimstone in hell. Status-conscious worldly Christians expect the social structure of heaven to be literally hierarchical. Some people will literally have more stars in their crowns and bigger mansions than others; some will be on God's right hand and others merely on the left. They could not endure a heaven in which all people are perfectly equal in the sight of God. Worldly Judaism requires a literal messianic kingdom in this world, with high status and great prosperity for the chosen people. Worldly Islam requires a literal erotic paradise like that described in the *Koran* (Sûrah XLV: 51-57 and LVI: 11-40); many suicide bombers are now dying for that! Worldlings in almost any world religion might be attracted to the prospect of an erotic paradise.

Worldly religion does not repudiate other worlds; it simply adopts a grossly empirical or worldly picture of heaven and hell, more so perhaps in Christianity and Islam than in Judaism. With one important qualification, it conceives of these otherworlds in this-worldly sensory terms. In heaven as it is on earth! The qualification is, in heaven restraints on acquisition imposed by scarcity and the recalcitrance of this-worldly matter do not exist. In the *Koran*, taken literally, restraints on sex do not exist in heaven, though it has no reproductive function.

Diamonds, pearls, and gold are valuable now because they are scarce, but literalism assumes that without being scarce they would still retain their value in a worldly heaven. A worldly heaven is an extrinsic sensory paradise, not a paradise of intrinsic loving, social, spiritual, or mystical union. It is filled with valuable sense objects—jeweled crowns, gates of pearls, golden thrones, strummed harps, splendid choruses, eloquent preachers, luxurious mansions, magnificent cities, and streets of gold; and it is populated with beautiful, sexy, accomplished, and successful people. It is the fair and happy land where their *possessions* lie. In more vulgar terms, heaven is the "Big Rock Candy Mountain" where all the hens lay golden eggs, and all the cops have wooden legs. Hell, too, is furnished with finite sense objects—fire, brimstone, instruments of torture, and rags instead of riches.

Popular revivalists and televangelists convert many worldly people because they preach an essentially worldly religion. Their *other-worldliness* is not *non-worldliness*, the rejection of security, status, and possessions (extrinsic values) as the supreme values of human existence, the true alternative to worldliness. Worldly people expect "only the best" for themselves both in this world and the next, but their "best" is only extrinsically good. They can conceive of nothing better. In heaven, their very earthy sensory treasures will be incorruptible, inexhaustible, immune to theft, and impervious to damage and corrosion by moth and rust. From religion, worldlings simply demand and expect *more of the same*. They assume that their extrinsic sensory value orientation would be perfectly at home in heaven (or hell), and that nothing there would make them non-worldly. Sensory/literal interpretations of heaven and hell express limited imagination, enslavement to and by literal-minded religious positivism, and devotion to value-objects that do not satisfy the soul.

God and the Image of God

> Mortals suppose that the gods are born (as they themselves are), and that they wear man's clothing and have human voice and body. But if cattle or lions had hands, so as to paint with their hands and produce works of art as men do, they would paint their gods and give them bodies in the form like their own—horses like horses, cattle like cattle. Ethiopians make their gods black and snub-nosed, Thracians red-haired with blue eyes.[80] Xenophanes

> Thou shalt not make unto thee any graven image, or any likeness of any thing that is in the heaven above, or that is in the earth beneath, or that is in the water under the earth. Exodus 20: 4

> Being then God's offspring, we ought not to think that the Deity is like gold, or silver, or stone, a representation by the art and imagination of man. (Acts 17:29, Revised Standard Version)

> When God is extrinsically valued he is valued as one among many, and compared with others of his kind. This, of course, is polytheism. Significantly, since extrinsic valuation deals with the things of the world, polytheistic gods are conceived in terms of mortals.[81] Robert S. Hartman

Popular worldly "anthropomorphic" concepts of God or the gods require that they have finite sensory bodies occupying some limited region of ethereal or earthly spacetime. God in the singular is *pictured* as a male father figure with a skin like one's own, as Xenophanes indicated. God has a deep masculine voice and a long white flowing beard, though not an explicitly displayed phallus, except in primitive nature religions. Ancient male fertility divinities were thus represented, and female fertility divinities were also physically well-endowed. Few people today want to be quite that literalistic about God's masculinity or femininity. Crude, vulgar, racist, sexist attempts at religious humor occasionally suggest that God is a "black woman" (or whatever racial, social, or sexual stereotype is relevant). Yet, God as a unique, infinite, all-inclusive, and omnipresent ultimate reality cannot be literally humanoid, much less black, white, male, female, Jewish, or Gentile. Picturing God as a finite, empirical, human-like object (making graven images) is precisely what was wisely forbidden by the second commandment in the Old Testament (Exodus 20:4) and by the New Testament (Acts 17:29).

During the iconoclastic controversies of the seventh and eighth centuries A.D., the *iconoclasts* claimed that representative art, particularly art that depicting God as humanoid, is contrary to the second commandment. The *iconodules*, their opponents, thought that this was OK. The iconoclastic controversy resurfaces every few centuries, even in Protestantism. John Calvin was an iconoclast; Martin Luther was an iconodule. In Christendom, historically, the worldly-minded iconodules won. Iconodules say that representative art is OK as long as its images are not worshiped and are understood metaphorically, symbolically, and non-literally as pointing to non-physical spiritual realities beyond themselves. They keep the images but do not construe them literally. Judaism and Islam take the second commandment more seriously and do not allow representative religious art in their centers of worship. Only abstract non-representative art is permitted.

The worldly portrait of God correlates closely with a worldly understanding of the divine image in humankind. According to the Bible, human beings were created in the "image of God" (Genesis 1:26-27; 5:1; 9:6; Colossians 3:10; II. Corinthians 4:35; James 3:9). St. Paul and other Christian theologians added that this image is tarnished if not obliterated by sin. Judaism, by contrast, finds the notion of original sin to be very strange, alien, and unscriptural. Old Testament texts that introduce the "*imago dei*" concept do not specify the point or kind of resemblance between us and God, and the Old Testament does not suggest that this image was ever lost. In the New Testament, Colossians 3:10 may suggest that we resemble God as knowers, but the wording is ambiguous; it may mean only that knowledge is helpful as we grow toward Godlikeness. If so, then nowhere in the Bible are we ever told how we resemble God or how God resembles us. All answers are merely human interpretations. But why should anyone select knowledge, cognition (systemic values) for special emphasis rather than "God is love" (intrinsic values)? II. Corinthians 4:3-5 says that Christ is the image of God, but how does Christ resemble God? Throughout the scriptures, God is said to have many human-like personal and psychological attributes, and human beings to have many god-like attributes—knowledge, love, mercy, anger, vengefulness, power, presence, *etc.* Choosing *any* of these for exclusive emphasis is clearly a matter of human interpretation and selective evaluation. Such evaluation needs careful consideration and proper guidance, like that afforded by formal axiology! The ultimate priorities of formal axiology and Christianity come together in the two love commandments of Jesus.

Historically, theologians gave many different answers to "How are we like God?" The image of God in humankind, our most essential human resemblance to God, has been construed *systemically* (the image of a rational knower), *extrinsically* (the image of a finite, physical, socially exalted masculine humanoid being), and *intrinsically* (the image of inwardness, love, empathy, compassion, total identification, inclusiveness, and euphoric mystical union/communion). Worldly religion conceives of our resemblance to God in extrinsic sensory/physical/social terms. God is portrayed as a physical, social, and sensory male, the "big man up in the sky," like the humanoid masculine gods of Greek and Roman polytheism, of today's Mormonism, and of much traditional representative religious art. Yet, this ignores the Genesis claim that both males and females were created in the image of God (Genesis 1:27). Also, God as humanoid could occupy only a limited region of a more inclusive system of spacetime, as do all human bodies, so the worldly God could not fill the heavens and the earth, would not be omnipresent. Worldlings try to imagine, depict, relate to, appease, and manipulate a finite man-like God.

God is "invisible," says some parts of the Bible (I. Timothy 1:17; Hebrews 11:27), which could be interpreted in many ways. Classical theologians interpreted this to mean that God is "incorporeal," meaning that God has no physical body at all. Though not emphasized traditionally, an incorporeal or immaterial God would have no anatomical parts or features, not even literal masculine or feminine ones. Biblical religion may have made verbal graven images, but not physical ones. The idolatrous statue of the golden calf (Exodus 32) was repudiated. Human-like physiology is often verbally attributed to God in the Bible (e.g., Exodus 33:20-23), in much popular religion, and in religious art. Such imagery encourages an extrinsic, physical, spatiotemporal, worldly view of our essential resemblance to God. We look like God; *God looks like us*! Much biblical imagery and religious art endow God with a face, hands, eyes, ears, with left, right, front, and back sides, and with literal physical masculinity—clothed, of course. Far too many people, worldly people, take this imagery quite literally rather than metaphorically. Are all biblical literalists stuck with this? Are all Christians stuck with this? Imagery should not just be dismissed; it can be extremely helpful devotionally if understood metaphorically or non-literally.

Many people pray to a God who is imaginatively depicted as a very large, handsome, potent, imposing, distinguished, elderly, corporeal, humanoid male with gray hair, a graying beard, a mouth to speak, ears to hear, hands with which to aid and create, and a skin colored like their own—like the God who reaches out his hand (a physical social gesture) to Adam in Michelangelo's painting on the ceiling of the Sistine Chapel. In words if not in substance, fundamentalism encourages people to take corporeal humanoid imagery literally, along with everything else—and thus to make graven images.

The dominant tradition in Christian theology explicitly repudiated the image of a physically humanoid God. Assuming Platonic mind/body dualism, St. Augustine ruled out any physical resemblance between us and God, or between any other physical objects and God, in these words:

> If ye are not able now to comprehend what God is, comprehend at least what God is not: you will have made much progress, if you think of God as being not something other than He is. God is not a body, not the earth, not the heaven, not the moon, or sun, or stars—not these corporeal things. For if not heavenly things, how much less is He earthly things! Put all body out of the question.[82]

Like so many other classical theologians, dualistic John Wesley also explicitly ruled out physical resemblances with God on the grounds that "God's image upon man, consists in his nature, not that of his body, for God has not a body, but that of his soul. The soul is a spirit, an intelligent, immortal spirit, an active spirit, herein resembling God, the Father of spirits, and the soul of the world."[83] Yet, dispensing with all physical images when thinking of God is almost impossible for worldlings. The perfectly viable alternative is to construe them non-literally.

How we conceive of God has serious implications for any religious ethics that requires us to be Godlike. The most prevalent worldly image of God is that of "The big man upstairs with the big stick." Extrinsic Godlikeness consists in being a powerful, demanding, vengeful, domineering, paternalistic alpha male who doles out rewards only to submissive subordinates—like the God of much but not all of the Old Testament. But is this really the most excellent way?

If Kierkegaard and many other theologians are right, worldliness is the most commonplace human mind-set, the most prevalent manifestation of natural or original sin, an unrefined but persisting value orientation that distances people from God. It is also *"maya"* in the Eastern religions and "inauthentic existence" in Western existentialism. Original sin and the worldly mode of evaluative consciousness are almost, but not quite, one and the same. Other perverse but persisting axiological orientations also keep people from God, like the ideological systemic value orientation explicated in the next chapter, and the many forms of despair, in addition to worldliness, identified in Kierkegaard's *The Sickness Unto Death*. The world's great religions at their best offer alternatives to worldliness; so do many philosophers from Socrates and the Stoics to Kierkegaard, Marcel, Ortega y Gasset, and Robert S. Hartman. During rare epochs, idealistic youth cultures seriously seek for alternatives. Even worldlings over thirty may yearn restlessly for a simpler and more meaningful life; but all that is another story, the one told in Chapter Three.

Spiritual Strengths and Weaknesses of Religious Worldlings

> *Do not be conformed to this world but be transformed by the renewing of your mind, that you may prove what is the will of God, what is good and acceptable and perfect.* St. Paul, Romans 12:2

> *Do not love the world or the things in the world. If any one loves the world, love for the Father is not in him. For all that is in the world, the lust of the flesh and the lust of the eyes and the pride of life, is not of the Father but is of the world. And the world passes away.* I. John 2:15-17

Worldly people are not "beyond redemption." They can be spiritually strong in extrinsic values and evaluations, and they can grow graceful in their non-dominant systemic and intrinsic values and evaluations. They can be excellent church and synagogue workers. They can make many positive contributions to spiritual fellowships. Their spiritual strengths are mainly practical, but they can make very important positive practical contributions to their own religious groups. They excel in doing, belonging, getting or receiving, and sometimes in giving. They can courageously commit themselves to religious outlooks, especially those that center on believing and acting in conventional or traditional religious ways—because "religion pays." They will join and work for almost any religious group that promises ample worldly security, prosperity, things, powers, prestige, and rewards, especially in this world, but at least in the next. They can also grow beyond this when properly encouraged and nurtured. They may attend religious services mainly to be entertained and think that this is worship, but they can also grow toward a deeper faith and practice. They can be vigorous and productive workers in their religious communities and in their chosen spiritual vineyards, especially if offered far greater rewards than those who do less. All spiritual communities need practical people, helping hands, good workers. Not every member of a religious body can be a spiritual egghead or bleeding heart! We have diverse spiritual gifts within one inclusive spiritual body, and everyone can grow where currently lacking.

Worldly religious people, like everyone else, have spiritual and moral weaknesses. Though their extrinsic capacities dominate, they still have lesser systemic and intrinsic capacities, and these can be cultivated. *If their systemic capacities are weak*, they may suffer much spiritual anxiety and frustration because their religious concepts and beliefs are confused, conflicted, or superficial. They may be cognitively or doctrinally shallow, undeveloped, and befuddled. They may not *understand* "what is good and acceptable and perfect" (Romans 12:2). Spiritually, they may "pay their money," so to speak, for "that which really is not bread" and work for "that which does not satisfy" (Isaiah 55:2). Yet, they can learn and be taught, especially if they are willing to put some time and effort into developing spiritual understanding and the religious affections.

Systemically underdeveloped worldlings are vulnerable in many ways. They are not usually very picky about religious beliefs or communities as long as they promise to pay off in the end. Jonathan Edwards asked, "What will not men believe if the thing believed makes for their worldly interest, and what will they not disbelieve when the belief makes against their interest?"[84] If they are systemically weak, worldlings mindlessly appropriate almost anything offered to them, religious or not, that seems to work or pay off extrinsically. They may avoid deep thinking about more profound intrinsic spiritual beliefs and attitudes, which they grasp only dimly and darkly. If the proper external authorities say that it all makes sense somehow, that is usually good enough for them. They "conform to the world," including the world of worldly religion. They are conventionally religious and participate in traditional religious communities that promise rewards. They let others make sense out of life for them because they can't make much sense out of it for themselves. They are not spiritually thoughtful, reflective, insightful, and creative. Their worldly religion does not empower them in such ways. They would have much more abundant spiritual lives if it did, but they can learn and grow. They can develop the non-worldly "mind of Christ" if they will. Effective spiritual guidance for them would center on growth in the knowledge of and love to God and all their fellow creatures. They need to grow spiritually, not only with their minds, but also in their hearts. And they can if they will, with God's help.

Consider one important example of how worldly-minded people can be very confused spiritually. They may be very uncertain about the nature, ranks, and roles of faith, works, and grace in salvation. Egoistic worldly people find that gift-giving with no expectation of payback is utterly incomprehensible, and this corrupts their understanding of spiritual faith, works, and grace. They combine worldliness with some degree of ideology and turn faith into a form of internal "works righteousness" that supposedly *earns and deserves* God's grace, salvation, earthly prosperity, and heavenly rewards. They think that having systemic faith (willfully believing certain doctrines) will *bring about* their salvation. They apply the worldly economic model of "paying the price" and "getting what you pay for" to faith and salvation. Systemic faith (effortful believing) is the payment; intrinsic grace and salvation are bought with it; in due time these will pay off extrinsically.

Worldly-mindedness, confined to an earning-and-being-paid model, misses the more appropriate intrinsic model of truly generous gift-giving (by God), accompanied by grateful receiving (by us), with no need to repay. But this does not mean that spiritual-minded people do not do the works of love. Intrinsic spiritual living *expresses* what has happened to Godly people, but it does not *pay for it*. Understood intrinsically, a God of love gracefully gives salvation to faithless sinners while they are yet faithless and sinful—for no price or condition at all, certainly none that we could ever pay. Having faith is like responding thankfully to a gift offered with no strings or conditions attached. Having faith, gratefully receiving God's free gifts, changes of heart, and doing the works of love are the effects, not the causes, of spiritual salvation. They are integral parts of that more abundant moral and spiritual life that *is* salvation and is its own reward, but this eludes worldly-mindedness.

If worldly people are *deficient in intrinsic values and evaluations*, it is partly because they so dearly love the *things* of the world. Their hearts as well as their minds may be weak, perhaps even hard, with respect to loving God, neighbors, strangers, and enemies, although this is where abundant living most clearly abides. They appraise people, not for their value to, for, and in themselves, not as unique individuals, not as equally loved by God, but for their usefulness to themselves, and they esteem God likewise for his usefulness. Because they know and value people as extrinsic things rather than as intrinsic conscious persons, they cannot love others deeply for their own sakes. Because they know and value themselves superficially, they cannot love themselves very deeply since a purely extrinsic self is the only self they have to love. They see God as the "big man upstairs with the big stick," so they fear and try to placate God, but they do not really love God for God's own sake. They just try to "use" and "appease" God to get what they want. God, too, is just a means to their worldly ends. And they try to be big men with big sticks!

Most real human beings, who are never pure worldlings, can to some degree identify themselves with and devote themselves lovingly and compassionately to others, but even then their loves are few—usually limited to kin and klan (clan), just as modern sociobiology indicates. The scope as well as the degree of their capacity to love, to evaluate intrinsically, is inordinately restricted. They may care intrinsically about "insiders," but not about "outsiders," and the circle of their insiders is very narrowly drawn. They cannot identify with or care about strangers and aliens. They assume that no aliens could be God's aliens. No outsiders could be God's outsiders. Most people in God's world just do not count. God loves only "my kind of people," the elect. They need a soul-transforming conversion.

Intrinsic evaluation involves identifying ourselves as fully as possible with those we love, so much so that the differences between us cease to matter or be noticed, though they do not cease to exist. Positively, this means that the good-making properties of those we love become our own good-making properties valuationally and psychologically, though not metaphysically or existentially. To the extent that we can identify profoundly with others, our own lives become richer in good-making properties. In biblical terms, we live "more abundantly" (John 10:10). The scope of a holistic saintly capacity for identification-with-others extends spiritually to and through the whole of creation and all the way to God. The richest and most abundant life we can possibly live involves "loving God with all our hearts, souls, minds, and strength," as well as "our neighbor as ourselves." Both of these "commandments" involve love—intrinsic evaluation. Their intrinsically valued objects are intrinsically good, ends in themselves. Loving God takes priority over loving people because God has infinitely more good-making properties than people. Worldly people and worldly churches are not able so to love. They do not take the goodness of God and all others into themselves and fully identify with them; thus, they do not comprehend, feel, live, or make available the most abundant life possible. Worldly and highly ideological churches, often combined, spend more time and effort teaching people who and how to hate rather than who and how to love.

Worldly people lack the courage, knowledge, and skill to love widely, deeply, and unselfishly, to value intrinsically, to give themselves completely, and to become one with the goodness that exists in all others and all of creation. In this way their lives are immensely impoverished; they do not live abundantly. They take very little of the goodness of others into themselves, especially outsiders, strangers, aliens. Proper spiritual aid and development would empower everyone for intrinsically abundant living, but worldly religion does not offer people such power. Real saints, who transcend, outgrow, and overcome the world, live more richly because their intrinsic spirituality gives them enough strength, concern, affection, compassion, courage, knowledge, and skill to care as widely, deeply, completely, and unselfishly as God cares.

Chapter Two
Ideology and Systemic/Ideological Religion

> Though the term ideology *has had a checkered career, today we understand it to refer to emotionally charged beliefs about the substance of the "good life," the most desirable orbit of human fellowship, the ideal form of social organization, or the conditions for the legitimacy of government—or all of these together. In the latter case we speak of an ideological* system, *such as Marxism.*
>
> *Every ideology contains, either explicitly or implicitly, two elements: a particular value and the assertion that social or psychological reality calls for the implementation of this and no other value.*[1] Max Mark

The word "ideology" has a checkered history. When coined by the French philosopher, Destutt de Tracy, in 1796, it named a positivistic worldly philosophy that aspired to derive all ideas from sensations. "Ideologues" became a term of derision when Napoleon used it to express the contempt that worldly men of action have for those who value ideas and thinking more than doing and achieving. Karl Marx also used the term pejoratively for the false consciousness of "brain workers" who first create fictional supersensible entities (conceptual constructs) like God, private property, and the divine right of kings and then mistake them for enduring realities. In time, Marx thought, ideologies (especially religions) come to serve the interests of ruling classes by rationalizing the economic and institutional arrangements through which their special privileges are secured. Since Marx, "ideology" has been given many meanings, not all of which are derogatory. Today the term frequently refers to any and all fundamental world views or "idea systems,"[2] especially if socially shared.[3] For our purposes, ideologists are understood to be systemically dominated individuals who wish to impose their belief systems on unwilling others through all available means, including force.

Defining Ideology and Ideologists

Ideology—thought constructions...without counterparts in reality.[4] Robert S. Hartman

> *To see everything under an ideological or a racial angle, as is done by the Birchers, the communists, and other ideologists is lack of sense of proportion and axiological astigmatism. It is an overvaluation of the systemic at the cost of the other two dimensions.*[5] Robert S. Hartman

Axiologically understood, "ideology" preserves its traditional pejorative function and much of its historical connotation. Ideologies are belief systems that center upon and overvalue non-empirical conceptual constructs, mistake them for ultimate realities, and assign the highest possible value to them. Ideologies are readily and regularly misused by those who would impose them upon everyone else at almost any price, but not all belief systems are ideologies in this sense. Our minds and beliefs can be used properly and well. We can have both intellectual integrity and competence as well as serious spiritual beliefs without being ideologists.

Although ideologies include systemic values and evaluations, they are not identical with them. Systemic values and evaluations are indeed very important and desirable. They can be either helpful or harmful, and not all cognitive beliefs count as ideologies. They are indispensable for human existence as we know it; but, according to the axiological hierarchy of value, for all their importance, they are less valuable than extrinsic values and evaluations, which in turn are less valuable than intrinsic values and evaluations. Thoughts about them have less value than the good things and valuable persons they symbolize. Ideologists reverse this hierarchy of value; ideas, beliefs, non-empirical conceptual constructs, have the highest value of all; both extrinsic things and processes and intrinsic individuated subjects of consciousness are subordinated in value to ideas, words, rules, formalities, and doctrines.

Ideologists may believe mistakenly that ideas and conceptual beliefs are far richer in good-making properties than they actually are, that they are as rich as intrinsic entities and the realities to which they point. Although ideologists *could* value ideas with systemic dispassion, *they tend to value them passionately, intrinsically, and to identify themselves with them wholeheartedly*. Ideologists reserve relatively passionless systemic detachment, or something even more extreme—indifference or hatred—for people and things.

In all ideologists, systemic value-objects predominate, but, like worldlings, they are never completely devoid of non-dominant intrinsic and extrinsic values and evaluations. They tend to value intrinsic and extrinsic value-objects systemically (dispassionately, all or nothing, reductively) and to value systemic entities (ideas, words, authorities, systems, formalities, rules, rituals, *etc.*) passionately, wholeheartedly, as if they had intrinsic worth. They regularly combine a passionate love of their own beliefs and theories with all or nothing, black or white thinking. Ideologists accept people who fit their systems, but they have only indifference or contempt for those who deviate. For ideological reasons, they are perfectly willing to degrade or destroy those who do not fit their systems. They disvalue intrinsic values, people, when they do not conform to their pre-conceptions. They are much weaker in the extrinsic and intrinsic realms of value than in the systemic, even when all three are present to some degree.

People dominated by an ideological mode of evaluative consciousness live only marginally in our common world of sensory entities (things) and individual conscious subjects (people). Ideologists live almost entirely in conceptual worlds of their own making and thinking, their own special "ivory towers." Their worlds consists largely of experientially empty conceptual constructs and fictions. Ideologists are maximally involved with minimally valuable entities and only minimally involved with maximally valuable realities.

Ideologists are far removed from worldliness, for they do not see or value things as things. They are also far removed from saintliness, for they do not see or value persons as persons. They are out of touch with practicality, common people, and common sense, for their extrinsic ability to evaluate concrete sensory reality is weak. They are also out of touch with saintliness, for their intrinsic ability to value human reality is weak. They are out of touch for God, for they value theological doctrines more than the God to which they point. When ideologists connect their conceptual or ideological universes to perceived physical and social worlds, they see particular things and individual persons only through ideological lenses. They view them merely as abstract ciphers in formal systems that either fit or don't fit. If they don't fit, they must be either ignored or exterminated. Sound beliefs are not dangerous; ideologists are.

Ideological Language and Values: Conceptual Constructs

> *Only with constructive concepts can one be absolutely certain that they contain all that their object does, for these constructs come about together with, and actually are, their object. They possess* complete *precision, for they are creations of the human mind itself rather than abstractions.*[6] Robert S. Hartman

Ideological language cannot be separated from ideological values, for they are identical. Ideological values refer only to themselves and not to anything beyond themselves. For ideologists, to exist is to be thought. I am thought, therefore, I am. Keep in mind that no one is a pure ideologist, for those in whom systemic values prevail still have some extrinsic and intrinsic values and capacities. Pure ideologists would attach positive value only to systemic linguistic or conceptual symbols, to highly abstruse systems that order thinking, and to non-empirical conceptual constructs like the state, sovereignty, territorial boundaries, the divine right of kings, the social contract, the state of nature, the general will, natural laws, the dictatorship of the proletariat, corporate persons, group minds, the Aryan race, the Fatherland, Dixie, the Absolute, the Messiah, the Second Coming, papal infallibility, and biblical inerrancy; the list could be extended indefinitely. Purely systemic entities, formal systems, conceptual constructs, and most religious and philosophical beliefs, are not abstracted from the sensory world; they are constructed by systemic minds. No real people are pure ideologists, but some come very close. Their ideologies prevail over people and practicality; they overvalue beliefs and undervalue or even disvalue people and the things of the world. Often they are ignorant of religious history, for as Marcus J. Borg notes, "The notions of biblical infallibility and inerrancy first appeared in the 1600s, and became insistently affirmed by some Protestants only in the nineteenth and twentieth centuries. Papal infallibility was affirmed only in 1870."[7]

Systemic constructs are not all bad or useless. Not all ideas and conceptual systems are ideologically perverse. Not all intellectuals are ideologists. Not all believers are dogmatists. Many ideas and beliefs are extremely helpful, indeed indispensable for human existence. As Robert S. Hartman recognized, logic and its axioms, (for example, the principle of non-contradiction, which says that propositions cannot be both true and false, and which implies that real things cannot both be and not be themselves), are absolutely essential for intelligible thinking and successful living.

Without the axioms, formulas, and theorems of mathematics, the natural sciences as we know them would not exist; all natural science would be Aristotelian, non-predictive, and ineffective; only their formal, logical, and mathematical features confer the power to predict and control.[8] Without such formalities, no empirical system of thought counts as a real science. Real science is much more than just collecting facts. Some popular and philosophical definitions of "natural science" stress its empirical fact-collecting side; but our knowledge of nature does not become genuine natural science until some systemic genius first discovers how to order empirical data using mathematical and/or logical formulas, and then actually creates and applies a relevant system of formulas to some empirical subject matter.

Axiology itself is a formal system of constructs that orders the realm of values and evaluations, as does no other system. *Nothing is wrong with systemic values until they are regarded and lived as supreme.* Axiology says of itself that it is less valuable than most of its subject matter. Robert S. Hartman wrote, "*My own philosophy has taught me the relative unimportance of my philosophy.*"[9] Systemic thinking as such is not inherently bad; ideological thinking that devalues persons and ranks systems over persons is bad. It is even worse when it spills over into action.

Ideological Values: Ideas vs. Persons and Things

> *A synthetic concept has a definite or finite number of properties....It gives rise to only two values, either perfection or non-existence, value or non-value. There are no degrees of value, such as good, fair, poor, and bad. Everything is either black or white.*
>
> *A systemic state or organization (the fulfillment of a synthetic concept) is authoritarian and dictatorial. You either belong, or you get out. Shades and differences of opinion and character are not tolerated. Individuality is cancelled. The one value is conformity, and the one disvalue, non-conformity, which leads to expulsion or "liquidation."*[10] Robert S. Hartman

> *I think it is clear by now that we are living in three worlds. We live in the world of the mind, we live in the world of the senses, and we live in the world of our inner selves.*
>
> *We live in the world of the mind. It is in our mind we think, we build systems. Here are all the sciences, all mathematics, astronomy, cosmology, physics, biology—here is the arsenal of our technological world. And there are people who live in the systemic world of the mind as their real world—the scientists. They live in the world of systemic value. Sometimes, in their delight over the systemic beauty of this world, they forget the world of everyday reality and of intrinsic values. They appear then in a spectrum of types from quiet absent-minded professors to noisy proponents of bigger and better bombs.*[10] Robert S. Hartman

Real ideologists may not be quite pure, but extreme ideologists would value themselves and others only as systemic entities. They would not value persons intrinsically, and they would be ready in a flash to sacrifice persons for ideological reasons. They have little interest in knowing concrete entities, and (like some philosophers) they could easily persuade themselves that individuals are unknowable. In a sense, individuals are unknowable in typically scientific ways. Usually, the natural sciences try to know less and less about more and more; they search for the most general and abstract features and laws common to the largest number of individuals; scientific knowledge proceeds by *omitting* properties until at last only a few very bits of abstruse information remain.

Self-knowledge and intimate knowledge of other persons and things proceed in just the opposite direction. Natural science is reductive of properties; axiological science, applied psychology, and personal self-knowledge are inclusive of properties. Knowing *individuals* involves learning more and more about less and less; it proceeds by *including* properties, by grasping the greatest possible number, range, and order of the concrete features of single or unique realities. Knowing people individually and intrinsically is very different from knowing them or applying natural science and mathematics to them. Real people are much more than mere numbers.

Extreme ideologists do not wish to know themselves or others; for them, the system is everything; the self is nothing. Just which system? Well, that varies from one ideologist to the next; but some ideological systems are both popular and pernicious. Consider one good illustration of how ideological scientism knows less and less about people until they finally know almost nothing. Some pseudo-scientists tell us that sexual or romantic love is *nothing more* than propagating genes. How much of immense significance they omit and miss, as anyone who has ever loved intimately knows perfectly well! Some ideologues say that we are worth nothing more than the cash value of the chemicals in our bodies. What do they ignore?

Systems may be valued in a great variety of ways. For the most part, because they are so deeply immersed in and enthralled by concrete existence, some historical saints, but not holistic saints, tend to disregard or even disvalue thoughts and systems. Worldlings, by contrast, value ideas and systems extrinsically; they see logic, algebra, geometry, computer programs, statistics, and other formal systems as *useful* in obtaining high status and greater prosperity. Ideologists are very different. They value constructs and systems intrinsically, as ends in themselves, as the most essential authentic realities, as their own ultimate values, as the only things they really love, as the only things really lovable.

Ideologists can be so deeply immersed in abstractions or conceptual constructs that they hardly live at all. They do not use systems to aggrandize themselves; they use and even abuse themselves to aggrandize systems. They willingly sacrifice money, position, practicality, respect, and love of family and friends for the sake of cognitively constructed systems (words or symbols), that is, for what they call "knowledge" and "truth." If their preferred system demands it, they willingly sacrifice their own lives for ideological fabrications (more words). They are like the perhaps fictitious German soldier during World War II who, upon discovering that he was adopted and genetically Jewish, presented himself to the nearest concentration camp to be tortured and executed! They may be like today's very real terrorists who blow up themselves and others for the sake of their beliefs.

Ideologists take the same attitude toward other human beings that they take toward themselves; they attach no more value to others than they do to themselves. No persons have value to them in and of themselves. Everyone exists only within and for the sake of the system; everyone should be forced to accept the system; and everyone can and should be sacrificed for the system, willingly or not, if the system demands it.

To pure ideologists, the concretely existing things of everyday experience have little or no utility value. They have little interest in practical values or in knowing or comparing the utilities of concretely experienced entities. Because *pure* ideologists have no interest in extrinsic usefulness, no purists actually exist, but *extreme* ideologists do exist who are largely oblivious to the world. Brute facts have a way of getting everyone's attention. Even Plato had to admit, reluctantly, that philosophers have to know enough about the concrete sensory world to be able to find their way home at night![11]

As much as possible, ideologists assign to both people and things only the value conferred upon them by the system of ideas or beliefs that happens to dominate their souls. To ideologists, people and things are mere functions or vacuous variables in black or white ideological schemes. Either people and things perfectly fit and function according to the system, or they are worthless. If systemically flawless, their existence is justified; if flawed, their existence is not justified, and they could or should be either ignored or eradicated. Ideologists sublimate their natural drive to dominance and place it in the service of dogmas. People and things are tiny specks or iotas in vast systemic wholes, and their value is determined solely by their place within some ideological scheme. If they serve or exemplify the system well, they have some value, however minute; but if they fail to serve or fit the system, they are worthless and may be extinguished without compunction. Regarded only systemically, Hartman says, people are "like the members of a synthetic class or system— terms within the whole, lieu-tenants, placeholders for formal relations. They have no extension and no intension of their own, but only through and by the system. In themselves they are zeros—as the zero in arithmetic is nothing but a placeholder."[12]

To illustrate, some ideologists think that people have very little if any worth because we are so very small physically in relation to the vastness of our *spacetime* universe. Others treat *history*, human knowledge of human events, as a vast system that gives meaning to everything. The philosopher G. W. F. Hegel lamented that nothing worth writing up in the history books occurs during eras when people are generally happy and at peace with one another; such eras of peace are the "blank pages" of history;[13] and they have no more value than that! Like General George Patton, Hegel loved war—because *history* is being made! He regarded Napoleon as the "World Spirit [God] on horseback." To make names for themselves in history, systemically minded individuals, who can find no other worth for themselves, will do desperate things like assassinating rock stars, congresswomen, or presidents.

Systemic ideological value-objects must now be considered in relation to ideological evaluation.

Ideological Evaluation: Cognition, Feelings, and Actions

> *Not all systemic valuation is evil. It is evil only when it is a transposition—when applied to situations where it is inappropriate. Many things in our individual and social life* must *be valued systemically. Scientific constructs must be valued this way, and the rigorous discipline of systemic evaluation in general is necessary for modern society and is precisely what...American education [is] lacking, as against European education. There are even life situations where systemic valuation is necessary: all situations where no play is allowed and it is a matter of either being or not being. Thus, when meeting a deadline, when making a train, when stopping*

> at a red light, or before a railroad crossing—you either do or you don't—and when you don't you miss, and sometimes [lose] your life. The saying that a miss is as good as a mile expresses systemic valuation. Systemic valuation is necessary in all situations that demand discipline....But where numerical order is important, as in tagging the right baby of the right mother, there is no badness in the systemic valuation.[14] Robert S. Hartman

Ideological evaluation involves something like systemic evaluation, but they are not identical. Systemic evaluation is often very desirable, a very positive thing when it values ideas properly, without overvaluing or undervaluing them. In saintly wholeness, it is combined constructively with extrinsic and intrinsic evaluation. Real saints know what they believe and what they are doing. They have intellectual integrity, and they are very practical. Knowledge and beliefs become ideological and undesirable only when employed to undervalue or disvalue people and things, only in transpositional situations that reduce people or things to mere systemic constructs.

Consider next how ideologists distort and pervert the cognitive, affective, and dynamic dimensions of systemic evaluation into something evil.

Ideological Evaluation and Cognition

> A circle lacking in a single one of the properties of the concept "circle" is not a circle. Constructions of the human mind thus have only two values, which we shall call systemic values: *either perfection or nonvalue.* This is the model of the black and white valuation of things, the simplest kind of valuation there is. Since it belongs to constructions of the mind it is obvious that when it is applied to actual things it "prejudges" them—it is the model of prejudice. This kind of thinking is based on the logical category of limitation; the variety of the world is limited to only two distinctions: A and non-A (e.g. white and non-white, Communist and non-Communist)....Systemic valuation is the model of schematic and dogmatic thinking.[15]
> Robert S. Hartman

All purely systemic values, ideological or not, are primarily cognitive. At one extreme, ideology employs concepts of a very special kind—conceptual constructs integrated into larger systems of conceptual constructs; and it makes very peculiar systemic judgments—reductive, rigidly dualistic, black or white, all or nothing. The "nothings" suffer the consequences.

Paradigm systemic concepts are so pure that they may not refer to empirical entities at all: points without magnitude, lines having an infinite number of parts or points, curves equidistant from a central point, lines with no thickness, bodies completely at rest, absolute sovereignty, infallibility. Purely conceptual constructs such as numbers and the laws of logic contain no empirical elements, but systemic concepts and evaluations gradually overflow into the empirical domain. Empirical elements like magnitude, lines, curves, and bodies are projected and integrated into

Ideology and Systemic/Ideological Religion   83

non-empirical contexts in expanded systemic thinking. Hartman gradually extended the notion of a conceptual construct to include the *definitions* of all empirical concepts like "chair" and "car." Actually, all concepts and beliefs are systemic values, whether they have empirical reference or not. Empirical definitions are composed of definite and limited sets of the perceivable properties of such things; their more inclusive expositions may consist of practically innumerable properties, but only a few of them are actually used in evaluation processes. Hartman enlarged the notion of "system" to embrace not only the pure formalities of arithmetic, algebra, geometry, logic, and axiology, but also what he called "pseudo-systems" that incorporate empirical elements,[16] like most of the systems mentioned in the next paragraph.

Many different kinds of systems exist: logical, scientific, circulatory, skeletal, philosophical, religious, theological, ecclesiastical, political, social, caste, racial, root, economic, industrial, military, *etc.* Systems of all kinds are available to ideologists, who treat them as conceptual schemes or frameworks for evaluating concrete things and people in reductive or minimizing ways. Ideological systems, possibilities for perverse systemic evaluation, are almost inexhaustible. We will now consider a few secular and religious ideological systems that are especially alive and pernicious in today's world.

All or nothing, either/or, black or white, perfect or worthless judgments are quite appropriate in purely formal systems. Except in "fuzzy logic," being a little bit self-contradictory is like being a little bit pregnant! The perfectionist aspect of systemic mentality has a legitimate place, but ideologists extend it far beyond its appropriate limits. The rigidly dualistic white or black racist mentality that operated in earlier America recognized no such thing as being a little bit black; the slightest bit of "Negro blood" made one entirely black, thus only fractionally human and subject to slavery, relentless discrimination, and ruthless exploitation. Racism today retains the discrimination and exploitation.

Ideological thinking and organization immensely and extravagantly finitize the significance of anything non-systemic. This is what is axiologically most significant about ideologists. Worldly individuals also inordinately finitize and thereby debase the worth of human persons, but ideologists carry finitizing and devaluing tendencies to ultimate extremes. Worldlings just have a slightly richer understanding of who they stigmatize.

Ideological evaluations are most troublesome when applied to persons. How are persons undervalued or devalued systemically by ideologists? Most humanly constructed "isms" incorporate ideologically systemic devaluations of concrete persons: communism, capitalism, Nazism, fascism, totalitarianism, militarism, nationalism, imperialism, racism, scientism, reductionism, dualism, materialism, authoritarianism, dogmatism, fundamentalism, *etc.* Ideological undervaluation or disvaluation is expressed by every label that stereotypes, pre-judges, and inordinately reduces and finitizes the significance of individual human beings, while ignoring the practically incalculable richness and worth of their actual good-making properties.

Ideological Evaluation and Feelings

> Systemic measurement is the abstract, formal kind of measurement used by the scientist, objective and detached.[17] Robert S. Hartman

Ideological evaluation should not be confused with systemic evaluation, despite their superficial resemblances. Systemic evaluation minimizes but never completely eliminates affective involvement, and this is often a very good thing. "Rational objectivity," "impartiality," or "disinterestedness," our paradigm words for proper systemic evaluation, can mean many things. They best suggest that beclouding emotions are so diminished and under control that they no longer resist or interfere with an honest and open-minded search for truth. Systemic evaluation falls toward one end of a continuum of human feelings; saintliness falls toward the other extreme; worldliness is somewhere in between; and the indifference or disvaluation of ideology are beyond all positive evaluation.

Indifference, the refusal to value at all, is not the same thing as rational disinterestedness. Indifference is off the axiological chart! Sadly, rationality is not always properly understood; some people confuse suppressing biasing, prejudicial, and obstructive emotions and feelings with suppressing all emotions and feelings. Indifference or apathy toward individual human beings is a moral vice that should never be confused with the intellectual virtue of dispassionate or fair-minded inquiry. Systematic rational inquiry should not be confused with ideological indifference, devaluation, or hostility. Ideologists are not rationally objective. Their thinking falls short of comprehensiveness. They are passionately blind about their selected ideas and systems and can be very hostile to intrinsically valuable people for ideological reasons. Affective indifference bears some resemblance to authentic impartial, objective, disinterested systemic evaluation; but it lies several steps *beyond* it. Passionate ideological commitment is obviously very different from systemic objectivity. With passionate prejudgment or prejudice, ideologists undervalue and typically disvalue those things and people who do not fit their cherished systems. Both indifference and vicious ideological extremism go far beyond systemic rational objectivity.

Ideologists intrinsically value or dearly love the abstractions in and for which they live and are willing to die. They have passionate positive feelings, not about things and people, but about words, ideas, and beliefs. They go far beyond minimal, rational, disinterested affective involvement with concepts and systems. They feel deeply or intensely about selected systems, principles, and intellectual constructs; they love them and fully identify with them. Yet, this is almost *all* that they feel positively about. They have either indifferent or negative feelings about people, animals, living things, and anything that just doesn't conform. Ideological disvaluation of people and things is very real and pernicious in our world today, including here at home.

The life of both rational and holistic saintly minds or souls involves all kinds of evaluation—systemic, extrinsic, and intrinsic. Rational systemic evaluation is that small part of cognition in which positive feelings are minimal but not non-existent. Proper systemic cognitive activity (impartiality) is indeed affectively Spartan by comparison with the affective effusiveness and comprehensiveness of saintly intrinsic evaluation, but the best of saints have it all. Rational disinterestedness is not inherently indifferent or hostile to genuinely intrinsic realities and values, but affectively misdirected ideologists are. Ideologists typically disvalue people who buck the system and challenge its authority and to things that just don't conform. Ideological attitudes are definitely not the same as rational, impartial, fair-minded, intellectual disinterestedness. Rational objectivity takes everything into account; it is comprehensive; but ideologists focus only on very small sets of good-making predicates and ignore the full richness of reality itself. Rationality is open-minded, but ideology prejudges everything and everyone as either conforming perfectly to a given system, or else as worthless or highly undesirable anomalies. An ideological system is a house of cards; if one small part collapses, there goes the whole thing. To preserve any meaning at all, perfectionistic ideologists must be intolerant and defensive. Rationality, by contrast, is unprejudiced and self-correcting. It just grows and expands when challenged. Ideological feelings and attitudes are readily expressed in ideological activity, as explained next.

Ideological Activity

> *In business, one can think immediately of many needs for an axiological X-ray. Take the idea of a worker. Systemically, a worker is a production unit, valued in time and motion studies. Extrinsically, a worker is one of a number of workers performing this, that, or the other function. This calls for incentives and leads to different kinds of compensation. Intrinsically, a worker is a human being with infinite value, and this again leads to entirely different consequences, such as the partnership of worker and employer in profit-sharing.*[18] Robert S. Hartman

> *In war the one who kills may not see or know what he is doing, or who he's doing it to. Under his uniform he's just a nice man like you or me who, without the slightest twinge of conscience, executes an order that results in death for other nice men like you or me, or our grandchildren. He's just part of the system; just doing his duty; just transporting the fire to the people. If he does his duty well, he gets a medal, because that's how the system works. A killer in peace, however, is not part of a system, not an arm of the state. He acts on his own, as an individual, and as such he is subject to the moral and legal law which he has violated; so...for him the electric chair.*

> *Why should this be so? Why do we as human beings tolerate, accept, yes, and applaud the killing of millions of men, women and children when it is done systemi-*

cally, and draw back in horror and moral outrage at the killing of one person when it is done outside that system?....We must stop the war system before it stops us.[19]
Robert S. Hartman

Systemic dynamics actively combines conceptual constructs that objectively have minimal value with people and things having immensely greater value. It can utilize any kind of system or pseudo-system. This is not always undesirable, but it can be when united with ideological prejudices and practices. To illustrate, we will briefly consider systemic dynamics in the business world, then in the military world. Both can manifest a systemic if not an ideological view of reality with corresponding reductive devaluations of people.

With rare exceptions, in today's *business* climate, worldliness is wedded to some ideology like "free enterprise," "free trade," "deregulation," "bureaucracy," or "capitalism." Most worldlings pursue wealth and status within the framework of a socially stratified workplace such as a factory, business corporation, governmental organization, or university. In an excessively extrinsic/systemic/ideological business environment, all "organization men" and ordinary laborers are ideally identical with all others. They can all be replaced by someone else without loss of value. No employee has unique or intrinsic value to a factory, a corporation, a governmental bureaucracy, or any institution as such. Neither do customers or clients. The "bottom line" is everything.

Economic organizations exact as much uniformity and conformity as possible for the sake of the "bottom line." When required by the profit system or by institutional regulations and objectives, any employee can be relocated, reassigned, replaced, or "downsized" without loss of systemic or extrinsic value. Employees, the basic human elements of extrinsic/systemic business systems, ideally should be as much alike as possible; they should be interchangeable and readily discardable, like the mindless components of assembly lines and mechanical systems. Employees are only slots in assembly lines. Bureaucracies and bureaucrats in both government and corporations are notoriously insensitive and unresponsive to the concrete needs of the individuals who work for them and the clientele that they supposedly serve. They see individual persons only ideologically through an economic, corporate, or bureaucratic mentality. "Red tape" is the ideological devaluation of intrinsic values, as are most rationales for war, terrorism, and genocide.

Ideologists typically *use* systems and intellectual constructs to devalue and then destroy people and things. Illustrations fill our history books. Innumerable historical instances of *militarism*, for instance, show how persons and property count for almost nothing in militaristic ideological systems. This is why military organizations need to be controlled ultimately by civilians, by real people who can better appreciate the true worth of individual persons and their belongings.

Militaristic and terrorist minds are immensely talented in inventing euphemistic conceptual constructs that dehumanize and depersonalize individual human beings. Torture of prisoners is nothing more than "enhanced interrogation." To militarists, individual soldiers are nothing more than expendable "recruits," "replacements," "cannon fodder," "grunts," "casualties," or "body bags." Slaughtered and maimed women and children are nothing more than "non-combatant casualties" or "collateral damage." Intrinsically, however, there is no real distinction between combatants and non-combatants, between soldiers and civilians. Every person is equally valuable intrinsically, whether fighting or not, whether in uniform or not. Militaristic systems reduce the significance of intrinsically valuable persons and things to systemic statistics: to numbered troops, divisions, armaments, terrains, casualties, and body counts.

Prejudicial ideological constructs, labels, and slogans are frequently used to enforce systemic military conformity. When we had military conscription, young men were conditioned to "go without thinking" when their draft summons arrived; and those who refused or conscientiously objected were branded as "cowards," "slackers" or "draft dodgers." Often they were jailed. Military training and drills aim at transforming predominately self-interested worldly-minded recruits into selflessly obedient systemically-minded soldiers, who nevertheless are expected to identify intensely with (to intrinsically value) members of their own small units or teams *because* this best serves the military system. A military system works most efficiently when its officers and enlisted personnel are thoroughly imbued with a militaristic ideology that reduces both themselves and their enemies to impersonal tokens and statistics. Those who serve the military system well are rewarded with symbolical systemic/extrinsic value tokens—decorations, ribbons, medals, statues, memorials, flags, and parades—extrinsic objects and processes imbued with systemic significance. The families of non-surviving heroes are awarded flags and gold stars. These symbolic keepsakes clearly do not compensate adequately for the extreme hardships and sacrifices that are made by individual soldiers and their families. Robert S. Hartman wrote,

> The problem, I think, is wrapped up in the question, "Why does a killer in war get a medal and a killer in peace get the electric chair?" My answer is that it's because killing in war is on the third level, the systemic level of value. It is part of the war system. It is "killing" rather than killing. In war you never kill a man, you "eliminate enemy forces," you "liquidate resistance," you "take the objective," you "put the enemy out of action." You are part of an abstract game. You don't even shoot. You "handle arms," and they are not yours, they belong to the United States.[20]

People go to war and abstain from war for many reasons, some intrinsic, some extrinsic, and some systemic. According to the hierarchy of value, intrinsic reasons for going to war or abstaining are the most compelling, extrinsic are next, and systemic reasons are the least compelling of all. Illustrations of each may be drawn from the 1861–1865 American Civil War and the 1991 Persian Gulf War.

Purely extrinsic reasons for war are commonplace, popular, easy to comprehend, but not easy to accept in good conscience. An important Federal or Union extrinsic reason for fighting the Civil War was to keep the Mississippi River open for commerce. A comparable Confederate reason was to grow cotton and other agricultural commodities using slave labor. Neither extrinsic reason really justified that horrible war or the institution of slavery. Nor did the senior George Bush's extrinsic "protecting our oil supplies," and "moving our economy out of a depression" justify the 1991 Persian Gulf War. All purely extrinsic reasons for killing unique human beings in war fail to pass the test of carefully considered conscience.

During the Civil War, Generals Grant and Sherman argued on purely extrinsic grounds that there are no morally significant differences between soldiers and civilians. No civilians are really "innocent" because they supply their soldiers with indispensable financing, rations, bullets, arms, and equipment. The effects of this assumption of extrinsic sameness were highly visible when Sherman marched through Georgia and South Carolina! A very serious intrinsic reason can also be given for thinking that there are no morally significant differences between soldiers and civilians: members of both groups are real persons, equally so. Every soldier and every civilian is a unique conscious individual having equal basic intrinsic worth. Putting uniforms on soldiers says in effect that they are no longer persons, so it is OK to kill them. Wearing a uniform is a license to kill or be killed because uniformed individuals are not real persons.

Intrinsic considerations are the strongest moral reasons for *not* killing, war or no war. Every soldier and every civilian on every side in all armed conflicts is a person with incalculable intrinsic worth, but this is disregarded when wars and battles are fought, as Hartman explained,

> In war, values are turned upside down. In time of war, the most honorable man is the one who kills the greatest number of people while in time of peace if he kills only one he gets the electric chair, is hung or shot or will spend a lifetime in prison. The war hero is the criminal during peacetime and viceversa. If one contends, as has been done on many occasions, that it is not people but soldiers that are killed in war, then one simply is saying that soldiers are not people, which happens to be the crux of the problem of war.[21]

Shooting enemy soldiers while fully understanding and appreciating them as unique individual persons would be morally difficult if not impossible. Killing them cannot be combined with loving our enemies. In the midst of the 1991 Persian Gulf War, Marine snipers explained that "They were trying to avoid thinking of their Iraqi opponents as men with families and children." One Marine Sergeant explained, "I try not to think about the other man's personal life....I concentrate on him being the enemy. If I were to give him sympathy, I don't think I would be effective."[22] We have difficulty understanding and appreciating the intrinsic value of our own soldiers, much less that of enemy soldiers. What it means to value a soldier intrinsically was well expressed in the epitaph on the grave of a soldier killed in World War I that has since become a somewhat commonplace epitaph.

> To the world he was a soldier;
> To me he was all the world.

Troops who have survived all the horrible sounds, screams, smells, sights, feelings, emotions, pains, stresses, blood, and guts of several battles are said to be "hardened," but what does this mean? In part it just means "experienced," but it mainly means "desensitized." Hardened troops have become accustomed and thus desensitized to such horrors and are able to endure them and afflict them on others more effectively. These horrors will likely come back to haunt them later during episodes of Post Traumatic Stress Disorder, but in the heat of battle, "hardened" soldiers suppress the intrinsic significance of killing and maiming real people.

Killing *anyone* on any side in any war destroys an intrinsically valuable person. This is an evil of immense proportions, of infinite proportions if we bring God into the picture, and this is the best available moral reason not to kill in war. But surely in *some* situations killing in war is justified; surely some wars are "just wars," most of us believe. Our deepest and most carefully considered moral intuitions tell us that under some conditions *protecting* intrinsic values from unjustified aggression is a sufficient reason for war. Killing seems justified when necessary as a last resort for eliminating slavery, preventing mass genocide, or defending oneself, one's loved ones, or other innocent persons against unjustified aggression. Killing is always incredibly harmful, but it is not always wrong, for some things are even worse. Yet, such considerations may be mere rationalizations that disguise our real reasons for war. President George H. W. Bush rightfully professed that we were preventing the massacre of innocent Kuwaitis by viciously aggressive Iraqis in the 1991 Persian Gulf War; but the complete sincerity such lofty sentiments is always in doubt when we act to prevent massacres only in countries with massive reserves of oil.

President Abraham Lincoln changed the purpose of the American Civil War from preserving the union to liberating slaves when, after the battle of Antietam in 1862, he issued the *Proclamation of Emancipation*. This *Proclamation* freed only the slaves of the Confederacy, not those in the Union; but it was the beginning of Lincoln's struggle to change the national purpose of the Civil War from a systemic "preserving the Union" to a morally intrinsic liberation of slaves and abolishment of slavery.

"People killing people to end slavery," may appear on the surface to be just another systemic reason for killing people because slavery, like war, is a systemic institution. However, values and disvalues combine on many levels; and a deeper axiological analysis shows that the institution of slavery allows real people to own and treat other real people as mere property. This systemic institution reduces the worth of an intrinsically valuable person to nothing more than an extrinsically valuable possession, as the "Dred Scot" Supreme Court decision of 1857 made clear. This is the main reason why slavery is morally objectionable. It dehumanizes, depersonalizes, and often destroys, like war itself. It reduces people to vacuous systemic/extrinsic variables having little or no unique identity, content, or value at all. It dehumanizes unique human beings.

Consider two historically significant *systemic reasons for going to war*: first, a Federal reason for the American Civil War, then a parallel Confederate reason.

President Lincoln repeatedly said that the primary reason for war against the Confederacy was "to preserve the Union." In the early years of the Civil War, this was his only public reason; he explicitly denied that it was a war to eliminate slavery; its only purpose was to preserve the Union. However, "the Union" is a purely systemic construct that exists only in people's minds; it does not exist in itself; we cannot go somewhere to inspect it, weigh it, or measure it; it has only the very finite constructed meaning that people give to it in their thoughts, beliefs, and corresponding practices. People have not always lived in nation states. States are relatively recent historical social constructs. "The Union" can be evaluated intrinsically with powerful feelings, as patriots tend to do, though it is only a systemic reality. No matter how much he valued it, Lincoln originally gave the weakest kind of reason, a merely systemic reason, "preserving the Union," for killing people in that ghastly war. Later he offered a better reason, an intrinsic reason—freeing the slaves.

Confederates (and today's lingering pseudo-Confederates) also typically denied that the "War Between the States" was about slavery. They offered another purely systemic rationale, "State's Rights," for fighting this war. Of course, this really meant "state's rights to have slaves"! This was merely a systemic rationalization for an economic system that annihilated and/or debased countless intrinsically valuable people—a system that reduced to chattel, to property, the enslaved persons who survived the brutal and often deadly processes of capture, enslavement, and transportation across the ocean. The survivors and their descendants were ultimately reduced to mere tokens in an oppressive economic system. It was a system that significantly devalued black slaves in relation to white citizens. In his "Cornerstone Speech" of 1861, Alexander Stephens, the Vice President of the Confederacy, spoke the honest truth: slavery itself was the real reason for secession from the Union and ultimately for the War. After discussing the "fundamentally wrong" idea of "the equality of the races," Stephens explained, "Our new government is founded upon exactly the opposite idea; its foundations are laid, its corner-stone rest, upon the great truth that the negro is not equal to the white man; that slavery subordination to the superior race is his natural and normal condition."[23]

White Southern religious leaders and followers had their own systemic religions reasons for slavery.[24] As they read and understood the message of the Bible, slavery was God's own and only proper way to order society and relations between management and labor, as the "Good Book" repeatedly illustrated and never condemned. It was also God's own way of introducing Christian beliefs to persons of African origin, so many slave owners rationalized that they were really doing them a great favor by enslaving them!

Because ideas are less valuable than persons, we are never justified in killing or enslaving persons merely for ideological reasons, even if these reasons seem benign. We are never justified in killing or enslaving people simply for the sake of systemic conceptual constructs like: "The Union," "States' Rights," "A New World Order," "The State," "National Security," "Sovereignty," "Patriotism," "Dixie," "The Fatherland," "White Supremacy," "The Superman," or anything of the sort, including religious constructs like "bringing on the Rapture"—a favorite theme of "left behind" religious ideologists.

Confusing Ideology with Spirituality

> *Then there appear confusions both in practice and in theory. The most fundamental, most consequential, and most prevalent such confusion is between systemic and intrinsic value—both equally unknown theoretically—which appears, in practice, in the confusion of systemic value with "spiritual" value, in the hypostatizations of national social, theological, and other ideologies as demanding man's supreme loyalties, and in theory, in the denial of the logical nature of intrinsic value.*[25] Robert S. Hartman

Ideologists superficially resemble saints in their self-less-ness and in their devotion to immaterialities, but these are very different kinds of self-less-ness and immateriality. Worldlings are extrinsically self-less, despite their selfishness, because they know themselves only as objects and not as subjects. Saints are intrinsically self-less, not because they do not know and value themselves as subjects, but because they are loving, compassionate, non-egoistic, self-giving, humble, and self-effacing. They at least know that they have a self to give! Extreme ideologists are systemically self-less because they fully identify themselves with their mental systems and so readily give up and sacrifice themselves to systemic values or belief systems. Like saints, they are non-egoistic, self-giving, and self-effacing; but the value-objects to which they give themselves are very different. Saints (and many heroic soldiers) willingly make sacrifices for the existence, lives, and well-being of concrete individual subjects of experience, action, and evaluation; ideologists enthusiastically sacrifice themselves and others to soul-less ideas, beliefs, doctrines, constructs, and abstract systems.

Ideologists are also self-less in the way they know themselves. They do not fully know themselves as embodied—hence their absent-mindedness, practical ineptitude, and accident proneness. Also, they do not really know themselves as subjects—hence their preoccupation with thoughts and their relative unawareness of themselves as thinkers and of the richness of their own inwardness. They know themselves and other people only as ideological factors in algebraic systems, but not as fully embodied conscious subjects or persons.

The seeming "immateriality" of both systemic and intrinsic values contributes to the confusion of ideology with spirituality. Intellectual systems and conceptual constructs are not things or process that can be perceived and known directly through the external senses. Like all other systemic value-objects, the number "two" cannot be touched, smelled, tasted, heard, or seen. Two *things* can, and our written numeral for it can, but not the number "*two*." The same may be said of inner conscious selves or souls, of an incorporeal God, or of a conscious God who is the soul of the world.

Yes, inner and spiritual realities do require outer and visible signs. Ludwig Wittgenstein's behavioral "criteria" for inner states of the soul were anticipated and required for centuries by theologians, who insisted that inner graces require external and visible signs and manifestations. But inwardness is not identical with its correlated external criteria. Even if thinking, intending, feeling, and willing or choosing are identical with material processes in the brain, with "motions in the head" as Thomas Hobbes put it, this is not obviously so, it requires much more proof than is usually offered, and that is certainly not the whole story if understood reductively. The perfect identity of brain and consciousness is not a deliverance of either direct or indirect observation. It is a theoretical construct or theory, even if it is true, and it may not be true. Even if cleverly defended and well supported, mind/brain identity is only a philosophical hypothesis, a systemic explanatory construct. No one really knows the exact relation between consciousness and brain; and matter really isn't what it used to be any more. Consciousness actually seems to be an invisible spatiotemporally extended field that surrounds and pervades the brain, without being strictly identical with it.

We exist only as embodied souls. Our physical systems, structures, and processes are integral to our total being and reality, even to our intrinsic existence and worth. Nothing is *wrong* with bodies, or with spatially extended consciousness embodied in brains or physical fields. Think about it: what is so horrible about being spatially extended? The alternatives to embodiment are not very attractive for many reasons. Think for a moment about what you would not be able to do if you did not have a body! Systems (ideas) are disembodied and causally ineffective unless acted on by embodied intelligent agents. Communication between souls requires embodiment and speech or signs. All action in the world requires embodiment. Aristotelian systemic "formal causes" are not "efficient causes." Abstract universals (repeatable properties) exist and act only in individuals. People are not disembodied, and neither is God if the universe is God's body and God is the soul of the world, as Process Theologians insist. So, the "immateriality" resemblance between ideology and spirituality is very superficial.

Some people relate to systemic constructs as if they were intrinsic values because they mistakenly associate the intrinsic with the spiritual and the spiritual with the immaterial. Material or physical objects and processes are directly encountered in ordinary sense experience, but not the systemic or intrinsic entities and processes in our thoughts or hidden behind our skulls. Because both systemic and intrinsic objects are in some vague sense "immaterial," these two kinds of value are easily fused and confused. Not every "immaterial" entity is an intrinsic entity having consciousness and intrinsic worth. All the concretely existing intrinsic entities we know are embodied, thus spatiotemporally extended. Mere ideas or beliefs have no minds, consciousness, feelings, purposes, freedom, actions, or values of their own. We should bet our souls on unique, property-rich, conscious, and embodied intrinsic realities, not on abstruse, property-poor, and disembodied systemic abstractions!

The value error of confusing systemic with intrinsic values is pernicious as well as commonplace. We are easily seduced into identify ourselves with systemic-mistaken-for-intrinsic realities. In ethics, this manifests itself as a deep commitment to moral principles and rules, but not to people, as ends in themselves. Here, people are made for the moral law, not the moral law for people. In religion, it appears as legalism or "rule worship," according to which people were made for the Sabbath, for God's rules, not the Sabbath and God's rules for people. Bibliolatry, another form of systemic idolatry, confuses God with "The Word" or "The Good Book," that is, with its conceptual meanings and doctrines, which truthfully only point to the reality of God.

The ideological mode of evaluative consciousness dwells in the realm of intellectual abstractions and constructions, mistakes their immateriality for intrinsic reality, and is out of touch with concrete existence. It commits what Alfred North Whitehead called "the fallacy of misplaced concreteness," the fallacy of mistaking abstractions for concrete realities.[26] It reifies and idolizes abstractions.

Ideologists are not necessarily intellectuals themselves. Yet, many but far from all intellectuals are ideologists. Ideologists have a well-developed capacity for recognizing and overvaluing intellect and its products—theories, systems, authorities, rules, doctrines, creeds, and dogmas—even if they have no part in creating them. Hartman wrote that "There is no necessary correlation between abstract intelligence and appreciation of such intelligence."[27] Just as worldlings are social snobs, ideologists are intellectual snobs. Even when they are not very bright or intellectual themselves, they may be intellectual-want-to-bes. They identify themselves with those who actually are, and they look down on those who are not.

Ideologists adhere rigidly to conceptual constructs. Philosophers, systematic theologians, college professors, and intellectuals are prone to be ideologists and to attach primary value to systemic entities, but not necessarily so. They may be indifferent to, confused about, or even downright hostile toward concrete existence, whether personal, social, or sensory in nature. Ideologists are largely "out of touch" with people and things, both extrinsically and intrinsically. They can be very clumsy when manipulating things, unduly prone to accidents, much confused about and unsuccessful in their social roles, poor at planning for the future, and ineffective in establishing meaningful interpersonal relations. When they try to relate to people and things, they often succeed in connecting only with abstractions, like the elderly doctor who spoke these words to Dostoevsky's Father Zossima.

> I love humanity,...but I wonder at myself. The more I love humanity in general, the less I love man in particular. In my dreams...I often make plans for the service of humanity, and perhaps I might actually face crucifixion if it were suddenly necessary. Yet I am incapable of living in the same room with anyone for two days together. I know from experience. As soon as anyone is near me, his personality disturbs me and restricts my freedom. In twenty-four hours I begin to hate the best of men: one because he's too long over his dinner, another because he has a cold and keeps on blowing his nose. I become hostile to people the moment they come close to me. But It has always happened that the more I hate men individually, the more I love humanity.[28]

By degrees, most people are worldlings, not ideologists. Both saints and true ideologists are few and far between. Nevertheless, a mean ideological streak exists somewhere in almost all of us. The left-brained systemic/thinking self is dominant in most scientists, philosophers, and intellectuals. Most ordinary people can easily tap into the ideological dimension of their own personalities, especially when enticed by charismatic ideologists. Some of these (like Alexander Stephens or Hitler) are politicians, but some are religiously prominent and influential. When combined, worldly and ideological mentalities are highly unstable. In fact, many people are very unstable and confused about their own values and evaluations.

Sub-cultures and educational institutions that place heavy emphasis on systemic cognitive abilities teeter on the brink of ideology. Non-intellectuals not living intellectually examined lives are said to have lives not worth living. Socrates claimed that a rationally unexamined life is not worth living, but he was wrong. It would be more accurate to say that a morally and spiritually vacuous life is meaningless and not worth living, for that is precisely how most such people experience it. Morally and spiritually good people not living intellectually or philosophically examined lives really can have very worthwhile extrinsic and intrinsic lives. They can be very creative, practical, loving, and compassionate people. Kenneth Keniston, referring to the intellectual elite, not to the masses, observed,

> We run the risk in America today of having only one hierarchy of human value: cognitive ability. With this approach both individuals and society pay a high price. Even for those who play the cognitive game well, the price is too often an atrophy of other human qualities which I suspect are, in God's eyes, far more important: morality, kindness, empathy, feeling, joy, imagination, playfulness, grace, artistic ability—to say nothing of love. And the price paid by those at the bottom is all too well known—children who by second grade have accepted the label of "losers" and who carry it with them forever.[29]

Ideologically oriented social orders have little place for intrinsically evaluating genuine intrinsic value-objects—animals, people, and God. Neither do ideologically oriented religions, churches, religious dogmatists, and fanatics of every description.

Systemic/Ideological Religion

> *Language is not an end but a means, and the end is communication with meaning and significance. The language of the Bible is meant always to point us to a truth beyond the text, a meaning that transcends the particular and imperfectly understood context of the original writers and our own prejudices and parochialisms that we bring to the text itself.*[30] Peter J. Gomes

Only a fine line separates the legitimate systemic (conceptual) aspects of spirituality from ideological religion. What can be said to clarify the differences? Legitimate systemic aspects of spirituality take their place as third in value-rank behind its extrinsic and intrinsic aspects. Ideological religion usurps that rank in many ways, now to be explored. Authentic spirituality uses words, symbols, and doctrines to point beyond themselves; ideological religion greatly overvalues and misconceives them as supreme goods, as ends in themselves.

Ideological religion excessively emphasizes correctness of interpretations, beliefs, doctrines, creeds, rituals, rules, laws, and formalities. Spiritual ideologists do not value these religious formalisms in purely systemic ways and relate to them only disinterestedly or impartially with their intellects. Most are devoted to them with all their hearts, souls, minds, and strength, to the neglect of the realities that they represent. There is a time and place for what Spinoza called "the intellectual love of God" in true religion, without lapsing into ideological religion; and there are many other ways of loving God. As Saint Thomas Aquinas recognized, although very few people have the time, talent, or intellect for objective philosophical theology, they can still be deeply spiritual by loving God and their neighbors.

Ideological purists value the idealized conceptual constructs of religion intrinsically, with all of their being, while not loving God and their neighbors. Even if somewhat developed intrinsically, extreme ideologists would not allow themselves to accept and love others who do not subscribe to the right doctrines and scriptural interpretations, or who do not participate in the right rituals or ceremonial formalities. They withhold affection from, shun, boycott, disinherit, ostracize, disparage, and consign to oblivion other people—including close family members—who do not accept, or who are exceptions to, their religious interpretations, ideologies, and formal practices. They care socially only for those who mentally conform.

Like fabled ostriches, religious ideologists like to bury their heads in the sand and segregate themselves and their loved ones into sheltered ideological communities where their favored dogmas, interpretations, and religious formalities will not be challenged. They may want public tax money to pay for home schooling their children or for private sectarian schools in which they will not be exposed to modern scientific truths like evolution and the vast age of the universe. They tend to hate religious outsiders and act hatefully toward them. They avoid, shun, and depreciate persons of other faiths. They shop only with merchants who advertise in the "Right-Religion Yellow Pages." They do not do unto religious outsiders as they would be done unto. If they are ideological Christians, they may diligently practice their own version of the Nazi injunction, "Do not buy from Jews." They think that God's love extends only to Christians (or to those of like persuasion, whatever that might be). The Inquisitions of the mid to late Middle Ages showed how vicious ideological religion can get. Better to torture people than that they not believe the right stuff!

Ideological religion emphasizes formalities over all else, but ideologies can take innumerable forms. We will now consider systemic/ideological approaches to God and the image of God, all-or nothing religious belief systems, and their rules and rituals. Systemic/ideological approaches to faith will then be contrasted with extrinsic and intrinsic approaches, and better alternatives will be identified.

God and the Image of God

> God, then, made man in His own image. For he created for him a soul endowed with reason and intelligence, so that he might excel all the creatures of earth, air, and sea, which were not so gifted.[31] St. Augustine

> Man is said to be in the image of God, not as regards his body, but as regards that whereby he excels other animals....Now man excels all animals by his reason and intellect; hence it is according to his intellect and reason, which are incorporeal, that man is said to be in the image of God.[32] St. Thomas Aquinas

> For the will of God is never irrational....We affirm that the Divine nature is beyond doubt impassible....But we say that the Lord Jesus Christ is very God and very man, one person in two natures, and two natures in one person. When, therefore, we speak of God as enduring any humiliation, we do not refer to the majesty of that nature, which cannot suffer; but to the feebleness of the human constitution which he assumed.[33] St. Anselm

> But how art thou compassionate, and, at the same time, passionless? For if thou art passionless, thou does not feel sympathy; and if thou dost not feel sympathy, thy heart is not wretched from sympathy for the wretched; but this it is to be compassionate. But if thou art not compassionate, whence cometh so great consolation to the wretched? How, then, art thou compassionate and not compassionate, O Lord, unless because thou art compassionate in terms of our experience, and not compassionate in terms of thy being.

> Truly, thou art so in terms of our experience, but thou art not so in terms of thine own. For, when thou beholdest us in our wretchedness, we experience the effect of compassion, but thou dost not experience the feeling. Therefore, thou art both compassionate, because thou does save the wretched, and spare those who sin against thee; and not compassionate, because thou art affected by no sympathy for wretchedness.[34] St. Anselm

> *Mercy is especially to be attributed to God, provided it be considered in its effect, but not as an affection of passion....To sorrow, therefore, over the misery of others does not belong to God.*[35] St. Thomas Aquinas

In unguarded moments, they may have had richer concepts of God and of God's image in us, but when classical theologians like St. Augustine, St. Thomas Aquinas, and St. Anselm discussed the "image of God" in humankind, they offered a purely *systemic* interpretation of it. We were made in the image of a completely impassive, unfeeling, disembodied, rational, all-knowing, and systemic God. A different but still systemic understanding of God was offered by philosophical minded rationalists like the Stoics, Spinoza, and Einstein, who identified God with reason in nature, with the systemic laws of nature, but not with a transcendent personal being.

In many respects, classical medieval and post-reformation theology was much more indebted to Plato, Aristotle, and other Greek philosophers than to the Bible. Most Greek philosophers were prejudiced against feelings, good ones as well as bad. They thought *all* feelings to be bad or at least inferior to pure reason and thus unworthy of Divinity. Aristotle insisted that God is unmoved, not just physically, but emotionally. God is "impassible," which means that God has no feelings, affections, emotions, or desires at all, especially not any that are distressing or painful. Aristotle's purely rational God thinks only indifferently, i.e., with no feeling at all, about thinking, but never about us or the world. Aristotle's God was not omniscient, for it knew and thought *only* about thoughts.

Many Greek philosophers believed mistakenly that reason is a distinct faculty that can function without any feelings whatsoever. They did not understand that true disinterestedness is not absolute uninterestedness, for it always involves a bit of interestedness. Classical Christian theologians fused and confused this Greek philosophical ideal of divine perfection as pure rationality devoid of all feelings with biblical religion and spirituality. They relegated the all-pervasive affective language about God in the Bible to the realm of impious and misleading metaphors and myths, none of which could be taken seriously. Classical theologians assumed unquestioningly that the Greek philosophers knew the literal truth about divine perfection, namely, that a perfect being would be pure intellect with no feelings whatsoever. When biblical words and phrases said otherwise, as they usually do, Classical theologians called them merely human and misleading metaphors, but not literal truths.

Early influential and prominent Christian thinkers adopted the Greek systemic ideal of divine perfection as pure reason without feelings. This logically entailed that God does not really suffer with or for distressed creatures, that God is not compassionate. That God suffers with us in our sufferings was the heresy of "patripassionism," meaning the "error" that God the Father has feelings. As St. Anselm explained, when Jesus suffered on the cross, only his human nature suffered, not his impassible Divine nature. Anselm said that when we think of *God as compassionate*, that means only that we experience God *as if* he were that way, even though *he really isn't!* St. Thomas Aquinas likewise insisted that God is merciful without feeling mercy; we experience God's mercy even though God doesn't have any! Try preaching that in Church on Sunday morning!

The Greeks also corrupted later Jewish thought about God. Moses Maimonides taught, according to Rabbi Abraham J. Heschel, that when God is called compassionate, "This does not mean that He feels compassion, but that He works deeds in regard to His creatures similar to those which with us would proceed from the feeling of compassion."[36] As Rabbi Heschel correctly indicates next, all of this is clearly a perversion of biblical religion.

> Far from insisting upon their effacement, the biblical writers frequently regarded some emotions or passions as having been inspired, as reflections of a higher power. There is no disparagement of emotion, no celebration of apathy. Pathos, emotional involvement, passionate participation, is a part of religious existence. The utterances of the psalmist are charged with emotion, are outpourings of emotion. Reading the prophets, we are stirred by their passion and enlivened imagination. Their primary aim is to move the soul, to engage the attention by bold and striking images, and therefore it is to the imagination and to the passions that the prophets speak, rather than aiming at the cold approbation of the mind.... The prophets thought of God's relation to the world as one of concern and compassion.[37]

The New Testament, as well as the Jewish Bible, also presents God's relation to the world as one of real concern, compassion, and love. Intrinsic religion positively values desirable feelings, both human and Divine. It does not divorce reason or religion from feelings. It does not conceived of the "image of God" as nothing more than impassive reason; that image also includes real affective love and compassion. Not all feelings are unworthy of God just because they are feelings. Intrinsic spiritualists do not say that God loves without loving, that God acts compassionately without being compassionate, that God seems merciful though really is not. Intrinsic spirituality was nicely captured by Alfred North Whitehead, who said that God is "the great companion—the fellow sufferer who understands."[38]

Popular Christianity and Judaism have always taken affective language about God and human beings in the Old and New Testaments very seriously and somewhat literally, even when qualified as analogical, that is, even when infinite differences between us and God are recognized. Intrinsic theologies do so as well; many systemic theologies do not.

Just how we conceive of God has great significance for religious ethics as well as for theology. Religious ethics requires us to be Godlike and to fulfill or actualize the image of God within ourselves, with God's help. Being Godlike in *systemic* theologies would *require us* to be purely indifferent or unmoved rational beings, to love without loving, to be compassionate without compassion, to be merciful without mercy, and so on. That is the very meaning of "Godlike," systemically (ideologically) conceived.

The Stoics took systemic or ideological Godlikeness to its logical conclusion; they insisted that we should be emotionally unattached and indifferent to everyone, even those who are closest to us in life—our spouses, children, and best friends. Something resembling this Stoic ideal persists in our popular culture's image of the "macho male" who does what he has to do without feelings or intense personal involvement in anything. The reason "Big boys don't cry" is not that they have feelings but suppress them. No, "real men" are impassive Greek gods; they just don't have any feelings at all! Only women and effeminate males have feelings. Does your religion say this? Would a truly good religion say this? Intrinsic spirituality avoids sexist stereotypes and domineering, requires us to be fully loving, compassionate, and merciful without qualification and to act accordingly because God is like that, and it is best for all that we be Godlike. A good religion affirms and does not repudiate the religious affections either in us or in God.

Given the Hartmanian hierarchy of value, systemic goodness is the least valuable form of goodness, though it is still very good. It has less value than extrinsic and intrinsic goodness. Thus, a purely systemic God would be the least valuable kind of God, one having much less value than an extrinsic and/or an intrinsic God. *God as nothing but reason alone without feelings* is definitely not that being than whom none more valuable (greater or better) can be conceived. "God is impassible" is about as far removed from "God is love" as you can get.

Beings with no feelings at all would actually have very few if any recognizable values, as illustrated by brain-damaged human beings in whom rational thought process have been severed from feelings.[39] A purely rational being with absolutely no feelings, Supreme or not, would attach value to nothing at all, not because it could not correlate properties with standards of goodness—even sociopaths can do that—but because it could never adopt and identify itself with any such standards. A God who is greater than a purely systemic divinity is definitely conceivable. Systemic theologies do not make good sense; intrinsic theologies do—intellectually, practically, and affectively. A being than whom none better can be conceived would contain all dimensions of value, not just the purely systemic dimension, and definitely not total affective indifference.

All or Nothing Belief Systems

> *The articles of faith stand in the same relation to the doctrine of faith, as self-evident principles to teaching based on natural reason. Among these principles there is a certain order, so that some are contained implicitly in others; and thus all principles are reduced, as to their first principle, to this one:* The same thing cannot be affirmed and denied at the same time, *as the Philosopher [Aristotle] states. In like manner, all the articles are contained implicitly in certain primary truths of faith, such as God's existence, and His providence over the salvation of man....For*

> the being of God includes all that we believe to exist in God eternally, and in these our happiness consists, while belief in His providence includes all those things which God dispenses in time for man's salvation, and which are the way to happiness; and in this way, again, some of those articles which follow from these are contained in others. Thus faith in the Redemption of mankind includes implicitly the Incarnation of Christ, His Passion and so forth.[40] St. Thomas Aquinas

Religious concepts, ideas, interpretations, and doctrines are bound together into systems or pseudo-systems. Although not as exact as logic and mathematics, religious ideas and beliefs have logical connections with one another. Some logically imply others, and some beliefs, like those of atheists or doubters, are logically incompatible with them. Many seriously held religious beliefs are incompatible with others. St. Thomas nicely expressed the *systems* aspects of systemic religious doctrines in the words above.

The "all or nothing" approach of systemic evaluation is nicely illustrated in the Thomistic doctrines that (1) the church is infallible because it derives its doctrine directly from God, who cannot be mistaken about anything, and (2) anyone who obstinately doubts even one doctrine of faith thereby rejects every doctrine of faith.[41] True believers must accept the whole package, the whole system of revealed doctrine as taught by the Church, or none of it, St. Thomas decreed. The impending consequences of accepting none of it (hell) would be quite unpleasant! Like other authoritarian ideologists, religious dogmatists intensely disvalue those who don't accept or fit their belief system. They usually consign them to hell. Ideologists are ideologist whether they are Christians, Marxists, Nazis, White Supremists, or whatever. Many vicious wars have been fought over religion. Religion can both offer and serve ruthless ideologies. As Robert S. Hartman observed, "Hitler's armies did not lack chaplains!"[42]

Jesus reportedly said, "He that is not with me is against me" (Matthew 12:30). He was probably talking about *personal* relationships, not about *doctrines*, for the doctrines of Christian orthodoxy had not yet been formulated. Today's Christian exclusivists proclaim that a person can be saved only by believing certain doctrines, their doctrines, about Jesus. Yet, having an intense personal relationship with doctrines is not the same thing as having an intense personal relationship with Jesus. Systemic black or white thinking oversimplifies everything. It becomes ideological when it overvalues doctrines and undervalues people at the expense of doctrines, typically through a rigidly systemic, person-degrading, dualistic, "all or nothing" mentality.

In its approach to religious beliefs, traditional Roman Catholic theology was intellectualistic and comprehensively systemic, and it ideologically disvalued dissenters. Faith was defined as a wilful act of intellectual assent in the absence of evidence. This was applied, not just to a single religious proposition, but to the whole system of intricately interrelated Catholic doctrines, which were all or nothing at all. Except for the Twentieth Century heresy of fundamentalism, Protestants for the most part, including today's evangelicals, understand faith primarily as intrinsic personal involvement with religious realities rather than as blind intellectual assent to religious doctrines. Fundamentalism, however, is exceptionally doctrinaire; it reiterates orthodox Catholicism's systemic view of faith as assent to dogma, but it centers this faith upon the infallible Bible instead of on the infallible traditions and teachings of the Church and the Pope. Reformation Protestants complained that Catholicism added new and unscriptural doctrines to those given in the Bible. Do Protestants, especially fundamentalists, add any of their own?

The final outcome is much the same for most religious ideologists—a complex system of dogma that must be accepted *in toto*—with dire consequences for nonacceptance. James Barr pinpointed the systemic dimension of fundamentalism (and other religious dogmatisms), as well as its "all or nothing at all" approach to hermeneutics, when he wrote, "According to the fundamentalist understanding, the whole Bible hangs together; all parts are related to all others. Any defect, any criticism attaching to any part, however small, is therefore a wound which injures the entirety."[43]

In contemporary fundamentalism, biblical literalism yields to or is transformed into inerrancy. A literal interpretation is just the one, metaphorical or not, that makes any biblical passage true and thus infallible. As Barr notes, fundamentalists are tied "not to the 'literal' meaning ... but to the 'plain' meaning, the meaning which is clearly the right one."[44] "Inerrancy," Barr says, "is the constant factor in all fundamentalist interpretation."[45] The crucial consideration is that everything in the Bible is true; this is the very meaning of inerrancy: "correspondence with external reality and events."[46] But to be true, an interpretation must harmonize both with pre-selected fundamental doctrines and with everything else in the Bible as filtered through fundamentalistic doctrinal lenses. Fundamentalists believe that the Bible, properly interpreted, is a logically and a religiously flawless system of harmonious affirmations that correspond with Ultimate Reality, "a final and fully expressive transcript of God's mind."[47] Making this claim work by actually harmonizing all seemingly conflicting texts isn't easy; it isn't even possible; it isn't even biblical, as Barr aptly and amply demonstrates.[48]

Fundamentalists, who insist upon biblical inerrancy, should not be confused with evangelicals, who affirm biblical inspiration but not biblical infallibility. Evangelicals also assign much more weight and value to the religious affections, whereas for fundamentalists, doctrinal correctness is the highest value.

In relating to doctrines, most fundamentalists, dogmatists, authoritarians, and ideologists do not manifest systemic detachment. They intrinsically evaluate their belief systems. In itself, this is not an undesirable thing; the trouble is, they do it at the expense of real people and other Christian values. Religious ideologists enthusiastically pillory dissenters, passionately burn heretics, and confidently consign all doubters and unbelievers to hell. They think in "all or nothing" terms, and they cannot see God's own grey area. Those who do not accept their beliefs *in toto* are worthless and beyond redemption, no matter how rich in good-making properties and bright and beautiful in spirit they otherwise are. Ideologists may detach emotionally from non-systemic realities, but their adherence to dogma is passionate and intrinsic, and their animosity to disbelievers can be fierce. Their faith is mainly in systemic faith itself, not in God. They love the forms but not the substance of religion with their whole being. Fundamentalists cannot comprehend taking scriptures seriously without taking them literally. They seem to love the scriptures more than they love the God of the scriptures. To them, inspiration without infallibility is inconceivable, and infallibility is more valuable than love to God and neighbors, especially those who are different or who disagree.

Even without affirming infallible and unrevisable doctrines, studying and thinking about the Judao-Christian scriptures can be immensely beneficial to seekers of moral and spiritual understanding, insight, growth, support, and help. These venerable and inspired sacred writings offer us a common reservoir of stories, metaphors, myths, and basic insights that have been central to our history, culture, and spirituality for many centuries. Most of us can grasp narratives easier than we can comprehend abstract theology and philosophy, and reflecting on narratives can lead to deeper thinking. Serious individual and group Bible study enables Christians and Jews to see how God worked with and through very flawed and undeserving human beings who were far removed from saintly perfection and absolute knowledge.

The Bible is a very honest and inspired book, even if not infallible. It shows how God brought as much goodness as possible from the sad, uninformed, and sinful predicaments into which our spiritual predecessors got themselves. By placing ourselves imaginatively into their shoes, we can learn valuable lessons about the depths of human nature, its complexity, its pliability and resilience under adverse and very different cultural conditions, its potentials for moral and spiritual experience and growth, and how God values and helps us. By identifying with them empathetically, we can learn to appreciate the profound worth of blemish lives. Wrestling with and thinking about their moral and spiritual puzzles, shortcomings, and successes can help us to grow morally and spiritually and to deal more appropriately and effectively with our own spiritual predicaments. The outcomes may not be infallible, but they can be immensely helpful and illuminating.

We can also learn much about how *not* to think, feel, will, and act from the people and ideas we meet in the scriptures. *They* were fallible, not infallible. Progressive revelation running through the Bible is often affirmed, but this recognizes that some biblical insights are more proper and profound than others. Understanding the struggles of unsaintly scriptural characters to gain higher and more adequate moral and spiritual insights, motives, and practices can give us both guidance and hope for ourselves. There we can find positive role models or examples that we can emulate today, but not every person in the Bible can be a role model for us, and not every word in the Bible is God's final word for us. Jesus told us that emphatically in his "Sermon on the Mount" (Matthew 5-7) where he challenged what had been said in the scriptures of old—what we call the Old Testament. By better understanding the means of grace by which flawed scriptural characters grew towards God and goodness, we can be empowered for our own moral and spiritual development.

Rules and Rituals

> By 'means of grace,' I understand outward signs, words, or actions, ordained to God, and appointed for this end, to be the ordinary channels whereby he might convey to men, preventing, justifying, or sanctifying grace.
> A sacrament is 'an outward sign of inward grace, and a means whereby we receive the same'.
> The chief of these means are prayer, whether in secret or with the great congregation; searching the Scriptures (which implies reading, hearing, and meditating thereon) and receiving the Lord's Supper, eating bread and drinking wine in remembrance of him; and these we believe to be ordained of God as the ordinary channels of conveying his grace to the souls of men.
> But we allow that the whole value of the means depends on their actual subservience to the end of religion; that consequently, all these means, when separated from the end, are less than nothing, and vanity; that if they do not actually conduce to the knowledge and love of God they are not acceptable in his sight, yea, rather, they are an abomination before him, a stink in his nostrils.[49] John Wesley

We need now to consider systemic religious forms, rules, and rituals. Ideologists identify spirituality with formalities, sometimes doctrines, sometimes rites and ceremonies. Systemic service to God can take the form of legalistic obedience to moral, social, dietary, or ceremonial rules, practices, and procedures. The legalistic version of Judaism that was represented in the First Century CE by the Pharisees was ideologically oriented toward purity and conformity in such matters. The Pharisees tried to live by, and up to, every letter of the law. They expected everyone else to do the same and thought themselves better than those who did not. Obviously, they failed, as does every rigid and ideological legalist and formalist. Systemic perfection is unattainable. Instead of giving comfort, peace, and salvation, the law condemns and produces anxiety, guilt, and fear of Divine retribution, as St. Paul well understood.

Both Jesus and St. Paul refused to identify the heart of spirituality with religious formalities, rules, laws, and rituals, but they supported them as long as they serve more valuable spiritual ends beyond themselves. Legalistic religion is "rule worship," where behavioral guidelines are seen as final ends, to be obeyed for their own sakes, rather than as flexible and helpful means to human grace and flourishing. Jesus insisted that the law and the Sabbath were made for man, not man for the law and the Sabbath (Mark 2:27). St. Paul thought that Jesus came to liberate people from bondage to biblical laws and ceremonies (Romans 8:1-4; Galatians 10-13). Jesus and Paul did not try to eliminate rituals, rules, and rule-following from the saintly life; they did not throw out the systemic commandments, but they subordinated them to and placed them in the service of intrinsically loving intrinsically valuable beings. Freedom from the law meant liberation from guilt, not license to disobey, unless there is a more loving way. From overbearing legalistic systemics, Christ came to set Christians free! Love fulfills the true intent of the law. Love needs the law; the law needs love. Loving people keep the commandments in loving ways as best they can with God's help, forgiveness, and grace.

Excessive preoccupation with correctness of and rigid conformity to ritual forms manifests an ideological spiritual orientation. Extremely systemic ideologists, religious or not, can be callously indifferent to human suffering and the intrinsic worth of individual human beings. Leo Tolstoy lamented "the spiritual condition of a Russian peasant who would rather die than spit out the Sacrament onto a manure heap, but who is yet ready to kill his brothers at the command of men."[50] Total absorption in formal correctness makes the intrinsic evaluation of concrete individuals nearly impossible; inflexible approximation to it makes loving difficult by degrees. Sticklers for ritual or doctrinal correctness unlovingly consign people to perdition for subscribing to incorrect doctrines, or for not being properly immersed, or for not observing the Sabbath on the right day of the week, or because their religious ordinances are administered by ministers who cannot trace their ordination and authority back through apostolic succession to St. Peter or some other Apostle, or for some other incredibly picky systemic reason.

In intrinsic religion, rules and rituals are not totally eliminated, but they are not ends in themselves, not valued only for themselves. Their forms are systemic; their practice is extrinsic; their motives and objects are intrinsic. They are *systemic/ extrinsic means* of grace, means to other ends beyond themselves, intrinsic ends. As John Wesley explained, you should "use all means *as means*; as ordained, not for their own sake, but in order to the renewal of your soul in righteousness and true holiness. If, therefore, they actually tend to this, well; but, if not, they are dung and dross."[51] Ritual forms belong to the systemic value domain; acting them out, ceremonial practice, combines them with extrinsic behaviors; their deepest significance as sources and expressions of love and devotion belongs to the intrinsic when they express and engender intrinsic union and identification with others.

When rituals and ceremonies seem dead or empty, their intrinsic significance is lacking. They are not working as graceful means to being and becoming a more loving person. Valuable objects and modes of evaluation may be combined in many ways. When religious rules and rituals are experienced as empty forms, systemic value-objects are being valued indifferently—without personal involvement. But when they are used to express, evoke, and celebrate deep feelings of communion with and love for God, Jesus, neighbors, strangers, other living things, and natural ecologies, systemic forms become extrinsic means to intrinsic goodness and divine grace.

In intrinsic saintly religion, religious rules, rituals, and ceremonies express and evoke powerful religious feelings of awe, wonder, adoration, praise, comfort, Sabbath peace and rest, loving affection, and a deep and heartfelt communions of saints with God and with one another. Here the forms and formalities of religion mediate between us and greater goodness. Love and practice need conceptual guidance, but love fulfills everything really important in the law, without its rigidity. The law was made for love, not love for the law. At times, individual devotional practices and communal worship services may be nothing more than empty forms and practices; they may be overvalued for their own sakes; but they can be so much more. They can be efficacious means of grace that help us to make contact with divine love and to carry it beyond our Sabbath moments into the whole of life.

Systemic, Extrinsic, and Intrinsic Faith

> *Let not your heart be troubled: ye believe in God, believe also in me.* Jesus (John 14:1)

> *Believe on the Lord Jesus Christ, and thou shalt be saved, and thy house.* Paul and Silas (Acts 16:31)

> *If I have all faith, so as to remove mountains, but have not love, I am nothing....So faith, hope, love abide, these three; but the greatest of these is love.* St. Paul (I. Corinthians 13:1, 13)

> We evangelicals contend that correct doctrine and faith in the veracity of the biblical revelation are not enough. We believe that to be "saved" and to have a right relationship with God, we must have a personal relationship with a risen and living Jesus. This is the *essential mystic dimension of being a Christian.*[52] Tony Campolo

Faith is a central spiritual concept, but theologians do not agree about what "faith" is or means, or about the precise value of spiritual believing and knowing. Many emphasize doctrines, interpretations, conceptual meanings, and intellectual assent. Others emphasize utility, broadly understood as actually living out one's deepest commitments, or narrowly understood as subscribing to any beliefs and regular practices that will insure eternal security, prosperity, prominence, and rewards in heaven and on earth. Others emphasize adoration, devotion, wonder, trust, love, and holistic commitment, along with helpful symbols, metaphors, guidelines, and their extensional meanings, referents, or realities.

"Having faith" can be understood or analyzed in all three value dimensions. Systemically it means (1) assenting cognitively to doctrinal beliefs. Extrinsically it means (2) practically living in Godlike or Christlike ways; practicing what you preach. Intrinsically it means (3) all of that plus loving and personally identifying with God or Jesus. "Believing on Jesus in order to be saved," so heavily emphasized by many Christians, can be construed in one, two, or all of these three ways. Is saving Christian believing (faith) just a matter of accepting certain doctrines or ideas about Jesus and God? Or is it that plus a great deal more? Doesn't it also involve actually living and acting socially like God or Jesus, where actions speak louder than words and manifest what we really believe? Isn't it even more than that? Isn't it also a matter of having an intense intrinsic loving personal relationship with God and Jesus as still-living persons or realities who exceed anything that we could ever think or believe about them?

Do some believers stop at the systemic level? Is the believing involved in being "saved" the intrinsic personal relationship expressed in daily doing and living, or is it merely systemic cognitive assent to doctrines, especially "fundamental" ones? Or, as some seem to think, is "being saved" just an extrinsic matter of getting a free ticked to heaven and reaping the heavenly rewards of it here and hereafter? Does faith-based salvation involve actually doing the works of love? Is it a new birth into intrinsic spirituality and personal communion with God, the first step in lifelong spiritual growth? Perhaps "believing in order to be saved" is *all of the above* in proper order or priority. If so, actually having faith is very complicated, and "faith" is a very complex concept! We must further consider faith in each value dimension.

Systemic Faith and Belief

> *When revelation is conceived as consisting primarily of communicated truths or doctrines, faith will inevitably be understood as consisting primarily in assent to these truths. Throughout a great part of Christian history it was so understood. Faith was thus primarily an exercise of the intellect, though the will also takes part; the will, according to Aquinas, moves the intellect to assent.*
>
> *Thus in the Middle Ages three elements were distinguished in faith:* notitia, assensus, *and* ficucia; *understanding, assent, and trust. The two former are clearly intellectual in nature, but the last is as clearly volitional. In what then does* ficucia *consist? The answer seems to be that prevailingly, and in spite of certain other commingling strands of meaning, it is understood as submission to the Church's teaching.*[53] John Baillie

A few systemic souls may keep their personal involvement with anything and everything as disinterested as possible, but thereby they lack deep or intense religious faith and feelings. Perhaps they confuse rational impartiality or disinterestedness with affective uninterestedness. However, religious ideologists typically relate intrinsically rather than systemically to their ideologies and creeds, and they use them to berate and degrade others who do not agree. Most are passionately involved with religious doctrines, and their systemic-like detachment (or worse) is reserved for people and things. *Intrinsic ideologists* care deeply about the one thing they take to be of real value: ideas, concepts, beliefs, dogmas, doctrines, rituals, forms, and formulas. They may or may not also relate intrinsically to other intellectual pursuits like philosophy, mathematics, physics, psychology, politics, government, etc.

Ideologists are often found in institutions like universities and monasteries that both nurture their cognitive capacities and shelter them from deep involvement with people and practical affairs. Ideologists are paradigm "ivory tower intellectuals" who, unlike worldlings, passionately care about ideas as such. They are intellectual snobs who, like Socrates, think that other kinds of life are not worth living. In religion, ideologists favor intellectual or cognitive approaches to religious faith; doctrines mean everything to them. They value dogmas wholeheartedly, as ends in themselves, at the expense of the realities toward which such religious beliefs point, that is, at the expense of God and everyone God loves.

St. Thomas Aquinas and most medieval theologians subscribed mainly to a systemic, cognitive, intellectualistic, and ideological view of the nature of faith. Their approach to faith was "scholastic." *Systemic faith* is firm cognitive assent to the truth of religious propositions. In defining faith, St. Thomas wrote: "Faith signifies the assent of the intellect to that which is believed."[54] Notice that acting and loving are not included in this definition. Such intellectual assent is determined by an act of will or desire, not by an act of reason like a philosophical proof. According to St. Thomas, even though revealed to us by God, who cannot be mistaken about anything, faith's doctrines lack a rational demonstration sufficient to convince anyone, especially determined doubters.[55]

St. Thomas knew that "faith" is connected indirectly with will, charity (love), hope, self-interest in happiness, infallible doctrinal revelation, things unseen, psychological certitude without rational evidence, virtue, salvation, and so on; but he defined faith to be primarily a function of intellect or cognition. Faith as such is definitely not affective or emotional; its proper targets are invisible intellectual objects. Reflecting on St. Paul's understanding of faith as "the evidence of things not seen" (Hebrews 11:1), here is how St. Thomas summarized his own position.

> Accordingly, if anyone would reduce the foregoing words to the form of a definition, he may say that *faith is a habit of mind, whereby eternal life is begun in us, making the intellect assent to what is non-apparent*....Whatever other definitions are given of faith are explanations of this one given by the Apostle. For when Augustine says that *faith is a virtue whereby we believe what we do not see*, and when Damascene says that *faith is an assent without inquiry*, and when others say that *faith is that certainty of the mind about absent things which surpasses opinion but falls short of science*, these all amount to the same as the Apostle's words: *Evidence of things that appear not*.[56]

The dominant medieval approach to faith was very systemic. It centered on concepts, doctrines, interpretations, systems, intellectual assent, and accepting propositional truths. Except for fundamentalists, Protestant theologians tend to subscribe to a quite different and much more intrinsic and person-related understanding of the nature of faith. Religions like Buddhism officially disvalue doctrines, though they sneak lots of them in through the back door. Gautama himself taught that metaphysical inquiries like "Does God exist?" are waste of time because they divert people from their primary spiritual task here and now—gaining relief and permanent release from suffering. Christians take doctrinal beliefs much more seriously, but not necessarily as seriously as the realities to which they refer. And they are (or should be) deeply engaged with those realities, not disengaged or detached from them.

Extrinsic Faith and Belief

By their fruits you will know them. Jesus, Matthew 7:20.

Faith without works is dead. James 2:20, 26.

Faith is believing things that no one in his right mind would believe.[57] Archie Bunker

We don't really stretch our faith; we don't believe for anything bigger. But God wants us to constantly be increasing, to be rising to new heights. He wants to increase you in his wisdom and help you to make better decisions. God wants to increase you financially, by giving you promotions, fresh ideas, and creativity.[58] Joel Osteen

If you want to prosper in your finances, put God first. If you want to prosper in your business, put God first. When you honor God, God will always honor you.[59] Joel Osteen

Religion or spirituality, like everything else, may be valued positively or negatively in any axiological dimension. Some people disvalue spirituality because they think that it is practically useless. Naturalistic atheists, for whom religious beliefs are just not true, say that efforts devoted to purely fanciful other-worldly religion are practically harmful because they siphon off and waste energy that would be better spent directed to real moral and social problems in this world. Pragmatic nonintellectual skeptics like Archie Bunker just think that religion requires us to believe things that no one in his right mind would ever believe. What a waste! Of course, not everyone agrees, and not everyone identifies faith with believing irrational things.

Our understanding of "faith" may include extrinsics as well as systemics. Spirituality is often correctly valued positively for its beneficial practical effects, some of which are thought to occur in this world, some in another world. Doing is always informed to some extent by thinking, so *extrinsic faith* at its best is *living out your religious ideas and beliefs*. Really believing the word means acting in accord with the word. Believing without good works is dead. Truly loving means doing the works of love. Having real faith involves much more than cognitively assenting to the truth of religious beliefs or doctrines. It involves acting on those beliefs, putting them into practice, practicing what we preach, living the idealized life. Real spiritually involves believing, practicing, and loving. We do not actually have faith if we are not willing to live out what we believe and if we are not intimately involved in trust, confidence, and love with personal spiritual realities. We hold back and do not act to the degree that we lack intrinsic commitment. Extrinsic "believing" just means "acting" or "being disposed to act." Grace without works is cheap grace. Without good works, faith is dead, so there is no faith without good works. Faith requires more than mere words or thoughts, and more than mere feelings and devotions. Actions are integral to the very meaning of "faith." Only faith *with* works is alive. St. Paul's three dimensional *faith* that *works* by *love* (Galatians 5:6) is the highest or best kind of faith.

Thinking about doing right or wrong activates many of the same parts of the brain as actually *doing* it; but far more is involved in *living out* our resolves. We put far more of our brains and our total intrinsic selves into "walking the talk" (our extrinsic plus our systemic selves) than into just "talking the talk" (our systemic selves alone). Far more value is created for ourselves and for others when we actually live up to our ideals, and far more evil is created when we actually do wrong or harm others than when we merely think about it. The value combination, systemic plus extrinsic values (or disvalues), has more positive (or negative) worth than systemic values (or disvalues) alone. In holistic saints, all three dimensions of value are combined in holistic faith.

A narrow, questionable, perverted, extrinsic and *worldly sense of "faith"* also needs to be recognized, one that focuses exclusively on practical benefits rather than on loving practices—on receiving rather than giving. *Worldly faith combines systemic believing with extrinsic rewards.* "Faith" in this worldly sense is *"using God to get what you want."* Worldlings assume that extrinsic prosperity and status will follow if they believe or cognitively assent to just the right doctrines and then act accordingly. Believing, for them, is not a way of expressing trust, love, and self-sacrifice; it is a means to gaining worldly wealth and success, their highest priorities. They ask not what they can do for God, but what God can do for them. They revere and fear God, not for God's own sake, not as the Ultimate Intrinsic Value, but because God is useful to them. God can do things for or to them. To them, God is the Ultimately Useful Extrinsic Value. Many people turn to God only when they are in big trouble and need God's help. "There are no atheists in foxholes," as we all know. But when trouble goes away, when they think God is no longer useful, they may turn away, fall away, backslide. *Worldly faith* is any kind of believing/doing that promises earthly and/or eternal security, prosperity, success, promotions, social prominence, gratification, revenge against rivals, and rewards to close allies. Popular preachers as well as religious institutions and groups often make such promises. This is the essence of *the prosperity gospel*. Being religious pays off!

Though practically astute, worldlings may be poorly developed conceptually or systemically, quite gullible theologically, and easily persuaded or tempted by prospects of worldly gains. They are not likely to be sticklers for particular doctrines or dogmas; almost any beliefs and attitudes will do as long as they promise security, success, position, prosperity, entertainment, pleasure, rewards, and revenge, here and hereafter.

Worldlings are impressed by numbers; if everyone believes or is being converted to something, they don't want to be left out or left behind. They like big churches, big revivals, entertaining "contemporary" services, and successful preachers. They accept uncritically the religious doctrines of their social group because they don't especially care about or tune in to beliefs and theology. They are enticed mainly by promised rewards, here and hereafter. In religious circles, they associate with those who preach a prosperity gospel. They want worldly results as soon as possible, and the sooner the better.

Does Godly living bring about salvation, or does salvation bring about Godly living? Do either guarantee worldly success? Religious people with a strong worldly bent may distort spiritual believing and doing into "works righteousness." They expect *to bring about* their own salvation, and its earthly and heavenly rewards, by believing and doing as required. Worldly people understand work and pay, punishment and reward; and they conceive of spiritual believing and doing accordingly. Spiritual doing may be costly, but it pays off in the end and earns even greater rewards, they think. By believing and/or working hard enough, they assume, they can *earn* their salvation and will *deserve* higher rewards. They interpret "Believe... and you will be saved" to mean that wilful believing is the condition upon which they merit or become worthy of salvation and its rewards. They do not understand "By grace you are saved through faith, not of yourselves, but as a gift of God." They don't see how God could love sinners, so they try to be righteous in order to earn God's love. They think you get only what you pay for.

Yes, believing and doing are spiritually important, but not as understood by the *worldly model* of pay-for-work. A more illuminating *intrinsic model* involves accepting, responding to, and expressing thanks for gifts freely given. Properly or intrinsically understood, spiritual believing, doing, and adoring *express* acceptance, trust, and gratitude, but they do not earn rewards. They are not like working for pay. They do not *cause* salvation; they are salvation's *effects, not its causes*. Intrinsic saints live righteously in grateful response to God,'s love, not in order to earn it.

Since they are committed to religious beliefs that promise status, prosperity, and worldly well-being, worldlings can become quite defensive about them because a lot is at stake. Ministers and religious leaders dealing with worldly church members should not expect them to be persons of deep intrinsic religious faith and feeling, at least not initially, but they can grow spiritually. If primarily worldly, they are not at first likely to have profound faith and feelings about anything except material objects, wealth, social rank and privileges, and their own ingroup. Yet, they can still belong, be loved, be nurtured, and grow spiritually.

Worldlings are the "nominal" Christians, or Jews, or what have you, who join up and attend religious services because it pays. They ask in order to receive. Their everyday interestedness level of involvement with religious beliefs and practices is marginal and practical. In Rabbi Harold S. Kushner's words, they think that "Observing the Sabbath is worthwhile because it enhances your efficiency at work. Resting one day makes you a better worker on the other six."[60] With their limited capacity for intrinsic evaluation, they love religion as a means to position and prosperity. Yet, just as real people are seldom purely extrinsic and worldly, so worldly religion is seldom merely worldly. Preachers of a prosperity gospel promise more than they can deliver, but they may also emphasize systemic and intrinsic faith as minor motifs. What are their deepest priorities? What are yours?

Intrinsic Faith and Belief

> *Whatsoever the generality of people may think, it is certain that opinion is not religion: no, not right opinion; assent to one or to ten thousand truths. There is a wide difference between them: even right opinion is as distant from religion as the east is from the west. Persons may be quite right in their opinions, yet have no religion at all. And on the other hand persons may be truly religious who hold many wrong opinions...but many of them are now real Christians, loving God and all mankind.*[61] John Wesley

> *Without faith we cannot be thus saved. For we can't rightly serve God unless we love him. And we can't love him unless we know him; neither can we know God, unless by faith. Therefore salvation by faith is only, in other words, the love of God by the knowledge of God, or, the recovery of the image of God by a true spiritual acquaintance with him.*[62] John Wesley

> *What faith is it then through which we are saved? It may be answered, first, in general, it is a faith in Christ—Christ, and God through Christ are the proper objects of it....It is not barely a speculative, rational thing, a cold, lifeless assent, a train of ideas in the head; but also a disposition of the heart.*[63] John Wesley

> *[Faith] is not (as some have fondly conceived) a bare assent to the truth of the Bible, of the articles of our Creed, or of all that is contained in the Old and New Testament. The devils believe this, as well as I or thou; and yet they are devils still. But it is, over and above this, a sure trust in the mercy of God, through Christ Jesus. It is a confidence in a pardoning God. It is a divine evidence or conviction that 'God was in Christ, reconciling the world to himself, not imputing to their former trespasses;' and in particular that the Son of God hath loved me, and given himself for me.*[64] John Wesley

> *Faith then was originally designed of God to re-establish the law of love....It is the grand means of restoring that holy love wherein man was originally created. It follows that although faith is of no value in itself (as neither is any other means whatsoever), yet as it leads to that end—the establishing anew the law of love in our hearts—and as in the present state of things it is the only means under heaven for effecting it, it is on that account an unspeakable blessing to man, and of unspeakable value before God.*[65] John Wesley

> *Also, he [Brother Lawrence] noted that there was a great difference between acts of the intellect and acts of the will. Acts of the intellect were comparatively of little value. Acts of the will were all important. Our only business was to love and delight ourselves in God.*[66] Brother Lawrence

> *Faith is: that the self in being itself and in willing to be itself is grounded transparently in God.*[67] Søren Kierkegaard

> *The desire which is so manifest among present-day thinkers to understand faith as personal trust rather than as assent to doctrine thus betokens no attempt to depreciate the high importance of sound doctrine in its own place.*[68] John Baillie

An intrinsic interpretation of "faith" takes religious beliefs seriously while emphasizing the primacy of love, trust, confidence, interpersonal relations, and commitment of the whole person—not just intellectual assent, and not just rewards. *Intrinsic faith is love for, adoration of, trust, confidence, and hope in, and wholehearted personal commitment to and identification with God.* Intrinsic faith is far more than cognitive assent to the truth of propositions. Intrinsic faith "takes it to heart." Intrinsic faith understands that the virtues of wisdom, belief, service, trust, hope, and love are not entirely separable; it involves all of these, just as hope and love also involve wisdom, service, trust, and beliefs. In the real world, human faith is always pervaded by degrees of reason or understanding, and human reason is always pervaded by degrees of feeling and faith. Reason and philosophy can never offer anything more than enlightened faith. Reason always presupposes unproven ultimate assumptions and involves "love of wisdom," *philos-sophia*, as well as trust, confidence, identification, curiosity, hope, and being put into practice. High degrees of these "sentiments of rationality" are present in intrinsic faith. So are interpersonal love and trust.

Intrinsic faith, emphasized by the New Testament and by many Protestant reformers, prevails among most Protestant theologians.[69] Systemic and intrinsic faith differ in at least two important ways: (1) The value-objects of systemic faith are dogmas, propositional beliefs, intensional meanings; but the value-objects of intrinsic faith are the extensional entities or realities to which dogmas and propositions presumably refer—God, Christ, and "Divine things." (2) The part of the soul functioning in systemic faith is either dispassionate intellect or passionate involvement with ideas alone, usually the latter. Without neglecting either cognition or action, the most relevant parts of the soul in intrinsic faith are affections and dispositions, particularly person-oriented trust, love, hope, awe, wonder, joy, and wholehearted empathic commitment, adoration, devotion, and identification-with.

Believe it or not, love, compassion, trust, hope, and other religious affections have been construed purely intellectually, cognitively, or systemically. Immanuel Kant branded as "pathological" all experienced feelings and emotions, even the good ones, even love itself. He thereby secularized and medicalized the old Christian heresy of patripassionism. His interpretation of Jesus's two "love commandments" entirely eliminated feelings.

> It is in this manner, undoubtedly, that we are to understand those passages of Scripture also in which we are commanded to love our neighbor, even our enemy. For love, as an affection, cannot be commanded, but beneficence for duty's sake may, even though we are not impelled to it by any inclination—nay, are even repelled by a natural and unconquerable aversion. This is *practical* love, and not *pathological*—a love which is seated in the will, and not in the propensions of sense—in principles of action and not of tender sympathy; and it is this love alone which can be commanded.[70]

Loving God and neighbor, according to Kant, means doing our duty just for the sake of duty itself (and not for the sake of God and neighbor, and with no affections, desires, or feelings whatsoever). He construed loving as the purely intellectual and volitional act of a noumenal ego, a purely rational and systemic self that exists beyond all time, space, causes, effects, feelings, and experiences. Dutifulness involves no feelings at all, (except the "rationally wrought" feeling of "respect" for the moral law). Kant erroneously denied that we experience a *desire* to do our duty, one that has to compete with other desires and feelings for prominence and dominance. For this reason, he thought, duty can be commanded, unlike "pathological" affections like love, sympathy, and compassion. Christians and other theists should be aghast at Kant's extreme intellectualizing of love! As Kant well illustrates, real love has no place in purely systemic faith, not even a passionate love of ideas or formal duties.

By contrast, combined with cognition and will, experienced love in its full array of feelings is the very essence of intrinsic faith. Jonathan Edwards was familiar with St. Thomas Aquinas; he preceded Kant and did not know his work; but he took a strong stand against just the sort of systemic intellectualizing of spirituality represented by both Aquinas and Kant. He located "true religion" *primarily* in the religious affections; and he warned against systemic over-intellectualizing.

> There is a distinction to be made between a mere notional understanding, wherein the mind only beholds things in the exercise of a speculative faculty; and the sense of the heart, wherein the mind don't only speculate and behold, but relishes and feels. That sort of knowledge, by which a man has a sensible perception of amiableness and loathsomeness, or of sweetness and nauseousness, is not just the

same sort of knowledge with that, by which he knows what a triangle is, and what a square is. The one is mere speculative knowledge; the other sensible knowledge, in which more than mere intellect is concerned; the heart is the proper subject of it, or the soul as a being that not only beholds, but has inclination, and is pleased or displeased. And yet there is the nature of instruction in it; as he that has perceived the sweet taste of honey, knows much more about it, than he who has only looked upon and felt of it.[71]

To say that we should love without affectionate feelings is to say that we should love without loving! Neither love nor dutifulness can be instantly commanded, but we can place ourselves in circumstances and make regular choices that encourage, develop, and support these dispositions and affections. Dispositions and habits can be created by regular choices. Sadly, we can also place ourselves in circumstances and make choices that detract from love and conscientiousness. Over the long run, and with sustained effort, we can cultivate and control our appetites and affections to a high degree, and for better or for worse; but if and when they come, love, compassion, conscientiousness, hope, trust, confidence, wonder, awe, joy, euphoria, ecstasy, intuitive insight, and other religious affections are gifts of spiritual grace.

Only systemic mentalities would *want to want* to do their duty for the sake of only duty; saintly intrinsic mentalities want to want to do their duty for the sake of people! And God! Only systemic mentalities equate faith with cognitive assent to the truth of propositions and regard that as necessary for salvation. The essence of intrinsic faith is a trusting, loving, joyful, committed, and active personal relationships with the realities of God, Jesus, or whatever is Ultimate. Words and doctrines symbolize, mediate, and facilitate, but they are secondary to loving, trusting, hoping, relishing, and whole-hearted or whole-personed commitment to Ultimate Spiritual Reality. In saintly religion, systemic religiosity is subordinated to and serves faith as loving, compassionate, committed, trusting, hopeful, joyful, responsible person-oriented intrinsic evaluation and service. H. Richard Niebuhr defined *The Purpose of the Church and Its Ministry*, as "THE INCREASE OF THE LOVE OF GOD AND NEIGHBOR."[72]

Paul Tillich defined both "religion," and "faith" in terms of "ultimate concern." For him, having faith and being religious are the same thing. "Faith," he wrote, "is the state of being ultimately concerned;"[73] and being ultimately concerned means loving God with all one's heart, soul, and might.[74] It is "an act of the total personality,"[75] not just intellectual assent. How different from Kant! Faith, for Tillich, is intrinsic spiritual evaluation—ultimate concern.

Criteria for judging the adequacy of beliefs within intrinsic saintly spirituality may be different from those of science, philosophy, history, psychology, etc. The purpose of doctrinal beliefs in intrinsic religion is to facilitate and inform open, informed, loving, compassionate, trusting, committed, hopeful, responsible intrinsic relationships with God, other human beings, all sentient beings, and all of creation. Beliefs that fail to do this, or that hinder it, are spiritually inadequate, inessential, and expendable. Systemic doctrines in intrinsic saintly spirituality are minimal, but they are not eliminated altogether. Saintly religion is holistic. It includes systemic, extrinsic, and intrinsic spiritual values. It does not eliminate all religious beliefs or duties or reduce religion to values and evaluations, but its gospel is doctrinally simple for the sake of love and its proper objects.

The ultimate saintly test for an acceptable spiritual belief is, "Will believing this help me to be or become a more loving person, a more intrinsic person?" Some religious beliefs make people less loving, more indifferent, contemptuous, or hateful; others make no real difference at all and are not worth worrying about. In very personal terms, when adopting or rejecting any religious belief, the essential *spiritual* questions are these: "What will I be like if I adopt this belief? Will I be more understanding, giving, accepting, forgiving, and loving? Or will I be more indifferent, prejudiced, grasping, alienated, estranged, snobby, contemptuous, hateful, or belligerent?"

In many sermons, John Wesley advocated a minimal doctrinal outlook grounded in love. He supported an extremely broad tolerance for diverse spiritual opinions, practices, and rituals. He preached that a "Catholic Spirit," the essence of universal Christianity, is the spirit of love for God and all God's creatures and creations. Some of Wesley's most celebrated words are, "'If thine heart is as my heart,' if thou lovest God and all mankind, I ask no more: 'give me thine hand.'"[76] [Compare II. Kings, 10:15.] His sermon on "Scriptural Christianity," Wesley said, deals with "'Christianity'; not as it implies a set of opinions, a system of doctrines, but as it refers to men's hearts and lives."[77] In his sermon "On the Trinity," Wesley professed his belief that God is three persons in one; but, he warned, these words are not applied to God in the Bible, and no one knows how to explain what these words really mean. Thus, he said, "I dare not insist upon any one's using the word Trinity, or Person."[78] As for the Incarnation, Wesley insisted upon just so much as God has revealed, and no more; God revealed that it happened but not the manner of it; and no one is required to believe "any mystery."[79] As for faith (as cognitive assent), Wesley said that it

> was originally designed of God to re-establish the law of love....It is the grand means of restoring that holy love wherein man was originally created. It follows that although faith is of no value in itself (as neither is any other means whatsoever), yet as it leads to that end—the establishing anew the law of love in our hearts—and as in the present state of things it is the only means under heaven for effecting it, it is on that account an unspeakable blessing to man, and of unspeakable value before God.[80]

For Wesley and all holistic saints, systemic faith as cognitive assent is a means or complement to the inner and outer workings of love. Doctrines and creeds are valued in intrinsic faith, but only to the extent that they promote love for God, for others, and for all creation. Intrinsic faith as love, trust, hope, peace, confidence, joy, commitment, interpersonal intimacy, and service does not completely eliminate religious concepts, laws, and doctrines; but it gives all spiritual formalities a relatively low priority. Systemic entities (concepts, doctrines, laws, and ritual forms) are not at the top of the saint's hierarchy of values; they are at the bottom. More about this in the next chapter, but within themselves spiritual saints are inherently and primarily loving persons. They act lovingly, feel lovingly, and believe lovingly.

Buddhism in the East and Positivism in the West officially disdain metaphysics (theories of ultimate reality), but they always sneak in basic assumptions about reality in general through the back door when everyone is off guard. The Buddhist view that selfhood consists of a succession of fleeting temporal occasions of consciousness is no less metaphysical than the view that selfhood consists of an enduring substance that underlies all our fleeting moments. Both views attempt to describe fundamental features of reality. Gautama Buddha was almost right in wanting to throw out (most) metaphysical, philosophical and theological questions and doctrines because they really do not contribute significantly to salvation— escape from suffering, as he understood it; but to his understanding of salvation, we might want to add: intrinsic evaluation—love, compassion, identification with others, and a truly worthwhile or abundant life. Metaphysics, philosophy, and systematic theology can be fun games for intellectuals, and they do not necessarily interfere with love. But love should always have priority—a hard lesson for intellectuals to learn.

Most of the issues philosophers fret about go nowhere, even if they are fun games for intellectuals. Serious and competent philosophical opponents are never convinced, and the history of philosophy is mostly just one Mexican stand-off after another. So is most contemporary philosophizing. (I write this after playing these games for almost a lifetime.) Philosophers just become fundamentalistic dogmatists who retreat into isolated rival and sometimes pernicious enclaves of like-minded souls.[81] A great deal more than *reason alone* is working in the souls of all philosophers. What they believe, and what they do not believe, seems to depend largely on what and how they value,[82] though the influence probably goes both ways.

Yet, some philosophical issues like those next identified really do seem to matter, at least for living a meaningful, worthwhile, and abundant life. Some truths or beliefs about reality are definitely presupposed by intrinsic valuing, living, and loving and cannot be disregarded altogether. Intrinsic faith always includes minimal systemic faith. For example, unless God exists, our love and service to God are pointless. Unless metaphysical pluralism is true, unless other minds or souls actually exist, unless reality is inherently social, we cannot love and act lovingly toward others, for there are no others; all others are just illusions, mindless machines, or indistinguishably one. And we may be an illusion ourselves, as some Eastern religions propose. Unless many relational and spatio-temporal selves and their experiences really exist in community and communion with one another, ethical interaction is impossible and unintelligible. Unless space, time, and causation are real, not just human illusions or appearances, morally significant action is impossible because it always takes place in spacetime, involves actors and choosers in spacetime, and causes beneficial or harmful effects. Ethics and spirituality presuppose the reality of the past, the creative indefiniteness of the present, and the openness of the future. If atheistic determinism or theistic predestination are true, we cannot choose or live freely, creatively, and responsibly. If and only if we love an infinite God and are loved by that God is our own value infinite. Unless human values and evaluations are supported and saved somehow by and within the ultimate nature of things, they are indeed ephemeral. If and only if the value of our unique reality is taken into God and preserved and cherished forever in God's faultless memory and love does our fleeting worth escape from the transience of all earthly or temporal goodness. These systemic theological and metaphysical matters are not trivial or irrelevant to morality and true religion, to religion at its best, to a spirituality that is richest in good-making properties, and to living a meaningful, worthwhile, and abundant life.

Many people have a natural bent for metaphysics, philosophy, and theology. They have a deep and ineradicable curiosity about the ultimate nature of things; and a profound spirituality should encourage, not discourage, these talents. It should constantly remind them, however, that there is much more to living, valuing, reverence, and devotion than mere intellect and systemics, and that the intrinsic is the real key to Ultimate Reality. Yes, God should be loved with our minds, but also and primarily with our hearts, strengths, and whole being or souls. Profound curiosity is a gift from God. The intellectual love of God, one path to spirituality, involves knowledge and the dispassionate quest for it. This has a legitimate place in true religion, even if many human intellects are too feeble, untrained, or busy for it. Intrinsic faith includes loving God with our mind, but also with all our soul, heart, and strength. It fuses intellect with loving affections, thoughts, and deeds directed toward neighbors, self, and all creation. It practices what it preaches, it knows what it is doing, and it cares profoundly and profusely. By approximation and degrees, this is exactly what happens in holistic saintly spirituality.

Defining "Good Religion"

> [...*True religion*] *is in every way suited to the nature of man; for it begins in a man's knowing himself: knowing himself to be what he really is—foolish, vicious, miserable. It goes on to point out the remedy for this, to make him truly wise, virtuous, and happy, as every thinking mind...longs to be. It finishes all, by restoring the due relations between God and man.*[83] John Wesley

Relatively recent researchers in the psychology of religion want to be "objective" about values in religion, which, for them, means *not trying to distinguish between good and bad religions.*[84] However, formal axiology offers a methodology for distinguishing between a good and a bad *anything*, including good and bad religions. A good thing has properties or attributes that correspond to all the elements (predicates) contained within the ideal or standard being applied to it. Good is concept or standard fulfillment, as Hartman said repeatedly; and bad things are those that fail to meet our standards. So what are our standards for "good religion"? Would we ever agree?

Objective systemic evaluation can distinguish between *good and bad approaches* to religion as well as *good and bad religions*. Impartiality or rational disinterestedness is the best approach for purely *cognitive* purposes. For purposes of *living* spiritually and *doing* what religion requires, an extrinsic approach would be best. For purposes of spiritual *devotion and identification* with God and God's creatures, an intrinsic approach would be best. The very best approach of all would be *holistic* and comprehensive, combining all three. In holistic saintliness, all due relations between God and human beings are restored and developed in every dimension of goodness.

We can disagree about whether anything (e.g., a religion, a denomination, etc.) is good either because we do not all employ the same standards, or because we are not adequately informed about whether something has the good-making properties required by its conceptual norms. An objective rational approach to questions of good and evil is possible; indeed, it is actual, once formal value theory is understood and employed correctly. Try to be clear-headed about what *you* would want from a good religion. What are the good-making properties of a good religion? Make a list of such attributes! Then measure extrinsic, systemic, and intrinsic religion (as developed in Chapters One, Two, and Three) by your own standards, and see what you get.

Here are some suggestions about how holistic saintliness might identify the good-making properties of a good religion. You may or may not agree, but if you disagree, try to be clear about why, about what values and evaluations underlie your disagreement, and about their true worth. Here are the main criteria by which the highest saintliness would measure the alternatives available and thereby identify a good religion:

1. Its primary value-objects would be unique conscious beings—God, all human beings, all animals.
2. All such intrinsic value-objects would be intrinsically evaluated, that is, valued intensely, lovingly, empathetically, compassionately, and with the fullest possible concentration on and self-identification-with-them.
3. Its secondary value-objects would be the bodily structures, processes and activities of living things, their social roles, and the rest of physical creation. Ultimately, after sufficient spiritual development, all non-living things would be intensely valued under God, as "sub-species of eternity."
4. Spiritual living, acting, and practice would support and express love and care for God, for all human beings, all animals, and all the rest of creation.

5. Its tertiary value-objects would be religious beliefs, doctrines, rules, rituals, and formalities, those that express and support love for God, all human beings, all animals, and all the rest of creation.

6. The ultimate spiritual criterion for accepting (or rejecting) proposed religious beliefs, doctrines, rules, rituals, and formalities is whether they support or are means to love for God, all human beings, all animals, and all the rest of creation.

7. All values and evaluations would be arranged according to the hierarchy of value, with the intrinsic coming first, the extrinsic ranked second, and the systemic ranked third; but none would be neglected or omitted; and all would be developed as fully as possible by each individual in accord with his or her personal gifts and talents.

8. It would enable its members to live abundantly, that is, to live the best lives they could possibly live—as rich as they could possibly be or become in intrinsic, extrinsic, and systemic values and evaluations.

What else do you think a good religion would include? What should be added? Should any of the above be omitted? If so, on what grounds? And what is the value of those grounds? Would a good religion be holistic saintly religion? How do these criteria apply to your religion? To other religions?

Religious Concepts and Beliefs as Symbols

And he saith unto them, But whom say ye that I am? And Peter answereth and saith unto him, Thou art the Christ. Jesus and Peter (Mark 8:29)

Like all other ideas, religious ideas, beliefs, and judgments may have both extensional meanings (the realities to which they refer) and intensional meanings (the words or concepts themselves). Consider concepts like "God," "Jesus," "Christ," "the Trinity," and then consider this judgment that combines them: "Jesus Christ is God, the Second Person of the Trinity." For the moment, consider only the meanings or concepts within this judgment, not its truth or falsity. In traditional Christian theology, "God," "Jesus," "Christ," and "the Trinity" are concepts that have intensional meanings; God is "the creator and sustainer of the universe"; Christ is "the Messiah, the anointed one, who was fully God and fully man"; the Trinity is "God as three persons in one substance." Much traditional Christian theology variously explicates these systemic or conceptual meanings, so go to that literature and study it for details.[85]

The early church struggled for several centuries before it arrived at any standardized interpretations of the biblical metaphors of "Messiah," "Son," "Word," "Lamb," *etc.* Systemic Christian orthodoxy evolved from conflicts among and compromises by many dissenting factions, and its doctrines are susceptible to many different interpretations. So it is also with every world religion. Religious concepts, judgments, and beliefs have conceptual or intensional meanings, and these have histories. They are words about which volumes of additional words have been written. They also presume to refer to something beyond themselves.

The realities to which words and beliefs refer are their extensional meanings. Extensional meanings or referents may be either extrinsic empirical entities or intrinsic spiritual entities. Both the definitions and the realities of "horse" and "mountain" are their meanings. The definitions and the realities of both "God" and "Christ" are their meanings. Their intensional meanings are conceptual; the realities to which these symbols refer are all-pervasive, like the laws of nature, logic, and mathematics. Some conceptual constructs are so profound that they tell us about universal reality. Scientists and philosophers are constantly amazed that reality, empirical or otherwise, is logical, mathematical, lawful, and penetrable by reason. Spiritual persons are constantly amazed that all of reality is pervaded by God.

In *The Idea of Revelation in Recent Thought*,[86] John Baillie noted a remarkable consensus among Protestant theologians that Christians do not believe primarily in *the truth of religious propositions*; instead, they believe in *the intrinsic religious realities* to which such propositions refer. Divine revelation, in this consensus, does not consist of doctrines and documents that God dictated; rather, it is the Divine Subject encountered within human subjects and human history. The Christian revelation is not the words of the New Testament; it is a person, the unique concrete historical Jesus, the Word made flesh. A once-existing person, the historical Jesus himself, the incarnate Word, is the definitive intrinsic Christian revelation, God's best attempt to communicate the essence of divinity to humanity. Jesus is God's best revelation of himself to us, intrinsic Christians believe. As unique, concrete, intrinsic persons, God and Jesus are far richer in properties than, and thus far more valuable than, anything that any books, creeds, interpretations, or doctrines could ever say about them. Any religious book, creed, interpretation, or dogma could be fallible due to the limitations, errors, distortions, and perversions of the finite and sinful human interpreters and writers who are on the receiving end of spiritual insights and revelations. The New Testament is the attempt by early church authorities to make cognitive sense of the Word made flesh, to answer the question of Jesus, "Who do you say that I am?"

This theological perspective implicitly presupposes the distinction between intensional (connotative) and extensional (denotative) meanings. According to it, Christians are primarily concerned about the realities, the extensional meanings or referents of spiritual words, concepts, interpretations, and affirmations, not the words themselves. Yet, their access to these realities is commonly mediated imperfectly by words, symbols, intensional meanings. Axiologically, conceptual symbols, words, or intensions are subordinate in value to the unique, concrete, intrinsic realities, the extensional meanings, to which they refer. Scriptures, doctrines, and creeds have a vital place within spirituality as systemic means of grace that point beyond themselves, but they are not intrinsic spiritual ends in themselves.

Spiritually, everything depends on our capacity to intrinsically evaluate or love that to which our concepts and interpretations point or refer. Some of our beliefs and interpretations are more refined than others; none are perfect, infallible, or absolutely complete. The disciples and other contemporaries of the historical Jesus had access to him through sensory perception and direct personal acquaintance. They saw, heard, and touched Jesus in the flesh as he made and divided history; but none of them were dispassionate scientific observers engaged in purely descriptive reporting. They constantly interpreted the significance of what they saw and heard either in light of their spiritual and/or moral preconceptions, or in light of new revelatory interpretations and insights. According to Kierkegaard, in conceptualizing or interpreting the Christ of faith, the literal and historical contemporaries of Christ had no significant advantage over us. Systemically, with respect to *interpreting* the spiritual and moral significance of Jesus, people today are in exactly the same boat with his literal contemporaries.[87] This is also true of our intrinsic capacity to identify with Jesus or God, and of our extrinsic capacity to act in a Christlike or Godlike manner.

What was the cognitive or conceptual spiritual significance of the historical Jesus for himself and for his contemporaries? This question is very difficult to answer. In his own quest for conceptual self-knowledge, Jesus must have wondered "Who am I?" He challenged his followers with, "Who do you say I am?" At first and for quite some time, they did not know what to think of him, how to conceptualize his significance, who to say that he was. Some eventually identified Jesus with the expected Christ or Messiah of faith, though he was very different from the Messiah expected by most Jews of his day and today. Also, their initial conceptual constructs or interpretations needed, and later received, much further penetration and elaboration. Theirs was a primitive theory, a *kerygma*, the earliest preaching, something occasioned by but not given by mere perception, something more than "Just the facts, Ma'am." In that respect, today's Christians and the literal contemporaries of Jesus are indeed all in the same boat. Archeology and fact-finding (e.g., finding Noah's ark) can never "prove" the Bible! St. Thomas Aquinas, to this day the official philosopher of the Roman Catholic Church, repeatedly emphasized that "The object of faith is something unseen concerning God."[88]

The New Testament and the history of early Christianity tell us how his contemporaries and immediate successors struggled to find the right words for what they experienced in Jesus, not only during his life, but also after his death. Some words, mostly metaphors like "Son," and "Lamb," "Vine," "Bread," rather than literal expressions, were then and are now more effective and appropriate than others. Members of every new generation must answer for themselves the question asked by Jesus, "Who do you say that I am?" We must find spiritually significant words, metaphors, and images suitable to our own time and place; but no one seems to have absolutely the last infallible word. Spiritual realities always surpass their symbols in meaning and worth. So do all physical and social realities.

Christians today cannot relate to Jesus in the total absence of symbols, ideas, words, beliefs, reports, and records drawn from the New Testament and Christian traditions, but they should love and identify with the *realities* of Jesus and God to which the *symbols* point. Christians may also have keen religious experiences and encounters that are sensitive to the intimate presence of God in Jesus, Jesus in God, and God's Holy Spirit within themselves here and now. Believers are convinced that God and the Word are more than just words; they are incarnate, they have extensions as well as intensions. The words point us toward something more, much more, but they are means to ends, not ends in themselves. Systemic values have less value than intrinsic values.

Chapter Three
Saintliness and Intrinsic/Saintly Religion

The collective name for the ripe fruits of religion in a character is Saintliness. The saintly character is the character for which spiritual emotions are the habitual center of the personal energy; and there is a certain composite photograph of universal saintliness, the same in all religions, of which the features can easily be traced.

They are these:—

1. A feeling of being in a wider life than that of this world's selfish little interests; and a conviction, not merely intellectual, but as it were sensible, of the existence of an Ideal Power. In Christian saintliness this power is always personified as God; but abstract moral ideals, civic or patriotic utopias, or inner versions of holiness or right may also be felt as the true lords and enlargers of our life.

2. A sense of the friendly continuity of the ideal power with our own life, and a willing self-surrender to its control.

3. An immense elation and freedom, as the outlines of the confining selfhood melt down.

4. A shifting of the emotional center towards loving and harmonious affections, toward "yes, yes," and away from "no," where the claims of the non-ego are concerned.[1] William James

As William James indicated, when the religious life bears its ripest fruits, saintliness is the result. But what is saintliness? Axiologically considered, the saints are those who give the highest priority to intrinsic values and evaluations, but is saintliness pure intrinsic values and evaluations with no admixture of the systemic and extrinsic? We now know that in worldliness extrinsic values dominate systemic and intrinsic values; only extrinsic objects are evaluated intrinsically. And from an ideological perspective, systemic values are dominant. Extreme ideologists evaluate systemic objects intrinsically and intrinsic and extrinsic objects either uninterestedly or disdainfully. Now we must ask, what and how do saints value? How do they relate to all three dimensions of value and evaluation? It is tempting to think that saintliness is pure and unmixed intrinsic evaluation, but for saints perhaps intrinsic values and evaluation are predominant, but by degrees extrinsic and systemic values and evaluations are also present. Ideally, saints are axiologically well developed, balanced, harmonious, and properly prioritize all three dimensions of value in all three ways, but there may be better and worse forms of saintliness.

Saintliness: Pure Intrinsic Evaluation, or Wholeness?

> *The fruits of religion...are, like all human products, liable to corruption by excess. Common sense must judge them....We find that error by excess is exemplified by every saintly virtue. Excess, in human faculties, means usually one-sidedness or want of balance; for it is hard to imagine an essential faculty too strong, if only other faculties equally strong be there to cooperate with it in action. Strong affections need a strong will; strong active powers need a strong intellect; strong intellect needs strong sympathies, to keep life steady. If the balance exists, no one faculty can possibly be too strong—we only get stronger all-round character. In the life of saints, technically so called, the spiritual faculties are strong, but what gives the impression of extravagance proves usually on examination to be a relative deficiency of intellect. Spiritual excitement takes pathological forms whenever other interests are too few and the intellect too narrow.*[2] William James

> *In persons of feeble or diffuse intelligence, however, and above all in victims of a self-regarding spirituality, this deep absorption in the sense of Divine Reality may easily degenerate into monoideism. Then the "shady side" of Illumination, a selfish preoccupation with transcendental joys, the "spiritual gluttony" condemned by St. John of the Cross, comes out.*[3] Evenly Underhill

At least two varieties of saintliness must be distinguished. The first is the incomplete saintliness of almost pure intrinsic value and evaluation where the extrinsic and the systemic are weak. The second is the more complete saintliness of wholeness in which the intrinsic comes first, but the systemic and the extrinsic are well developed and expressed as fully as possible. Both forms appear implicitly in the above quote from William James's *The Varieties of Religious Experience*. Our task now is to make an informed choice between them with respect to their value or desirability. Evelyn Underhill, following St. John of the Cross, called the first "spiritual gluttony." As James indicated, "Common sense must judge them."

According to William James, some saints are more admirable, thus more saintly, than others. Many historical saints had grave character defects, and most thoughtful religious people today would not wish to emulate them. The second of his two chapters on "Saintliness" was titled "The Value of Saintliness"; but, he said, it might have been called the "Critique of pure Saintliness."[4] As a Pragmatist, James noted that saintliness does not always bear good fruits.[5] Jonathan Edwards appealed repeatedly to "By their fruits ye shall know them" (Matthew 7:20) as the most reliable way to distinguish between real saints and non-saints or lesser saints.[6] James, who relished first-hand religion, not tradition, added, "not by their roots".[7]

James's critique of pure saintliness focused on both practical extrinsic ineffectiveness and lack of systemic or intellectual development. Either or both of these can transform the virtues of saintliness into the vices of Fanaticism and Asceticism, he thought. As Underhill intimated, excessive spiritual sentimentality that neglects the two other value dimensions can turn a saint into a "spiritual glutton," or into what someone else called a "love slob." In earlier times, predominant intrinsic spirituality was called "enthusiasm." It was heat without light, feeling without knowledge, reflection, and intellect, zeal and passion without fruit or good works. The main problem with oddball saints is their deficiency of balanced development, James explained. No one of our spiritual value capacities can be overdeveloped, but any particular one can be greatly out of balance when others are underdeveloped. To avoid spiritual weaknesses, real saints must develop all their evaluational capacities in proper proportions and put them to good use.

Saintliness and Ideal Spiritual Self-realization

> *Intrinsic is better than extrinsic value, extrinsic better than systemic value.... The hierarchy of value is a evaluation of value.*[8] Robert S. Hartman

> *The most valuable value, that is, the value that fulfills the concept 'value' most fully is intrinsic value.*[9] Robert S. Hartman

If "saintliness" connotes the supreme ideal of human or Christian spiritual evaluation and self-realization, at least two possibilities must be explored. One type of saintliness, here called "intrinsic saintliness," involves primarily intrinsic evaluations and values but is very weak in extrinsic and systemic evaluations and values. A second type, here called "holistic saintliness," involves a balanced wholeness of well developed intrinsic, extrinsic, and systemic evaluations and values. Which type is best?

The richest and most commendable type of *self*, the most saintly self, is the holistic self that values and expresses itself appropriately in all three value dimensions. The richest kind of *value* is intrinsic value; but the richest kind of *self* is not a purely inner intrinsic self; it is a whole and balanced self living as fully as possible in all three dimensions of value. Why so? Because if all three dimensions of value are well developed, more good-making properties are present in the soul. Saints should ideally develop their systemic, extrinsic, and intrinsic capacities, all three; their lives are much richer in goodness, more admirable, better, and more saintly when they do. Holistic saintliness includes all value dimensions. It takes them all up into itself and makes them holy. It is the richest life conceivable in both quantity and quality of positive or desirable good-making properties.

The intrinsic self or person is the whole self or person, not just some inner or private part. Realizing or actualizing our intrinsic self requires actualizing all of our capacities for value and evaluation. Hartman wrote, "Intrinsic evaluation means dedication of the whole person and all its capacities. It means fully living persons."[10] He explicitly supported axiological balance in every situation in order to avoid value astigmatism or distortion. As he explained,

> The three value dimensions must be seen in equal proportion and not out of proportion with the other. That is to say that in each situation the three dimensions of value, the personal, the practical, and the theoretical have to be seen equally clearly in order for the valuing person to have a clear picture of the situation. If one of the dimensions is seen more clearly and the others less clearly, or one less clearly and the other two more clearly, we have what is called *axiological astigmatism*. In [some cases] the situation is not seen *clearly* since the three value dimensions are not equally focused.[11]

David Mefford, a former student of Hartman's, consistently advocates balanced evaluational wholeness as the supreme ideal of ultimate self-realization. He writes,

> When we define an ideal of value realization for the human self, we can use it as a norm for measuring differences in people. We can also use it as the basis for a disciplined program for self-development. That ideal is the *balanced integration* of all three axiological dimensions....The axiological ideal is attained when persons value each self value capacity, integrated with equal and balanced emphasis, as a complete whole, forming a harmonious unity between self and world.[12]

Balanced wholeness really is compatible with the insight that intrinsic values and evaluations are in some sense supreme. Balanced wholeness does not abandon the hierarchy of value; "The best *self* is the balanced self" is quite distinct logically from "The best *value* is intrinsic value." These are not conflicting claims; their logical subjects are different. The best self values well and appropriately in all three dimensions, not just one or two, and achieves "a harmonious unity between self and world."

How can anyone value competently in all three dimensions but still acknowledge the superiority of the intrinsic? That all three evaluational capacities should be *equally developed and emphasized* does not imply that all three should be *valued or ranked equally*. Balanced self-development in all value dimensions is deeply harmonious with the axiological superiority of intrinsic values and evaluations. As another former student of Hartman's, Richard Leggett, suggested in an unpublished paper, we should value all people intrinsically, but we need not and should not do so *merely* intrinsically.

> How should we go about in the world valuing individuals (persons)? Obviously, there are problems of application here: We live in the ordinary world of ordinary

language and to function in it we must extrinsically value persons as members of certain classes (also sometimes systemically, but my comments should hold for both). We *should*, of course, value individuals *intrinsically*—this is dictated by the system since intrinsic evaluation is the best (richest in properties) kind of evaluation, and anything less with respect to individuals is disvaluation. Yet my students *are* students, the bar keeper *is* a bar keeper, and June *is* a cook; and I must value them accordingly in order pragmatically to function in the world.

I suggest a Kantian sort of 'compromise': Just as Kant says that we should treat people not *merely* as means but also as ends in themselves, I say that we should value people not *merely* as members of certain classes but also as unique individuals. Of course, it is hard to do both at once just as it is difficult intrinsically to value persons whom we have just met—most of our intrinsic valuing is of friends. Hence, my suggestion breaks down into the following: When we value extrinsically we approach the object with a certain concept. For example, I approach a watch knowing what (I believe) a good watch to be; I approach a waitress knowing what a good waitress is; I approach a student (hopefully) knowing what a good student is; and so on. Now, I suggest that we approach persons not merely extrinsically with a class concept but at the same time intrinsically with a singular concept. But this singular concept must in a sense be *empty* (which in a sense is no concept at all). The concept is fulfilled by experiencing the person; and since an integral part of this continuum of experiencing is qua butcher, baker, etc., I can at the same time 'subordinately' value him or her extrinsically. Basically speaking, this amounts to an attempt to avoid imposing restrictions on the person's individuality, an attempt to allow each individual wholly to express her or himself to us. In this way we leave open the possibilities for ourselves and others to increase the richness, the value, the meaning of our lives infinitely. If we are restrictive in our approach then we might keep individuals from realizing their concepts of themselves. To do so would be a disvaluation since we are valuing them as something less than they really are.[13]

Leggett maintains that, though difficult, we can concurrently evaluate in all three dimensions. No doubt, geniuses at saintliness can do this; and perhaps all of us can at times. Even if we can't evaluate in all dimensions simultaneously, those of us who, as Hartman might say, are mere "boy scouts of evaluation"[14] can learn to do it successively, while still respecting the hierarchy of value and treating persons always as ends and never *merely* as extrinsic means or as systemic cipher s. As the author of *Ecclesiastes* suggested, "To every thing there is a season, and a time to every purpose under the heaven" (Ecclesiastes. 3:1). There is a time for valuing people intrinsically, as well as a time for valuing them extrinsically and systemically. Balanced wholeness discerns the proper times for each without abandoning the hierarchy of value or losing sight of the intrinsic worth of individuals. Leggett suggested that singular concepts (proper names of unique persons) should function at times *somewhat like* variables or open-ended concepts, taking account of both the definiteness of past selves and the indefiniteness, freedom, and creativity of present and future selves. Would this be the saintly way to do it, the axiological ideal? Would everyone's sinfulness require us to qualify this ideal?

Intrinsic values and evaluations pervade saintly religion. It is both formed and largely constituted by them. Saints are disposed to evaluate everything intrinsically (except intrinsic, instrumental, and systemic evil), but even saintly persons cannot sustain peak intensities of intrinsic evaluation at all times. William James noted that mystical experiences are transient; they usually last for an hour or much less; and mystics, frustrated by their inability to sustain them, undergo "the dark night of the soul." Some memory of them remains after they are gone, and this modifies "the inner life of the subject between the times of their recurrence."[15] Peak experiences of intrinsic evaluation are also transient, but their influences and memories linger and can be pervasive. When saintly individuals "come down from the mountain top" and revert to weaker intrinsic or to merely extrinsic or systemic evaluational modalities, they may or may not experience them as "the dark night of the soul"; but the rest of life is likely to be deeply colored by the memory and soul-transforming power of intrinsic evaluation experiences, even when they are not present in their fullest vividness and intensity. The disciples of Jesus wanted to stay on the mountaintop of direct intrinsic communion with God, but he would not let them.

A Critique of Purely Intrinsic Saintliness

> *It is one of those fables which out of an unknown antiquity convey an unlooked-for wisdom, that the gods, in the beginning, divided Man into men, that he might be more helpful to himself; just as the hand was divided into fingers, the better to answer its end.*
>
> *The old fable covers a doctrine even new and sublime; that there is One Man,—present to all particular men only partially, or through one faculty; and that you must take the whole society to find the whole man....The state of society is one in which the members have suffered amputation from the trunk, and strut about so many walking monsters,—a good finger, a neck, a stomach, an elbow, but never a man.*[16] Ralph Waldo Emerson

> *The entire man, who feels all needs by turns, will take nothing as an equivalent for life but the fullness of living itself.*[17] William James

> *For as we have many members in one body, and all members have not the same office: So we being many are one body in Christ, and every one members of one another. Having then gifts differing according to the grace that is given to us.* St. Paul (Romans 12:4-6)

In many ways, and for many good reasons, saintly wholeness is far superior to or better than the "spiritual gluttony" of saints of pure intrinsic evaluation. Consider the following case for this judgment.

1) The foremost reason is that the life of saintly wholeness is indeed richer in good-making properties than the life of purely intrinsic evaluation because it develops and uses a greater number and kind of human evaluational capacities; it actual-

izes our systemic and extrinsic as well as our intrinsic capacities. It also contains a far greater profusion of value-objects, extrinsic and systemic as well as intrinsic. The whole person is much more fully and richly developed, exercised, and fulfilled. This can happen without sacrificing the superiority of the intrinsic. Lower values and evaluational capacities can be taken up into higher values and evaluational capacities; and we can learn to evaluate systemically, but not merely systemically, extrinsically but not merely extrinsically, intrinsically but not merely intrinsically, just as Leggett suggests.

2) Purely intrinsic saints, devoid of extrinsic and systemic capacities, would never survive for very long in this harsh world. Real saints always have some effective coping and thinking skills. To survive, they must have sufficient extrinsic self-maintenance skills to groom, feed, and nourish themselves, to provide clothing and shelter for themselves, to avoid natural and social dangers, even to reproduce and raise children, for real saints need not be celibates, recluses, or monastics. Saints must have sufficient extrinsic and systemic *savoir faire* to survive. Otherwise, God, the universe, themselves, and other people would be deprived of their long-life contributions, the intrinsic goodness of their existence, and the joy and exuberance of their own intrinsic, extrinsic, and systemic evaluations.

Saints deficient in systemic and extrinsic development often do incredibly stupid and self-destructive things. William James noted that some historical saints licked the sores of sick people under their care.[18] This is not a wise survival strategy! Day and night, Jerusha, the saintly, beautiful, and exceptionally promising daughter of Jonathan Edwards, nursed tubercular David Brainerd, to whom she was engaged, through the last few months of his life. Very shortly after his death, she also died most prematurely from tuberculosis at the age of seventeen. At that stage in the history of medicine, she was probably "in pitiful ignorance of the risk she incurred,"[19] as one author suggested; but many saints have done similar self-destructive things fully knowing the risks and with few if any efforts to minimize them. Saints who do not develop and employ their extrinsic and systemic capabilities effectively undervalue and undercut their own intrinsic, extrinsic, and systemic worth, and they do not long endure. Common sense says, "You can't take care of others unless you take care of yourself," and saints need a little common sense. Holistic saints make daily sacrifices and perhaps even the ultimate sacrifice of their lives for others, but not pointlessly, prematurely, stupidly, or unnecessarily. As required by Jesus's second commandment, they love themselves. Only by doing so can they love others.

3) Purely intrinsic saints would be parasites upon society. Some monastics pay their own way extrinsically by baking and selling bread, but many actually are parasites who survive only by begging. Yet, begging itself is a paltry extrinsic skill, and some beggars are better at it than others. Monastics often depend heavily on the generosity of others to meet their own most basic physical and social needs.

Monastic societies are actually just microcosms of their larger macrocosmic social worlds. Systemic and extrinsic values are inevitably re-created within monastic communities, even where people retreat into them and withdraw from the world in order to dispense with ideological and/or worldly cares. Commenting on the monastic movement, H. Richard Niebuhr noted,

> Even if no use were made of another inheritance besides that derived from Jesus Christ, the needs of the withdrawn community would lead to the development of a new culture. Invention, human achievement, temporal realization of value, organization of the common life—all must go on in it. When the dogmas and rites of social religion have been abandoned, a new dogma and a new ritual must be developed, if religious practice is to go on at all. Therefore monks work out their own rituals in the monasteries, and Quaker silences become as formalized as masses.... When the state has been rejected, the exclusively Christian community has necessarily developed some political organization of its own; and has done so with the aid of other ideas than those derived from the injunction that the first shall be the servant of all. It has called its leaders prophets or abbots, its governing assemblies quarterly meetings or congregations; it has enforced uniformity by means of popular opinion and banishment from the society....Prevailing property institutions have been set aside; but something more than the counsel to sell and give to the poor has been necessary, since men had to eat and be clothed and sheltered even in poverty. Hence ways and means of acquiring and distributing goods were devised, and a new economic culture was established.[20]

Human survival always makes demands upon our systemic and extrinsic capacities. Even people who renounce them covertly re-affirm and re-invent them. Non-intrinsic domains of value and evaluation must be taken *seriously*, even if they are not *ultimate*. The alternative is death! Saints must have cognitive and practical coping skills, even though lower in value than their intrinsic capacities. Saints are ineffective precisely to the extent that their extrinsic and systemic selves are underdeveloped and underemployed. Monastics who renounce systemic and extrinsic values end up reaffirming them, often ineffectively.

4) Purely intrinsic saints would be unable to contribute anything to society, to other individual persons, or to God. Total repudiation of extrinsic values and evaluations would create a spiritually dead zone of quietistic faith with no works. Real saints, whole saints, need not be celibates, recluses, or monastics. Whole or holistic saints can support and participate in society and ordinary life. They can affirm the goodness of and participate family life; they need not be Christ-like in bachelorhood and celibacy, *or* monastic (and un-Christlike) in withdrawing almost completely from the world. They overcome the values of worldliness; they do not live mainly for things or for glory. But they can immerse themselves into the ongoing life of the world, partly just to live it, partly to try to make it better, partly because God gave it. Real holistic saints are active performers in the dance of life. They are

in the world, that is, deeply involved, but not *of* the world, that is, not devoted solely to worldly goods, practices, and customs.

Without using the technical language of value theory, H. Richard Niebuhr said that Jesus himself did not advocate a life of purely intrinsic values and evaluations.

> Though he commanded his disciples to seek the kingdom above all else, he did not advise them to scorn other goods; nor was he indifferent to the institution of the family, to order in the temple, to the freedom of the temporally oppressed, and to the fulfillment of duty by the powerful. The other-worldliness of Jesus is always mated with a this-worldly concern; his proclamation and demonstration of divine action is inseparable from commandments to men to be active here and now; his future kingdom reaches into the present.[21]

5) Purely intrinsic saints would be very vulnerable to duplicity, exploitation, malice, and every other human vice. They would lack adequate cognitive and pragmatic self-protective abilities. Decent people would not take advantage of saintly innocence and incompetence, but evil people would. Saintly passivity and non-resistance to evil practiced by Mahatma Gandhi and his followers eventually freed India from British rule, but only because the British were basically decent people. These tactics would not have worked against Hitler and the Nazis, or Stalin and fanatical Communists.

Not only would saints weak in systemic knowledge be vulnerable in self-care and self-protection, they would also be weak in understanding faith, religion, and spirituality themselves. Most of us Americans today tell ourselves and others, particularly pollsters, that we are profoundly spiritual people. The trouble is, as well documented by Stephen Prothero, our "faith is almost entirely devoid of content. One of the most religious countries on earth is also a nation of religious illiterates."[22] Needless to say, most of us are far from being holistic saints! Holistic saints love God with all of their minds, as well as with all their hearts, strength, and souls.

Systemically weak saints would also be ineffective in helping others. Hartman maintained that to be effective, decent people must learn how to organize goodness. In his autobiography, he deplored the fact that evil people like the Nazis knew how to organize evil, but good people do not know how to organize goodness. When the Nazis were breathing down his neck before he escaped from Germany using a false passport in 1933, Hartman posed these questions:

> I thought to myself, if evil can be organized so efficiently, why cannot good? Is there any reason for efficiency to be monopolized by the forces of evil in the world? Why is it so difficult to organize good? Why have good people in history never seemed to have had as much power as bad people? I decided I would try to find out why and devote my life to doing something about it.[23]

People with weak systemic and/or extrinsic capacities (many good people) have never been able to organize goodness very well, and they never will. Only genuinely whole persons can do it, but few there be! If for no other reason, saintly wholeness is superior to purely intrinsic saintliness. Love slobs and mystical gluttons never get the job done!

6) Purely intrinsic spiritual gluttons would likely misdirect their love. Instead of loving God, other people, and all of God's creatures, they might love only love itself. They might just be love slobs. They love the pleasure, delight, and ecstasy of their own immediate mystical or spiritual experiences and assurances, but not God and others as the intentional objects of such experiences and assurances. Their intrinsic capacities are self-feeling-centered, not God and people centered. They love only their own loving experiences, mystical experiences, ecstatic feelings, assurances, and spiritual bliss. This is the main reason why their love does not carry over into the rest of life. They love only love and rapture. They seek and find the bliss of nirvana with no content, no object, no God, no people, no responsibilities.

Many of the foregoing difficulties with purely intrinsic spirituality apply to both mystical and monastic withdrawal from thinking and ordinary living. Mystical experience takes many forms; but the mysticism of pure consciousness that isn't conscious of anything is its emptiest and most escapist form. St. Thomas Aquinas's "beatific vison" of God involved only systemic knowledge and contemplation, but no love, emotions, affections, or actions. It was almost solipsistic, not social, (just God and me—reminiscent of "Just Jesus and me" in "On the Jericho Road"). It has no social dimension, no communication or rejoicing with other human souls, no kingdom of ends, no communion of the saints. This vision of God includes God, but not anything or everything that God loves. However, if what God loves cannot be separated from God himself, a purely solitary systemic vision of "only God" would be incredibly incomplete if not completely incoherent.

A better, richer, more complete vision of God is conceivable: God's consciousness is the richest-in-content form of consciousness, not the poorest. God's consciousness includes systemic, extrinsic, and intrinsic knowledge and their objects. It includes all of creation, every creature, every creative act of God, every concrete manifestation of God's love and compassion. The most godlike forms of God-consciousness, whether mystical or not, would be those that are richest in every dimension of goodness. They would be the fullest, not the emptiest, in content.

Mystical nirvana is wonderful, or so we are told by those who have experienced it; but, as William James noted, it never lasts. After an hour or so at most, mystics find themselves back in ordinary consciousness, modified in various ways by memories of mystical rapture. During intervals between mystical ecstasies, some mystics live and love more vigorously, more intensely, more systemically, extrinsically, and intrinsically; but others experience only the "dark night of the soul" and yearn for yesterday's rapture. Quietistic love slobs regard intervals between ecstasies as miserable wastes of time, as unwelcome intrusions. They languish and do not think or act. They do not allow their religious ecstasies to transform and enrich the rest of life. They love only the ecstasy, their own feelings of love, their own devotional experiences—but not God, people, and God's world. Saintly wholeness is much to be preferred! According to Emil L. Fackenheim, there is a place for mysticism in Judaism and Christianity, but for both a purely "mystical flight from the world" is unacceptable because "God has made the world for man to live in, not to flee from."[24]

By degrees, almost everyone has some capacity to identify evaluationally and psychologically with others. Even people who are less than saints have within themselves the beginnings of a profound spirituality, one which can culminate in complete identification with God and all of God's creations; but our intrinsic identification capacities need to be developed. Identification spirituality should not be confused with ecstatic mystical emptiness. They resemble one another in some ways, but the differences are profound. Almost everyone experiences fleeting moments of intrinsic union when they profoundly identify with their work, reading, music, games, teams, belongings, thoughts, beliefs, heroes, role models, spouses, children, friends, and loved ones.

During these identification-with-something moments, we are so concentrated and involved that we have little or no sense of self or time, so both identification experiences and mystical experiences are in some sense self-less and time-less. During psychological/axiological identification, differences between self and other are not noticed and no longer matter, and time seems to "stand still," but individuals and time do not simply disappear. When we love and identify intrinsically with others, we endure through time and remain who we are in our full uniqueness and completeness while in intrinsic union with those we love; our existential realities do not merge, even when our separateness and differences are not consciously noticed and no longer matter.

Mystics of ecstatic emptiness say that they experience existential or metaphysical selflessness, timelessness, absorption, and identity or perfect union. Perhaps they confuse identification with absolute identity, but we should not make that mistake. Ecstatic emptiness has no content, or so those mystics say; but spiritual identification takes the full richness and concreteness of the others into oneself, where it is cherished and does not dissolve or disappear into pure unity without content or diversity. A transformed self is present and "found" in both types of experience while the isolated self of ordinary selfish consciousness is "lost." However, a newborn spiritual/identification self is full of good-making properties, not empty of them, whereas the ecstatic/empty mystical self has no properties at all, or so we are told. Which has the most value? Holistic saints achieve and practice identification spirituality, not narcissism, spiritual gluttony, escapism, or emptiness.

Holistic saints recognize that intrinsic values and evaluations are highest, but they develop and deploy all their evaluational capacities as far as they can, relative to their own uniqueness. Relatively few people, if any, fully realize the goal of saintly wholeness. Most approximate it only by degrees. All of us have ongoing strengths and talents, weaknesses and failures, even after we and God have done our best to make us whole. After doing our best to achieve saintly wholeness, some of us will still be best at systemic tasks like thinking, teaching, and writing, some at extrinsic tasks like doing the works of love, getting the job done, and some at intrinsic tasks like loving devotion to and identification with God, other people, and all of creation. But all of us can use our strengths to express our love for God and God's creatures in our own limited, human, and uniquely personal ways.

The ideal of saintly wholeness can be a measuring rod that shows us how our underdeveloped lives are impoverished, where we need to grow in the love and knowledge of God and others, how we can act to express this love effectively through good works, and how further self-development can enrich our own and all other realities. Saintly wholeness is an ideal to which spiritual minded individuals aspire; but, as St. Paul realized, it is best achieved in and by entire communities or social bodies whose diverse members belong to one another, identify with one another, complement one another's strengths, compassionately correct and forgive one another's errors, and effectively compensate for one another's deficiencies.

Defining Holistic Saintliness and Saints

> *Indeed geniuses in axiology may well be saints, "saint" being defined as an axiological genius both in knowledge and action. To be a saint is a profession, like any other; it is the identification of self with every other self.*
>
> *The more intelligent a person is the better he or she will know how to value, for the more and wider concepts he or she considers; the most intelligent sees all* sub species aeternitas....*The* saint *is the genius of intrinsic evaluation, of ethics, applied to people.*
>
> *Only saints can fully live [the] infinite range of the self. A saint is a person who puts his whole power, all the resources of himself, into his own goodness, a man who has discovered his oneness with all creation, all men, all animals, even all things. He lives within the depth of everybody and everything. He is a man of infinite compassion. The deepest intrinsic goodness is to live so deeply and transparently within ourselves that we live deeply and compassionately with every human being, indeed every living being—indeed, every being. As St. Francis said to Brother Leo when he tried to extinguish the fire on St. Francis' coat: "Brother Leo, be careful with Brother Fire." Or as Albert Schweitzer, who felt pain at having to kill the bacteria when he did an operation. Compassion is one touchstone of moral value.*[25]
> Robert S. Hartman

Holistic saintliness includes all dimensions of value and evaluation, intrinsic, extrinsic, and intrinsic, developed as fully as humanly possible. Axiologically understood, saintliness is primarily but not exclusively the disposition to evaluate intrinsically all genuinely intrinsic value-objects, as well as all of creation. Genuine intrinsic value-objects are unique unified conscious centers of experience, activity, and evaluation like people, animals, and creation's God. Evaluating them intrinsically means wholly identifying with them emotionally, cognitively, volitionally, and behaviorally. It finds expression in feeling, doing, and knowing.

Love, compassion, and empathy are key words for intrinsic evaluation in ordinary discourse. Jonathan Edwards claimed that love is the most basic spiritual virtue, from which all other virtues are derived; and it is "the sum of all religion."[26] In saints, capacities for intrinsic evaluation are exceptionally well developed, even if they always fall somewhat short of perfection. Saints realize that unique conscious beings are truly valuable in themselves. They comprehend that repeatable abstractions like pleasure, knowledge, preference-fulfilment, and dutifulness are not intrinsically good, but they are good for us. Such good-making properties immensely enrich the lives of the individual centers of consciousness who actually are intrinsically good. Saints value themselves and others intrinsically; they love themselves, they love others as themselves, they love God's creation, and, most of all, they love creation's God.

In loving God, holistic saints come to love all that God loves. They do not isolate or separate God from all that God loves. The disposition to evaluate intrinsically tends to spread beyond its native home, which is intrinsic values proper. Ultimately, it extends to everything—to bacteria, the lilies of the field, the birds of the air, every living thing; to inanimate entities like Brother Sun, Sister Moon, Brother Wind, Sister Water, and Brother Fire, Mother Earth, Sister Death; to sunshine, lightning, mountains, valleys, planets, comets, stars, works of art; even to illuminating abstractions, axioms, systems, laws, rituals, ceremonies, and formalities. Yet, the propensity to evaluate everything intrinsically has appropriate limits, even in holistic saints; as Jonathan Edwards indicated,[27] it does not extend to intrinsic, systemic, and instrumental evil. When not otherwise explicit, this qualification applies to all references in this book to valuing "everything."

The degree to which we approach truly comprehensive intrinsic evaluation is the degree to which we approximate holistic saintliness. Historically, degrees of holistic saintliness are well represented by people like Jesus (the paradigm holistic intrinsic evaluator), St. Francis of Assisi, Albert Schweitzer, Mahatma Gandhi, Toyohiko Kagawa, Martin Luther King, Jr., Mother Teresa, and Desmond Tutu. Most were not perfect, but they came much closer to holistic saintliness than the rest of us. Jesus probably came closest to loving and valuing intrinsically everything that exists, as God does; and in this respect he was one with God, the man most fully and uniquely attuned to God. He was the man who most fully identified himself with God, and with whom God most fully identified Himself—thus most fully man and most fully God—identity through intrinsic identification.

Saintly Values: Self and Others

> *Recognize in thyself something which I wish to say within, in thyself; not within as if in thy body, for in a sense one may say, "in thyself." For there is in thee health, thy age whatever it be, but this in regard to the body. In thee is thy hand and thy foot; but there is one thing in thee, within; descend into thyself, go to thy secret place, thy mind, and there see, if thou canst, what I wish to say. For if thou art far from thyself, how canst thou come near to God?*[28] St. Augustine

> *"Know thy God" (I Chron. 28:9) rather than "Know Thyself" is the categorical imperative of the biblical man. There is no self-understanding without God-understanding.*[29] Rabbi Abraham J. Heschel

St. Augustine advised would-be saints to enter into the depths of themselves. Little progress in spiritual self-development can be made until we abandon our natural absorption in and attachment to the external extrinsic sensory world and turn toward inward intrinsic self-knowledge and self-transformation. We must turn our attention inwardly toward our distinctively intrinsic selves, our own unique consciousness, and its contents, structure, and activities. We should learn who we are, not merely physically and externally, but mentally, spiritually, and internally. Worldly people find this difficult, and if most people are primarily worldly, then most find it difficult. Yet, no one is purely worldly and beyond all hope.

The worldly phase of consciousness is spiritually undeveloped and not far removed from the more primitive animal awareness from which it emerged. For the most part, both sub-human animals and worldly persons are engrossed in external things, social roles, status, and hierarchies. The have not made the Augustinian inward turn. They know and value things, social dominance, and libido gratification, but little else. They know themselves primarily as things, bodies, and social functions and relations. Despite their short-sightedness, acquisitive worldly people can look a bit further into the future than most animals; but both animals and worldlings are almost completely absorbed in and attentive to externalities, including their own bodies. Without really knowing themselves as conscious minds or souls, worldly people yearn, at least semi-consciously, for peace of mind or soul, for deep self-knowledge, and for God. Yet, they are weak in inwardness and subjectivity. Primarily, they know themselves and others as objects, not as subjects, and they live and act accordingly.

St. Augustine advised people who would come near to God to enter into themselves, to get to know themselves as conscious subjects, not as merely extrinsic objects. They must know themselves immediately, not just indirectly through mirror images and the eyes and opinions of others. They must learn to exist within themselves and not merely outside, beside, or beneath themselves. Saintly people who live in and with God are directly acquainted with themselves as unique, personal, conscious individuals living out their lives before God. They no longer see themselves as mere bodies playing out social roles before the world, though they are not oblivious to that. Yet, they do not become purely cognitive minds living only their own private thought worlds, thinking only about thinking, like Aristotle's god. Saints know themselves directly and concretely as individuated social beings. They intrinsically value themselves as ends, as intrinsic goods, despite all their self-acknowledged faults. Self forgiveness, forgiveness from others they have wronged, and divine forgiveness enter into their saintly sense of self-worth. The spiritual gift of forgiveness can and should find expression in all three value dimensions—with the head, in deeds, and with the heart, thus, with whole soul.

Saints are able to withdraw their attention from the world of external things and from what others think of them. They know how to focus their attention directly upon their inner conscious selves, upon their own thoughts, feelings, desires, emotions, intuitions, and volitions. Some can even attend to their own attending. Such inwardness is best cultivated in long hours of solitude, meditation, concentration, self-reflection, introspection, and prayer.

Because they know and value themselves intrinsically, saints are better qualified and prepared to know and value others intrinsically, to recognize others as intrinsic goods, as unique subjects, as ends in themselves. They are able to love other people as fully as they love themselves because they regard others as conscious subjects like themselves, not as mere objects or things. Worldly people, not inward subjects even to themselves, can change, become self-aware, and awaken to inwardness, self-knowledge, and intrinsic self-evaluation. Sleepers, awake! Kierkegaard said that the most important kind of truth is just this sort of subjectivity. He wrote, "The truth is the subject's transformation of himself."[30] Introspection, inwardness, and withdrawal from the world into oneself, are pre-requisites for and constituents of saintliness.

Sanctification (saint-making) is ongoing, something to be "worked out," as St. Paul suggested. Saints live and develop in time, and they know it. Their sanctified time becomes the fullness of time, rich in goodness. Knowing and valuing oneself directly as a conscious subject is difficult and requires sustained time, effort, and solitude (with God). Once initiated, it can be nurtured by intense concentration, social mentoring, the communion and encouragement of other saints, and no small measure of divine grace. At least, the saints think so, and they live accordingly.

Saints are keenly aware of living out every moment of their lives as unique individuals existing directly before, within, and in communion with God. Such profound awareness is intrinsic faith. Sometimes it comes in solitude, away from other people, sometimes in the presence of and in community and communion with others, sometimes in helping others, sometimes in gardening or walking in the woods, sometimes in deep thought, but always in the presence of God. Saintly wholeness is the richest in goodness, the most intense, and the most fully developed kind of human consciousness. Within themselves, the saints find God, and in finding God, they find and gain everything and everyone. St. Augustine would agree with Rabbi Heschel that adequate self-knowledge involves God-knowledge.

Saintly wholeness does not merely use God and other people to gain worldly riches and acclaim. For saints, spirituality has neither a prosperity-conferring function nor a dominance-conferring function. Before God, we cannot hide behind sham, pretenses, vanity, and externalities. Before the One unto whom all hearts are open and from no secrets are hid, we can only be ourselves. Before God within us, we are constantly stripped of all pomposities, pretenses, and self-deceptions. Before God within us, we are all sinners who deserve self-respect and the respect of others because God loves us, forgives us, and dwells within us. While we are yet sinners, God knows and values us intrinsically, despite our faults. Being Godlike means doing the same. God loves *all other people* who are yet sinners, *not just us*! Should we do no less? In saintly theism, being valued intrinsically by God is our most significant asset or good-making property. It is a relational property. Without God, we have intrinsic worth; within God's love, we have equal and infinite worth.

Saints think that being valued intrinsically by God means that all people have basic equal worth in the eyes of God, and this profoundly affects their own relations with other human beings. It affects how they think about, feel about, and act toward others. Unlike saints, most people do not love others as themselves; far too many do not even know or love themselves intrinsically. In the depths of sin, people are either indifferent to most others, or they ardently despise them, especially outsiders. This is perfectly natural, as modern sociobiology indicates. Saintly religion aspires to move us beyond this "natural man" (and woman), defined by Rudolf Bultman as "man prior to faith."[31] Because God is immanent in nature, and we are within nature, being transformed into a saint is a natural human possibility; but it is not a natural human probability. Few there be who find it! Yet, even worldly people can come to their senses, to themselves, and realize that worldliness is hell, lostness, emptiness, despair, forlornness, and loveless alienation—the most prevalent and miserable form of original sin. Religious hope for the end of the world is for the end of worldliness.

The Bible says emphatically in both Testaments that God is no respecter of persons (Deuteronomy 10:17, Romans 2:11, Colossians 3:25, and elsewhere) and that we should not be either (Deuteronomy 1:17, 16:19, Leviticus 19:15, Proverbs 24:23, I. Peter 1:17, and elsewhere). Not being a respecter of persons is not the same thing as not respecting persons, that is, not recognizing the intrinsic worth and basic rights of persons. In the biblical sense, being a "respecter of persons" means something extrinsic; it means giving extra weight to and placing extra value upon worldly distinctions like rich and poor, intelligent and not so intelligent, high and low social class or status, slave and free, male and female, Jew and Gentile, and the like. Worldlings *are* respecters of persons; they give special respect and favors to "top dogs" because they think they have more comparative worth than "underdogs." They aspire to be top dogs themselves. Saints are not extrinsic respecters of persons because they see and value persons in their uniqueness, where every person has equal worth, and each person is incomparable. Pure worldlings and ideologists cannot do this. Most of us fall somewhere in between.

People obviously differ in race, color, creed, wealth, power, prestige, talent, productivity, intelligence, usefulness, and so on. For these reasons, we are not all of equal worth in the eyes of the world. Worldlings reduce individual worth to extrinsic social worth—usefulness to other people and to themselves. By worldly standards, we are not all equally valuable extrinsically, that is, equally useful to others, especially to those who would merely use us. And others are not equally useful to us. By worldly standards, employing only extrinsic distinctions to determine human worth is perfectly sane. To worldlings, a President is obviously worth more than a peasant or a field hand, and a winning football coach has much more value than a second string quarterback or a philosophy professor. Saints, by contrast, see no difference in our basic intrinsic worth before God or before themselves, though they know that some people are more godlike and live more abundantly than others. By saintly standards, the world is deranged because it measures human worth solely by extrinsic worldly distinctions. Worldlings tune in only to extrinsic worth, whereas saints are attuned to total worth, intrinsic worth, infinite worth, before God. Whole-istic saints weigh extrinsic and systemic worth only in ways that respect intrinsic worth, including spiritual worth. They are not respecters of persons.

Jesus was at least as deeply devoted to tax collectors, businessmen, laborers, sinners, paupers, beggars, prostitutes, and thieves as he was to the high and mighty, to persons of means, wealth, respectability, and repute. If he were alive today, with what outcasts, underdogs, and "low down people" would he associate and eat his meals? What does Christlikeness require of today's Christians? With which of "the least of these" would he affiliate today? His parable of the workers in the vineyard (Matthew 20:1-16)[32] is utterly incomprehensible to worldlings, but to saints it expresses the most appropriate way to value other people because it does not allow worldly distinctions of status and affluence to stand in the way of love and respect. In this parable, some laborers work a full twelve hour workday, some three fourths of the day, some half of it, some a fourth of it, and some only one hour; yet, all receive the same wages, as each individually agreed to in advance with the vineyard owner. When those who worked longest found out that they received no more pay than those who worked only one hour, they "grumbled" and said to the owner: "You have made them equal to us who have borne the burden of the day and the scorching heat" (Matthew 20:11-12). That is precisely the point! Worldlings are "offended" by equal basic human worth! The intrinsic equality of every incomparably unique person in the sight of God is precisely what worldlings cannot comprehend; but holistic saints can. Saints get it!

Equality before God means that God values dogmatic ideologists just as much as God values greedy worldlings, and that God values both just as much as he values saints. It means that God loves dogmatists, worldlings, and saints equally, even if they do not all love God equally. No matter what our differences are, no matter if some are smarter than others, some more practical than others, some more loving and devotional than others, God loves all equally. While we are yet sinners, God loves us all equally! God "desires all men to be saved and to come to the knowledge of the truth" (I. Timothy 2:4). All men and all women!

A longstanding tradition in Judaeo/Christian theology affirms that all people are equally sinful and equally valuable in the sight of God. Saintly spirituality affirms equal human worth and tries to make it so in human practice, especially in those areas where it really counts. Without denying the immense extrinsic and systemic diversity and inequality of human beings, and without denying that some people are more saintly than others, saintly wholeness posits a deep basic core of equal intrinsic worth in every personal life. Thinkers of the Seventeenth and Eighteenth Century Enlightenment expressed universal human equality philosophically in terms of equal basic human rights and respect for all unique persons. Human rights protect the core of unique human conscious existence from being intruded upon or obliterated by others. Theologians view equal basic worth and rights as a consequence of God's equal and universal love for all. Many saints extend respect and rights deeply into the animal kingdom, and God's love to everything that God has made.

Regarding everyone as having equal intrinsic worth is not the same thing as having equal duties toward everyone. We should, and saints do, equally respect everyone's basic moral rights; yet, loving everyone as a unique person means valuing everyone concretely and uniquely given their own personal histories, interests, projects, and situational duties and responsibilities. Yet, saints have special duties to their children, loved ones, and close friends that they do not have to everyone in the world. Saintly love is not just an abstraction; it applies to everyone in the fulness of their being, personal concerns, stories, and distinctive commitments.

Saints do not identify either God or Christ with culture. Saintly spirituality constantly stands in judgment on religious, political, and social establishments and injustices in every era. Saintly spirituality rejects the idea that God favors worldly opulence, power, success, status, and acclaim—that God is an extrinsic respecter of persons. All such worldly goods can be gained, and the soul still be lost. Saintly religion focuses on the total person, especially on soul, consciousness, the inner affective self; but it does not neglect the mind, the thinking self, or the body and the outer or public self with its circumstantial station and duties. It refuses to identify souls with mere externalities, as does behaviorism, positivism, and worldliness; and it refuses to identify souls with mere internalities, as does metaphysical idealism and mind/matter dualism. It acknowledges and rejoices in the fact that all souls are embodied, that souls and bodies exist in indissoluble unity, and that souls are formed or created only in social settings. Christian saintliness affirms the social resurrection of embodied consciousness, not the immortality of disembodied and disengaged Platonic minds.

Saintly spirituality is creative; it is socially and morally active and innovative. It lives out on a human level the image of God as creator. It includes a vision of a better way, a kingdom of peace, cooperation, and equality that is *in* but not *of* the world. It invokes the aid of a divine power capable of transporting even worldlings and ideologists from loveless indifference, suspicion, misunderstanding, snobbery, and alienation into membership within a loving community of mutual union, acceptance, affirmation, and respect—a beloved community, a fellowship and communion of mutually supportive saints. Loving, forgiving, and cooperating with other equals before God is the best way to live. It is better than competition and violence, better than social climbing, better than lording it over losers and social inferiors, better than revenge, better than worldly success, better than haughtiness, better than ideological indifference or condescension. Love, the kingdom of God within, can transform the world without. Holistic saints act in informed ways to implement this conviction. With enlightenment and passion they do the works of love. They have the faith that works by love (Galatians 5:6).

Saintly Evaluations: Feelings, Cognition, and Actions

> *I have observed from time to time, that in pure love to others, i.e. love not arising from self-love, there is a union of the heart with others; a kind of enlargement of the mind, whereby it so extends itself as to take others into a man's self: and therefore it implies a disposition to feel, to desire, and to act as though others were one with ourselves.*[33] Jonathan Edwards

> *'Tis the nature of true benevolence to desire and rejoice in the prosperity and pleasure of its object; and that in some proportion to its degree of prevalence.*[34] Jonathan Edwards

> *Love of* benevolence *is that affection or propensity of the heart to any being, which causes it to incline to its well-being, or disposes it to desire and take pleasure in its happiness....Beauty in the object is not always the ground of this propensity;...there may be such a thing as benevolence, or a disposition to the welfare of those that are not considered as beautiful; unless mere existence be accounted a beauty....Love of* complacence *[by contrast] presupposes beauty, for it is no other than delight in beauty; or complacence in the person or being beloved for his beauty.*[35] Jonathan Edwards

> *Since I do not abstract in intrinsic valuation, I concentrate on the thing as it is, I am fully concentrated on this one thing. For this reason, intrinsic valuation when applied to things brings about aesthetic valuation; the artist is fully concentrated on the thing he creates. He and the thing are empathically related; they form one unit. Applied to persons this valuation is ethical; it is complete involvement of one person with another, complete concentration of one person on another; the persons are sympathetically related and form one unit. We may call this relationship between persons* Community.[36] Robert S. Hartman

Saintly evaluations are primarily intrinsic evaluations, though holistic saintliness also includes contextually appropriate extrinsic and systemic evaluations. Intrinsic evaluation involves emotion, cognition, and dynamic activity. So do extrinsic and systemic evaluations by degrees, but intrinsic evaluation is momentously affective. It is intensely loving, empathetic, compassionate, affective identification-with-loved-ones. Yet, it is not entirely affective, because loving and compassionate emotions are not mere feelings. They are intentional feelings, which means that they include cognitive awareness of and responsiveness to their objects, even if some loves are only "free floating," seeking objects, but not always finding them. Holistic saintly intrinsic evaluation is not blind; it incorporates thought, information, truth, beliefs, doctrines, and knowledge. It is not inactive or quietistic; it does the works of love. It practices what it preaches.

At one stage in his career, Frederich Schleiermacher equated religion with pure feeling totally devoid of all knowledge and action. He wrote, "Ideas and principles are all foreign to religion,"[37] and "Religion by itself does not urge men to activity at all. If you could imagine it implanted in man quite alone, it would produce neither these [moral] nor any other deeds. The man...would not act, he would only feel."[38] His saints would be love slobs or spiritual gluttons, but Schleiermacher was wrong for many reasons. For one thing, like other kinds of feeling, spiritual feelings have identifiable intentional objects; they are always feelings *of* something, love *of* someone, union *with* an Ultimate that has good-making properties. Our feelings of absolute *dependence* are *on something*, on God. Furthermore, as Jonathan Edwards insisted, our religious affections do express themselves in godly and righteous living and acting. Salvation is not earned by good works, but it is expressed in and through good works. Without works, faith is dead. Without ideas, faith is dumb.

Saints know or experience things that others do not know or experience. The intentional objects of spiritual knowledge are conscious subjects. Saints know themselves and others as unique subjects, not merely as objects. Their most valued intentional objects are conscious subjects. They both know and delight in uniqueness, combined with inwardness, combined with an uncountable host of other good-making properties. They understand the true nature of well-being, they know how to express spiritual knowledge in action, and they act on such knowledge. They *know* something about the religious entities or realities to which they are ultimately devoted and on which they ultimately depend. As Hartman indicated, saints are geniuses of evaluation "both in knowledge and action." Acting, feeling, and knowing are all integral to holistic saintliness. Systemic faith and intrinsic evaluation are dead without works and blind without information. Intrinsic evaluation is loving something or someone with all of one's heart, and soul, and mind, and strength. Holistic saintliness involves much more than heart alone, soul alone, mind alone, or strength alone. It is all of them all at once—whole-soul involvement and fulfillment.

Our complete identification or union with God is always limited by our finitude. Our union with God does not make us God, not even in our most profound spiritual or mystical experiences. Human identification with God is not complete identity with God. When we "see God," we do not acquire all of God's good-making properties in their completeness. Experiencing union with God does not make us omniscient, omnipotent, omnipresent, uncreated, everlasting, indestructible, or anything remotely resembling that. It only makes us as knowledgeable, loving, and Godlike as we can be at that moment in our finitude, but what does that mean?

Jonathan Edwards, a genius at cognitive analysis, often analyzed the immensely complex concept of "love." He did not just throw the word around thoughtlessly, as we often do ; he really wanted to know what it meant. Read again the quotes from Edwards at the beginning of this section. Paraphrasing and summarizing his analysis, we may say that loving "any being" (any x) includes:

1) a profound emotional heartfelt sense of union with x,
2) a knowledge of both oneself and x as individual conscious selves or subjects,
3) a mental, psychological, or axiological "enlargement" that takes x into oneself,
plus enduring dispositions:
4) to feel the unity of x and oneself,
5) to desire the unity of x and oneself,
plus enduring benevolent dispositions:
6) to act as if x is one with oneself,
7) to desire the prosperity of x,
8) to desire the sustained pleasure or happiness of x,
9) to rejoice, delight, and take pleasure in the existence, prosperity, well-being, and/or happiness of x, in proportion to the degree of each,
10) to delight and rejoice in the beauty of x, that is, the harmonious and "amiable" symmetry and proportion of x's properties, and
11) in particular cases, the sensible and vigorous exercise and activation of all of these capacities and dispositions.[39]

Here, says axiology, the "x" being loved could in fact be an insentient thing like a mansion, a sunset, a work of art, or a belief system, even though such objects are not unique conscious subjects, thus not ends in themselves. Most properly, however, "x" is a conscious being like oneself, another person, another sentient being (an animal), or God. Even physical things may be loved (idolized) as if they were persons, as we well know from experience. Loving is intrinsic evaluation, a function of the whole person; it is not mere feelings, not just spiritual gluttony, not cold intellect, and not mindless and/or heartless frantic activity. True love exercises all the valuer's capacities for positive attachment to and identification with the beloved. People with no knowledge of God cannot love God, for "God" has no content. People who do not know themselves cannot love themselves, for "self" has no content. People who do not know their neighbors and strangers cannot love them, for "neighbors" and "strangers" have no content. People who have no understanding of "well-being" cannot promote or value it for they do not know what it is; and they cannot eschew "ill-being" precisely because they have no comprehension of it.

Cognitive elements in intrinsic evaluation are indispensable, even though intrinsic evaluation *largely* consists of feelings, emotions, desires, affections. This understanding of the primacy of feeling in intrinsic evaluation is akin to Jonathan Edwards's definition of "true religion" as something which *"in great part, consists in holy affections."*[40] The *other small but not insignificant parts* are spiritual beliefs, information, knowledge, cognition, and benevolent behaviors or good works. The religious affections are all grounded in knowledge, he insisted, and they are inevitably expressed in actions. Yet, the *greatest and most significant part* of true religion definitely consists in holy affections, for "The Holy Scriptures do everywhere place religion very much in the affections; such as fear, hope, love, hatred [of wickedness], desire, joy, sorrow, gratitude, compassion and zeal."[41] All of these affections have cognitive intentional objects, involve knowledge, and manifest themselves in the perseverance of the saints in Godly and righteous living.

Sin, by contrast, says Edwards, consists "very much in hardness of heart," by which "is plainly meant an unaffected heart, or a heart not easy to be moved with virtuous affections, like a stone, insensible, stupid, unmoved and hard to be impressed."[42] People without deep feelings do not have true religion. They are not saints. Intrinsic evaluation consists in great part of powerful feelings, but holistic saints do not divorce these feelings from knowledge or information, and they express them in ethical acting and spiritual living. Worldlings and ideologists, who are deficient in intrinsic evaluation, have hard, unaffected, insensible, stupid, uninformed, unmoved, hard to impress, and stony hearts! They do not care about or act to help others, especially outsiders.

For saints, the very real physical and ontological differences between self and others do not cease to exist, but phenomenologically they seem to disappear in peak gestalt experiences of mystical, affective, and social union. They do not cease to exist, but they cease being noticed and emphasized. No one ever becomes totally one with another existentially or ontologically, but differences between subject and object, self and others, cease to matter to holistic saintly virtuosos of intrinsic evaluation.

Saintly Values: Things and Status

> God is in all things, and that we are to see the Creator in the glass of every creature; that we should use and look upon nothing as separate from God, which indeed is a kind of practical Atheism; but, with a true magnificence of thought, survey heaven and earth, and all that is therein, as contained by God in the hollow

of His hand, who by His intimate presence holds them all in being, who pervades and actuates the whole created frame, and is, in a true sense, the soul of the universe.[43] John Wesley

[The pure in heart] now see him by faith (the veil of flesh being made, as it were, transparent), even in these his lowest works, in all that surrounds them, in all that God has created and made. They see him in the height above, and in the depth beneath; they see him filling all in all.
The pure in heart see all things full of God. They see him in the firmament of heaven; in the moon, walking in brightness; in the sun, when he rejoiceth as a giant to run his course. They see him 'making the clouds his chariots, and walking upon the wings of the wind.' They see him 'preparing rain for the earth', 'and blessing the increase of it'; 'giving grass for the cattle, and green herb for the use of man'. They see the Creator of all wisely governing all, and 'upholding all things by the word of his power'.[44] John Wesley

One of the things that makes us human is our ability to sense that an anniversary, a birthday, a holiday is different from the days around it. Physically, one book is no different from another. We, in our humanity, can see some books as sacred. God is the source of our unique human ability to recognize the invisible qualities that make some objects, some buildings, some blocks of time sacred.[45] Rabbi Harold S. Kushner

While many of us tend to see the world as divided into the holy (the realm of the religious) and the profane (the ordinary, nonreligious, meaning everything else; the word profane *literally means outside or in front of the church), theologian Martin Buber taught that the division is really between the holy and the non-yet-holy. Everything in God's world can be holy if you realize its potential holiness. One of the fundamental teachings of Judaism is that the search for holiness, for the encounter with God, is not confined to the synagog. Everything we do can be transformed into a Sinai experience, an encounter with the sacred. The goal of Judaism is not to teach us how to escape from the profane world to the cleansing presence of God, but to teach us how to bring God into the world, how to take the ordinary and make it holy.*[46] Rabbi Harold S. Kushner

The counterpart of this secularization, however, is the sanctification of all things. Now every day is the day that the Lord has made; every nation is a holy people called by him into existence in its place and time and to his glory; every person is sacred, made in his image and likeness; every living thing, on earth, in the heavens, and in the waters is his creation and points in its existence toward him; the whole earth is filled with his glory; the infinity of space is his temple where all creation is summoned to silence before him. Here is the basis then not only of a transformed ethics, founded on the recognition that whatever is, is good, but of transformed piety or religion, founded on the realization that every being is holy.[47]
H. Richard Niebuhr

Saintly Jews, Christians, Moslems, Buddhists, Hindus, and others know how to surmount the familiar distinction between the sacred and the secular by *making everything sacred*. For them, everything is a sacrament, and God is all in all. Worldly people move in the opposite direction; they secularize everything, and ideologists intellectualize everything. Perfect saints would revere, respect, adore, love, prize, cherish, identify with, and delight in everything (except evil) in its full concreteness, uniqueness, and inherent being and dignity. Whatever is, is good, just as St. Augustine said. Achieving this level of ethico-religious development for most people is a lifelong struggle. Making all things holy, including oneself, (sanctification) is gradual and incremental. It requires enormous spiritual effort, growth, and Divine grace.

Intrinsic spirituality increasingly objectifies itself extrinsically in things, events, and practices. God is found initially in special places. Shrines, churches, cathedrals, temples, synagogues, or scenic vistas tend to evoke a sense of mystery, awe, reverence, sublimity, and corresponding humility, abasement, and repentance. Particular historical events like the Exodus, Mt. Sinai, or the birth, life, death, and resurrection of Jesus, may manifest God's presence and acts. Special physical objects or "ornaments" like the ark of the covenant, crosses, minoras, robes, vestments, altars, rosaries, bread, wine, incense, and religious art may be infused with sacredness. Ritualized practices like kneeling, bowing, hand-clasping, genuflecting, singing hymns, reading sermon texts, preaching, praying, and standardized "orders of worship" can be imbued with intrinsic spiritual significance that evokes, embodies, sustains, and expresses the presence of God.

In saintliness, spirituality spreads beyond special times, places, and things, and into the mundane. Godliness becomes a total way of life, and all things, practices, activities, events, and people become holy. Whatever is, becomes sacramental and sacred.

As James W. Fowler pointed out, Christianity struggled for centuries before it finally recognized that all occupations (except inherently sinful ones) are callings from God. For many centuries, the distinction between sacred and profane occupations prevailed in Christendom; the priesthood and monasticism were sacred, and everything else was profane. Fourteenth Century German mystics like Meister Eckhart and Johann Tauler first expressed "an understanding of *all* human work as having the dignity, potentially, of a call." Without invoking works-righteousness, Martin Luther popularized the idea that "any work, any office, if offered to God in faithfulness and gratitude, can be a fitting form of partnership with God in behalf of the neighbor."[48]

The saintly capacity for intrinsic evaluation tends to spread beyond its native home amid unique, unified centers of conscious experience, activity, and evaluation. In saints, it gradually spreads and extends to everything. Saints are disposed to evaluate everything intrinsically. St. Augustine proclaimed that "Whatsoever in any degree is, is good."[49] As the song writer and performer Ray Stevens crooned,

"Everything is Beautiful in Its Own Way." So everything is, at least to saints. Many people transcend worldly values sufficiently to value intrinsically *a few* highly select people, things, labors, avocations, practices, and other activities; but saints exist at the ultimate extreme of axiological enlargement and evolution. Truly blessed among human beings, they can value and identify themselves with everyone and everything before and within God. For that, they live richer lives, they live more abundantly, and they have so much more to give back in return.

Our Natural Environment

> John Wesley did more than suggest that animals will be with us in "the new heaven and the new earth." Using Romans 8:19-22, where the Apostle Paul said that all of creation works for redemption, as well as the creation accounts of Genesis, Wesley preached that animals *will be with us in eternity.* He believed that since God's creation was originally in harmony and unity, and since God will one day restore all *of creation to that original state, then animals will be part of that new heaven and new earth promised in Revelation. But Wesley did not believe that we should just wait for that day to value all of God's creation. He believed that God is bringing all of creation "nearer and nearer" to the day it will be set free, so we too, in our lives* now should *"imitate him whose mercy is over all his works." We do this by treating all that God created in more compassionately just ways* because *they are valuable, in and of themselves, as God's creation.*[50] Tony Campolo

Saints and worldlings have radically different perspectives on the environment—the world of nature and non-human living things. For worldlings, "inanimate" nature and "lesser" forms of life exist merely to be exploited in the human quest for profit, affluence, entertainment, pleasure, comfort, and dominance Not so for saints. Because they regard every living thing as existing for its own sake, saints try to minimize their own destructiveness, their own behaviors that harm, debilitate, frustrate, or exterminate other living things. Saintly reverence for life manifests itself in many ways, including *creation care*. Eastern religions proclaim that every non-human living thing has the dignity of a human person because each once was or soon will be reincarnated as a human being. Such religious myths actually can facilitate intrinsic evaluations. Of course, subscribing officially to an ideal, and actually living up to it, are two very different things, just as much so in the East as in the West. In neither the East nor the West do ordinary people live up to their highest ideals, to their own cultural, religious, or personal norms of saintliness, morality, and spirituality.

Saints minimize the exploitation of life by life, especially by themselves, even when this cannot be eliminated entirely. Their asceticism has a point; it is life affirming. They choose to consume only minimal quantities of lower forms of life. They deliberately eat "low on the food chain." They try to live by what the Eastern religions call "*ahimsa*," non-violence, not just toward people, but toward everything. Respecting non-human nature, vegetarians are closer to saintliness than typical human omnivores. Hindus and Buddhists say that those who live by violent occupations cannot become saints or be saved, especially butchers! To appreciate why, read Gail A. Eisnitz's 1997 book titled *Slaughterhouse: The Shocking Story of Greed, Neglect, and Inhumane Treatment Inside the U.S. Meat Industry*![51]

Saints celebrate the inherent dignity and worth of every creature of God in many ways. Saint Francis preached to the birds and spoke winning and calming words of friendship to the attacking wolf. In his presence, non-human animals displayed an uncanny absence of fear and caution; they somehow sensed that St. Francis would respect their existence and not exploit, injure, deceive, or destroy them,[52] as would most men and women of the world. Many people actually have this sort of trustworthy communion with animals. How close are they to saintliness? Can maturing saints be recognized by their ways with animals?

Saintly (but not perfect) Albert Schweitzer contended that western ethics has been too human-centered. Even when universalized to include all members of the human tribe, our capacity for intrinsic evaluation is still too limited, too provincial. Even after all human beings have been included within the moral community, a further "widening of current views" is required, Schweitzer contended. We need an ethics of "reverence for life" that embraces ethical responsibility "towards all that lives," he held. "The time is coming," Schweitzer predicted, "when people will be astonished that mankind needed so long a time to learn to regard thoughtless injury to life as incompatible with ethics."[53] Our ethical and unethical relations with non-human animals are complex, but saints are very reluctant to take from any living creature the only life that it will ever have.

Renouncing It All

> Now the individual begins, not indeed by relating himself at one and the same time absolutely to the absolute *telos and relatively to relative ends, since through being fast in the immediate he is in precisely the opposite situation; but he begins by exercising himself in the absolute relationship through renunciation. The task is ideal, and has perhaps never been completely realized by anyone....In order that the individual may sustain an absolute relationship to the absolute* telos *he must first have exercised himself in the renunciation of relative ends, and only then can there be a question of the ideal task: the simultaneous maintenance of an absolute relationship to the absolute, and a relative relationship to the relative.*[54] Søren Kierkegaard

Becoming a saint is not easy, and no one ever said that it is. Saintliness involves acknowledging one's sins and shortcomings before God, which many of us have too much pride to do. It also involves giving up all absolutistic attachments to finite and relative values, including the material and social goods of worldliness and the dogmatisms of ideology. Initially, saintly spiritual development can be wrenching, the cause of great suffering, as Kierkegaard emphasized. "No pain, no gain" applies to saintly spirituality.

A negative saintliness of pure renunciation frequently manifests itself in the religions of the East and elsewhere. It renounces, it even disvalues and disdains, all concrete existence. It may even try to renounce and disvalue evaluation itself—for the sake of pure emptiness. The ideal of total renunciation was greatly admired and commended by Western pessimists like Arthur Schopenhauer.[55] It prevailed in Stoicism, in much religious asceticism, and in many of the religions of Asia. But it was deplored and repudiated as "life-denying" by Albert Schweitzer.

Total renunciation can free people from bondage to the values of worldliness and ideology. It can liberate from preoccupation with things, status, ego, and doctrines. But it has nothing positive to put in their place—except for its own assumptions and hidden doctrines, and its sometimes favored passion, compassion. Taken with utmost seriousness, it gives people no reason to live, to act, to choose, to think, or to feel. When extremely negative saints give up extrinsic evaluation, they may take refuge in indifference to everything. This indifference resembles systemic rational detachment but goes far beyond it. Those who merely renounce everything do not move on to intrinsic evaluation. Many Buddhists, Hindus, and the Greek and Roman Stoics advocated universal non-attachment, though most of them slip compassion in by the back door. Intense intrinsic involvement with anything is explicitly or officially repudiated. We should not even be emotionally involved with or attached to those who are closest to us in life, they say. To avoid being hurt by the accidental loss of beloved human intimates, or of cherished things or beliefs, negative saints may deliberately give up loving and cherishing altogether. Purely negative saints would have no courage to be, to love, to help, or to live. Yet, they often inconsistently commend compassion and actions flowing from it.

A negative saintliness of pure renunciation could be an essential first step in transcending worldliness and ideology, a temporary but necessary step in the wrong direction, a step backward before going forward. Kierkegaard and many others thought so. But, judged axiologically, because it is essentially negative and empty, pure renunciation cannot be the final step in spiritual self-realization. Emptiness or total indifference to everything is an unsatisfying and unsatisfactory ultimate ideal. Positive saintly wholeness, by contrast, is completely life affirming, not completely life denying. It has not lost or repudiated the courage to be, to affirm, to commit, to act, to choose, to know, to relieve suffering, and to love intensely. A good religion is much more than indifference, emptiness, or the emptiness of emptiness.[56] A good religion makes a place for abundant living, not for the impoverishment of total renunciation.

Whether some *stages of religious development* are better than others can be addressed clearly and unequivocally by axiology. Axiology defines "better" to mean "richer in good-making properties." The same rational process that differentiates between good and bad religions can also tell us that some stages of spiritual

150 *Spiritual Values and Evaluations*

development are better than others, specifically, those richer in good-making properties, and the richest are the best. This book shows that an extrinsic religiosity or spirituality that practices what it preaches is richer than ideological systemic spirituality that merely preaches; and holistic saintly intrinsic spirituality is richest of all. It is richer than both renunciation and a purely internal intrinsic spiritual gluttony. Holistic saints, not those of pure renunciation, are the ones who live most meaningfully, helpfully, and abundantly.

Having It All

> *By faith I make renunciation of nothing, on the contrary, by faith I acquire everything.*[57] Søren Kierkegaard

> *I closed my eyes, soothed. A quiet, mysterious pleasure took possession of me—as if all that green miracle around me were paradise itself, as if all the freshness, airiness and sober rapture which I was feeling were God. God changes his appearance every second. Blessed is the man who can recognize him in all his disguises. At one moment he is a glass of fresh water, the next your son bouncing on your knees or an enchanting woman, or perhaps merely a morning walk.*
>
> *Little by little, everything around me, without changing shape, became a dream. I was happy. Earth and paradise were one. A flower in the fields with a large drop of honey in its center: that was how life appeared to me. And my soul, a wild bee plundering.*[58] Nikos Kazantzakis, from *Zorba the Greek*

> *If the doors of perception were cleansed, everything would appear to man as it is, infinite.*
> *For man has closed himself up, til he sees all things thro' chinks of his cavern.*[59] William Blake

Saints do renounce worldly values as the sole or supreme meaning and purpose of human existence; yet, strangely, unless their ethico-religious development is arrested at the stage of renunciation, saints get back everything that they renounce, and then some! Curiously, everything is returned to them once they have sought and found the loving kingdom of God, the kingdom of intrinsic ends, values, and evaluations. Kierkegaard thought that this is possible only by virtue of the absurd. His "knight of faith" renounces everything, just as Abraham renounced Isaac; but then, like Abraham, he then gets everything back again by virtue of the absurd.[60]

Without regressing into the absurd, the theory of value with which we are working offers a better way, a more excellent way. It gives a perfectly rational explanation for why saints can have it all. Holistic saints place an even higher value on things and social structures than worldlings, not because it is absurd to do so, but because they fully actualize their capacities for intrinsic evaluation, which purely extrinsic worldlings, systemic dogmatists, and saints of pure renunciation do not do.

Saints see everything secular as sacred; they see God as all in all. They see God as fullness, not as emptiness.

Holistic saints also actualize their capacities for valuing extrinsically and systemically, but always as subordinated to the intrinsic. Actual saints are not all exactly alike, even though all are virtuosos of intrinsic value and evaluation. Some are better at extrinsic rather than systemic tasks, some better at systemic rather than extrinsic tasks, some equally good at both, and some are very proficient in all three dimensions. Saints have different gifts, but they are members of one another. They value everything (except evil) intrinsically without abandoning the hierarchy of value. The exuberance and vitality of their intrinsic sensitivity overflows into the extrinsic and systemic realms. Holistic saints value everything intrinsically while being proficient in all types of evaluation. Each saint does this uniquely in her or his own distinctive way, so all positive intrinsic evaluation formulas apply to them in their own special circumstances.

Saints comprehend the immense inherent worth of inwardness, individuality, and spirituality to which worldlings are blind; they value intrinsic values intrinsically. Saints can also evaluate extrinsic things intrinsically. This enables them to perceive and relish the things of the world just as they are, but in a new, innocent, and unselfish light. All of us know what it is like to value *some* physical things intrinsically; we greatly cherish special material gifts or objects received or inherited from significant others; we know that gift-giving and receiving can combine the intrinsic with the extrinsic; we understand that *things* can be expressions of *love*. Saints see *all* positive realities as expressions of God's love—intrinsic people and animals, systemic beliefs, rules, laws, formulas, and rituals, and extrinsic objects, possessions, positions, the natural environment, and human behaviors. As St. Augustine said, "Whatever is, is good," according to its degree of being, but only the saints fully understand and appreciate this. Only the saints truly get it!

Positive value-combination-wholes can have more value than their component parts in isolation or merely added up separately. The wholes can be better than the sum of their parts. Dimensional values can be combined with one another in ways that either enhance value (compositions), decrease value (transpositions), or remain unchanged. A Valentines day gift of candy or flowers combines extrinsic physical objects—candy or flowers—with the intrinsic love of one person for another. It expresses that love, thereby increasing value. Here, the love of one person for another is combined with an extrinsic object to produce a new and greater value combination—a gift expressing and amplifying the love of one person for another.

In the book of Matthew, Jesus asks two closely related questions, "Which is greater: the gold, or the temple that has made the gold sacred?" (Matthew 23:17), and "Which is greater: the gift, or the altar that has made the gift sacred?" (Matthew 23:19) These words of Jesus can be analyzed axiologically. Temples and altars are value combinations; in them, systemic beliefs and intrinsic devotional spirituality are united with physical extrinsic structures. They *combine* systemic, intrinsic, and extrinsic values; and that *inclusive value* combination has more spiritual worth than the extrinsic gold or gift objects have *alone*. Temples and altars take extrinsically valuable gold and gifts into themselves and make them sacred, as parts of complex spiritual value combination wholes. United with spirituality, these systemic/extrinsic/intrinsic value combinations have much greater worth than gold or gift objects taken separately or in isolation.

Temples, altars, and gold viewed as "offerings" are extrinsic physical objects positively imbued or combined with systemic symbolic meanings. They are more than just extrinsic buildings, furniture, and gold alone. When functioning even deeper as something "sacred," another layer of value is added, God and the intrinsic, with its intense spiritual and social bonding and affection.

For many people, spiritual objects, symbols, and means of grace fail to function optimally. Someone may just see extrinsic church building, furnishings, ornaments, and cash, and fail to imbue them with symbolic spiritual meanings or values. Someone else may see both the extrinsic objects and their conceptual meanings but fail to integrate them into a profound intrinsic worship experience that encounters the sacred. The temple and the altar *should* function to make the gold and the gift sacred; they do so when functioning optimally, but this does not always happen, as we all well know. Sometimes, gold is just gold, not something offered freely to God. Sometimes, gold is not combined with spiritual beliefs and attitudes. Sometimes when gold is combined with spiritual beliefs and attitudes, the intrinsic level of sacredness, God's presence, is not quite reached. Saints have greatly enhanced capacities to see the systemic (symbols and beliefs) and the extrinsic (physical altars and offerings) within the context of the intrinsic (the sacred, the sacramental, the personal, the Divine). They can see all things as belonging to God, as pointing to God, as manifesting and symbolizing God's presence and glory, as existing in, before, and within God, and as valued by God.

Whole saints have it all, but not a worldly way. They are not ascetics of mere renunciation, but they may voluntarily adopt a relatively "low standard of living," measured by worldly standards of social status and material goods, in order to minimize the negative impact of their own existence upon other people and other forms of life. Saints intensely value all things, all living things, all physical things, but not egoistically. For worldlings, physical or material things personally owned and "improved" mean everything. Saints approach material things through a richer, higher, and ultimately more fulfilling kind of experiencing, a higher stage or degree of evaluative consciousness. In and through things, they find and worship God. They can simply let material things be or else give them away; they do not have to possess or "improve" them to delight in them and find God's presence in them. They can enjoy and relish things just as they are, not because or only when personally owned or flaunted.

Genuine aesthetic sensitivity is the un-self-interested intrinsic evaluation of perceptual objects and processes. Aesthetics may lead beyond worldly values and in the direction of saintliness if expanded into moral and spiritual sensitivity. That beauty can lead us to God is a very old and respected idea. Saints regain everything, even the physical and the bodily, even beauty, through their greatly enhanced capacities for evaluating and experiencing all things intrinsically, including extrinsic actions, objects, structures, and processes. To them, all things are sacred.

Worldly people are somewhat blind in their dealings with things, social roles and realities, and social hierarchies, even though worldly treasures mean everything to them. They inordinately finitize the significance of that which they value most. They tend to see everything merely as a means—mainly to enhancing their own short-sighted self-interests, narrowly understood, or to promoting the interests of a very few others about whom they really care. By contrast, saints experience things, social orders, and ideas as having incalculable spiritual significance. Their sensitivity to the measureless complexity, interrelatedness, and symbolic significance of natural objects and social processes far transcends narrow practical self-interests. Quite apart from security and self-aggrandizement, saints can perceive and value empirical entities and processes, as well as social and intellectual systems, in their vast internal complexity and external relatedness, and in their relations to God. They perceive, comprehend, and feel in depths that are hidden from non-saints. For saints, the doors of perception are cleansed, open, intrinsic, and fulfilling, whereas the perceptions of worldly people tend to be ego-centered, sordid, obstructed, crudely utilitarian, and ultimately unsatisfying. Worldlings do poorly what they do best—valuing the things of the world! For them, things have so few good-making characteristics; for saints, things have so many!

Søren Kierkegaard's lowest aesthetic stage along life's way, composed of "indifferent" extrinsic values and evaluations, is merely "dethroned" but not eliminated when higher ethical and religious stages of evaluative consciousness are attained. In advanced spiritual stages along life's way, intrinsic values and evaluations prevail. Of the more advanced ethico-religious stages, he wrote, "It does not follow by any means that the aesthetic is excluded....The ethical personality is concentrated in itself, so the aesthetic is absolutely excluded or excluded as the absolute, but relatively it is still left....The whole of the aesthetical comes back again in its relativity."[61] According to Kierkegaard, "The aesthetical returns again," after a person learns to "contemplate existence under ethical categories," and "only then does existence become beautiful,...only in this way can a man succeed in saving his soul and gaining the whole world, can succeed in using the world without abusing it."[62]

Holistic saints do not ignore the extrinsic or the systemic. They bring complex religious beliefs and devotional practices and habits with them when they evaluate the things of the world. Their cognitive orientation (perhaps temporarily suspended in peak intrinsic experiencing, perhaps not) colors the significance of everything that they experience. Under the aegis of their more advanced spiritual concepts and beliefs, their capacity for intrinsic evaluation extends to all things; but so much more is involved than aesthetics. They see things "*sub species aeternitas,*" as Robert Hartman suggested. This does not mean that everything exists or is predestined from eternity; it means that all things manifest or reflect everlasting realities, values, and evaluations in time. Things can become almost limitless in their symbolical significance, for everything (except evil) can be a metaphor for God. Everything can be a thin place through which God shines. All things are ultimately contingent upon God for the basic conditions of their existence, and all things are loved and pervaded by God. Saints are attuned to the infinite within the finite, to the divine within the mundane, to the whole within the parts, to the parts within the whole, to the omnipresence of God, to the sacredness of all in all. They strive to use the world minimally without abusing it. They get back everything that they renounce.

In his book on *St. Francis*, Nikos Kazantzakis gives these words to that saint: "God has become rain and is raining on the world. O Lord, what joy! What happiness! Look how earth, rain, and the odors of dung and the lemon trees all combine and become one with man's heart!"[63] Clearly, things, perceptual objects and processes, have far richer meanings for saints than for worldlings. Saints may actually attribute an infinite number of good-making properties to things by virtue of their relations with God. This may or may not be poetic exaggeration; but saints tend to talk and think in metaphors, not in straightforward prose, which is never adequate for saintly purposes. Just the right metaphors, at the right time, and in the right place, can help intrinsically to bridge the gap between us and God. Conceptual metaphors are moral and spiritual bridges to God and goodness.

Two of Buddhism's primary objectives are: (1) liberation from bondage to *samsara*, which is rebirth into the pluralistic and temporalistic mundane world of ordinary everyday things, processes, and people, and (2) the attainment of *nirvana*, the highest form of enlightenment, bliss, and blessedness. In Mahayana Buddhism, when the highest form of enlightenment is achieved, an enlightened person realizes that *samsara is nirvana*![64] Abraham Maslow's account of peak experiencing explains how and why. Take a look at it sometime for yourself.[65]

Thus surprisingly, saints are more, not less, sensitive to the value, meaningfulness, and worth of external perceptual entities, processes, and actions than men or women of the world. Enhanced evaluational sensitivity and imagination are integral to the saintly stage of evaluative consciousness. The exhilaration of saintly self-transcendence finds repeated expression in the world's greatest literature, religious and otherwise.

Not uncommonly, when extrinsic and systemic entities are intrinsically valued, we may speak of them, by metaphorical extension, as intrinsic values. When people identify themselves with works of art or with philosophical or theological systems, these extrinsic and systemic value-objects take on a kind of relational intrinsic worth as parts of the whole, "x's being intrinsically valued by person p." Non-conscious entities, the "things" of the world, including great works of art and the sublime in physical nature, do not have intrinsic worth simply in themselves, as do individuated centers or subjects of consciousness or experience. Yet, they may enter into and become parts of greater (more valuable) spiritual intrinsic wholes.

The Scope of Saintly Evaluation

The virtues which must be practiced, at least generally, by rude men, so that they may associate in a body, are those which are still recognized as the most important. But they are practiced almost exclusively in relation to the men of the same tribe; and their opposites are not regarded as crimes in relation to men of other tribes. No tribe could hold together if murder, robbery, treachery, &c., were common; consequently such crimes within the limits of the same tribe "are branded with everlasting infamy"; but excite no such sentiment beyond these limits.[66] Charles Darwin

The commandments of the decalogue contain a special precept about the honor due to our parents (Ex. 20:12). Therefore we ought to love more specially those who are united to us by ties of blood....We ought out of charity to love those who are more closely united to us more, both because our love for them is more intense, and because there are more reasons for loving them. Now intensity of love arises from the union of lover and beloved: and therefore we should measure the love of different persons according to the different kinds of union, so that a man is more loved in matters touching that particular union in respect of which he is loved. And, again, in comparing love to love we should compare one union with another. Accordingly we must say that friendship among blood relations is based upon their connection by natural origin, the friendship of fellow-citizens on their civic fellowship, and the friendship of those who are fighting side by side on the comradeship of battle. Wherefore in matters pertaining to nature we should love our kindred most, in matters concerning relations between citizens, we should prefer our fellow-citizens, and on the battlefield our fellow-soldiers.[67] St. Thomas Aquinas

True virtue most essentially consists in benevolence to Being in general. Or perhaps to speak more accurately, it is that consent, propensity and union of heart to Being in general, that is immediately exercised in a general good will.[68] Jonathan Edwards

'Thy neighbor'; that is, not only thy friend, thy kinsman, or thy acquaintance; not only the virtuous, the friendly, him that loves thee, that prevents or returns thy kindness; but every child of man, every human creature, every soul which God hath made: not excepting him whom thou has never seen in the flesh, whom thou knowest not, either by face or name; not excepting him whom thou knowest to be evil and unthankful, him that still despitefully uses and persecutes thee. Him thou shalt 'love as thyself'; with the same invariable thirst after his happiness in every kind, the same unwearied care to screen him from whatever might grieve or hurt either his soul or body.[69] John Wesley

> *But the stranger that dwelleth with you shall be unto you as one born among you, and thou shalt love him as thyself.* Leviticus 19:34.

The first two quotes above say something very different from the last three. Most real people, particularly those who received a decent measure of mothering or intrinsic nurturing as infants and children, are capable of some degree of intrinsic evaluation. Worldliness, ideology, and saintliness are axiological types to which actual people only approximate. By God's prevenient grace, most real but unsaintly people, even if predominately worldly, are capable of genuinely loving, having compassion for, identifying with, and making unselfish sacrifices for at least a few other people, their own "in crowd," but definitely not for everyone. Our initially limited capacity for intrinsic evaluation may spread and spill over into a keen aesthetic appreciation for works of art or for sublime natural vistas. And we may relate in wonder and awe to many works of human intellect. Still, when spiritually undeveloped, our loves are few, and we experience most of life and reality as dull, prosaic, mundane, and secular. God has made us restless...

Saintly people, by contrast, differ immensely from the rest of us in the *scope* of their capacity for intrinsic evaluation, in *how much* of everything and everyone they value intrinsically. This difference in scope is facilitated largely by their spiritual convictions and experiences. How do saintly people work out and express their relations with other people and with their non-human environments?

As anticipated by Charles Darwin, modern sociobiology and evolutionary psychology[70] tell us that although we are disposed to worldliness by nature and inheritance, we are nevertheless also social animals. We have a natural conscience of sorts that tells us the difference between right and wrong, and we have limited natural capacities for unselfishness, compassion, and empathy. Within limits, we are naturally disposed to be cooperative and altruistic, first on a reciprocal basis, eventually perhaps on a genuinely unselfish basis, with the kin and kind, mates and playmates, with whom we live and grow up. As we mature, our altruism and compassion may spread to members of slightly larger social in-groups. But this is usually as far it goes. Outsiders are beyond consideration, if not harshly considered. They have no moral standing with us.

Most "social contract" theorists of the origin of ethics and civilized society make the great mistake of basing this contract entirely on egoism or self-interests. The philosopher John Rawls is a good example of this. But egoism completely ignores our nature as social animals with inherent and sincere but limited capacities for unselfish interestedness in the interests of others. In genuine altruism, compassion, and empathy, my interests are in your interests; and my self-interests (interests possessed by myself) are partly constituted by your self-interests (what benefits you). This naturally unselfish part of myself (and yourself) may originally be quite meager, but it is open to growth and development, and by the grace of God we can choose to help make it so.

Most of us today are not significantly different from our hunter/gatherer ancestors with respect to the limited *scope* of our capacities for intrinsic evaluation. Our natural disposition to value intrinsically only a few persons who are close to us in life has immense survival value and evolutionary significance; but it does not make us saints, for its scope is too narrow, too provincial. As primatologist Franz de Waal acknowledges, "Human history furnishes ample evidence that moral principles are oriented to one's own group, and only reluctantly (and never even-handedly) applied to the outside world."[71] Darwin earlier said basically the same thing, as in the previous quote from him. The primary task of moral and spiritual development, the task of becoming a saint, consists largely in overcoming the naturally limited *scope* of our capacity for intrinsic evaluation.

Jonathan Edwards anticipated the findings of Darwin and contemporary sociobiologists and evolutionary psychologists. He did not contend that "natural men" under sin are total egoists with no conscience and no capacity at all for loving others unselfishly. No, in their natural state, all human beings have an inborn moral sense that discerns the difference between good and evil, right and wrong; and most people are capable of genuinely loving and making unselfish sacrifices for a small handful of other people. As Edwards conceded, some people "by natural instinct or by some other means, have a determination of mind to union and benevolence to a particular person or private system, which is but a small part of the universal system of being." A person's natural propensity toward unity with and benevolence toward others may extend beyond mere self-love and take in "half a dozen more, and...extend so far beyond his own single person as to take in his children and family." It may reach "further still to a larger circle," but it still "falls infinitely short of the universal system, and is exclusive of being in general."[72] Natural benevolence and good will are "limited to a particular circle of beings." Because they are narrow in scope, these natural virtues are radically different from the universal "true virtue" of the saints, Edwards believed.

Our natural propensity to take care of ourselves first, then those closest to us, is not necessarily a bad thing. St. Thomas Aquinas thought this to be a law of nature ordained by God. This really is the most efficient way imaginable to get the job done. We can take care of ourselves and those closest to us in life much more effectively and efficiently than we can take care of people living down the street or on the other side of the world. We can recognize and respect the basic human rights of all much more easily than we can feel and act upon love for all. Even love must be expressed concretely to specific individuals with all their definiteness and distinctive personal stories, preferences, projects, and local commitments. It also expresses the lover's own personal responsibilities to those most affected by what he or she actually does. The real spiritual problem for most people is that moral concern, compassion, and benevolence stop too soon. Spiritual development expands the scope of our loves far beyond kin and kind. It goes far beyond the call of ordinary duty and moves us toward what Jonathan Edwards called "true virtue."

True virtue "consists in benevolence *to Being in general*;...it is that consent, propensity and union of heart to Being in general, that is immediately exercised in a general good will."[73] True virtue "consists in agreement or consent of being to being,"[74] Edwards said. It is general or universal, which means that it extends to everyone and everything that has being (except for that which is hostile to the being of others or self—intrinsic, instrumental, and systemic evil). The scope of intrinsic evaluation for non-saints is inordinately finite, but in the saints it approaches infinity. The scope of *philosophical* ethics is also universal (as in Kant's ethics, for example); but most real people are no closer to living philosophically than they are to living spiritual or saintly lives. Most people don't, but saints and many philosophers do make the "inner circle" all inclusive. Saints don't just talk or theorize about it; they really live it. A few philosophers may even be or become saints, however improbable!

Jonathan Edwards recognized the limited benevolence of most ordinary people. Our constricted natural benevolence correlates with our deep and abiding propensity to divide people into superiors/inferiors and insiders/outsiders, and with our dispositions to detest, exploit, humiliate, repress, and eliminate subordinates and strangers or outsiders. As Edwards remarked, even if genuinely unselfish, constricted natural benevolence "will set a person against general existence, and make him an enemy to it"; it will "pursue the interests of its particular object in opposition to general existence"; it "puts down being in general."[75] By nature, our loves are few, and this can have extremely harmful and evil results.

Once the constricted scope of our natural capacity for intrinsic evaluation is understood, we can easily comprehend how Nazis, Mafia bosses, and hit men can be loving and affectionate parents and devoted family men with good "family values." Their capacity for intrinsic evaluation is not non-existent; it is just extremely confined or limited in scope. Loving and affectionate villains can be "good providers" for those they love; but to be good providers, they callously exploit, deprive, disdain, or annihilate other people, outsiders. In order to exploit their victims so viciously, they compartmentalize or develop multiple personalities; they reduce outsiders to systemic nothings, to nobodies, or to mere means to ends not their own. They deliberately choose to know as little about them, their virtues and talents, their sufferings, and their deprivations, as possible. Only then can they treat them extrinsically as mere means, or systemically as mere numbers or statistics. Their ideologies tell them that people don't count.

Where do we get our general hostility to outsiders and the paltry limits that we naturally impose on membership in our own ethical community? Contemporary evolutionary psychologists and sociobiologists ground these flaws in human nature as it evolved in, through, and from our hunter/gatherer ancestors, whose genetic image we still bear. Tribalism had survival value for early human beings. As Hans Mohr indicated, "We are (almost) ideally equipped by nature for life in the Pleistocene [Ice] and the Stone Age, but ill-adapted for conditions in the modern world.

On the way to a cultivated paradise we are always stumbling over our ancient genes."[76] Mohr further explained,

> The dark side of our biological nature has grown up within the brutality of conflict between groups: the bloody battle for existence at a time when our "primary nature" was developing, between the tribe and merciless Nature—but above all between groups of people. Endless fighting for tribal integrity and dominance determined the lives of our forefathers. All favorable ecological niches were already occupied in early Neolithic times. The carrying capacity in relationship to the productivity of those times had been reached. Expansion could only take place at the cost of other groups. The brutality of group conflict is well documented by both prehistory and early historical tradition. Most territorial conquests in the history of *Homo sapiens* were accompanied by genocide. Wholesale murder—*wherever* one cares to open the horrifying pages of our history! The victory of the children of Israel over the Midianites, so graphically described in the 31st Chapter of Numbers, will serve us as an example....Xenophobia and a militant sense of territorial right are everywhere characteristic of human conduct. The cultural modification of these propensities should not deceive us into forgetting that they are only with difficulty overcome, lying dormant in our nature and at any moment ready to break out.[77]

Jane Goodall discovered that we share our genocidal genes with our nearest primate relatives, the chimpanzees, who rage lethal war periodically on the nearby clans with whom they compete for territory and females.[78] Revenge is sweet for them, also, as it is for us, unless we are saints. Do spiritual and moral saints ever *completely* overcome their natural worldly passions for aggression against those who have what we want, and for revenge against others who have wronged them? In all likelihood, no human being is ever perfect in this or any other respect, but the saints overcome aggressiveness and revenge far more than the rest of us. They know how to make peace and to forgive others time and again, while relying on God's willingness to forgive their own lingering inability to forgive. They seek peace and reconciliation, not revenge. They are peacemakers, not warmakers. They build up, not tear down. They repudiate the distinction between insiders and outsiders.

So, the theologians were right all along; something is seriously and stubbornly defective about us human beings in our normal, natural, undeveloped, "original" state. The "natural man and woman" exist in a state of war, not against all, but against most, that is, against outsiders. They have a very long way to go down the lengthy road of spiritual growth and development. Patricia A. Williams, an insightful contemporary philosophical theologian, identifies the exceedingly limited scope of our natural moral concerns, together with our natural hostility to outsiders, with original sin itself. She writes:

> People do love themselves and their relatives more than those in equal or greater need. It is this fact about humanity that strongly supports the existence of original

sin, the sin inherent in human nature due to the action of natural selection, the sin of exclusive self-love leading to self-aggrandizement, nepotism, and greed; the sin of exclusive in-group pride, promoting out-group belittlement, deceit, racism, slavery, and genocide.[79]

Darwin, de Waal, Mohr, Williams, Jonathan Edwards, and so many others, discerned correctly that "by nature" we do not extend morality beyond kinship and tribe. Against such human nature, philosophers of ethical "universalizability" and saints of "true virtue" have been fighting a losing battle. Most human beings do not acknowledge in attitude and practice that *all people* have equal moral rights, are neighbors to be loved as we love ourselves, and should be treated as we would have them treat us. We do not naturally value *all* human beings intrinsically, much less all sentient beings, and even less all living things and the whole of God's creation.

Our natural moral provincialism has as much psychological force today as it did with our hunter/gatherer ancestors. It underlies the prejudicial ideologies and practices that dominate the lives of humankind, ranging from narrowly conceived "family values" to religious exclusivism, holy wars, terrorist assassinations, suicide bombings, road rage, cruel and pervasive snobbery, high school and beyond social cliques, bullying, condescension, snobbishness, and the violence and bloodshed of street gangs. It is present in regionalism, nationalism, patriotism, colonialism, slavery, racism, terrorism, Nazi and Serbian style "ethnic cleansing," sexism, ageism, and homophobia. This ancient dark side of human nature is expressed today in our insatiable appetites for war and genocide, holy or not, in our abiding suspicion of and animosity toward outsiders, strangers, and illegal aliens. It underlies our persisting propensity to mistrust, misunderstand, disvalue, deprive, and destroy those who are beyond the pale of our pathetically limited capacities for true virtue, sympathy, compassion, understanding, loyalty, and love toward all.

Today we try to re-channel the grim endowments of the "natural man and woman" into less destructive activities like violent entertainment, intensely competitive business practices, ferocious athletic contests, and abiding rivalries, athletic and otherwise. Violent television programs and movies feed our natural appetite for aggression and brutality hour after hour, businesses try to "kill the competition," and the objective in athletic contests is to "murder the bums." Most of us have not overcome the dark side of human nature. The saints have, or at least they are well on the way.

Original sin consists partly in indifference, but mainly of powerful natural dispositions to be disrespectful, violent, and barbaric toward others, especially subordinates and outsiders. Facing honestly up to this in no way commits us many things usually associated with original sin—the literal existence of Adam and Eve in a Garden of Eden without death, struggle, or pain. Yet, we really do have a natural bent to sinning that keeps us from loving God wholeheartedly and from loving others, especially strangers and outsiders, as we love ourselves. These dark features of human nature do block the ascent of our souls to God and obstruct the creation of a universal moral/spiritual kingdom of God on earth. With much personal effort, supplemented by divine grace and the ongoing social support of saintly communities, the dark side of human nature can be overcome to a significant degree. No matter how low we start on the scale of ethico-religious development, we are responsible and justly blamable if we do not try our best to become holistic saints.

As John Wesley believed, even when they can't do it in their finitude, saints are at least disposed to love everyone, including people they have never met. Human finitude and persisting sinfulness prevent real saints from actually loving every individual person whosoever. The best saints don't even know most people on earth, and no one knows specific members of future generations. Saints have many special affections for and duties to people close to them in life that they do not have to everyone on earth, as St. Thomas Aquinas rightly discerned. Yet, we recognize as saints those persons who most closely approximate the ideal of empathetic and compassionate self-identification with the well- or ill- being (in compassion) of all others. *Saintliness consists largely in the inclusive range of the saints' capacities for intrinsic evaluation, in the vast scope of what Jonathan Edwards called their "holy affections."*

The Language of Saintly Evaluation

> *In formal axiology, the language of intrinsic value is a private language, which does not mean that it is no language, but that it is a language in a definite logical sense: that of using singular concepts whose intensional structure is infinite in a precisely defined way.*[80] Robert S. Hartman

> *Things corresponding to [singular concepts] are unique. Uniqueness is the intensional counterpart to extensional singularity. The predicates of such intensions may be words of infinite meaning, that is, words which may mean any other word in the language. Such words are metaphors. A metaphor is a set of predicates used as a variable. Hence it can, in principle, replace every other word of the language....A conjunction of a finite number of metaphors is a poem or a poetic novel. The fulfillment by a thing of a singular concept, understood in this sense, constitutes intrinsic value. Intrinsic value is the valuation of poets and artists, lovers and mystics, magicians and advertisers, chefs de cuisine and politicians, creative theologians and scientists. It is emphatic—and empathic— valuation.*[81] Robert S. Hartman

> *Abstract, verbal, unambiguous communication may be less effective for some purposes than metaphorical, poetic, esthetic, primary process techniques.*[82] Abraham Maslow

What is the basic language of saintly intrinsic evaluation? It employs two linguistic forms, (1) singular concepts or unicepts, and (2) metaphors. Each has a slightly different function within complex intrinsic conceptualization.

(1) Singular concepts are *proper names* and the *personal pronouns* that serve as variables for proper names. Such words have intensional (conceptual) meanings, and they do far more than just designate or pick out particulars. The full intensional meaning of a proper name, or its corresponding pronoun when so applied, is the total set of integrated predicates that correlate with all the actual properties of the individual person named, plus her or his (largely unknown and undecided) potential properties that may eventually be actualized. In the broadest sense, it includes everything that a person was, is, and might become, especially everything with which he or she profoundly identifies. It covers a person's entire nature, experiences, thoughts, feelings, actions, and history—the complete story of his or her life.

The full meaning of our lives is *the full meaning of our individual names*. That meaning cannot be expressed merely in terms of our common humanity or nature, our rationality, our morality, our positions and social roles, our thoughts and beliefs, or our general metaphysical properties like being and becoming, actuality and potentiality, effect and cause. It is all of these and more; it is *our uniquely integrated total property inventory*. In practice, we never really know ourselves completely, much less other persons, partly because there is just too much to know, partly because our memories are so weak and selective, and partly because as living persons we are still in the making. But, the more we know and deeply appreciate the full depths of ourselves and others as unique individuals, the more meaningful and saintly is our existence.

What is our integrated total property inventory? It includes both our descriptive property inventory and our evaluational or axiological property inventory. *Descriptively*, we have all the qualities and relations of our systemic thoughtful selves, our extrinsic practical selves, and our intrinsic loving selves. These properties are so vast that they are beyond our comprehension, though comprehending them (self-knowledge) is worth a try. Our integrated total selves partly consist in our *evaluational* or axiological selves, especially our capacities for identifying intensely with selected ideals, practices, realities, and future possibilities. But what are the limits of our capacities for identification? Whatever they are, they set the limits of our intrinsic evaluational property inventory (but not our total property inventory). William James was very interested in our evaluational identifying-with properties, and he discussed them at length in his *Principles of Psychology*. He introduced the topic with these words:

> In its widest possible sense, however, a man's Self is the sum total of all that he CAN call his, not only his body and his psychic powers, but his clothes and his house, his wife and children, his ancestors and friends, his reputation and works, his lands and horses, and yacht and bank account. All these things give him the same emotions. If they wax and prosper, he feels triumphant; if they dwindle and die

away, he feels cast down,—not necessarily in the same degree for each, but in much the same way for all.[83]

James did not connect these thoughts with saintliness, but he recognized that and how people properly define themselves, usually inordinately, through that with which they identify. In this sense, the saints have or are the richest possible selves, and non-saints have or are relatively impoverished selves. The saints take all the good-making properties of everything and everyone into themselves and make them their own. Saints intensely identify with all goodness, wherever it is, and no matter whose it is, and make it a part of themselves. They unite spiritually, morally, and evaluationally with all good-making properties in all. So what kind of a self are you? To answer you must know yourself, including everything with which you identify and make fully your own. The quest for self-knowledge attempts to know the complete meaning of our proper names.

(2) In addition to proper names and personal pronouns, *metaphors* belong conspicuously to saintly language, largely because of their role in intrinsic evaluation. "Metaphorical language," as broadly understood here, includes similes, myths, poetry, and all symbolic or non-literal expressions. Metaphorical language, said Hartman, functions like a variable in logic; it is an empty place marker that simultaneously means both everything and nothing,[84] but this needs to be qualified somewhat because metaphors do have some definiteness of meaning. Metaphors like "a peach of a girl" or "a peach of a peach" (Hartman's examples) are used to stretch the mind, stimulate the imagination, inspire insights, establish connections between the familiar and the unfamiliar, express and evoke powerful feelings of empathy, love, and deep concern, motivate to action, and help bring about personal identification and intrinsic evaluation.

Of course, degrading, devaluing, systemic and transpositional metaphors also exist in great profusion, as does prosaic poetry. Some metaphors are employed systemically to reduce rather than to increase sensitivity to value. Aaron Katcher and Gregory Wilkins explain how this can happen when familial metaphors are extended to cover animals.

> But the use of the category "kin" to describe our reciprocal relationships with animals or plants implies the category of "not kin." And "not kin" can devolve into the category of "vermin" and remorseless destruction can follow.
> The category of vermin implies that certain animals or plants (weeds are plant vermin) can or must be exterminated. There is no longer any concern for their persistence. Extinction becomes a desirable end. Our tendency to view an animal or plant as utterly bad, or unnecessary, or valueless is accentuated by the metaphorical use of animals and nature that is so fundamental a part of all languages. In metaphor a being is stripped of its behavioral complexity and refined into the reflection of a single attribute, even one as broad as "good" or "bad."[85]

Using metaphors or any form of language to degrade, though common, is morally and spiritually questionable. In our rude and inconsiderate social order, demeaning language runs rampant, but here we will concentrate on those positive moral and spiritual metaphors that enrich rather than diminish what and how we value others and all things. We turn now to intrinsically constructive metaphors, to intrinsically positive poetic or symbolic language.

Looseness, ambiguity, indefiniteness, and variability do indeed characterize metaphorical language; but metaphors are not infinitely loose, ambiguous, indefinite, and variable. Usually, metaphors are carefully chosen to connote and communicate *some* definiteness, along with much openness, of meaning. Effective metaphors hang upon one or more points of resemblance. They are bridges to somewhere, not to nowhere, or to everywhere. Good metaphors have some degree of preciseness and appropriateness. They combine definiteness with indefiniteness. They can be analyzed and re-stated either in other metaphors or in non-metaphorical "demythologized" discourse. When we call a girl "a peach," we intend to suggest that she is sweet (another metaphor), attractive, luscious, beautiful, and so on; we mean to communicate very positive things about her. A peachy girl is definitely not ugly, fetid, unattractive, aesthetically unappealing, and the like; so metaphors that communicate effectively cannot be given just any interpretation whatsoever. They are not just empty place markers into which anything whatsoever can be inserted. Their meanings can be misconstrued or misinterpreted, which would not be possible if they literally mean both everything and nothing. In interpreting them we can make hermeneutical mistakes, focus on irrelevant similarities, or fail to make or get the point.

The constricted language of ordinary prose is exceptionally inadequate, saints find, to express, communicate, and bring about profound intrinsic appreciation for and identification with the practically limitless complexity, significance, beauty, truth, and goodness of concretely existing beings, human and non-human. Prosaic meanings are too circumscribed to express the practically inexhaustible richness of good-making properties in concrete realities, especially personal realities. Literal language does not do justice to the immense aesthetic, moral, and religious sensitivity of the saint's powers of evaluation. Profoundly spiritual persons tend to use language metaphorically, mythically, or poetically rather than prosaically.

Words in ordinary speech are given extraordinary meanings and powers when used as metaphors. For both speakers and hearers, metaphorical symbols can indeed stretch minds, stimulate imaginations, inspire new insights, persuade intellects, establish connections between the familiar and the unfamiliar, express and evoke powerful feelings like empathy and concern, motivate actions, and precipitate personal identification-with. Metaphors can provoke, communicate, and express intrinsic evaluations.

Metaphors may personify what they depict in order to express or evoke intrinsic evaluation effectively. Our wives, husbands, dogs, guns, and pickup trucks may have metaphorical pet names as well as proper names. Concrete personal individuality is the original and proper domain of intrinsic values and the native home of intrinsic evaluations. Personifying words and images are often used metaphorically to move non-personal entities over into the realm of the intrinsic and facilitate their intrinsic evaluation. Using language metaphorically, St. Francis personified *things* in order to express and communicate his non-worldly intrinsic appreciation for "Brother Sun," "Sister Moon," "Brother Wind," "Sister Water,""Brother Fire," "Mother Earth," "Sister Sickness," and so on.

Yet, a word of caution is in order. When rampant imagination and exuberance personify and assign individuated awareness to everything, this verges upon animistic superstition. At times, intrinsic evaluations need strong corrective doses of tough-minded systemic and extrinsic reflection. Of course, valuing everything intrinsically as sacred (but not necessarily as animated or finitely ensouled) is not superstition; it is a Divine gift if God is everywhere and all in all. Only in that theological sense do holistic saints personify everything. They need not believe that aggregates like rocks, rivers, and trees have their own finite conscious or unconscious spirits or souls.

Worldlings use ordinary language prosaically and literally to manage, finitize, and diminish the significance of people and things; saints use ordinary words metaphorically to celebrate, rejoice in, and amplify significance. Saints have poetry in their vocabularies as well as in their souls. *Purely intrinsic* saints (who do not actually exist) would *never* use ordinary prose at all; they would speak only in metaphors of praise, delight, and thanksgiving without ceasing! Music, myth, and the poetic language of the King James translation of the Bible (purged of its errors, of course) would be the languages of heaven (metaphorically speaking)!

What musicians, poets, mythologists, prophets, preachers, and saints want to say always exceeds the bounds of ordinary, empirical, literalistic language. They stretch the meaning of ordinary sounds and words and make them mean much more than they usually connote. Saintly words say more than they can say. Human words and thoughts are never large enough for God or the whole realm of "Divine things." The saints use mundane class-words that apply conventionally to many similar things to relate conceptually to realities that are utterly unique, mysterious, and incommensurably precious. For saints, good art, including the art of words, celebrates inwardness, uniqueness, concreteness, and sacredness. Historically, many saints excelled in music and the language arts, but there is no good reason why they should not excel in any art forms that celebrate the richness and sacred significance of concrete reality just as it is. Even juggling and tweeting can be sacred if God is all in all.

Saintly Spiritual Metaphors

> *For ordinary consciousness, for consciousness in its ordinary formation, religion exists essentially in these modes, as a content that primarily presents itself in*

sensible forms, as a series of actions and sensible determinations that follow one another in time and then occur side by side in space. The content is empirical, concrete, and manifold, its combination residing partly in spatial contiguity and partly in temporal succession. But at the same time this content has an inner aspect—there is spirit within it that acts upon spirit.[86] G. W. F. Hegel

Every *theology is dependent for the clarification of its concepts upon a pretheological understanding of man that, as a rule, is determined by some philosophical tradition.*[87] Rudolf Bultman

Theology does its reflective and constructive work by way of metaphor. The etymology of the word "metaphor" is helpful: the Greek meta, *"across, over, beyond," and* pherein, *"to bear or carry." Metaphor, we may say, is the use of an evocative representation of something from our common experience to "carry us over" toward experiential participation in something otherwise not accessible to our experiencing.*[88] James W. Fowler

Metaphorical language is not only the language of poets proper, but of all those who want to express intrinsic value, lovers and mystics, magicians and advertisers, chefs de cuisine and politicians, theologians and scientists.[89] Robert S. Hartman

Metaphorical language is the language of the Bible.[90] Robert S. Hartman

According to the philosopher Hegel,[91] religious language is typically that of myth, but he did not intend to belittle religious language when he so characterized it. He treated myths very affirmatively and sympathetically. He did not equate myth with falsehood or deception, as we often do. Mythical language, he thought, expresses the most profound religious concepts and feelings through sensory images employed metaphorically. Mythical language is the figurative, sensory, representational, metaphorical expression of profound non-sensory truths about spiritual reality. When myths are taken literally, the spiritual is lost, and only sensory meanings remain. So, religious myths, religious language, should not be taken literally! And we should not be fundamentalists! Where more precise thinking is called for, the truths embedded in myths should be re-expressed, if possible, in a more adequate language that does justice to their spiritual meanings and feelings without confusing the spiritual with the purely sensual, as worldlings and literalists are inclined to do. Of course, Hegel wanted to transpose everything into his own philosophy; and we do not what to make that mistake!

"Demythologizing," as it is called today, tries to derive more exact ideas from ancient myths, but some religious thinkers have reservations about its success. H. Richard Niebuhr feared that all demythologizing is just re-mythologizing into the myths of our own century or time and place.[92] In some sense, this is clearly not true; meanings in figurative language can often be abstracted successfully and reexpressed adequately in less ambiguous and misleading non-figurative language. But Niebuhr may have meant only that when we try to connect the "literal truths" of our own time and place with the figurative mythical and metaphorical language of the past, we never completely escape cultural relativism, our own finitude, and the need for Divine judgment and correction. This is a valid point. Nevertheless, some of our modern myths, many from the natural sciences, for example, can be and usually are much more effective, precise, and accurate than ancient ones. Some are much less misleading, much clearer, much better thought out, and much better confirmed by experience than the myths of yore, taken literally.

Extreme skeptics claim that we don't know anything about anything, but they can react practically to such doubts in at least two different ways. One is that since we can't know anything, we can't prove anything, so we should not believe anything. The other is that since we can't know anything, we can't disprove anything, so we can believe anything we want to believe. Either no one can prove us right, so nothing goes, or no one can prove us wrong, so anything goes. Both approaches commit the *ad ignorantium* fallacy, drawing conclusions from ignorance or knowing nothing. Once we realize that no conclusions follow logically from ignorance, we have already moved away from extreme skepticism and are appealing to something that we actually know. There must be a happy medium somewhere between these two responses to extreme skepticism. What is it?

Even at their best, philosophy and theology formulate systematically only the philosophical and religious truths that we can comprehend in our own time and place. To a degree, Hegel was right: "It is absurd to fancy that a philosophy can transcend its contemporary world as it is to fancy that an individual can overleap his own age, jump over [the island of] Rhodes."[93] Systematic theology has the same limits. Still, we can try, and some tries are better than others. We can and should give it our best shot. Creativity often transcends the given and the expected quite successfully, especially with the help of metaphors! We don't have all the answers, but we have made some philosophical and theological progress. God may reveal himself more clearly today than in the past as we learn to think about God more clearly. Divine revelations may not yet have come to an end. God may still have more to show and tell.

Charles Sanders Peirce's "fallibilism," as he called it, accurately affirms that "Our knowledge is never absolute but always swims, as it were, in a continuum of uncertainty and indeterminacy."[94] A continuum is infinite, Peirce realized, and so is the uncertainty of all human knowledge; but this does not excuse us from doing the very best that we can. We really can push back some of the darkness that surrounds us. We must be as logical, precise, thorough, clear-headed, consistent, comprehensive, creative, and competent as possible when doing value theory, philosophy, metaphysics, and systematic theology. We should also be as metaphorical or poetic as possible when doing devotional theology and practice. Ideally, even devotional language should be grounded in a sound systematic theology that seriously thinks as clearly as possible about the reality and nature of God.

Our most careful systemic efforts in theology and philosophy can yield only an enlightened faith, not certainty or omniscience. We can push back the darkness, but not all the way to infinity. As best we can, we must decide how to relate to, evaluate, and identify ourselves with enlightened faith and to accept and not browbeat ourselves if we are believers in the face of uncertainty. Now we can understand why God values faith so much, and why we should ourselves: when all is said and done, there isn't anything else! Not even if it is the measly impoverished faith of a naturalist or a skeptic! Yet, all does need to be said and done, and we should not give up too quickly on trying to understand and think clearly about divine things. Enlightened religious faith cannot be reduced to value theory, even though values and evaluations are essential to such enlightenment. Spiritual and philosophical truth may coincide ultimately with beauty and goodness, but they are not perfectly identical. Arguments, evidence-giving procedures, conceptual analysis, reflective insights and intuitions, and creative inspirations or revelations are all integral to enlightened faith and to rationality itself, broadly understood. As Thomas Jefferson discerned, we are accountable not for the rightness but for the uprightness of our decisions about what and how to believe.[95] By degrees, reason is always infused with faith, and faith is always infused with reason.

In religious contexts, ordinary words do not have their ordinary literal meanings. Spirituality gives them uncanny meanings. The scriptures use language metaphorically, symbolically, mythically. Saintly religion was never fundamentalistic or literalistic about religious language. It understands heaven, hell, and the kingdom of God in mystical and social but not in purely literal sensory terms. Jesus frequently used words metaphorically, not literally. When he said we should our neighbors as ourselves, he did not mean for us to take "neighbor" literally, meaning only those who live next to us, or at least very nearby. No, "neighbor" for him meant "every child of God," as John Wesley put it, every person on earth. Jesus also corrected the young man who tried to take literally his metaphor of being "born again." This happens not literally and physically but metaphorically and spiritually.

Saints know perfectly well that heaven contains no literal pearly gates and streets of gold, and hell contains no literal fire and brimstone. Heaven is being ultimately with and in God, and hell is being ultimately without God; but even these powerful expressions have extraordinary meanings. Saintly religion employs ordinary language to conceive of and express things that are not ordinarily conceivable and expressible. Being ultimately in and with God involves a plurality of souls sharing a profound and harmonious communion and union with God and with one another, but in this world this happens only in the midst of great uncertainty. Heaven is not a purely sensory paradise, even if the saints are re-embodied in glorified, resurrected, and perceptible bodies. Nor is it purely systemic emptiness with no objects to revere, for God in his fullness is there with and in the saints. The ultimate treasures are mysterious, spiritual, non-sensory, and mythical. The saints use sensory imagery, things seen, to think and talk metaphorically about things unseen. Religious metaphors are ways of thinking and talking about realities that are too mysterious and tremendous for ordinary words.

To some degree, most of us can demythologize sensory, metaphorical, religious language without great difficulty. When God is called a "rock" and a "fortress" (Psalms 18:2), even professed biblical literalists have enough good sense not to take these words literally. Most of us realize that these figures of speech mean that God is powerful, enduring, reliable, foundational, and protective. Just how much so is another matter, and getting to the depths of this one moves us up to another level of theological abstraction and reflection, one that employs more exact but still imprecise technical, systematic, non-sensory, non-metaphorical terms like "omnipotence," "everlasting," "eternal," "morally immutable," and "triumphant over evil" (perhaps ultimately but clearly not immediately). To deal with these issues and with others like human responsibility, freedom, spontaneity, the actual existence of evil, and why good people suffer, we translate our theological metaphors into very abstract philosophical notions like "being" and "becoming," "substance," "attribute," "accident" (Aristotle and St. Thomas Aquinas), or "existential situation," "authenticity," "personal responsibility," "nothingness," "demythologizing," "existential interpretation" (Martin Heidegger and Rudolf Bultman), or "actual occasions," "events," "creativity," "freedom," and the "primordial" or "consequent" natures of God (Alfred North Whitehead, Charles Hartshorne, and John B. Cobb, Jr.). Such high abstractions, and many others like "theodicy" and "eschatology," are quite unavoidable for those who would think carefully, deeply, clearly, and systematically about theological issues. But these are not the words or language of worship and devotion. For that, metaphors work much better.

Bridging the gap between myth, metaphor, and systematic theory runs the risk of remythologizing, but some myths and metaphors are definitely more appropriate and much less misleading than others. Metaphors at any level of abstraction may be misinterpreted, but no viable alternative exists to using the conceptual framework that we find most meaningful and adequate in our own time, place, and stage of cognitive and spiritual development. We can only do our best, not better than our best. Selecting a philosophy or theology from the available menu is never an entirely rational process. It depends in part on each person's historical circumstances and personal proclivities and values. Here, self-knowledge is vitally significant. Your philosophy and theology depends heavily on who you are, and who you are depends on what and how you value. So who are you? What and how do you value? Ultimately, all philosophical and theological commitment is autobiography.

Philosophers nicely illustrate this. To which thinkers did our philosophy professors expose us as being worthy of serious consideration? Graduate students usually take seriously what their professors took seriously. Were we educated, by the grace of God, in an environment that made Whiteheadian process philosophy a live option for us; or were we stuck with something really cruddy like David Hume, Martin Heidegger, Ludwig Wittgenstein, Logical Positivism, John Dewey, or Jacques

Derrida? Of course, all of them are well worth studying, so long as the philosophical curriculum is balanced with the study of less worldly or skeptical thinkers, but this does not always happen. Many departments of philosophy and theology or religious studies adhere rigidly to narrow party lines, often worldly and naturalistic, or systemic and abstruse, sometimes fundamentalistic, sometimes openminded. Fortunately, the worst of this was not so at The University of Tennessee, where I taught for over thirty years. We were always free to do our own thing without censures or pressures to conform, but this is not the case everywhere. Even philosophers are pressured to conform to the fads and fashions of their own time, place, and department. The degree to which they succumb or resist depends ultimately on who they are and what and how they value.

Philosophical and theological metaphors can be drawn from all aspects of life and human experience. Different metaphors resonate for different people; some are lively in some places and times but deadly in others. Today's urban children have never seen sheep may profit little from "The Lord is my shepherd"; neither may those who know from life on real farms that shepherds protect sheep in order to mature and fatten them for slaughter! Similes and metaphors are always imprecise and are easily misinterpreted; someone may seize upon the wrong element of resemblance. Children whose fathers died before they were old enough to know them, or whose fathers abused and abandoned them, or who are raised entirely by single mothers, cannot fully appreciate "Our Father..." Still, personal and familial metaphors like "Person," "Spirit," "Father," "Mother," "Son," "Daughter," "Sister," and "Brother" are usually very potent.

Many metaphors from nature are perennial spiritual favorites and usually resonate—"light" and "darkness," "day" and "night," "winter" and "spring," "roots" and "fruits," "gold" and "dross," "pearls" and "pigs," "diamonds" and "dung." Political metaphors that were correct in biblical times are dated in our own. Would God as "Governor" work today? Does God as "King," "Lord," or "Prince" stir many hearts in democratic societies? God as "President" would be ludicrous for most of us because most Presidents we have known during our lifetimes had too many imperfections. We are not likely to hear: "The Lord is my President; I shall not want." Even in a democracy, the image of "Citizen Jesus" would be prosaic, irrelevant, and inefficacious. An excessively systemic "God as the World Wide Web" might work for many today! Many respond very positively to football analogies and metaphors, but others are turned off by them. If you have not noticed, there are no football analogies or metaphors in the Bible. Ministers, priests, rabbis, theologians, and philosophers sadly discern that they cannot be and say all things to all people, that their homilies and similes will not resonate with all hearts and minds.

Some intellectuals may attend religious services and read devotional literature expecting religious language to be employed always with the precision, clarity, abstraction, and accuracy of systematic theology or the philosophy of religion. For everything there is a season; systematic theology has its time and a place, but probably not in worship services or devotional literature where narratives, metaphors, and myths are much more effective. Once the metaphorical nature of much religious language is recognized and appreciated, many of the problems that intellectual have with religious discourse should just dissolve and disappear. Even intellectuals must recognize that many good things (intrinsic and extrinsic values) are much more valuable than beliefs and words (systemic values), metaphorical or not.

In devotional discourses, metaphors cannot be so irrelevant, deviant, imprecise, or indefinite that they turn people off or fail to communicate anything, but different people are turned on and off by different imagery, and it will always be so. Devotees gravitate toward particular religious communities that use metaphors congenial to their own spiritual values, ideas, beliefs, and practices. Devotionally, and without taking everything literally, sermons, songs, prayers, hymns, anthems, creeds, confessions, offerings, rituals, sacraments, and ceremonies celebrate the intrinsic worth of individuals and facilitate and renew the intrinsic evaluation of God, divine things, and our fellow creatures. Effective devotional practices and discourses bring us to the love of God, of one another, and of all of God's creation. Systemic-minded scholars, adept at the intricacy and lucidity of philosophical or systematic theology, still need the myths, metaphors, and narratives of devotional theology to express, evoke, and communicate their love for God as All in all.

As contemporary evolutionary psychology allows, we are by nature capable of loving, of evaluating intrinsically; but we naturally or usually love only members of our own family, clan, or tribe. Both secular philosophical ethicists and religious moralists attempt to draw us out of our moral parochialism and expand or universalize the scope of our moral concerns. To accomplish this, metaphors drawn from the family, the hard core of intrinsic social experience, have always been powerful and helpful—ever since Alexander the Great first introduced the idea of *universal* human "brotherhood" in order to further his territorial ambitions. The biblical metaphor of God as universal "Father" helps to bridge the enormous psychological and moral gaps between the immediate clan and all the rest of humanity; so do metaphors of universal brotherhood and sisterhood. The still-in-clan metaphor of "neighbor" expands the scope of love, of intrinsic evaluation, beyond the immediate family; it can be stretched metaphorically, as Jesus did, far beyond clan, tribe, race, and nationality; but "enemy" really pushes the envelope!

To expand and intensify our intrinsic spiritual sensitivity, narratives, metaphors, poetry, and myths tend to work well, but not always perfectly. Much religious language functions both metaphorically and effectively: it stretches minds, stimulates imaginations, provokes novel insights, persuades intellects, establishes connections between the familiar and the unfamiliar, expresses and evokes powerful feelings of empathy and ultimate concern, motivates action, and facilitates personal identification with objects of spiritual veneration—Father God, and all our brothers and sisters in all creation.

God and the Image of God

> Finally, there is intrinsic valuation of God, where the person is fully involved in God as a being personally approachable. Here we have true religiosity, mysticism, and religious existentialism such as Kierkegaard's.[96] Robert S. Hartman

> *The relation of* this *God to* this *man, the relation of* this *man to* this *God, is for me at once the theme of the Bible* and the essence of philosophy.[97] Karl Barth

> Hence, God must be thought not only as existing but as supreme value. He is the value of values.[98] Robert S. Hartman

> As man is created in the image of God, so God appears in the image of man. The logical structure of the spiritual world is similar to the logical structure of man....God is, potentially, the world's self-fulfillment. As the world becomes morally and spiritually better, ever more transparent to its own self, it becomes more and more God-like. The world is, so to speak, God's body and mind, and God is the world's Self. Thus, in the degree that the world improves and enriches itself, it improves and enriches God's creation and thus confirms God's own goodness and mastery—his sovereignty over creation.[99] Robert S. Hartman

> *God is love.* I. John 4:7 and 16.

> *He [Jesus] is the image of the invisible God*. St. Paul, Colossians 1: 15

> *Now God is love; therefore they who resemble Him in the spirit of their minds are transformed into the same image. They are merciful even as He is merciful. Their soul is all love. They are kind, benevolent, compassionate, tender-hearted; and that not only to the good and gentle, but also to the froward. Yea, they are, like Him, loving unto every man, and their mercy extends to all His works.*[100] John Wesley

> *By salvation I mean, not barely (according to the vulgar notion) deliverance from hell, or going to heaven, but a present deliverance from sin, a restoration of the soul to its primitive health, its original purity; a recovery of the divine nature; the renewal of our souls after the image of God in righteousness and true holiness, in justice, mercy, and truth. This implies all holy and heavenly tempers, and by consequence all holiness of conversation.*[101] John Wesley

> *Above all remembering that God is love, he [the Christian] is conformed to the same likeness. He is full of love to his neighbor: of universal love, not confined to one sect or party, not restrained to those who agree with him in opinions, or in outward modes of worship, or to those who are allied to him by blood or recommended by nearness of place. Neither does he love only those that love him, or that are endeared to him by intimacy or acquaintance. But his love resembles that of him whose mercy is over all his works. It soars above all these scanty bounds, embracing neighbors and strangers, friends and enemies; yea, not only the good and gentle but*

also the froward, the evil and unthankful. For he loves every soul that God has made, every child of man, of whatever place or nation.[102] John Wesley

Contrary to the Freudian hypothesis,...God is evidently perceived as more similar to one's mother than one's father.[103] Lee A. Kirkpatrick

How are human beings made in the "image of God"? Our answers reveal how we and the theologians view both God and ourselves, and what we or they really value in both. Logicians tell us that "resemblance" is a symmetrical relationship, which means that it goes both ways. If A resembles B, then B resembles A. If we resemble God, then God resembles us, but how? Theologians give very diverse answers, based largely on what they value most.

As explained earlier, many traditional theologians think that we were created in the *systemic image of God*. We are Godlike with respect to our rational and cognitive capacities and their objects—knowledge, truth, doctrines, beliefs, etc. We exist in the systemic image of a purely rational and impasssive God, they say. Systemic values are intellectual values, and theologians who value intellectual goodness above all else conceive of our resemblance to God, and God's resemblance to us, in intellectual or cognitive terms. Traditional systemic-minded theologians explicitly ruled out any extrinsic physical and all intrinsic affective resemblances between us and God. God is "incorporeal," has no body, so there can be no bodily resemblance, they said; and all feelings are imperfections, so there can be no affective or emotional resemblance between us and God. So what is left? Reason alone, said the Greek philosophers and innumerable Christian theologians who were more influenced by them than by Biblical religion.

Worldly theologies, by contrast, suppose that God resembles us *extrinsically*. God has a very large, distinguished, and powerful humanoid physical/social body. Most theologians deny it, but many ordinary believers conceive of God as the "big man upstairs with a big stick," and in their heart of hearts they assume that God *looks like* us. We exist in God's bodily image. We sit, so God sits on his throne; we have right and left hands, and so does God. We have a face, a nose, eyes, and ears; so does God, and one day we will see his face. Some of us are literally male, and so is God. Human males are literally powerful, domineering, jealous, and vengeful, and so is God. Of course, God always have the same color skin that we have. Since any given God occupies only a finite space and time, there is plenty of room for many gods; so polytheism is an extrinsic possibility and probability.

Intrinsic theologians and holistic saints locate our resemblance to God primarily in our inner *intrinsic capacities and their scope*. They do not think of God as purely impassive systemic reason alone, even though God is all-knowing and unbiased. Instead, God is the all-inclusive reality who is also passionately creative love, universal and unconditional in scope. To exist fully in God's intrinsic image, we must be literally loving, merciful, kind, benevolent, compassionate, forgiving, joyful, tender, supportive, responsible, reliable, and creative, like a good mother, or like Jesus, who must have been very much like his own mother. And such intrinsic words must apply analogically or metaphorically to God. To be Godlike, the scope of our intrinsic virtues and affections must extend to every person and to all the rest of God's works, and we must be co-creative creatures of our creative God. Finding a pre-twentieth-century theologian who is willing to say explicitly that we are made in the image of God as love is very difficult, but John Wesley said so very clearly and often. See the quotes from Wesley at the beginning of this section.

In saintly religion, real feelings of love, compassion, empathy, delight, trust, and all the religious affections are perfections, even if Greek philosophers and medieval theologians enthralled by them regarded them as imperfections. St. Anselm correctly captured the spiritual meaning of God as a perfect or supremely worshipful being in the formula, "That Being than whom none greater (better, or richer in good-making properties) can be conceived."[104] To flesh out what this means, we have to trust our most profoundly reflective value insights and intuitions. Anselm sometimes got the details wrong, however, especially when he judged that real compassion is an imperfection, and that we experience God as if he were compassionate, even though he is not.

More definite and specific meanings for Anselm's abstract formal axiom of Divinity are offered by individual worshipers and their interpretive communities. Everyone who believes in God may agree on Anselm's abstract formula, God is the best of the best, but they do not agree on the details, and the Devil is in the details. Or maybe God is in the details! Theologians do not agree about which "attributes" count as God's good-making or perfection-making properties, or exactly what these attributes mean, even when they use the same words. How we conceive of God's specific perfections or good-making properties depends largely on what kind of persons we are, on what and how we value, which is why self-knowledge and value theory are so important even for theology.

If we don't just absorb it socially and unthinkingly, we construct our concept of God as "the best of the best" out of our own ultimate values. We project our ultimate values onto ultimate reality and into our interpretations of scripture. St. Anselm's "official" view of "God" was systemic/rational—God as impassive knower; but it should have been systemic/ extrinsic/intrinsic—God as knower, God as creator and actor, and God as love and compassion. Otherwise, something greater or better, something richer in good-making properties, would be conceivable.

Psychological projection does not necessarily invalidate the final results of religious reflections. John Hick indicated that when Sigmund Freud pronounced our concept of God to be a projection of our father-image (really, our mother/ father image) onto the cosmos, "He may have uncovered the mechanism by which God creates an idea of himself in the human mind....Clearly, to the mind which is not committed in advance to the naturalistic explanation, there may be a religious as well as a naturalistic explanation of the psychological facts."[105] In other words, God is nothing more than an illusory psychological projection only to those with closed minds who are already atheists, naturalists, or skeptics. Otherwise, such "projection" can be understood as God's way of providing us with a rudimentary natural knowledge of God. So, let us project boldly but carefully and axiologically, with no qualms of Freudian guilt about it! Traditionally, analogical reasoning about God was commonplace and greatly respected. An axiological frame of reference can make it even more respectable.

Value projection definitely is involved in the way people conceive of the *details* of divine perfection. Extrinsically oriented worldlings think that a perfect being is one who looks like themselves and who has the systemic knowledge and extrinsic power to insure their worldly well-being; they can conceive of nothing greater; even their "other world" is axiologically worldly, filled with mansions, pearls, gold, and other mindless but glittering things. Ideologists think that a perfect being would be purely and totally rational, thus devoid of all actions and affections (like Aristotle's utterly unmoved and impassive mover). They think that without any desires or feelings we ought to simulate only his systemic rational image and obey his formal commands for their own sake, but not for the sake of people; they can conceive of nothing better. Saintly persons tend to conceive of God as fully embodied—omnipresent but not humanoid, as supremely social—thus creative and interactive, as totally rational and well informed, and as completely personal, conscious, loving, compassionate, empathetic, faithful, forgiving, creative, joyful, and intrinsic. God is the supreme systemic/extrinsic/intrinsic Evaluator of all Values who could not not exist, and who includes, preserves, and cherishes forever within himself all created values and evaluations in all dimensions. God is the most fully systemic rational knower, but not merely that. God is also extrinsically and omnipresently embodied, creative of, and immanent in the world, in spacetime; God fills "the heavens and the earth," but not merely that. God is also intrinsically or spiritually one with all in love, compassion, justice, and all spiritual affections.

Christianity insists metaphorically that God is embodied in a special way, both in Jesus, the word made flesh, the still living and our best image of God, and in the Church, the resurrected body of Christ. *Intrinsically, Jesus fully identified with God; intrinsically, God fully identified with Jesus.* Intrinsically, Jesus was fully God and fully man through psychological/axiological identification (and perhaps in other ways beyond the scope of this book). Other religions recognize God's special embodiment in other avatars. In saintly spirituality, God's extrinsic and systemic value dimensions are always in harmony with but subordinated to God's loving and creative intrinsic nature. God is the first and the last word. God is everywhere. God is love. Saints can conceive of nothing greater. Can you?

Fortunately, the theory of value with which we are working provides a rational framework for assessing the validity of value-laden projections of human values onto God. God as the-supreme-systemic-extrinsic-intrinsic-reality-that-includes-all-else, and who could not fail to exist, wins the contest, for nothing richer in good-making properties can be conceived. Additional considerations may help us to understand this better.

Systemic theology's traditional emphasis on "impassive" rationality as the point of resemblance between us and God was tied to an anthropocentric exclusivism that is now outdated for many reasons. Theologians once thought that human beings are the only rational animals; and since no other animals were rational, this had to be image of God because we have it but they don't. However, Charles Darwin correctly discerned that degrees of rationality extend deeply into the animal kingdom; so rational resemblance no longer insures theological speciesism.[106] Most recent thinkers give Darwin credit for discovering that other animals are rational by degrees. However, long before Darwin, John Wesley figured this out: "What then makes the barrier between men and brutes? The line which they cannot pass? It was not reason. Set aside that ambiguous term: exchange it for the plain word, understanding, and who can deny that brutes have this? We may as well deny that they have sight or hearing. But it is this: man is capable of God; the inferior creatures are not."[107]

God loves individuals in other species besides ours. Many of them exist by degrees not only in God's rational or systemic image but also in God's extrinsic and intrinsic images. If we truly resemble God in our capacities for love, mercy, kindness, benevolence, compassion, tenderheartedness, supportiveness, courage, loyalty, dependability, and responsibility, then many non-human animals were also created in the affective/creative/parental/moral image of God. Massive evidence now indicates that many non-human animals manifest these largely affective intrinsic virtues and dispositions, but mainly only in relation to species, clan, and kin—just like us![108]

Further, we now know that at least some sub-human animals, primates in particular, can understand simple moral and social rules, obey them, intentionally break them, and socially enforce them; so rule-based morality for the common good no longer provides a basis for species favoritism.[109] Of course, as with us, many social animals break the rules! Some animals manifest God-like morality, but to a lesser degree than many if not most human beings. In non-human animals, moral capacities, positive affections, and social virtues are mixed together with heavy concentrations of indifference, hatred, competitiveness, egoism, insensitivity, hard-heartedness, mistrust, aggression, cruelty, predation, and vicious destructiveness to individuals belonging to other species, and to outsiders, subordinates, and "inferiors" within their own group or species; but in those respects, they are also exactly like us! Writing about animals, Frans de Waal says,

> Lack of concern for other species is to be expected, given the virtual absence of attachment. Animals often seem to regard those who belong to another kind as merely ambulant objects....Hunters judge the hunted by caloric rather than emotional value, and even if other species are not perceived as food, usually nothing is to be gained by investing care in them.[110]

Worldly people, not far removed from our hunter/gatherer ancestors, relate this way most of the time, not only to sub-human animals, but also to subordinates and aliens or strangers within our own species. Nothing is to be gained by investing in them, they think. Natural non-human animals and unregenerate human beings are not saints. But in small ways and by degrees, both non-human animals and human beings are children of God and made in God's image, the image of embodied love, creative virtue, and intelligence! John Wesley expected to see his faithful horse in the final "new creation," along with other transformed animals. Many people today hope to be reunited some day with *their* deceased pets, but what if all creatures are *God's* beloved pets?

According to most Christian theologians, our human resemblance to God is obscured if not obliterated by sin; and the image of God, the image of comprehensive love, must be restored or created by religious conversion and a prolonged process of sanctification—saint-making, spiritual growth. Jonathan Edwards was close to the truth in holding that the real difference between saints and non-saints lies not in the kind but in the degree and scope of their capacities for intrinsic evaluation.

Of course, degrees and magnitudes can be so great that they almost amount to differences in kind. We are rational systemic knowers; but, unlike God, in our finitude none of us can envision all possibilities for creative activity or comprehend and recall every concrete detail of all possible and actual worlds. We are embodied extrinsic doers, but none of us fill heaven and earth. Most of us have some ability to love a few others responsibly, but few of us love intensely and universally, as do God, Jesus, and the most developed saints. We are all co-creators with God, some more so than others, but none of us can create an entire universe. God is the most complete systemically, extrinsically, and intrinsically good reality conceivable; and we are but shadows and images of such divine things. We are metaphors for God, always inadequate, but made in God's image.

Unlike worldly religion, saintly spirituality does not picture God as a finite humanoid sensory object occupying a circumscribed region of the spacetime of this world or of heaven. Saints do not conceive of God in crassly or literally extrinsic terms, even when they employ metaphors for God drawn from the universe, or from masculine or feminine human embodiment, or from human social roles and actions. Saintly references to God as "He," "She," "Father," "Mother," "King," "Queen," or "Shepherd," are metaphorical, not literal, but they help to bridge the gap. Anthropomorphic God-talk suggests analogies, stretches our imagination, incites creative insights, and expresses and evokes intrinsic evaluation. God is embodied as spatiotemporal omnipresence, the soul of and beyond the world, but not as a gigantic humanoid male. Humankind's theomorphic image is primarily psychological, axiological, moral, intrinsic, and spiritual rather than physical. Our resemblance to God also extends far beyond mere rationality, which is why animals and human infants, poor in reason but rich in other good-making qualities, also directly reflect images of God.

Properly understood and qualified, physical imagery may be relevant to understanding God and our own theomorphic image. God is not a finite yet colossal man-shaped sensory object. God as omnipresent is incarnate within and manifested to some degree by every sensory entity, including every human and non-human body. The universe is the temple of God and the body of God. Intrinsic spirituality recognizes human bodies, living bodies, and ultimately all bodies, as temples of God. God is there in physics and chemistry as well as in biology and psychology. Saints take the *omnipresence* of God very seriously; but the Ultimate Being who "fills heaven and earth" (Jeremiah 23:24), the One "in whom we live and move and have our being," (Acts 17:27-28), and whose body the Universe may be, can't have a humanoid body because the universe as a whole just isn't shaped that way!

Saintly spirituality both universalizes and individuates. All unique men and women are brothers and sisters under the loving fatherhood/motherhood of God, metaphorically speaking. Saintliness extends "the neighbor" and "the tribe" to strangers, enemies, all humankind, and well beyond. Biblical figures clearly had to struggle in order to arrive at a genuinely universal religion; and the Bible is largely the story of that struggle.

For Jonathan Edwards and all who recognize God's infinity and omnipresence, God is the ultimate intrinsically valuable object of true virtue and intrinsic evaluation. True virtue is universal love to being in general, which includes every particular being within God, because "God himself is being in general." In created beings, consent and union to Being in general "implies agreement and union with every particular being, except such as are opposite to Being in general, or excepting such cases where union with them is by some means inconsistent with union with general existence"[111] Further, "In God the love of himself, and the love of the public are not to be distinguished, as in man: because God's being as it were comprehends all. His existence, being infinite, must be equivalent to universal existence."[112]

For some, Edwards's position may be too close to pantheism for comfort. Process Theology or "panentheism" introduces the attractive qualification that creaturely events enjoy a fleeting present moment of self-creative independence and freedom before perishing to themselves, lapsing into the past, and becoming immortalized in God. God has the power to empower us to make and originate our own creative choices, to be co-creative creatures with himself. Thus, we are responsible and accountable for what we choose and do, for what we make of ourselves.

Keen sensitivity to the omnipresence, all-inclusiveness, pervasiveness, and universal availability of God, enables saints to see every person, every living creature, every natural entity and process, as intrinsically, perhaps even infinitely, valuable because in time they manifest aspects of eternity to which worldlings are blind and insensitive. Saints value *things* even more than worldlings! They apply all their powers of evaluation—intrinsic, extrinsic, and systemic—to everything.

When valuing the things of the world, saints bring in their love of God and their beliefs about God. Saints discern an infinite God condensed into and reflected by each and every finite reality, where the part is equal to the whole, according to transfinite logic. Saints find God concentrated into every single thing valued intrinsically, macrocosm reflected in microcosm, creation reflecting Creator, the world's contingency requiring God's necessity, God incarnate in human flesh, God in the sacramental bread and wine, God in the flames of the minora, God in the scent of incense, God in the milk in the firkin, God in the daily bread, God *as* all *in* all. Many mystics, like the poet William Blake, experience God within intense sexual sensuality. To those who have a "sense of the divine," as William James put it, "the smallest details of this world derive infinite significance from their relation to an unseen divine order."[113] Saints are sensitive to the infinite in the finite, and the finite within the infinite. God's omnipresence has profound devotional significance.

Saints think metaphorically of human bodies as "temples" of God, fit to be "living sacrifices" unto God. Human bodies are not just useful material machines or mechanisms, as worldly philosophers believe. Nor are they miserable prisons for disembodied immaterial souls, as dualistic Platonic/Cartesian thinkers believe. God is both passively and actively present in every embodied person, in every embodied creature. Every cup of water given to an insignificant "nobody" slakes God's thirst, and every cup withheld causes God to suffer, for God identifies with all creatures and is present in all. God always rejoices with those who rejoice and suffers with those who suffer. God is equally present in all human beings of every race, color, creed, national origin, social standing, sexual orientation, or ideological persuasion, including those with "the least" worldly status or standing (Matthew 25:40). No systemic or extrinsic "powers and principalities" can separate any person or thing from the love of God. God is even there in our enemies, and there too God must be loved. God never wins a war, for God suffers and dies with every person on all sides. God is killed in every slaughter, including the slaughter of animals. God dies every natural death, and is reborn in every physical birth and spiritual rebirth. God's eyes look back at us through the eyes of every animal, of every enemy, and of every person who is poor, suffering, abused, unjustly treated, or slaughtered during war or peace. Much of the language here is metaphorical, but these images connote and communicate profound spiritual truths.

Conclusion: Saintliness as Salvation

> *Even St. Augustine, who is generally supposed to favour the contrary doctrine, makes that just remark,... 'He that made us without ourselves, will not save us without ourselves.'*[114] John Wesley

> *The salvation which is here spoken of is not what is frequently understood by that word, the going to heaven, eternal happiness. It is not the soul's going to para-*

dise....It is not a blessing which lies on the other side of death, or (as we usually speak) in the other world. The very words of the text itself put this beyond all question. 'Ye are saved.' It is not something at a distance: it is a present thing, a blessing which, through the free mercy of God, ye are now in possession of.[115] John Wesley

If worldliness is *maya*, original sin, and inauthentic existence, then what is the saintly mode of evaluative consciousness? Is it salvation? Yes, it is a substantial part of just that, even if not the whole of it. The saints merge salvation with sanctification, ongoing growth in grace. A brief concluding summary may help to make that clearer.

Holistic saints use all of their brains. They are the richest and the most fully developed human selves, and for this reason they live *the most abundant human lives, understood axiologically as lives that are richest in good-making properties in all dimensions of value*. Saints value all concrete entities intrinsically, even if for some purposes they also evaluate them extrinsically or systemically. To them, whatever is, is sacred. Limited only by their innate individual proficiencies and proclivities, their values and evaluational capacities are developed and utilized as fully as possible in all three value dimensions.

Holistic saints satisfy their most basic biological needs as simply, efficiently, and unpretentiously as possible. This leaves them free to fulfill their intellectual, moral, and spiritual potentialities. They know how to live well without living extravagantly. Unlike men and women of the world, they are content with and thankful for what they have, even small things. They are sufficiently well developed extrins-ically to be competent human beings who can cope effectively with the physical and practical demands of everyday life. They pay their own way in more ways than one, but they also know how to accept help and gifts from others graciously and thankfully. They find God in physical things and activities as well as in mental and spirit-ual realities and activities. They find God in good works, the arts, play, work, business, profit, and honor. They love, cherish, respect, develop, exercise, protect, utilize, and maintain their own bodies and those of others as temples of God, not as temporary prisons. They highly esteem physical embodiment and discern that being spatially extended (materiality) is desirable, not objectionable or deplorable. Matter is good because God created it and created us out of it, and there is a lot more to matter than most people think. We were literally created out of dust—stardust (exploded supernovas). To saints, nothing is wrong with extrinsic realities and values as such; they are objectionable or problematic only when rated higher than intrinsic realities and values. Properly ranked, but not overrated, the world is very good indeed.

Holistic saints also develop their minds as far as time and circumstances permit. They are sufficiently well developed intellectually not to be stupid, naive, vulnerable, or easily deceived and exploited. They know how to study and are eager to learn. Where called for, they practice tough love, informed by knowledge and discernment. They are good at distinguishing effective from ineffective means to ends. They recognize and avoid irrationality and superstition. They are enlightened. They find God in learning. The truth sets them free, even scientific truth, and they are not afraid of it. If they have special intellectual talents, they make the most of them and contribute creatively and insightfully to a great variety of intellectual disciplines. Their intellectual powers and virtues are complemented by intellectual humility and open-mindedness. They are fallibilists, not dogmatic ideologists. Their humility is both an intellectual and a spiritual virtue. They rank moral and spiritual goods higher than cognitive values, higher than philosophy and theology, higher than doctrines and beliefs. Saints are not dogmatists; they place philosophical and theological beliefs in the service of love. By such fruits, truth is known. Their ultimate spiritual criterion for the acceptability or unacceptability of a religious idea or belief is whether accepting it will help them to be or become more loving persons. Many religious beliefs and faiths are very unloving, but only those that nurture love abide.

The ancient myth that human reason was corrupted by the Fall contains a large measure of truth. As Irenaeus indicated, the Fall is, in reality, a lack of self-development. As infants, we start low, not high, in the scale of moral and spiritual development. Extreme worldliness ties human reason and its concepts exclusively to sensations and practicality and divorces them from intense feelings, intuitions, introspection, and serious moral and spiritual thinking. Everything else is meaningless. It makes little or no place for systemic and intrinsic knowing. Systemic ideology, by contrast, disassociates from sensations and divorces rationality and conceptuality from experience, action, feeling, introspection, and concrete living. With passion, it favors theoretical knowledge for its own sake and devalues extrinsic and intrinsic knowing.

Reason is indeed fallen, inadequate, and incomplete at the levels of worldliness and ideology; but saintliness makes it whole. Reason can be redeemed, restored, and sanctified, as Jonathan Edwards maintained. Reasoning and conceiving can be functions of whole persons, and holistic saints can integrate them harmoniously with all other positive functions of the human soul including sensing, feeling, introspecting, intuiting, believing, acting, and concrete living. Saintliness does not indulge in psychological compartmentalization; it makes an honored place for redeemed rationality, for holistic systemic, extrinsic, and intrinsic knowing. Without being enslaved by any of them, whole and mature saints master the technical logics and languages of the disciplines for which they have special talents, plus the ordinary prosaic logic and language required for maneuvering through the world, plus the intensional logic, uniceps, and metaphors essential for intrinsic evaluation, aesthetic appreciation, ethical commitment and action, and spiritual sensitivity and devotion.

Holistic saints know and value themselves and others directly and internally, not just indirectly and externally. They can attend directly to their own inner experiences, feelings, intuitions, activities, and processes. They have an inwardness that worldlings lack. They know who they are and what they want out of life, and it isn't all just for themselves. They fully realize that inner, spiritual, and intrinsic graces stand in need of outer, behavioral, and extrinsic signs, indications, and expressions.

Holistic saints value themselves as well as others intrinsically. They attach immense worth both to themselves and to others. They are not egoistically competitive and acquisitive. They overcome selfishness, but not by undervaluing themselves intrinsically. Selfishness involves both overvaluing oneself and undervaluing others. Saints do not undervalue others or overvalue themselves. They are cooperative citizens of the Kingdom of God, the kingdom of equals and ends, the kingdom of those who love one another as they love themselves, and who love God with all that they are and have. They creatively actualize non-competitive values like love, knowledge, social justice, mercy, generosity, humility, cooperation, kindness, and compassion, as well as aesthetic and intellectual goods that can be shared with others without loss to themselves. They do not play zero sum games where they can gain only if others lose. They intrinsically evaluate not only people and animals (intrinsic values) but also knowledge and truth (systemic values) and all physical actions, things, and processes that show God's handiwork (extrinsic values). They see and find God everywhere in everything. For them, everything is sacred, every place is a shrine, and every day is a holy day.

Holistic saints control, subdue, or eliminate vicious appetites and instincts that conflict with saintly virtues, beliefs, actions, and affections. They are liberated from psychological defensiveness and pretense. Gradually, the sanctification process takes away their bent to sinning. They are not short-sighted; their lives have continuity; they confront the future with expectation and hope. They trust in God. The interests and affections that abide in them and gradually prevail through sanctification are integrated harmoniously into very long range rational, moral, and spiritual plans of life that include the well-being of self, others, and all creation. They practice creation care. The process philosopher/theologian, Charles Hartshorne, argued that a kind of unselfishness is present in long-range selfishness, because the present self makes sacrifices for the love of its own future that resemble sacrifices made in loving other persons.[116] Saints gladly make such sacrifices for self and others.

Holistic saints closely identify with all things, and all things with God. They manifest identification spirituality. They practice the presence of God. For saints, all concrete conscious individuals are inherently valuable, as is every genuinely intrinsic relation with all creation. They respect people and all sentient creatures as ends in themselves. Where possible they avoid using people and animals as mere means to extrinsic or systemic goals. They understand and cherish people and animals in their unique and inherent dignity and worth, especially those with whom they have intimate contact and for whom they have personal responsibility. All living things trust them. They are trustworthy. They trust in God.

Holistic saints are true to themselves, not their sinful selves, but their redeemed, enlightened, developed, and righted selves; and they hope and pray that other people will be faithful to the best that is in them and to what God expects of them. Their actual properties correspond significantly with their ideal predicates; their conscience largely approves of who they are, that is, of who they have become with God's help and forgiveness. They have an easy conscience before God. Saints know and value themselves intrinsically. Intrinsic evaluation involves concept fulfillment; saints live up to their high ideals and self-expectations. They are good people.

Correlated with our total and integrated self-predicate inventory (our total self-concepts) is our total and integrated self-property inventory (our total concrete reality). Our self-property inventory is always incomplete because we are still creating ourselves; our self-predicate inventory is even more incomplete to us because, unlike the saints, most of us do not know ourselves very well.

Holistic saints combine repentance and deep humility with high self-esteem, self-respect, and self-love, the basis for loving others as self. They ultimately ground their self-love in God's grace, forgiveness, and love for them, despite their lingering finitude, ignorance, errors, sins, and temptations. They openly reveal themselves to others without guile, pretense, and affectation. They love God most of all and serve God as best they can. In being loyal to God, they are loyal to God's loyalties; in loving God, they love all that God loves. Their faith is alive, not dead, for their works express their faith. They do the works of love and mercy. They have the courage to be, to feel, to do, and to believe. In giving, they receive more than they give, not as their aim or objective in giving, but as serendipity and grace. They know how to count their blessings. They are real people. They exist authentically.

Holistic saints recognize that we are by nature social beings and that our ultimate happiness must be realized in community and communion with others. They recognize their own profound needs for adult attachments and social support in moral and spiritual growth. They contribute as best they can to the betterment of society and to the preservation and improvement of its most desirable social arrangements and institutions. As much as humanly possible in their distinctive circumstances, they live cooperatively in peace and harmony with themselves and others, and they work diligently for social justice. Their inner and outer serenity and ecstasy surpass all understanding. Yet, they are troubled by the troubles of the world. They carry crosses and bear burdens. They are compassionate and suffer with those who suffer. They are aesthetically, morally, socially, and religious sensitive, imaginative, and creative; and they share these gifts and their fruits with others. Their moral, aesthetic, social, and spiritual intuitions are in accord with the highest enlightenment, rationality, morality, and spirituality. They practice what they preach, what they know to be right and good. They are fulfilled, filled full with goodness.

Holistic saints use their whole brains. They are not just half-brained people. As time and their natural talents allow, they develop and use their left-brain systemic capacities for thought, reason, conceptualization, systematization, inquiry, and knowledge. They search for truth and find enough of it for abundant living. They also develop and use their left-brain extrinsic capacities for sensing, classifying, predicting, acting, controlling, and prospering, not only for themselves, but also for others. They develop and use their fore-brain, right-brain and mid-brain intrinsic capacities for intuitive insight, spiritual sensitivity, aesthetic appreciation, and moral involvement. They optimize their right-brain and mid-brain capacities for loving, caring, empathy, compassion, forgiveness, identification with others, and euphoric union with and delight in God, their neighbors, and all of creation.

Their intrinsic evaluation is all-inclusive in scope. They rejoice and delight in each and every being, or at least those who consent to and do not harm the being and well-being of others. Their own harmless pleasures are of the very highest quality. They are genuinely happy people. Euphoria is largely a right-brain and mid-brain function, and the saints use their whole brains. They sustain an intensity of intrinsic feeling, awareness, and exuberance unimagined and unapproached by worldlings. In loving extravagantly, they know the exalted happiness for which God made them. Their bliss in and with God is beatitude.

Holistic saints live *more abundantly*. By identifying themselves with God, others, and all creation, they take the good-making properties of God, all people, all living things, and all else into themselves and make them their own. They alone live truly abundantly. For them, life, time, space, and all of existence are filled with intrinsic sacred meaning, final worth, and a taste of eternity and infinity. For them, the earth and the heavens are full of God's glory. They never have to kill time, for they live creatively and constantly in the *fullness* of time. They are the salt of the earth, the light of the world, the true image of God, the most authentic shadows and images of divine things. They are our best hope, perhaps our only hope, for the extended future of humankind. Not to live so is sin; so to live is salvation.

Four

Moving Up From the Dark Side

> *All perfection in this life hath some imperfection bound up with it; and no knowledge of ours is without some darkness. An humble knowledge of thyself is a surer way to God than a deep search after learning; yet learning is not to be blamed, nor the mere knowledge of anything whatsoever, for knowledge is good, considered in itself, and ordained of God; but a good conscience and virtuous life is always to be preferred before it.*[1] Thomas À. Kempis

> *Sinner awake! Know thyself! Know and feel, that thou 'wert shapen in wickedness, and that in sin did thy mother conceive thee', and that thou thyself hast been heaping sin upon sin, ever since thou couldst discern good from evil.*[2] John Wesley

> *And, first, repent, that is, know yourselves. This the first repentance, previous to faith, even conviction, or self-knowledge. Awake, then, thou that sleepest. Know thyself to be a sinner, and what manner of sinner thou art.*[3] John Wesley

> *Of all kinds of knowledge that we can ever obtain, the knowledge of God, and the knowledge of ourselves, are the most important. As religion is the great business, for which we were created, and on which our happiness depends; and as religion consists in an intercourse between ourselves and our Maker; and so has its foundation in God's nature and ours, and in the relation that God and we stand in to each other; therefore a true knowledge of both must be needful in order to true religion.*[4] Jonathan Edwards

Theologians, philosophers, and psychologists have stressed the importance of self-knowledge, not only for daily living, but also for religion and the spiritual life. Yet, the thoughts, feelings, emotions, desires, decisions, and deeds of which we become aware in the pursuit of spirituality and self-knowledge are not all positive. As we endeavor to know ourselves and draw closer to God, we eventually gain a fuller consciousness of our own unthinkable thoughts, dark desires, disturbing emotions, detestable decisions, and deplorable deeds. We become more aware of and sensitized to the harms that we have inflicted upon other people and other living things. We come to understand how flagrantly we have violated our own highest ideals, how far we fall short of holistic saintliness. We realize that we really have been "foolish, vicious, and miserable," as John Wesley put it.

In good conscience, we cannot affirm, positively identify with, and delight in (intrinsically value) *all* that we are and have been and done. Self-knowledge does not always paint a pretty picture, especially when measured by God's standards, or by saintly standards. We begin to realize that much of self, much of what we are and have been, must somehow be changed, overcome, repented of, forgiven, redeemed, reconciled, transcended, overcome, diminished, or eliminated. Spiritual growth inevitably passes through phases of honest self-examination, self-devaluation, and moral or spiritual guilt, during which moral weaknesses and personal transgressions are recalled, repented of, and repudiated. Intrinsic saintly spirituality views our serious blemishes as sins against God; but it assures us that despite all of our shortcomings, we can be reconciled, redeemed, and restored. Eventually, with God's help and by God's grace, we can come to accept ourselves, love ourselves, forgive ourselves, and value ourselves intrinsically, despite all our personal faults and flaws.

Historically, religion has been an effective personal and social force in helping people to face their shortcomings honestly, penitently, and redemptively. Yet, religion as a social force always functions in conjunction with inner personal psychological dynamics, with natural and socially developed intellectual, moral, and spiritual evaluational capacities, and with individuated conscience and enlightened evaluative standards. We will consider first the role of conscience in grounding the dark side of self-knowledge.

Guilty Conscience

The self-reflective and self-directive part of a person is usually called the person's conscience. In the case of a person our definition [of "good" as "concept fulfillment"] may thus be formulated: "x is a good person if x is as x's conscience demands" or "x is good if x follows his [or her] conscience."...The norm for the intrinsic value is the person's conscience; to be a "good himself" he must first know himself, be a co-knower with himself of himself.[5] Robert S. Hartman

I have moral value in the degree that I fulfill my own definition of myself. This definition is: "I am I." Thus, in the degree that I am *I, I am a morally good person. Moral goodness is the depth of man's own being himself. That is the greatest goodness in the world. If everyone of us and everyone in the world would just be himself and follow his own inner self or as we say, the voice of his conscience, then everything would straighten itself out, all the problems would just fall by the wayside. We wouldn't listen to false prophets, to politicians, to those who want to use us for their own ambitions. We would just be, and be ourselves. We would know the true values.*[6] Robert S. Hartman

In the social field we are very adept. But we fall far short of living in the full depth of ourselves.... We live rather shallow lives. We are not fulfilling ourselves. We are only living a small fragment of ourselves. We are *not, really. We don't live what we could be.*[7] Robert S. Hartman

We may understand by conscience a faculty or power, implanted by God in every soul that comes into the world, of perceiving what is right or wrong in his own heart or life, in his tempers, thoughts, words, and actions.[8] John Wesley

Conscience is an inner light, a still small voice within that tells us the difference between right and wrong, virtue and vice, good and evil. It lies within the deep core of our inner intrinsic self. Ideally, it decrees and directs how we ought to develop ourselves and live systemically, extrinsically, and intrinsically. Some people have so little self-awareness that conscience hardly functions at all. Others are attuned only to the extrinsic or systemic aspects of conscience. But with increasing self-knowledge and psychological maturity, conscience in three dimensions sets standards for what self and others ought to be, think, do, and feel. Our "ought" is integral to our "is." Conscience measures self and others by its norms, some of which it assumes to be universally valid. If mature, sane, and morally developed, a *good* self is true to itself, true to its norms; but we are not always or equally in touch with our deepest and best selves, and we do not always live up to and fulfill our normative self-concepts. We often need moral guidance and direction from others who have more insight than we do into what is best for ourselves. When conscience compares our actual properties with our ideal properties, it usually finds us wanting, *a topic thus far greatly neglected by philosophical theories of value.*

The contents of conscience are presumably derived partly from universal human nature ("Follow nature!"), which in turn, according to the theologians, is ultimately designed by and derived from God. Of course, "Follow nature" can be bad advice, for some parts of human nature should not be followed, for example, our passion for revenge. Yet, "follow conscience," which is also part of our nature, may be good advice. God seems to have worked through evolution to create conscience within us. The appeal to human nature is troublesome; even this gift from God has been corrupted by sin, the theologians say, and the "natural man and woman" must be overcome and transcended to some degree, not simply affirmed as is. But what tells us which way to go as we strive to overcome our natural disposition to err, our natural bent to sinning? This brings us back to considering conscience in three dimensions, the presumed universal and valid part of our nature, the "inner light," the still small voice of God within, which has the authority to rule and overrule our wayward parts. Ideally, *conscience comes in three dimensions*, systemic, extrinsic, and intrinsic.

In brief, systemic conscience tells us to seek knowledge and obey the rules, extrinsic conscience tells us to be useful and practical, and intrinsic conscience tells us to be intimate and loving. *Systemic conscience* requires us to seek knowledge and truth persistently, honestly, and dispassionately. It tells us to master and conform to the highest laws of God, nature, society, logic, mathematics, morality, spirituality the state, the church, and other beneficial institutions. *Extrinsic conscience* requires us to live up to the expectations built into our social roles and to gain, save, and give as much wealth and status as we can without harming others in the process. *Intrinsic conscience* requires us to cherish and identify with people and all conscious beings in their full richness and uniqueness, to regard and treat them as ends in themselves, and to act upon our highest moral and spiritual beliefs and insights. A fully *enlightened conscience* includes all of the above. Our *actual conscience* is where we are now in our own maturation process, the often defective still small voice that we actually hear.

Some of these dimensions of conscience may be more developed than others in actual conscience. Some segments of actual conscience are doubtless derived from society with its partly corrupt culture and somewhat tainted religious environment. In part, actual conscience also expresses our own unique personal experiences, preferences, choices, and self-formed habits of self-expectation. Since we are social beings, the values of others are often reflected by this still small voice within us. Sometimes, others may know better than we do about what is best for us. Sometimes, they may also influence us for the worst. After due, careful, thoughtful consideration and consultation with others, we may be able to move toward a state of "reflective equilibrium" or "enlightened conscience" that better enables us to refine and prioritize our norms. A fully enlightened conscience is three dimensional. It may repudiate some of the standards by which we formerly measured ourselves and others, while accepting much of what we have been given. After due consideration, we can affirm, internalize, and identify ourselves with the norms that are sanctioned by deep-level or ideal conscience. Conscience, the locus of our deepest values, lies within the center or core of who we really are. An enlightened conscience is well informed, fair minded or impartial, free from overwhelming internal and external compulsions or coercions, including unconscious determinants, and intuitively attuned to the universal human values or norms that presumably lie within the deepest level of human and individual selfhood. William James thought that no sharp distinction can be made between sensitivity to the depths of human nature and sensitivity to God.[9]

Sadly, the values that we affirm in our more reflective or enlightened moments are not always the values by which we actually live. Knowing what is right is not necessarily doing it or living it. St. Paul was correct about that; we often do what we know we should not do, and we do not do what we know we should. Socrates and Plato were mistaken in thinking that we always do what we know to be best. Even if we affirm the three dimensional hierarchy of positive values in our Sabbath moments of reflective conscientiousness, most of us may actually live out our lives as worldlings who idolize worldly success, or as ideologists who idolize ideas. We should but do not always affirm in actual thought or in deeds that people are more valuable than things, and that things are more valuable than mere ideas of people and things. Fortunately, people who live in sin and darkness have occasional glimpses of great light, of a more excellent way. God has not left us without help and guidance.

A well formed three dimensional conscience both affirms and condemns much of what we actually are. When the "oughts" of mature three dimensional conscience and self-knowledge are applied to our past and present selves, we find that we have vices as well as virtues, pains as well as pleasures, weaknesses as well as strengths, and all of these partly constitute our total reality. Adequate knowledge of self always includes an awareness of "mental pains" that ideally we ought not to suffer: despair, depression, sadness, distress, fear, terror, jealousy, hatred, cruelty, boredom, loneliness, alienation, resentment, disappointment, grief, anxiety, inadequacy, insecurity, confusion, uncertainty, doubt, regret, shame, and guilt. All mental pains involve disvalues and disvaluations, often of our past and present selves and our personal circumstances. Painful emotions like guilt and despair indicate that we devalue our miserable present selves. Through them, we recognize and express our dissatisfaction with ourselves, our situations, or our reactions to our situations. We may be stricken or overcome with grief, guilt, sadness, despair, or other pains of soul.

Appropriate self-knowledge also includes an awareness of our motivation to commit most if not all of the seven traditional "cardinal sins"—pride, covetousness, lust, anger, gluttony, envy, and sloth. By such things we are constantly tempted. Whether these "deadly" sins are "original" or not is largely irrelevant in one sense, for there is very little originality in sin! People keep making the same old mistakes over and over again in every generation. Every new generation has to start all over again almost from moral and spiritual scratch. But they are "original" in the sense that they are deeply embedded in the human nature that we have inherited.

Not only our deeds but also our thoughts and feelings have a dark side that can be traced back to our evolutionary origins. Traditionally, "original sin" connoted a universal condition of value-depravity that distances us from God, into which all human beings are born. Even if we don't like the traditional terminology, we still have to admit that something within us regularly distances us from God. Value theory and evolutionary psychology can help us make modern sense of original sin as a universal disposition to value wrongly, a universal failure to develop our natural but seldom dominant capacities for valuing intrinsically all the intrinsically valuable realities that deserve to be valued intrinsically.

The actuality of *original sin* in this axiological sense does not require or presuppose a literal biblical Adam and Eve who fell out of an idyllic Eden where there was no death, suffering, conflict, or evil. More literally and accurately, *all of us just start low and fail to grow axiologically or evaluationally as we should,* as the church father, Irenaeus, suggested in the Second Century A. D. As today's evolutionary psychologists and sociobiologists indicate, our natural egoism and tribalism, plus our natural fixation on practical physical things and social status, have immense short-term survival and reproduction value and thus are usually stronger than equally natural but normally weaker rationality, unselfish altruism, and ethical respect for and identification with others. Also, as we grow up, we absorb and internalize the beliefs and practices of our morally corrupt social and religious orders, where wrongdoing is institutionalized and perpetuated collectively. Neglectful and abusive caregivers in the early weeks and months of life, and bad upbringings thereafter, can inhibit or corrupt the development of conscience and the practice of acting morally. Overcoming our personal and collective shortcomings is a matter of getting our priorities straight, in spite of all such obstacles. The insights of value theory into how to order actual conscience and prioritize our values and evaluations can be immensely helpful. So can the insights of morally and spiritually mature saints and truly saintly religious groups—the real communion of the saints.

Our thoughts, decisions, deeds, and feelings, even the dusky ones, do not just happen to us; they largely constitute and are integral aspects of who we actually are. We are the integrated totality of *all* our properties. It is often said, "We should hate the sin but love the sinner," but this is really too simple-minded to be true. We can affirm parts of what we and others are without affirming everything; but we cannot unreservedly affirm some parts of who we are. *We are,* in part, our sinful dispositions, desires, emotions, thoughts, choices, and deeds, just as the theologians have traditionally said. They partly constitute our very being, our total reality; they are not just extraneous facts about us. In part, as sinners, we are our sinful dispositions and deeds; they are integral aspects of our total property inventory. They need to be replace by saintly dispositions and deeds, but how do they become integral parts of what we might become? This chapter addresses this issue.

If we are our total integrated property inventory—all our properties, internal relations, and their configurations—this clarifies the venerable theological claim that sinfulness is not accidental; it is integral to our very existence. Psychotherapists try to free us from irrational and inappropriate guilt. Some psychotherapists, enamored with moral relativism, think that nothing is right or wrong for there is no such thing; others, convinced of hard determinism, assume that none of us are responsible for any decisions we ever make. However, sometimes guilt feelings are quite appropriate, not pathological, precisely because some actions are objectively wrong. Sometimes, we are in fact guilty because we have knowingly and freely chosen to do wrong. Our enlightened conscience tells us that many of our freely-made decisions and the behaviors that issue from them are not what they ought to be. Judged by social, moral, spiritual, aesthetic, and rational standards, we, like St. Paul, do that which we ought not to do, and we do not do that which we ought to do (Romans 7:15). We knowingly and voluntarily err by both commission and omission. Correspondingly, sometimes we are in fact innocent, either because we have been forgiven of wrongdoing, or we have knowingly and freely chosen to do what is right.

In axiological terms, *systemically*, we have not sought knowledge and truth persistently, honestly, and dispassionately; our thinking has been prejudiced, confused, distorted, unclear, inconsistent, incoherent, illogical, lacking in both comprehensiveness and simplicity, and inadequately informed by persistent study, reflection and experience. We have not adequately mastered or conformed to the highest or most carefully considered laws of God, nature, society, logic, mathematics, morality, spirituality, the state, the church, and other beneficial institutions; and we have not applied these rules appropriately to our own circumstances. Our rationality is corrupted, and systemic conscience condemns us.

Extrinsically, we have not lived up to the expectations built into our social roles; we have not been good employers, employees, entrepreneurs, consumers, competitors, parents, children, siblings, and so on; we have not made enough money, acquired enough property, or climbed high enough on the ladders of social class and material success. We have not *acted* upon our highest moral and religious beliefs and insights. We have not adequately considered the consequences of our deeds. We have hurt others in pursuing our own interests. We have not followed John Wesley's recommendation to gain all we can, save all we can, and give all we can.[10] Our practicality is corrupted, and extrinsic conscience condemns us.

Intrinsically, we have not fully appreciated and identified with either ourselves, all other persons, God, and the animals as intrinsic ends in themselves—and acted accordingly. We have not adequately rejoiced and taken pleasure in the inherent beauty and goodness of their reality or of our own. We have not respected and delighted in their autonomy or in the uniqueness of their own perspective on existence, especially if they are very different from ourselves. We have neither identified ourselves with their well-being nor acted effectively to sustain and enhance them. We have had little compassion for those who suffer, especially the "least of these" among us. We have not rejoiced with those who rejoice and suffered with those who suffer. We have not been sufficiently grateful for our own existence or that of others. Our ability to love is impoverished or corrupted, and intrinsic conscience condemns us. Holistic intrinsic conscience contains systemic and extrinsic conscience within itself, and it assigns systemic, extrinsic, and intrinsic values to their proper place within the hierarchy of value. We are not always true to ourselves, and we are not always our best selves to be true to. Our self-constitution, self-concepts, and self-expectations have been corrupted by nature, sin, and society. We do not always grasp or fulfill our best concepts of ourselves.

If we fulfill our ideal self-concepts only by degrees, does that mean that we have intrinsic worth only by degrees? Does it mean that some people, those true to themselves, have more intrinsic worth than others? Perhaps there is a minimal level of human intrinsic worth below which no human being falls and in terms of which all people have equal rights and equal intrinsic worth, but on top of that some people are clearly much better developed internally, more intrinsically fulfilled, more moral, more saintly, than others. All of us have the same basic equal worth as the great saints, e.g., St. Francis and John Wesley, but internally we are not as fully developed morally and spiritually as they were. All of us have equal basic worth in the eyes of God, but some of us are more saintly and thus live more abundantly internally than others.

Inadequacy and evil are within us. We may be rotten almost to the core, but goodness is also within us. We are born conflicted, both good and bad. We stay that way for much of our lives, but we need to and can change for the better and leave our iniquities and our old inadequate selves behind. We need to replace our sinful by saintly dispositions and deeds. But how?

Conversion and Self-reformation

> *Let us hereafter, in speaking of the hot place in a man's consciousness, the group of ideas to which he devotes himself, and from which he works, call it the habitual center of his personal energy. It makes a great difference to a man whether one set of his ideas, or another, be the center of his energy; and it makes a great difference, as regards any set of ideals which he may possess, whether they become central or remain peripheral in him. To say that a man is "converted" means, in these terms, that religious ideas, previously peripheral in his consciousness, now take a central place, and that religious aims form the habitual center of his energy.*[11] William James

> *They that are truly converted are new men, new creatures; new, not only within, but without; they are sanctified throughout, in spirit, soul and body; old things are passed away, all things are become new; they have new hearts, and new eyes, new ears, new tongues, new hands, new feet; i.e. a new conversation and practice; and they walk in newness of life, and continue to do so to the end of life.*[12] Jonathan Edwards

Conversion is not necessarily a spiritual or religious phenomenon. People change, develop, reform, and relapse in many fundamental ways, for many reasons, and from many influences and causes. All *reformers,* dedicated to facilitating fundamental changes in other people's value orientations, are *converters.* They try to promote desirable changes in manners, social customs, morality, aesthetics, education, psychology, science, religion, or whatever. Parents try to correct, change, and mold their children. Psychiatrists, psychologists, counselors, environmentalists, educators, philosophers, priests, ministers, rabbis, and evangelists are professional converters. All aim at bringing about fundamental changes in the hot spots of some other person's consciousness. Our present concern is with *spiritual conversion*, change, and growth, something emphasized by all the major world religions. Illustrations to follow will come mainly from Christianity but partly from Judaism, both biblical and beyond.

Being converted always involves self-knowledge of who we were and are, of who others (including God) want us to be, of who we ourselves aspire to be, of what conscience requires of us, and of how to make the transition from here to there. Conversion is always *from* something (immaturity and/or wicked ways and their guilt), but it is also always *for* something (maturity and/or a new moral and spiritual birth and outlook). Conversion introduces or at least prioritizes values and evaluations in novel ways or configurations. It transforms beliefs, attitudes, feelings, desires, dispositions, goals, purposes, and intentional actions. It modifies not only *what* we value, but *how* we value as well. It makes actual what was only potential. It rearranges our priorities.

Dramatic spiritual conversions became exceptionally conspicuous with the advent of Protestant revivalism in the Eighteenth Century, particularly during the Great Awakening of the early 1740s. Largely through the writings and worldwide influence of Jonathan Edwards and John Wesley, the Great Awakening set models and standards of expectation and success for Protestant revivalism and conversion that endure to this day. For predestinationists like Edwards, spiritual conversion is an important but not an infallible "sign," "assurance," or bit of "evidence" for being among the *very few* elected by God for salvation and heaven. For him and many other Protestants from his day to our own, what C. C. Goen called the "morphology of conversion"[13] was and is of great significance, for they wanted to discern their destiny. Wesley, a universalist, thought that *everyone* is among the elect, and we don't make it only because we refuse what God has to offer, beginning with conversion, and continuing lifelong with spiritual growth or sanctification.

Must authentic spiritual conversion be sudden, almost instantaneous, and very dramatic; or can it be gradual, serene, and slowly cumulative? Revivalism tends to produce the quickie variety; but, even when it is slow, gradual, untheatrical, and incremental, conversion alters the most basic value structures and orientations of human consciousness and conscience. Human personalities are structured largely if not entirely around the objects we value and our ways of valuing them. Values and evaluations form the "habitual center of our energy," as William James would put it. They are at the heart of spiritual conversion, and of all the rest of life.

Spiritual conversion, at least the quickie Protestant variety, typically begins with a guilty conscience, a deep conviction of sin, accompanied at times by great fear or terror, often expressed historically through weeping, wailing, and gnashing of teeth. Usually, people are either unaware or only dimly aware of their dark side, of the evil propensities within; but revivalistic preaching is carefully calculated to activate conscience and help people recognize and confess their iniquities and shortcomings. Revivalists try to induce both a profound sense of guilt before God and an overwhelming fear of Divine retribution, but their preaching culminates with offers of relief and rehabilitation through Divine grace, justification, forgiveness, and reconciliation. Religion is not the only social force that can make us aware of our shortcomings, but it clearly accentuates them and makes us keenly aware of them, especially if and when we first "get religion."

Biblically oriented converts tend to measure themselves by biblical standards, some of which are genuinely internalized for the first time at conversion. In many ways, they see themselves as falling short of the glory of God and as condemned when measured by God's laws and by their own enhanced or redeemed consciences. Anything is good to the extent that it fulfills the standards or concepts applied to it. If people measure themselves and others by internalized biblical standards, they find everyone, themselves included, to be considerably less than good. We may have some, but never all, desirable good-making characteristics. Religious extremist find us to be no good at all; we are totally depraved; our only side is our dark side. To them, we have no good-making properties whatsoever, especially in our "natural" or pre-conversion state. Even without total depravity, even when through God's prevenient grace given to all there is much goodness within us, people generally fall far short of the mark of their high spiritual calling.

The dark side of self-knowledge clearly discloses that we have indeed knowingly and willfully broken the Ten Commandments (Exodus 20:3-17 and Deuteronomy 5:7-21). We have had other deities, other ultimate concerns, besides God, the Only Ultimate Reality. We have made and bowed down to graven images, to false finite gods like prosperity, status, and ideology. We have taken God's name in vain. We have not kept the Sabbath Day holy. We have dishonored our parents. We have murdered and committed adultery, at least in our minds and hearts (Matthew 5:28). We have stolen, even if it was only petty theft. We have borne false witness, even if most of our lies were little and white. We have coveted the success, status, belongings, and sexual partners of others. We have disobeyed what Jesus called the First and Second Commandments (Mark 12:29-31); we have not loved God with all our hearts, souls, minds, and strengths; and we have not loved our neighbors as ourselves. These two commandments belong just as much to Judaism and Islam as to Christianity; they were first given in the Old Testament (Deuteronomy 6:4 and Leviticus 19:18), even if they were not in the Top Ten. Jesus knew the scriptures and cited them. Also, we have not loved our enemies (Luke 6:35); and we have not done to others as we would be done unto (Luke 6:31).

Not everyone cares, but the list of biblical action-guiding rules that every person has violated could go on and on. In addition, we have also failed to observe innumerable ceremonial and perhaps less appealing action-guiding rules given in the scriptures. This might or might not be objectionable. These days, most people do not even know they exist, including those who claim to accept *everything* in the scriptures equally, literally, and non-selectively. The Old and New Testaments are filled with implicit if not explicit rules for celebrating the Passover, for making burnt and unburnt offerings, for conducting feasts, fasts, marriages, circumcisions, Sabbath observances, baptisms, the Lord's Supper, and so on. Orthodox Jews are more observant of some biblical ceremonial rules than orthodox Christians; but all of us are very selective, often intentionally so, about the moral, devotional, and ceremonial scriptural rules that we take seriously and try to observe.

The Bible sets very demanding and often conflicting standards, as do the scriptures of all the world religions. Conscience, honesty, practicality, and rationality require us to make many legitimate exceptions scriptural norms or rules. Scriptural laws both guide and condemn us, as religious converts well understand. The dark side of self-knowledge, that we have many vices, that we are sinners, goes hand in hand with guilt, the depths of despair, and the fear of God. Conveniently, biblical religion offers an escape from such awe-full emotions. "Terror preaching," as Kenneth P. Minkema called it,[14] culminates with offers of relief, salvation, justification, release *from* guilt and bondage to sin, and a new spiritual birth *for* love to God and neighbors. Conversion offers a release *from* old values and evaluations (sin and bondage to sin) and a new beginning *for* better values and evaluations—salvation and sanctification.

Being converted or born again is more than getting a free ticket to an otherworldly paradise. Here and now, in this world, true conversion creates new personalities—transformed, released, reborn, and sanctified souls with new values, priorities, and evaluational capacities. Salvation is today. Sanctification takes forever.

The value dimensions of spiritual conversion will be explored later, but next we must consider *being choosy about scriptural rules that identify sinfulness*. By which religious or scriptural norms do and should we today judge our moral and spiritual successes and failures? Which scriptural rules should we take seriously, and which not? Which ones truly identify our dark side? Those who insist that we should take them all with equal seriousness, i.e. as "infallible," just don't know what they are talking about. They just don't know what is in the Bible, and they certainly do not know themselves very well. Consciously, subconsciously, or unconsciously everyone is choosy about what counts as sinfulness; but not everyone admits it. We can be convinced that sin in general is disobedience to God, and that God identifies specific kinds of sin in the scriptures, yet still puzzled about exactly what scriptural guidelines to take seriously.

Deciding What Counts as Sinful

> *Both sides [in the Civil War] read the same Bible and pray to the same God, and each invokes His aid against the other.* President Abraham Lincoln, Second Inaugural Address

> *To maintain that slavery is* in itself sinful, *in the face of all that is said and written in the Bible* upon the subject, with so many sanctions of the relation by the Deity himself, does seem to me to be little short of blasphemous! It is direct imputation upon the wisdom and justice, as well as the declared ordinances of God, as they are written in the inspired oracles, to say nothing of their manifestation in the universe around us.[15] Alexander H. Stephens, Vice-President of the Confederacy

> Slavery is wicked—wicked, *in that it violates the great law of liberty, written on every human heart*—wicked, *in that it violates the first commandment of the Decalogue*—wicked, *in that it mars and defaces the image of God by cruel and barbarous inflictions*—wicked, *in that it contravenes the laws of eternal justice, and tramples in the dust all the humane and heavenly precepts of the New Testament.*[16] Frederick Douglass, Abolitionist

The ethico-religious standards, concepts, rules, and laws by which we measure ourselves are systemic entities that exist only in our minds, even if also written down in books or on tablets of stone. They are conceptual constructs that can be deconstructed, modified, revised, qualified, repudiated, or affirmed. They have only an intramental reality and transcend every empirical approximation to them, but they can be applied to every relevant situation. Though they exist only as conceptual constructs, with them we can bring order, direction, virtue, goodness, spirituality, and well-being into what would otherwise be behavioral chaos. Action-guiding moral and spiritual rules and "laws" are standards by which we measure conduct; they can be fulfilled in various degrees; and they can both direct and condemn us.

Some people prefer to affirm *moral rules that are popular with philosophical ethicists*. For example: we should act to maximize goodness, or act on rules that would have the best consequences if everyone acted that way, or avoid inflicting harm, or always treat people as ends in themselves and never merely as means, or treat similar situations in similar ways, or redistribute desirable basic things to the least advantaged members of society. Like religious rules, philosophical rules both direct us and condemn us. No matter their source, rules rebuke us when we fail to live up to them, so even philosophical ethics has its dark side and identifies specific kinds of wrongdoing as well as rightdoing.

Our immediate concern is with *rules or norms derived historically from religious or scriptural sources*. Some of these seem plausible, some not, but how do we separate the good ones from the bad ones? Most Western monotheists affirm selected moral and ceremonial action-guiding rules from the Old and New Testaments. In the bright light of self-knowledge, scriptural norms show that we have not always been true to ourselves, and that we have often disobeyed God's commands. But how do we decide what God has commanded? Most Christians go the scriptures for answers, but which scriptural norms should we affirm? Which ones really do identify specific kinds of sinfulness?

Whether we admit it or not, everyone is and should be very choosy about the biblical rules that we accept as valid and binding. The same is true of social and philosophical rules. For many reasons, everyone ignores or repudiates many biblical norms, even those who profess otherwise. We do not try to pattern our behavior in accord with them, and perhaps we should not. We do not judge ourselves or others to have sinned in violation of some of them. So we pick and choose, but how?

Religious people do not measure themselves by many strange scriptural norms of *other* religions. In fact, they measure themselves only by a chosen few of the norms present in *their own* religion. For many good reasons, this is inescapable, even when not acknowledged. Fundamentalistic Jews, Christians, Moslems, and others who insist that every word of scripture is equally inspired, valid, inerrant, and literal are really very selective about the theistic, moral, and ceremonial scriptural norms they recognize and emphasize. They, along with non-fundamentalists, do not regard violating some if not all of the following rules as sins, even though the Bible, taken literally and in its entirety, clearly does. As that great Jewish lyricist and theologian Ira Gershwin told us, the things that we are liable to read in the Bible "ain't necessarily so."[17] As stated below, these rules are slightly paraphrased, though not inaccurately. Do you accept them all at face value?

– We should not eat pork (Deuteronomy 14:8).

– We should exact a life for a life, an eye for an eye, a tooth for a tooth, a hand for a hand, a foot for a foot, a burning for a burning, a wound for a wound, a stripe for a stripe (Exodus 21:23-25; Leviticus 24:19-20).

– We should not charge interest (usury) on money loaned or invested (Exodus 22:25).

– Those who curse God, who strike or curse their father or mother, who are witches, who have sexual intercourse with animals, or who sacrifice to idols, should be put to death (Leviticus 24:14-16; Exodus 21:15, 17; 22:18-20).

– We should make animal sacrifices to God (Exodus 22:20-24; Leviticus 1, 3).

– We should exterminate all the people—men, women, children, infants, and all their animals—who occupy the land that God has promised to us (Deuteronomy 20:16-17).

– Males should not go to war or attend to any business for one year after they are newly married (Deuteronomy 24:5).

– We should sell all that we have, give it to the poor, and follow Jesus (Matthew 19:21).

– We should forsake our houses, parents, brothers, sisters, spouse, and children to follow Jesus (Luke 18:-28-29; 12:51-53).

– We really should not marry, but we may do so if and only if we are burning with passion (I. Corinthians 7:7-9).

– We should cut off our hands and feet if they are involved in sinful activities (Matthew 5:30; 18:8).

- We may buy and inherit slaves (Leviticus 25:44-46)
- We may sell our daughters into slavery (Exodus 21:7-8).
- Slaves should be obedient to their masters, and masters should be good to their slaves (Ephesians 6:5, 9).
- Women should not adorn themselves with braided hair, gold, pearls, or costly array (I. Timothy 2:9).
- Women should not speak aloud in church (I. Corinthians 14:34-35; I. Timothy 2:11).
- Women should never teach in church or have any authority over men (I. Timothy 2:12).
- Married women should be subject, subordinate, or obedient to their husbands in *all* things (Ephesians 5:22-24).
- Divorces are permissible only when one's spouse has committed adultery (Matthew 5:32; 19:9).
- Adulterers should be put to death (Leviticus 20:10).
- Homosexuality is wrong (Leviticus 18-22; 20:13; Romans 1:26-27; I. Corinthians 6:9; I. Timothy 1:10).
- Homosexuals should be put to death (Leviticus 20:13).

Many if not most Christians today do not accept and live by the troublesome biblical norms here identified, but if not, we are being very selective. Our problem is, how do we select? Evangelicals and most other Christians who are not biblical infallibilists should have no difficulty facing up to this. Only those who affirm biblical infallibility should be disturbed, and they should ask themselves, "Do I really believe that violating all of these rules would be sinful?"

Do you personally find compelling any of the following reasons for rejecting such biblical commands? All of the following "rationalizations," if they are such, permit us to deal selectively (and effectively?) with those parts of the scriptures that we find troublesome.

Some Old Testament rules were countermanded by the New Testament, for example that we should require an eye for an eye, or that we should not eat pigs or other "unclean" foods, and that we should be circumcised (Matthew 5:38-39; I. Timothy 4:4; Acts 15). Jesus and the Christian Bible say that we should not believe everything in the Bible! It ain't necessarily so! Revelation is progressive! If later and better commands set aside earlier commands, they are not all equally valid and infallible. How should we decide which is which? How did Jesus decide when he preached the Sermon on the Mount?

Some commands like making animal sacrifices, selling everything and abandoning family to follow Jesus, and not marrying unless burning with passion, were meant to apply to someone else, not to us, we think. They apply only during particular eras, or only to particular biblical figures, or only to extraordinary saints but not to ordinary believers. They apply only to monastics who take vows of poverty, or only to Christians if we are Jews, or only to Jews if we are Christians. They applied only during the short interim before the immanent "Second Coming," but not over the long haul. Most Christians who affirm Christlikeness (I. Corinthians 11:1; Ephesians 5:1; I. Peter 2:21) and ask: "What would Jesus do?" have no intention of imitating his celibacy, bachelorhood, childlessness, homelessness, poverty, and martyrdom. Imitators of Christ are very selective! And they should also ask, "What would Jesus think?" and "Who and what would Jesus love?"

The command to make animal sacrifices to God applied only during the Old Testament era, Christians believe; and the sacrifice of Jesus on the cross brought that to an end. Jews do not agree about the Jesus part, but for the most part they too no longer sacrifice animals to God. It was repudiated in Psalms 51:16-17. Scripture countermands scripture.

The command to massacre the inhabitants of the promised land does not apply to us, most of us think; but our American forebearers definitely appealed to it and other biblical texts to rationalize their massacre of 100 million American Indians in what Kurt Kaltreider calls "The American Indian Holocaust."[18] Extremists in Israel today appeal to this command and others to justify killing and taking land from the present inhabitants of much of the "promised land," the Arab Palestinians. Anyway, on reflection, most of us have serious moral and spiritual reservations about any and all massacres. Divinely ordained massacres are not easily reconciled with "Love your neighbors as yourselves," "Love strangers as yourselves," and "Love your enemies."

Some rules, like an eye for an eye, were never meant to be taken literally in the first place, says Rabbi Harold S. Kushner.[19] Jesus told us not to take it at all (Matthew 5:38-42), so the Bible contradicts the Bible. Most Christians, even those who profess that everything should be taken literally, really believe that many biblical pronouncements (for example, the anti-family-values, and the self-mutilation rules cited above) were not meant to be taken literally and seriously by anyone.

St. Paul qualified his prohibition of marriage, saying that those who are burning with passion can do it; but what if we are not burning with passion and just want family values, opposite-sex companionship, and children? Paul thought that the world would not last long enough for that; but he was wrong.

Despite what the Old Testament says, most Jews, Christians, and Moslems today fully expect to be paid interest (usury) on the money that they invest or lend to others—or to be paid interest disguised as fees. Actions speak louder than words and betray the conviction that surely God never inspired *that* rule! And didn't Jesus say that worldly prosperity would be added to those who first seek the kingdom of God (Matthew 6:33)? Did he mean only the necessities of life, not all the luxuries?

More seriously, maybe prohibiting all divorces except where one's spouse has committed adultery is just too narrow minded, unrealistic, and impractical, as is forbidding all males to go to war or to attend to business for one year after they are newly married. And why weren't newlywed women excused from work and war for a year? How chauvinist can biblical rules get? And why not divorces just for "irreconcilable differences" if they are truly irreconcilable?

The Old Testament clearly authorized slavery. Unlike the pro-slavery majority in the pre-Civil War South, most American Jews and Christians today do *not* believe that slaves should be obedient to their masters (even if and when they are "good to them") because they repudiate slavery altogether, something the Bible never does. Slavery was a well established institution in the Old Testament, and what St. Paul said about slavery actually supported and encouraged it in the minds of pre-Civil War slave holders. Still, St. Paul conceived of a more excellent way, the way of love, in which the distinction between slaves and free would be abolished. The Bible often sends mixed messages, and both sides in serious controversies can quote it, just as Abraham Lincoln said.

Infallibilists take a systemic all-or-nothing approach to the scriptures. They say that they believe that everything in the Bible is equally inspired, acceptable, valid, literal, and true; but most of them just do not know what is in the Bible! They may condemn cursing God and parents, adultery, and homosexuality on biblical grounds, but they almost *never go all the way* with the Bible on such issues. The Bible does not just condemn such people and practices; *it requires that people who engage in them should be put to death* (Exodus 21: 15, 17; Leviticus 20:10, 13; 24:14-16). Do you really think that *not* putting them to death would be sinful? Or would putting them to death be the sinful thing? Wouldn't that be very unloving?

Today's biblical literalists or inerrantists do not advocate the *execution* of adulterers, homosexuals,[20] and those who curse God or who strike or curse their parents. Would you really want to live under a theocratic government that enforces and carries out these Biblical laws? If all adulterers (including those divorced on non-biblical grounds) were executed, as required by Leviticus 20:10, how many of them would be your friends, relatives, neighbors, and maybe yourself? Would you personally survive such a holocaust? Matthew 5:32 says that if a divorce is not based on adultery, all divorced persons who remarry, and those who marry them, are adulterers. Do you believe that, and are you ready to execute all such persons? People who are not willing to put homosexuals, adulterers, and those who dishonor their parents to death are definitely not going all the way with the Bible. But isn't there a more excellent way, a more loving way? Today, many westerners are appalled at the harshness of some of the Islamic laws in the Koran—without realizing that many laws in the Bible are equally as harsh, if not more so. Is the violation of *all* biblical rules and laws really sinful? Or would obeying them be sinful?

If we are not willing to go all the way with the Bible on executing such offenders, is it not because our own deepest values, our most carefully considered conscience, tells us that the Bible is just wrong about some things? Remember, even the Bible itself says so! Even Jesus said so in discussing what had been "said of old," Matthew 5. Our general reverence or respect for human life, and our love and compassion for particular human beings, may either require or forbid us to obey the

Bible, depending on which parts we area considering. Conscience can help us identify what is believable in the Bible and what is not. So can love. So does formal axiology! We love ourselves, our children, friends, and people in general too much to kill them when they engage in homosexuality, adultery, and dishonor of parents. Jesus said that love fulfills the law, and he was very selective about which laws to accept. If you doubt this, just read the Sermon on the Mount in Matthew 5.

People who claim not to be selective about biblical texts usually are, but they do not like to admit it, especially to themselves. Most Christians today do eat pork. They do not live by St. Paul's decree that women should be reduced to total silence in church, or that women must be completely subordinated and obedient to men in the home, in church, and in all things. Blatant sexism is now correctly assessed and condemned as immoral. Even St. Paul conceived of a more excellent way in which gender makes no difference. Slavery, racism, sexism, and homophobia were acceptable, given the culturally relative norms of First Century Israel, and some of these got into the Bible. Yet, most if not all of these practices are not morally acceptable to us today, given our presumably more reasonable, enlightened, conscientious, loving, and compassionate moral outlook.[21] Jesus, Peter, and Paul insist that biblical systemic and extrinsic distinctions between persons are of no moral and religious consequence (Matthew 19:30; 20:1-16; Acts 10:34; Galatians 3:28; Ephesians 6:5-9; Colossians 3:11; Timothy 6:1-2; Titus 2:9-10)? Doesn't the Bible itself often tell us that we should not accept everything that is in the Bible?

Biblical norms, requirements, and practices may be dismissed for many other reasons: perhaps their meaning is unclear; the translations are bad; they are being taken out of context; the interpretation does not harmonize with the author's intentions, or with the main thrusts of biblical religion; the passage was not in the original text but was added by a later scribe; the words were *mistakenly* attributed to an authoritative source like Moses, Jesus, or Paul; or there is a more excellent, a more loving way. Maybe Moses did not write the first five books of the Old Testament. Maybe Jesus never uttered the uncharacteristic black or white systemic judgment that "He that is not with me is against me" (Matthew 12:30); in Mark 9:40 the wording is, "For he that is not against us is for us," which isn't nearly as harsh. Maybe Jesus never claimed that only those who believe in him can be saved (Acts 4:12; Matthew 11:27); if he did, maybe he meant having a loving personal relation with him rather than believing orthodox doctrines about him;); maybe, as Peter Gomes thinks, the words translated as "homosexual" in both testaments originally applied only to specific, transient, and exploitive kinds of homosexuality. If so, the Bible does not condemn faithful, committed, loving, and monogamous homosexuality based upon impulses grounded in biology and/or early childhood experiences, and over which homosexuals have no choice or control. Maybe the rule that women cannot speak in church was not in Paul's original letter to the Corinthians but was added by a later scribe or copier.[22] Even so, that does not settle the question of divine inspiration. Maybe God inspired only the most loving and compassionate parts of it. Maybe God's revelations are progressive, which means that what God commanded for an early era was later set aside by what God inspired for a more advanced era. Or maybe God's revealed messages were occasionally distorted by sinful, unloving, ignorant, or culturally limited and deprived human receivers. We have to decide for ourselves. Maybe value theory can help.

The most important reason for repudiating some biblical action-guiding rules is that they do not match or measure up to our deepest, best informed, and most carefully considered values and evaluations—and most particularly the two biblical love commandments. If biblical religion has a heart, this is it. Some scriptural rules and practices are just plain unconscionable and unloving. In good conscience, not every person in the Bible can be a role model for us, and not every principle can be our guide. We often hear that we must give up certain biblical practices like slavery, racism, polygamy, sexism, and vengeance because they are incompatible with deeper biblical principles like loving others as ourselves;[23] but how do we decide what counts as an objectionable biblical practice and what counts as a deep biblical principle? Why aren't slavery, sexism, and revenge the deep natural and biblical principles, with love functioning only within that rubric? That was the way things worked for St. Paul and for slave owners in the ante-bellum south. The Southern Baptist Convention views the subordination of women that way today.[24] Yet, Southern Baptists are not ready to return to thoroughly biblical slavery and polygamy, to hush women *entirely* in church, to give them absolutely no authority whatsoever over men, and to stop them from braiding their hair or wearing gold, pearls, and costly garments. Do or should Baptist and other Christian husbands really practice the absolute control of wives by their husbands? Would it be sinful *not* to keep them in subordination? This is very doubtful. Their consciences and their wives wouldn't allow it! St. Paul assumed that masters should be good to their chattel slaves, that husbands should be good to their totally submissive and obedient wives, and that love should be expressed only within the context of those broad, deep, and divinely ordained but repressive social hierarchies. Do you agree? Or is there a more excellent way, a more loving way?

Presumably, *our own* deepest and most carefully and considered values, the most reliable aspects of admittedly fallible conscience, distinguish deep and enduring principles from transient, relative, and objectionable social and religious practices. Clearly, some biblical rules take priority over others; some are very profound; but others are irrelevant, unrealistic, uninformed, or downright immoral. Again, how do we distinguish between sound and unsound scriptural rules, or determine which rules have priority when conflicts occur? Many people believe that without the Bible we could not know the difference between right and wrong, but in reality we may require the carefully refined intuitions and reflections of enlightened conscience, (extra-biblical knowledge of right and wrong), to decide what to accept and what to reject in the Bible! As John Wesley recognized, "There are some Scriptures which more immediately commend themselves to every man's conscience"[25] than others.

The scriptures of the world religions almost universally affirm the value of truth, so their devotees should be able to appeal to extra-scriptural sources of truth on scriptural grounds. Formal Axiology is an extra-scriptural source that sheds light on which behavioral rules in the scriptures to accept, which to repudiate, and how to rank the many rules that do make good sense. Applied axiology accords almost perfectly with the two love commandments of Jesus, and some people may just want to stop there. If so, good enough; but others may want to go a bit deeper, if only for a better understanding of love and its most proper objects.

Robert S. Hartman claimed that axiology is independent of theology and that it can supply theology with a valid theoretical "frame of reference."[26] According to the hierarchy of values with which we are working, the intrinsic takes priority over the extrinsic, which, in turn, has priority over the systemic. These rankings are fundamental and universal mandates of reflective or enlightened conscience, and they are the highest goals of "true religion." After very careful consideration, enlightened conscience the world over affirms Hartman's hierarchy of value. All three dimensions of positive value have great worth, but the intrinsic is more valuable than (richer in good-making properties than) the extrinsic, and the extrinsic is more valuable than the systemic. The hierarchy of values is not culturally relative. Multicultural data obtained from testing with the Hartman Value Profile (HVP) show that in their more reflective moments, and with only relatively minor deviations, people the world over almost universally affirm the hierarchy of value.[27] This is true even if most people fall short and actually live as worldlings and ideologists in their less reflective moments. Perhaps axiology can refute wholesale value relativism, though more work remains to be done.

Applied to ethics, the hierarchy of values generates or correlates with moral rules such as: (1) we ought to develop ourselves, and help others to develop themselves, systemically, extrinsically, and intrinsically; (2) we ought to value all persons, including ourselves, intrinsically and never merely extrinsically or merely systemically; and (3) we ought to choose courses of action that sustain or increase value and avoid actions that decrease value in all dimensions. Not doing so would be wrong. Considered spiritually, not doing so would be sinful.

Such value insights are so fundamental, so profound, so essential and universal to our humanity, individuality, and enlightened conscience that they should be deliberately taught regularly and repeatedly in our public and private schools, as well as in our religious institutions and homes. Biblical counterparts to them can easily be found and selected. Our entertainment media should emphasize them instead of sex, greed, hatred, bullying, coercion, and violence. Due to almost universal human perversity this is not likely to happen, though it should. Persuading members of the world religions, and denominations or sects within them, to affirm and act upon these axiological insights is the surest and soundest path to ecumenicism, peace on earth, and good will toward all men, women, and children.

Rules as such are only systemic goods, but they can help, inform, and direct us intrinsically, extrinsically, and systemically. The most acceptable rules given to us historically by the world religions and by our own cultures direct us to respect the immense intrinsic worth of and the basic rights of conscious individuals as we act toward and upon them. We have also inherited more questionable rules and practices that instruct us to treat some people and almost all animals as if their worth is merely extrinsic or systemic, or to disvalue them completely. Which rules are best? We must choose. Even if God inspired and authorized them, sinners wrote down the scriptures; and they put both the worst and the best of themselves into them. We have to decide which is which.

Some biblical rules may direct us erroneously to treat people and animals as if their worth is merely extrinsic or systemic, but other biblical rules clearly say otherwise. Enlightened conscience cannot affirm scriptural or social rules that debase and devalue conscious individuals. "Love your neighbors, strangers, even your enemies" values people intrinsically. "Destroy, ostracize, exclude, avenge, enslave, manipulate, exploit, suppress, or subordinate people," as the Bible sometimes commands, disvalues intrinsically valuable human beings, and animals almost always get the worst end of every such bargain.

During biblical times, slavery was not based on race. Whether based on race or not, all slavery, including scriptural slavery, by definition reduces people to things, to property, to merely extrinsic goods. The ancestors of those of us who grew up in the South believed in slavery on biblical grounds. Contemporary racists and sexists also devalue people. All prejudices manifest a systemic reductionism that is blind to the abundance of human and individual goodness. Human witches, zoophiles, homosexuals, slaves, women, unbelievers, and offenders of every description, are actually unique persons who, even with their flaws, are immensely rich in desirable traits or good-making properties. They are also equally loved by God. Their immense value is conspicuously debased or devalued when their total worth is reduced to nothing more than a small handful properties that prejudiced people dislike, and everything else about them is ignored. Loving our enemies, wives, husbands, neighbors, strangers, etc., should always take priority over killing or debasing metaphorical Canaanites and literal witches, zoophiles, parent-debasers, deviants, strangers, aliens, and unbelievers. In a civilized society, loving and respecting others as equals, especially in church and within marriage, the family, and friendship, should always take priority over squelching or subordinating people because of differences in gender, race, ethnicity, or other extrinsic or systemic irrelevancies.

Taking the hierarchy of value as our theoretical frame of reference also shows up the dark side of self and self-knowledge. By both axiological and the best of biblical standards, we often engage in morally and spiritually objectionable practices. The brute facts show that we are almost universally disposed so to do. Awareness of our dark side can prompt us to seek profound changes in our fundamental value orientations, beliefs, standards, motives, dispositions, and practices. We could selectively quote scripture to support such changes; but in some instances, sinfulness does not consist in disobeying biblical rules; it consists in obeying them!

New Birth and Sanctification

> We shall give you the difference between this spiritual knowledge of divine things and the knowledge of divinity that natural men have as to the effects of it.... This spiritual knowledge transforms the heart, the other doth not. The believer hath got such a sight and such a knowledge of things that, ever since, he is become quite another man than he was before. It has exceeding altered his internal tempers and disposition. The knowledge that he has is so substantial, so inward, and so affecting, that it has quite transformed the soul and put a new nature into the man, has quite changed his very innermost principles, and has made things otherwise, even from the very foundation, even so that all things are become new to them. Yea, he is a new creature, he is just as if he was not the same, but were born again, created over a second time. That light and knowledge has been let into his soul that has so affected him that he has a new nature, just as if a new spirit were infused into that body; of an angel of darkness has made an angel of light of him; has brought the image of God upon him; has made him of an heavenly temper and an angelic mind; has sweetened and mollified his dispositions; and of an heart of stone hath made a heart of flesh, of bitter has made sweet, and of dark has made light. This the effect of true and spiritual [knowledge] of divine things.[28] Jonathan Edwards

Spiritual conversion, as understood in this book, is not a matter of proselytizing from one religion to another—something quite rare in some religions like Judaism.[29] Rather, it is the fundamental change of values that takes place in the soul when people begin to take spirituality very seriously. Conversion in Judaism is like the transformation of Jacob into Israel, something that takes place within and in the presence of God. In Christianity it is being "born again." *Sanctification* (saint-making) is the additional process of ongoing growth in grace, beliefs, practices, commitments, affections, and value enrichments that follows conversion. It is the lifelong process of saint-making, of growth in holiness. Throughout their lives, saints continually "press toward the mark of the high calling of God," as St. Paul put it (Philippians 3:14).

The standard Christian "morphology of conversion" proclaims that by the grace of God we can be changed from bad people into better people; we can be "born again" metaphorically and internally, though not literally and physically. Our dark side can be replaced with light. We can grow into and toward the light. Subjectively, this involves repenting of our sins, being reconciled to God and others, gaining a sense of being forgiven by God, other people, and ourselves, transforming our affections and priorities, learning to do the works of love, becoming active members of the body of Christ, thinking more Godly or Christlike thoughts, and rejoicing and delighting in divine things, not just earthly things. It involves coming to love God most of all and our neighbors as ourselves, instead of mostly loving wealth, social honors, and/or cognitive beliefs. This new birth is spiritual or psychological, not physical, though it doubtless affects the brain. As theologians claim, it involves marvelous new objective relationships with God and all of God's creations, with all of life and existence. Subjectively, psychologically, and spiritually, the change is largely evaluational, the subject matter of this book.

New value-objects and immensely enhanced valuational capacities come to assume the "hot spot" in the religious convert's consciousness, and these grow richer, deeper, and more inclusive as sanctification proceeds. Axiologically, being born again means making a transition, a leap, (1) from consciousness dominated by extrinsic or systemic values and evaluations into a newly structured consciousness in which intrinsic values and evaluations prevail, and (2) immensely expanding the range or scope of who and what is valued intrinsically. By nature, we value very few beings intrinsically; by saving and sanctifying grace, we come to value everything and everyone, including God, intrinsically. In redeemed souls, love and compassion prevail over all else, though the all else remains and is also redeemed.

Every religion, denomination, congregation, or individual convert may flesh out the specific value-transformations involved in "getting religion" somewhat differently. But every such variation can be analyzed according to the relative position and weight given to systemic, extrinsic, and intrinsic values and evaluations. This perspective on values provides a powerful systematic framework for understanding all religious phenomena. Coverage here cannot be exhaustive, but we will now summarize some of the themes of previous chapters as related to spiritual conversion.

First, in all conversion, whether spiritual or not, old *values*, that is, objects of value, are replaced by new ones. The primary value-objects of converts, the ones to which they give the most attention and emphasis, are changed, often drastically. This may happen swiftly, but not always. Where extrinsic (worldly) or systemic (ideological) values once prevailed, intrinsic values now reign supreme.

Worldliness is the most common pre-conversion spiritual/psychological stance, according to most theologians. Worldliness has an identifiable value structure. The primary value-objects of worldly, natural, pre-converted people are extrinsic physical self-preservation, material or physical things, social status, libido gratification derived from extrinsic entities and processes, revenge for threats to worldly well-being and prosperity, rewards to those who contribute to their worldly success, and aggression against those who have what they want. Worldly values are often called "temporal" goods, but axiologically they are extrinsic goods. Men and women of the world tend to reduce other values like systemic ideas and intrinsic people to extrinsic values; they see and use them only as means to *tangible* ends. They devote their lives to acquiring, possessing, and flaunting prestigious sensory objects—land, houses, furnishing, automobiles, clothing, luxuries, and so on, and the money necessary for owning them. They value people and ideas instrumentally. Other people and ideas are useful to them in acquiring security, property, prosperity, success, status symbols, social power, dominance over others, extrinsic pleasures, reciprocal altruism, aggression, and revenge.

Religious converts put their former worldly or temporal values on the back burner, repudiating or at least dethroning them; and newly valued intrinsic objects like their own souls, other souls, and the Ultimate Divine Soul, assume the hot spot in their valuing consciousness. They finally realize that there is no profit in gaining the world and losing their souls—a difficult thing to comprehend, apparently. Despite our natural self-centeredness, most of the time we attach too little value to persons, including ourselves. Worldlings do not realize that individual souls, unique centers of conscious experience, choice, activity, and evaluation, are the only things that are intrinsically good or valuable for their own sakes.[30]

Second, converts begin to view and *evaluate* everything and everyone differently. Not just what they value but how they value changes. They acquire new or immensely enhanced capacities for valuing everything, especially intrinsic realities (God, people, animals). They discover that their capacities for intrinsic evaluation were exceedingly weak prior to conversion. They realize that their former valuational strengths were primarily extrinsic and/or systemic. Or, if they were already strong intrinsically, they recall that their intrinsic energies and passions were directed almost entirely toward extrinsic material things and social status, or toward doctrines and conceptual symbols, or toward only a very few insiders. Idolatrously, most of them mainly the things of the world with all their hearts, souls, minds, and strengths. These were their ultimate concerns. With "true religion" comes enhanced capacities for intrinsic evaluation, for cherishing all conscious beings as ends in themselves, and for feeling, acting, and thinking or believing accordingly. Intrinsic evaluation capacities develop and intensify as sanctification proceeds. Love and compassion grow and grow, and they encompass more and more.

Spiritual-minded people are not the only ones capable of valuing intrinsically. People who do not consider themselves very spiritual may be more spiritual than they give themselves credit for being, especially if they have greatly enhanced intrinsic evaluational capacities. Spirituality awakens and enlivens a person's capacities for deeply cherishing God, other people, her or him self, animals, and all living things (e.g., Albert Schweitzer's "reverence for life"). Converts can see that all unique and irreplaceable conscious individuals have immense worth before God and within themselves.

Not only are their *capacities* for intrinsic evaluation, for loving and rejoicing in the being of self and others, enhanced, but the *scope* or range of entities valued by converts also expands immensely as sanctification intensifies and enlarges the soul. Our natural capacities for empathy, compassion, and caring deeply and unselfishly for others are very limited. Contemporary sociobiology indicates that the scope of our natural altruistic capabilities usually extends no further than to insiders, to kin, friends, allies, and clan, but certainly not to all souls. Spiritually reborn persons are enabled to care more deeply and unselfishly for strangers, outsiders, aliens, enemies, everyone, everything. They can also act accordingly, guided by appropriate moral/spiritual rules, beliefs, and religious practices, and supported and encouraged socially by the communion of the saints. God-likeness consists in being like God, who in his omnipresence includes, embraces, and cares for all, and for whom there is no distinction between outsiders and insiders.

Why should religious people want to fulfill "the law," to follow carefully selected moral/spiritual systemic rules, the ones that fulfill the laws of love? Religious people are immensely diverse, and they follow rules for many different reasons. They may (mistakenly?) value rules or principles intrinsically as ends in themselves, as did the philosopher, Immanuel Kant or the ancient Pharisees. They may (mistakenly?) view rules, or obedience to them, as effective means to achieving spiritual objectives like earning their own salvation, or meriting exalted religious rewards here or hereafter. Believing that religion pays, they may employ selected moral and spiritual rules as extrinsic means to worldly prosperity, success, and glory. They may simply affirm "the law" systemically, impartially, or disinterestedly as true and valid. They may see behavioral guidelines as tried-and-true extrinsic or useful means for bringing about the beneficial results that are desired by God and godly persons. They may strive to fulfill the law because they have been "born again" and regard selected scriptural rules as proper guidelines for expressing the intrinsic virtues of born-again souls.

To born-again converts, ethico-religious virtues are either new or immensely enhanced old capacities and dispositions for loving, caring for, empathizing with, being compassionate toward, concentrating on, and identifying with others. Converts cease being dominated by left-brain functions and begin to live also in their right-brains, mid-brains, fore-brains, and whole-brains. Their evaluational capacities are increasingly integrated into the comprehensive wholeness of intrinsic self-knowledge and self-expression. Carefully selected biblical rules are affirmed and acted upon, not as the causes of, but as the effects of, their own salvation. The transformations of character that constitute salvation and sanctification refocus on new loved ones, new ultimate concerns, and newly awakened and expanded evaluational capacities.

Mixed Blessings

A Christian is so far perfect as not to commit sin.[31] John Wesley

A perfect Christian...is one who loves the Lord his God with all his heart, with all his soul, with all his mind, and with all his strength. God is the joy of his heart,

> *and the desire of his soul....For as he loves God, "so he keeps His commandments": not only some, or most of them, but ALL, from the least to the greatest.*[32] John Wesley

> [Christian Perfection is] *the loving of God with all our heart, mind, soul and strength. This implies that no wrong temper, none contrary to love, remains in the soul; and that all the thoughts, words, and actions are governed by pure love.* John Wesley[33]

> *The children of God are delivered from the bondage of sin by new birth. This does not mean complete freedom and absence of temptation. A ceaseless battle goes on, to exercise the saints and help them to understand their weakness. There is still a spring of evil in every born-again man, which gives rise to sinful desires and actions. Wrong appetites still flourish and, even though resisted, incite us to lust, greed, ambition and other vices....Sin no longer reigns, but it still remains.*[34] John Calvin

> *The most valuable value, that is, the value that fulfills the concept "value" most fully, is intrinsic value....Any direction away from intrinsic value is negative, any direction toward or beyond it, positive. In the positive direction lie goodness and its intensifications, in the negative direction badness and its intensifications. The former, we might say, is the direction of enhancement, the latter that of debasement.*[35] Robert S. Hartman

Sin is a matter of valuing wrongly, no matter what else it involves (e.g., violating God and other people). Do some of our sinful dispositions persist after soul-transforming conversion? Theologians disagree. Most agree with John Calvin that by degrees sinfulness, valuing wrongfully, persists even after making a new spiritual beginning and being set on the right road. Learning to value rightly requires ongoing sanctification, growth in grace, working out our salvation, lifelong spiritual development, and constant vigilance. Increasing spirituality and holiness may be interrupted by periodic lapses or backsliding. Converts strive for perfect intrinsic evaluation, perfect love, all compassion, absolute obedience to the love commandments, and abundant living; but they seldom if ever achieve complete perfection. Christian perfection is the end state or goal of the process of sanctification—growing in holiness—the final state of fully mature Christians, not the present state of all Christians, especially newborn "babes in Christ."

Spiritual development is almost always accompanied by some degree of spiritual pride, a "Holier than Thou" attitude toward spiritual "inferiors"; and intellectual development is almost always conjoined with subtle vanity, a "Dumber than I" attitude toward others. Feigned humility often masks spiritual pride, as in the title of the fictional book titled *Humility, and How I Achieved It*. Self-knowledge honestly acknowledges covert and overt vices as well as virtues. Vices and virtues are usually impure and mixed in this life. Saintly goodness is usually tainted by sin and despair, except perhaps for a very few very mature saints. Striving for perfection differs infinitely from achieving it. Even the slightest flaw destroys perfection, for perfection is all or nothing. Only God has it. Today, most ministers emphasize only "striving for perfection."

In this world, spirituality is always a mixed blessing. Its finest elements are almost always mixed by degrees with their opposites. Knowledge is mixed with ignorance, clarity with confusion, faith and confidence with uncertainty and mistrust, strength with weakness. Temptations and yielding to them linger in redeemed souls. Spiritual gladness is mixed with sadness. Spiritual happiness is diluted by crosses, by a tragic sense of life, and by a keen sense of evil in the world, in nature, in us. New converts become keenly aware of sinfulness in human society, in human institutions and practices, in other human beings, and in themselves. William James said that there is always something "solemn" about the profound spirituality that involves "happiness in the absolute and the everlasting." James wrote, "A solemn state of mind is never crude or simple—it seems to contain a certain measure of its own opposite....A solemn joy preserves a sort of bitter in its sweetness; a solemn sorrow is one to which we intimately consent."[36] Compassion is clearly such a mixed blessing. Compassion is suffering with others who suffer, but suffering is suffering, even if both benevolent and fulfilling. Primary suffering is never good; but suffering with suffering, secondary suffering, compassion, is profoundly fulfilling. Compassionate suffering with others who suffer is joyful, deeply satisfying, and incredibly consoling; but it is not pure bliss. Saints rejoice with those who rejoice and suffer with those who suffer, so spirituality isn't all sweetness and light. It is a mixed but solemn and profound blessing.

Valuing rightly is difficult to do and sustain. Living or acting correctly is even more difficult. No one ever said these are easy. Valuing correctly involves ranking ideas and systems lower than things, processes, and social status, and ranking people, animals, and all centers of conscious experience, knowledge, choice, action and evaluation above all else. Valuing rightly involves ranking intrinsic values and evaluations over extrinsic, and extrinsic over systemic, as further explained and defended in the Appendix to follow. Valuing rightly is constantly mixed with valuing wrongly. We may lose it (backslide) after gaining it; and we constantly need self-transformation, repentance, forgiveness, and reconciliation.[37] Before God, we never have a completely clear conscience.

Learning how and what to value correctly is an integral part of authentic religious conversion, of overcoming the dark side, of gaining a properly refurbished soul. Conversion does not always take. Desirable moral and spiritual values evaluations come and go. Many religious converts soon backslide, fall from grace, and revert to less desirable values and habits of evaluation. From the time of the Great Awakening of the 1740s, surprised and chagrined revivalists saw (and still see) many converts revert to their former wicked ways after a few days, weeks, or months. Describing the long-run consequences of revivalism, Jonathan Edwards put it graphically: "The high affections of many seem to be so soon to come to nothing, and some who seemed to be mightily raised and swallowed with joy and zeal for a while, seem to have returned like the dog to his vomit."[38] This repulsive dog/vomit simile is entirely biblical (Proverbs 26:11; II Peter 2:22).

Aside from grace, at least two spiritually significant determinants (both of which manifest grace) help to sustain newly acquired values and evaluational capacities. One is the willingness of individuals to practice regularly until their new value focuses, behaviors, and attitudes become habitual or "second nature"—an Aristotelian point. The other is social encouragement, support, and expression—the "communion of the saints"—a Christian point.

Although many religious converts soon fall by the wayside and revert to their wicked ways, some really do undergo dramatic and enduring changes in what and how they value. A vision of the intrinsic goodness of God and their neighbors begins to prevail over extrinsic mammon and ego. Their largely right-brain and min-brain capacities for intrinsic evaluation, love, empathy, compassion, creativity, joy in the well-being of others, euphoric delight in all positive aspects of creation, and intuitive insight are immensely enhanced. Their actions express their new or improved ethico-religious affections, and their thoughts and beliefs bring them joy and peace beyond comprehension, even if tinged with sadness, solemnity, sacrifices, and crosses. They experience ecstatic but solemn happiness, mixed with a tragic sense of life and evil, in their new relations with God and others. Self-knowledge of personal shortcomings, together with sincere repentance, self forgiveness, the forgiveness of and reconciliation with others they have wronged, and Divine forgiveness and restoration, really do clear the way for positive value transformations. Sinfulness is forgiven but never completely forgotten. *Soul-rebirth* may take place very suddenly or very gradually; either way, the felicitous results are the same. *Soul-growth* takes forever.

Sanctification, becoming a holistic saint, is a lifelong process requiring enormous effort, devotion, commitment, cooperation, community support, and divine grace. Conversion is only the beginning of the right road, not its end. Old habits and values die hard, especially those of worldliness and ideology. Becoming a saint is a lifelong process, and few if any reach the ultimate goal of perfection in this life. By degrees, saintliness and saintly values and evaluations are within us all along the way, but so are their opposites. Saintly values and evaluations are there to be further cultivated and nurtured. Success in such value transformations determines the degree to which we live abundantly in what and how we think, say, do, feel, and love. Our *journey* is an integral part of our final *destination*; *now* is an integral part of *eternity*; salvation is today. This is the day of our salvation, just as St. Paul said.

Other-religious and Extra-religious Transformations

> *If the idea of salvation is given any experiential content, in terms of, for example, human renewal, liberation, re-creation, becoming a new creature, or achieving an authentically human existence, then it is manifestly the case that such transforming experiences occur outside as well as inside Christianity.*[39] John Hick

Whether or not they use the word "conversion," the world religions take personality-transformation very seriously and strive to effect it. Real conversion is personality-transformation, which is largely value-transformation. Most if not all religions emphasize both the need to change the objects we most value and to develop our higher evaluational capacities. Idolatry consists in supremely valuing the wrong objects, and the more passionate this is, the worse it is. The world religions may disagree about exactly what we should value most; but, on a very abstract level, they tell us, says John Hick, that we should learn to value "the Real" or a transcendent "Eternal One."[40] Just what this means can vary immensely from one religion to another.

The world religions probably agree more about *how* we should value Ultimate Reality than about *what* exactly it is. God is the Ultimate in the monotheistic religions, but some religions like Humanism and Hinayana Buddhism are not theistic. Ancient Greek and Roman religions were polytheistic. Still, they might agree that we should take the Ultimate with utmost seriousness; we should value it intrinsically, with all our souls. Paul Tillich said that being ultimately (or profoundly) concerned about something that gives meaning to life, and to which all other concerns are subordinated, is the defining characteristic of "religion."[41]

Surveying the world religions to find minimal common denominators by which "religion" can be defined reveals that (1) being grasped by ultimate concern and commending it to others, (2) giving meaning (or value) to life, and (3) dealing with the origin of and cure for evil, come very close to being religious universals.[42] These common traits of religion involve values and evaluations, as well as ontological commitments. Particular religions usually involve more than value-enhancement; and enhanced values and evaluations may be achieved in secular as well as religious ways.

Spirituality may not be the only way of being or becoming deeply involved or committed, or finding meaning or value in life, or resolving questions about good and evil, or learning to love deeply and unselfishly. Liberal education, psychotherapy, and good mothering, fathering, or caregiving may do so in their own ways. At the level of meta-ethics or axiology, philosophical value theory analyzes these concepts and tries to explain what they mean. Ethics and spirituality proper offer definite answers to ultimate questions about values and evaluations. Spiritual conversion brings about a repudiation of evil in oneself and others, as well as deeper personal involvement with and commitment to what is positively valued, whether systemic objects like rules and beliefs, extrinsic objects like material things and social rankings, or intrinsic objects like unique centers of consciousness, ranging in complexity all the way up to an infinite God. But spirituality is not the only way to get there, or at least part of the way. Even the study of value theory can help.

Many successful "secular" approaches to desirable human values and evaluational transformations are now available, and religious institutions have no monopoly on them, even if they are their best and most effective custodians. Can you think of any efficacious secular approaches in addition to liberal education, psychotherapy, good parenting, and value inquiry? All of these approaches vary in effectiveness and availability. Aside from good parenting, the religions of the world have probably been more successful than anything else. This is likely to continue, and some religions may be better at this than others. Most ordinary people find religion to be more accessible and effective than other sources of value formation and transformation. The secular *Hartman Value Profile* can also be used to measure and facilitate value transformations, whatever their source, and the *Christian Values Profile*[43] can be used to measure and enable Christian spiritual transformations.

Some approaches to spirituality bring the secular into the religious. Viewed spiritually, all of the above are manifestations of God's prevenient grace. From this perspective, God's presence, grace, and activity are in all constructive processes and realities, even when spirituality and God are not consciously or expressly acknowledged. No purely natural persons are absolutely devoid of grace; some degree of common, preparatory, or "prevenient" grace is available to all, for God loves and influences all, whether they know it or not. Unacknowledged sacred realities may be present and active even in the "secular" study of value theory, the practice of psychotherapy, good mothering or caregiving, and every beneficent institutional, social, and personal process and practice that helps people adopt better values and become better valuers. The world's major religions concretize value transformations for particular cultures and individuals. Enhanced capacities for intrinsic evaluation, and new or renewed appreciation for the Ultimate are deeply colored for Jews by Abraham, Moses, and the Exodus, for Christians by Jesus and Paul, for Moslems by Mohammed, for Buddhists by Gautama, and so on.

We philosophers would like to transcend the limitations of our time and place, but no one ever does so completely. Yet, we can make creative advances that push back the darkness. By degrees, we are all products of the broad cultural environments that have shaped us both philosophically and spiritually. Whether deeply thoughtful or not, most young Christians grow up to be adult Christians, most Jews to be Jews, most Moslems to be Moslems, most secularists to be secularists, and so on. There is nothing wrong with that, even if it is constantly being modified by multiculturalism. All people are shaped within and by their given religious culture, even those who define themselves by animosity to religion. When serious expressions of religious belief, worship, and practice take concrete form and find social expression, they do so in historically definite ways, and all of us just have to make the best of what we have been given and what we can create out of it.

No one lives an ethico-religious life, or any kind of a life, "in general" or "in the abstract." Even the most reflective moral and spiritual persons eventually find, after much consideration and many trials, that they are more comfortable with one style of spirituality rather than another (or with no spirituality at all). Not every mode of spirituality is a live option for everyone. Within broad and diverse spiritual traditions like Judaism and Christianity, deeply reflective adults may find that they are most at home with Orthodox, Reformed, or Conservative Judaism, or with Baptist, Presbyterian, Methodist, Unitarian, or Roman Catholic Christianity, or with some other historically determinate variety and community of spirituality, though not necessarily the exact one in which they grew up. This need not mean that they regard other religions or denominations as inherently inferior, or that they concoct theological or philosophical excuses for disvaluing other historical expressions of spirituality. It simply acknowledges our finitude and historicity.

Everyone's spiritual values and evaluations (or the absence thereof) must take some definite historical form. Each unique person's concreteness or definiteness is partly derived from his or her culture or sub-culture. Deep always calls and answers unto deep in historically definite and relative ways. From human limitations and historicity, no one can totally escape. Individuality is very real; but, for inherently social beings, our uniqueness is inescapably finite, relational, social, and historical, and we can never be who and what we are in absolute social isolation or independence. To one degree or another, all of us are members of one another, and this is a good thing, not a bad thing.

Value Theory and Spiritual Personality Types

> *To sum up all, the natural man neither fears nor loves God, one under the law fears, one under grace loves him.*
>
> *From this plain account of the threefold state of man, the 'natural', the 'legal', and the 'evangelical'—it appears that it is not sufficient to divide mankind into sincere and insincere. A man may be sincere in any of these states.*
>
> *'Examine yourselves', therefore, not only whether ye are sincere, but 'whether ye be in the faith.' Examine narrowly; for it imports you much. What is the ruling principle of your soul? Is it the love of God? Is it the fear of God? Or is it neither one nor the other? Is it not rather the love of the world? The love of pleasure? Or gain? Of ease; or reputation?....These several states of the soul are often mingled together, and in some measure meet in one and the same person. Thus experience shows that the legal state, or state of fear, is frequently mixed with the natural; for few men are so fast asleep in sin but they are sometimes more or less awakened....In like manner, the evangelical state, or state of love, is frequently mixed with the*

legal. For few of those who have the spirit of bondage and fear remain always without hope.[44] John Wesley

Earlier discussions in this book briefly explained, and the following Appendix will explain further, that axiology recognizes three types of value (*what* we value) and three of evaluation (*how* we value), systemic, extrinsic, and intrinsic. All six may be combined with one another in an immense variety of ways; and they are in fact so combined in every existing human personality. John Wesley anticipated this in describing the legalistic, the natural or worldly, and the evangelical or loving stages of spiritual development. These correspond closely with systemic, extrinsic, and intrinsic value orientations or combinations of them, and Wesley wisely noted that they are usually intermixed.

In all persons, complex values and evaluations tend to combine into relatively stable patterns. This is why we have generally stable and enduring personalities or characters, and why personalities profiles may help each of us to "Know thyself." Even with somewhat pliable personas, we and others can make many fairly accurate predictions about what we will be like in the future, what we will choose and do, and what and how we will value. An aura of uncertainty and unpredictability always remains, not just because we lack information, but because we are free and creative, and character is not a done deal until death do us depart.

Important spiritual thinkers, both East and West, say that not all people possess the same grade or level of selfhood. Kierkegaard, for example, thought that some people have more self, more consciousness, greater awareness, larger souls than others. Value theory can shed some light on this claim. The basic structure of human consciousness is organized around values and evaluations, and these differ significantly from person to person. Our conscious individuality exists and develops in time. It is not a finished and polished whole, not a "done deal." It must be developed and completed. The world in which one person lives and values may be quite different from that in which another person lives and values. This depends upon the condition, type, and developmental stage of the value consciousness through which each unique person relates to what exists and to what ought to be. Irreconcilable differences may exist between human beings, not only about what ought to be, but also about what actually is or exists, for one person may simply "see" more and be more of a self than another. Spiritually developed people (holistic saints) see more, live more abundantly, and love more abundantly than spiritually undeveloped people (worldlings and ideologists). They have larger or more inclusive souls. That is a very good reason for striving for perfection in all three value dimensions.

Holistic saints most value the intrinsic and disvalue the *dominance* of the extrinsic, the systemic, or anything else that detracts from intrinsic wholeness, but they do not repudiate practicality and thoughtfulness. Instead, they try their best to develop them, too. Note that *developing* all evaluational capacities adequately or equally is not the same as *valuing* them equally. The three dimensions of value are not all equally valuable, but they are equally or adequately developed in well balanced saintly personalities. Whole persons can accept the hierarchy of value, which affirms that intrinsic values are the *best values*, while recognizing that developing all three evaluational capacities equally, or at least adequately relative to their own uniqueness, yields the *best personality*.

The preceding chapters focused on value dominance, but they gave relatively little attention to the exact ordering of subordinate value dimensions. Thus, they do not give a complete analysis of all possible spiritual value types. They showed how excessive value dominance produces lopsided personalities, and how slightly warped personalities produce, express, or unite with, lopsided religions or spirituality. Chapter Three showed how even saints can be unbalanced, but not the best of them. It explained why saintliness ought to be balanced or holistic and how holistic saintly personalities express spiritual wholeness and live most abundantly. Did you find your own personality and spiritual type somewhere in the preceding pages?

Some but not all readers will now want to delve more deeply into the axiological theory employed here to explain such things. This is done next in the following Appendix. You may or may not want to read it.

Appendix

Axiology, Self-knowledge, Values, and Evaluations

Robert S. Hartman, a Twentieth Century axiological genius, died very prematurely in 1973. Since his death, members of the Robert S. Hartman Institute for Formal and Applied Axiology have carried on his work, refined and improved upon his reflections, and extended applications of his value theory into many disciplines, as anticipated but not accomplished by Hartman himself. This book has applied his theory to spirituality, but now we need to look more carefully at the theory itself.[1]

Hartman anticipated that his axiology or value theory would some day be applied to most intellectual disciplines, but he did not live long enough to see this happen. In his lectures and in his seminal book, *The Structure of Value*, he taught that "As the proof of the pudding is in the eating, so the proof of a value theory is in the application."[2] You have almost finished reading this book which, speaking metaphorically, invited you to a spiritual feast. It gave you a chance to try out this theory of value for yourself and to see if its axiological frame of reference helps you to understand different types of spirituality, especially your own.

Hartman's approach to axiology was *formal*. This distinguishes him from other axiologists. He wanted to create a science of values, a universally valid logical or methodological framework that could better organize our thinking about values and evaluations. Its axiom or first principle is his definition of "value" or "good," which is, "*Value is concept or standard fulfillment.*" This means that anything is good if it is as it is supposed to be, if it has all the properties that it is supposed to have. To find out whether something is good, we must first have a relevant ideal or standard for it in our minds. Some specific conceptual or ideal set of good-making features must be there in our minds to tell us what it is supposed to be like. Then, we must apply this conceptual ideal to what we are evaluating by experiencing it and matching it with its ideal. If the thing being evaluated has all the good-making features or properties contained in its concept or ideal standard, it is a good thing. Things may fulfill their norms by degrees, so some things are good, others only fair, average, poor, or no-good, depending on their degrees of concept or standard fulfillment. This definition is formal and rational, not empirical or natural. Because it is formal, it does not commit the infamous "naturalistic fallacy," where goodness is identified with some natural property like pleasure or preference. It applies to all kinds or dimensions of value and evaluation.

Hartman's widely used "secular" personality analysis instrument, the *Hartman Value Profile* (HVP), may be viewed on the Hartman Institute website, http://www.hartmaninstitute.org. It has proved invaluable to many people in gaining relevant knowledge of self and others. The HVP is used mainly in the business world to determine the suitability of applicants for jobs, whether they are likely to stay in them (retention), whether employees should be moved or promoted to different positions, and how to develop training programs to help present or future workers compensate for their value deficiencies. Psychotherapists also find the HVP invaluable for diagnosis, prognosis, and tracking personality changes. Anyone who takes "Know thyself" seriously will find the HVP to be an invaluable tool. A *Christian Values Profile* (CVP) based on Hartman's theory is now available at http://www.christianvaluesprofile.com. It reveals where people now are in their own spiritual development and what they need to do to move forward with it. A now published handbook or guide goes with it—*Developing Your Christian Values: The Christian Values Profile*.[3]

Most of Hartman's writings are hard to understand, but they contain many exceptionally lucid passages that effectively communicate his essential value vision. Quotes from Hartman appeared at the beginning of many earlier sections and sub-sections of this book, and more will follow. If some of these seem less lucid than others, the ensuing discussion should clarify their meaning.

In the formal theory of value (axiology) employed in this book, there are three kinds of value and three kinds of evaluation. We must now examine and defend these more carefully.

Three Kinds of Value

> *Value...is defined as a formal relation, namely, the correspondence between the properties possessed by a subject and the predicates contained in the intension of the subject's concept.*[4] Robert S. Hartman

> *To measure value by meaning means, then, to use meaning as a measuring rod which fits the thing and from which the number of the value of the thing can be read off. Meaning as logical intension, or as a set of predicates, is, precisely, such a*

standard of measuring. Just as the units of the meter are the centimeters, so the units of an intension are the predicates it contains. This set of predicates is compared with the set of properties actually possessed by the thing; and the thing has value in the degree that the set of its properties corresponds to the set of predicates in its intension; just as the thing has length *in the degree that the units of length it possesses correspond to the centimeters contained in the measure of its length, the meter.*[5] Robert S. Hartman

According to formal axiology, things have value or are good when they fulfill the set of normative expectations, standards, or concepts that we apply to them. To understand this, note first that value measurement is the rational process of determining whether something conforms to standards located in our minds. To measure anything's value, we must get to know its features, properties, or attributes, then apply an ideal standard to it to determine how well it measures up to or fulfills that standard. Things can measure up to our ideal expectations completely, by degrees, or not at all, so there are many degrees of standard fulfillment or goodness. Some things are completely good; others are only fair, average, poor, or worthless, depending on the degree to which they fulfill the standards we apply to them. Some undesirable things may also fulfill standards for badness or evil that go beyond mere privation or lack of properties.

To be conscious of anything is to value it. All consciousness is evaluative consciousness. Everything of which we are conscious belongs to one of at least three categories or dimensions of value: extrinsic, systemic, and intrinsic. These three dimensions of value contain their own appropriate value standards or measuring rods, as next defined and explained. Most people are more attuned to extrinsic values, practical values, worldly values, than to any of the others, so this is a good place to begin.

Extrinsic Values

Abstraction "draws off" properties common to at least two things. These properties are denumerable, for they must be abstracted one by one;...but there is an infinity of such possible properties. Referents of such concepts are the things of the everyday world. Each such thing has potentially an infinite number of properties in common with other such things...but in practice valuation will turn upon only a few of these properties....What is valued is not the thing in itself but its possession of the class predicates. Fulfillment by a thing of an abstract concept constitutes extrinsic value.[6] Robert S. Hartman

The subjects of extrinsic *valuation are everyday things and persons...in space and time....These empirical things are valued in the degree that they have the fullness of their class attributes. They are better when they have more attributes and worse when they have less.*[7] Robert S. Hartman

> *Every way of classifying a thing is but a way of handling it for some particular purpose. Conceptions, "kinds," are teleological instruments.*[8] William James

Philosophers say that extrinsic values are means to ends; they are useful in getting other things that we want. Extrinsically valuable things are good with respect to their kind and degree of function or usefulness.[9] Our external senses tell us about things, processes, and actions in public spacetime that are or might be useful in achieving our goals. Useful things in our common world are extrinsic value objects. Footballs, basketballs, goal lines, goal posts, hoops, cars, clothes, food, drink, our own bodies, and the bodies of plants, animals, and other people are all extrinsic values. We use our bodies to kick footballs, bounce basketballs, charge or defend goal lines, earn a living, paint a portrait, write a novel, teach a lesson, make a sale, wear clothes, and wine and dine. Extrinsic value-objects exist in the common, public, sensory world of space and time that we share with others. We can see, touch, smell, taste, and hear them. So can other people and other sentient creatures like non-human animals. Extrinsic value-objects are useful things, processes, and activities located in our common everyday world of sense experience (as opposed to our dreams and imaginations). They have survival value, but they are also useful in many other ways. Extrinsic values are good precisely because they are useful or instrumental in getting what we want, including more and more physical things.

Within their empirical classes, valued objects can be compared and contrasted with other good things. Some coins (quarters) will buy more than others (pennies or dimes). Some books contain more information than others. Some philosophical and axiological systems are more illuminating than others. Some cars run more efficiently or ride more comfortably than others. Some workers are more productive than others. Some philosophers are better thinkers and teachers than others. Some coaches are better motivators and guides than others. Some athletes are more physical, quicker, and otherwise more proficient than others. When athletes compete for the same position on a team, coaches compare their talents and performances to determine which players best fulfill standards essential for winning athletic games and contests. When comparing people only with respect to their usefulness, we are considering only their extrinsic but not their intrinsic worth. Purely extrinsic evaluation makes no place for appreciating people intrinsically for their own sakes.

Extrinsic value-objects can be immensely complicated. Using our raw senses plus magnifying instruments to reach the minute level of basic physical particles and motions, how long would it take us to describe everything that there is to know about just one golf ball or baseball bat, along with its every useful relationship with everything else in our common world? How many books would that fill? Be thankful that we do not have to master all of this information in order to use balls and bats effectively! Most of the time, sensory experience filters out biologically and practically irrelevant data for us. We have evolution and God to thank for that! But the more we know about extrinsic realities and how to control them, the more practically effective we can be.

Systemic Values

> The whole realm of what we call systemic value is new to value theory.[10] Robert S. Hartman

> Finite intensional sets (definitions) define formal concepts (synthetic concepts in the sense of...Kant's Logic). The things corresponding to them are constructions of the human mind, such as geometrical circles. Such things either fulfill their concept or else they are not such things; they either are or they are not what they are said to be. There are no good or bad geometric circles. A circle lacking a single one of the properties of the concept "circle" is not a circle. Constructions of the human mind thus have only two values, which we shall call systemic values: either perfection or non value.[11] Robert S. Hartman

> The subjects of logical or systemic valuation are things in a minimum relationship: as elements of a system or as schemata. A schema is less real than any empirical thing....What counts in a system is the system and its procedures and nothing else. This goes not only for the system's victims but also for its agents. They act as elements of the system and as nothing else.[12] Robert S. Hartman

Systemic value objects can be useful, but they do not exist in public spacetime. They are not physical things that we can touch, see, hear, smell, or taste. They exist only as concepts and beliefs in our minds. Examples are: definitions of perfect triangles, circles, squares; moral, legal, logical, and mathematical concepts and rules; philosophical and religious beliefs, doctrines, and dogmas; and social and spiritual ritual forms. Of course, all of these can be expressed in print.

Definitions are systemic value-objects. They identify the properties or qualities that something must have in order to belong to its class. Definitions are products of human evaluations and purposes. The defining essence of anything is what is most important or valuable to us for recognition and communication purposes. Conventional definitions express common human values and purposes; scientific and technical definitions express scientific and technical human values and purposes. The systemic common features of non-systemic entities like businesses, products, activities, or persons are the essential elements they must possess to be classified as such things at all. Systemic value-objects are not recollected from some prior existence in a realm of pure ideas, as Plato thought. Instead, we create or construct them with our minds. In their purest and most abstract form, they exist only in our minds. We cannot see or touch them, but we can make less than perfect copies of them that can be ordinarily experienced.

Purely systemic value-constructs (logic, math, geometry, etc.) exist only mentally, but we can use them to order chaos. Scientists are constantly amazed at the uncanny effectiveness and power of mathematics in understanding the world of nature. Systemic thoughts are always much simpler than the extrinsic things to which they apply; they do not have as many good-making (or bad-making) properties. Pure conceptual constructs can be defined with great precision in only a few words. Every true instance of purely formal construct is flawless. A circle that deviates slightly from being "a closed curved line with no thickness at all, every point of which is equally distant from its center" is not really a circle. The circular circumference of every existing wheel, basketball, and baseball is slightly flawed. None manifest perfect circularity, so technically they are not really circles at all, even if we so name them in practice and ordinary language. If we play basketball or baseball, we want our balls to approach the ideal as closely as possible. We don't want to play with lopsided balls. Manufacturers of spherical balls, circular wheels, or round auto tires, know that people will not buy these products if they are significantly out-of-round. Formal systemic value constructs like those of mathematics and logic can help us to order our world. They can provide us with regulative ideals to which we try to approximate in practice, but we cannot actually create or achieve systemic perfection. Usually a close approximation is good enough for practical or extrinsic purposes.

Not all systemic value-objects are formal technical constructs. Many definitions, for example, are of ordinary physical objects, processes, and activities, or of psychological objects, processes, and activities. All such value-objects possess many properties not contained in their definitions. Selected sets of these extra-definitional properties are called "expositions." They function as good-making properties, so not every instance of them is flawless; they can be exemplified by degrees. Some instances are good, possessing all of their expositional good-making properties, but some are only fair, average, poor, or worthless, depending on the degree to which they fulfill our expectations. In addition, many of our mental words or concepts apply to unique individuals—words like proper names, personal pronouns, and metaphors. We have words for unique intrinsic value-objects. More about this later.

Intrinsic Values

> *If systemic value is the value of* Perfection *and extrinsic value that of* Goodness, *singular or* intrinsic value *is the value of* Uniqueness.[13] Robert S. Hartman

> *The subjects of* intrinsic valuation are non-empirical things, or rather empirical things in their non-empirical aspects. They are, as such, neither in time nor in space. Each thing here is regarded as unique....Extrinsically seen, a woman is one among many beings of such and such a shape, features, and "build." Intrinsically seen, a woman is "the only one in the world," "the one and only," "there is nothing like her," "she is Woman."[14] Robert S. Hartman

Intrinsic value-objects are final ends; they are good in, of, for, and to themselves, good for their own sakes. Extrinsic values are good as means, and systemic values are good as symbols. Out of them we construct conceptual knowledge, clarity, and orderliness; but only intrinsically valuable realities are ends in themselves.

What kinds of things are intrinsically good? Answers to his question have been debated for centuries. Philosophers usually conclude, after much thought and debate, that intrinsic goods exist only in or as conscious awareness, or as desirable abstract and repeatable features of or within consciousness. A pure metaphysically materialistic or behavioristic world without consciousness would have no values in it at all. Many say that intrinsic goods are consciously experienced repeatable pleasures, or happiness (defined as a surplus of pleasure over pain for an extended period of time), or conscientiousness (dutifulness), or virtues like courage, temperance, justice, mercy, love, faith, and hope, or knowledge and contemplation, or self-realization, or fulfillment of interests or desires, and so on. However, these universal or repeatable qualities exist only within the conscious awareness of unique individuals who attach value to them. None of them can exist or be contemplated in isolation from individuated consciousness to determine whether or that they are desirable strictly "in themselves." We are always there doing the contemplation and the evaluation, and they can exist only in conscious individuals like us. They are not *intrinsically good* (in themselves); they are only *good in and for* us. We are intrinsically good; they are only intrinsic-value enhancers.

Consciousness is evaluation. All things considered, intrinsically valuable entities are unique conscious centers or subjects of experience, thought, activity, choice, feeling, and evaluation. Our lives can be enriched in the many ways just mentioned. God, people, and animals are intrinsically valuable by degrees. Their relative degree of intrinsic worth is too complex to be considered here.[15]

Intrinsically valuable beings are real, unique, conscious, organically integrated totalities. They are the most proper objects of intrinsic evaluation. However, both systemic ideas and extrinsic things can be valued intrinsically, that is, *as if* they were intrinsically good. *How* we value them can resemble how we ought to value divine and human persons and animals. Both inanimate things and ideas can be personified and valued passionately, as if they have intrinsic worth in, to, and for themselves. Inanimate things and thoughts can at least be considered and appreciated in their wholeness and uniqueness, their total property inventory; and we may personify them, which means that we can relate to them as if they were intrinsically valuable persons. We can fully delight in them, identify ourselves with them, emotionally embrace and cherish them, give them proper names, and make them evaluationally one with our own being. Inanimate things and activities can be evaluated intrinsically even though they are not intrinsic values, not conscious individuals. In a great athletic team, the distinctive talents, efforts, and contributions of individual players and coaches are combined into a unique whole to form the team's distinctive "personality," something greater than the sum of its parts. Team members may wholeheartedly give themselves, their talents, and their efforts to their teams, identify with them, and internalize them as integral parts of themselves and their own personal worth. Fans may also identify with them, so that when their team wins, they are winners (and when their team loses, they are losers).

People may also identify themselves intrinsically with many social wholes or units—families, tribes, communities, nations, universities, churches, synagogues, *etc*. Sublimely beautiful physical entities like mountains, canyons, homes, paintings, sculptures, airships, sea ships, the seas, and so on, may be valued intrinsically in ways most appropriate to, and having their native home in, our relations with conscious individuals.

Most essentially, every individual conscious subject is intrinsically valuable. We are unique unified centers or subjects of consciousness, self-awareness, self-knowledge, self-activity, and self-valuation. Things and thoughts have no such good-making properties of their own. During fleeting moments of self-awareness, we have concepts of ourselves, and we consciously experience ourselves. We experience, we think, we feel, we are active, we are valuing subjects; and we know and value ourselves directly. We assign kinds and degrees of value or disvalue, however great or small, to everything of which we aware. Our personalities are structured by what and how we value.

Our lives can be enriched by happiness, dutifulness, virtue, knowledge, self-realization, and in so many other intrinsic-value-enhancing ways. These non-unique repeatable properties are good in and for us, though not good merely in themselves. Their absence impoverishes us; their opposites diminish us. Think about what our lives would be like if totally devoid of all intrinsic value enhancers—pleasures, feelings, happiness, virtue, knowledge, self-realization, and so on. Think about what they would be like if filled completely with their opposites— pains, apathy, anomie, vices, ignorance, self-stagnation. In our for-the-moment-complete but ever-increasing temporal totality, we are intrinsically valuable, unique, conscious persons. We exist as ends, not merely as means. What evidence supports this?

The Hierarchy of Value

> *Systemic value, extrinsic value, and intrinsic value are the three value dimensions. They constitute a hierarchy of richness, intrinsic being richer in qualities than extrinsic value, extrinsic richer in qualities than systemic value. "Richer in qualities" is the definition of "better," "poorer in qualities" is the definition of "worse."*[16] Robert S. Hartman

> *The hierarchy of value [is] based on the fact that, since value is defined as the fulfillment of a connotation, the more of a connotation there is to be fulfilled the higher is the value.*[17] Robert S. Hartman

Which type of positive value is most valuable—extrinsic, systemic, or intrinsic? Does this question have a rational answer? Our discussion began in Chapter One with extrinsic values, not because they have greater worth than the others, but because to most people they are the most obvious and familiar. A rational and natural pre-systematic hierarchy of positive values is built into us, into human nature some axiologists suggest, by evolutionary pressures and processes.[18] Theists would add that God also had a hand in this. In our most deeply reflective, self-aware, and conscientious moments we can become aware of and affirm this hierarchy of positive values, but most of the time we are not very reflective, self-aware, or conscientious about our values and evaluations. We are usually very confused about what and how we value. Religion can help. Axiology can help.

In abstract philosophical terms, the *hierarchy of positive values* affirms that *intrinsic value-objects have more worth than extrinsic value-objects, and extrinsic values have more worth than systemic value-objects. Ranking from greatest to least worth, first comes intrinsic, then extrinsic, then systemic value-objects.* Some kinds of value-objects are better than others, have more good-making properties than others, though all can be very good. In application, this means that *people are more valuable than things, and things are more valuable than mere ideas of people or things.* "People," understood intrinsically, includes both to our common or generic humanity and our full unique individual concreteness and definiteness. "Things," understood extrinsically, includes all physical objects, processes, and bodily actions. "Ideas," understood systemically, refers to all conceptual or cognitive objects, thoughts, beliefs, constructs, rules, principles, formulas, forms, doctrines, beliefs, ritual patterns, systems, etc. The mere idea of any good thing is never as good as the corresponding desirable reality to which it refers; and the mere idea of any bad thing is never as bad as the corresponding undesirable reality to which it refers.

The hierarchy of positive values affirms that some things are better than others, and it tells us which ones. In the corresponding hierarchy of disvalues (negative values), some things are worse than others. Ideas of (words about or symbols of) evil people and events are less bad than the real evil people themselves, just as ideas of (words about or symbols of) good people and events are less good than their corresponding realities. The idea of (word-meaning for) a serial killer is less bad than, has fewer bad-making properties than, a real serial killer; and the idea of a killer hurricane is less bad than a real killer hurricane.

Why are some kinds or instances of value more valuable than others? Why should we accept the hierarchy of value? Hartman suggested that this so is because some values have "more of a connotation" than others. This means that some valuable entities have more "good-making properties" than others, and that the concepts by which we measure them are richer in positive meanings or connotations than their lesser counterparts. Some good things are better, richer, and more enriching than others. The best way to see this is to get in touch with our deepest and most enlightened preferences and consciences. Many strategies can help us do this. Consider the following.

Which would most enrich our lives, the idea of a sports car or a real sports car, the picture of a champion's trophy or a real trophy, the blueprint of a house or a real house? Most people who think seriously about it (except Plato!) would judge that we would be better off with an existing extrinsically desirable reality than with nothing more than the mere thought or idea of it. Existing extrinsically good things are more important or valuable than their corresponding systemic images, symbols, or abstract patterns. Ideas of (meaningful words for) positively desirable things are less valuable than the real things themselves. Mere ideas of good people and beneficial physical objects and processes are poor substitutes for the realities to which they refer. Correspondingly, mere ideas of vicious people and harmful things like earthquakes and wars are less bad or hurtful than the realities to which they refer.

Given a choice between the thought of or even the imaginary mental image of a friend, spouse, or puppy, and a real friend, a real spouse, or a real puppy, which would we prefer, all things considered? Which would be best? Most thoughtful people would prefer the existing intrinsic realities over their conceptual symbols ("friendship," "spousehood," or "puppyhood,") even when these are particularized as much as our imaginations will permit. Purely verbal, imaginary, or fictional friends are never quite as good as real ones. Intrinsic realities (real people) are more valuable than their corresponding systemic realities (ideas of people). Ideas of them are also less valuable than real animals, God, cars, food, and tools, so systemic entities belong on the bottom of our threefold hierarchy of value-objects. Because he is infinitely rich in goodness, God is infinitely more valuable than any of our religious beliefs or doctrines about God, even if one of these beliefs is that God is infinite.

Accounting adequately for animals may require a fourfold or tenfold hierarchy of value, with most animals (for example, those below the great apes) having lower degrees of intrinsic goodness. Human beings are typically much richer in good-making properties than sub-human animals, if only by degrees and not in kind. Some animals are very intelligent, but we are much more so. Some great apes and grey parrots have been "educated" and taught how to use elemental sign and spoken languages. Intelligent chimps and many other "uneducated" animals use primitive symbols, if only sensory images, to understand that some things are useful as means to ends, and they can act accordingly. Still, we greatly outshine them in cognitive capacities, symbolism, and devising complex means to our goals. Many animals are very good parents who selflessly love and make sacrifices for kind and kin, but we have the capacity to love *all* our neighbors in God's whole creation, even though we usually do not because we stick with kind and kin. Even within species, some members are much richer in such good-making ways than others. Animals are beyond the scope of this book, which concentrates on ideas, things, and people.

Why are people better than mere things, and things better than mere ideas? That ideas or word-meanings are less positively valuable than things and people goes counter to the prejudices of many intellectuals, especially philosophers, scientists, and religious dogmatists. This issue deserves some serious thought. Values involve meanings (to be fulfilled). Meanings are mental contents or predicates that exist in minds (intensions) and have corresponding properties in things (extensions). Things may actually have the properties that we think that they have. *More* positive or negative meanings indicate *more* positive or negative values. So, which is more positively meaningful (fulfills more good-making concepts, intensions, or criteria), the thought or blueprint of a house or a real one, the idealized image or thought of a dearly beloved spouse or a real one, a dream lover or a real one? Which would we prefer to live in, or to live and sleep with? The answer should be fairly obvious. Actualized empirical and intrinsic realities are far richer in desirable properties, in positive meanings, and thus in positive value, than our ideas of or symbols or words for them.

When we compare the value of good things and good people with the value of our ideas about them, these realities are clearly richer in desirable properties than, and thus better than their corresponding ideas, words, or numbers. Yes, some ideas are very valuable, not only our thoughts of things, but also our ideas of moral obligations, regulative ideals, and spiritual duties. Moral and religious ideals like the Ten Commandments or the duty not to inflict harm on others have enormous positive consequences when followed, so are they not better than things? Keep in mind that something can be very valuable indeed, yet less valuable than something else.

We should not confuse the value of ideas or word-meanings as such with value of the consequences of deliberately acting upon them. We should not confuse value-ideals with their valuable results when put into practice. We should not confuse simple values with complex value combinations. We should not confuse the systemic with the extrinsic value or usefulness of ideas and ideals. Moral and religious ideals may or not be acted upon; logically, their consequences are only possible but not actual. Much more is required for their realization. Particular results are not parts of or inevitable outcomes of general ideas or ideals as such. Getting desirable results from regulative guidelines requires that they be *combined* with favorable causal conditions and human decisions and actions. Holistic combinations or compositions of ideas (e.g., systemic guidance) with beneficial results, favorable conditions, moral decisions, and effective actions have immense worth; but their collective value should not be confused with the value of systemic guidelines alone, of mere ideas as such. Are the ideas of positive goods as good as, better than, or less good than the realities to which those ideas refer? Is the specific idea of good consequences as valuable as the good consequences themselves? Obviously not. The doctrine or "table" of the Ten Commandments is less valuable than actually living in accord with them. Moral theory is less valuable than moral persons.

This does not mean that positive systemic values (concepts, ideas, beliefs, rules, etc.) are somehow trivial or unimportant just because they belong at the bottom of the axiological hierarchy of positive values. On the contrary, they are or can be extremely important or valuable; but in a forced ranking system containing only three value dimensions, I, E, and S, the S dimension has the least inherent worth, the fewest good-making properties. Something can be very good without being the very best of all.

If systemic values belong on the bottom of our hierarchy of positive values, which of the other two, intrinsic or extrinsic values, belongs in the middle? Again, we must get in touch with our deepest preferences and insights of conscience. Suppose that an adored brother or a son is a pilot in the U.S. Air Force, and our country is at war mainly to protect its supplies of oil. Would we want our pilot, our son, to risk or lose his life for this oil? Is his life worth just so many barrels of oil? If he is killed in this war, would giving his life for so many barrels of oil be a fair exchange? Does the value of unconscious extrinsic realities ever equal or surpass the value of conscious intrinsic realities? Of course, everyone's sons and daughters, including those of our enemies, are just as valuable intrinsically as our own. Considering the value of moral persons, Immanuel Kant pronounced them to be "without price." They cannot be replaced or their loss adequately compensated for by some extrinsic/systemic treasure like money[19] or oil. (Usually, however, Kant seemed to value "moral law" as such more than the persons who exemplify it.)

The hierarchy of positive values is deeply embedded and expressed in many common beliefs and social practices. For example, our legal system rightfully gives people more protection than property, and property more protection than beliefs. The penalties for killing people are much more severe than the penalties for stealing property or criticizing their thoughts. Freedom of speech means that there are no legal penalties at all for disagreeing with someone, for disvaluing or criticizing someone's beliefs. In well ordered legal systems, positive value-objects having the greatest worth are the most protected, and value-objects having the least worth are the least protected. Some values fall in between these extremes. Lesser criminal harms receive proportionately less severe legal penalties, and the most serious harms carry the highest penalties.

In earlier discussions, we saw that some people devote their lives to accumulating great wealth and living in luxury. Their "materialistic" or "worldly" way of life consumes so much time and energy that they experience few if any deep and intimate relationships with other human beings. They die neglecting and without really loving their parents, spouse, children or friends, and without respecting or really knowing themselves. For a profusion of extrinsic values, they sacrifice all intrinsic values. They achieve the goods of life, but not a good life. They are rich in things but poor in soul. In gaining the world, they lose their souls. Would you want to be such a person? Perhaps you already are!

Are desirable extrinsic realities richer in positive meanings or good-making properties than positive intrinsic realities? Or is it just the reverse? Comparative value problems are difficult. Both things and people can be almost inconceivably complex in good-making properties or meanings, but consider this. Are we human beings simpler or more complex in good-making properties than circles or spherical volleyballs? The answer should be very obvious, but if not, you should get to know yourself and your own worth better than you do! Just how rich in good-making properties are we as unique persons? How many books would it take to describe absolutely everything desirable about us, our inherent attributes, and our relations to everything else in the universe? Our worth in good-making properties is practically incalculable, though not infinite. Only God's worth is infinite.

We are constituted by our inherent properties, their distinctive configurations, and our internal relations to innumerable other physical things, happenings, people, and living things. Our integrated totality of properties and relations makes us who we are. All three value dimensions exist in us, and their integration, configuration, and unification make each of us a unique person who is never exactly duplicated by anyone else. Internal relations enter causally and constitutively into a thing's composition; external relations are conceivable and knowable but inoperative in making something what it is. Our causal relations with our parents and early caregivers are highly constitutive of and internal to who we are, but our relations with people we have never heard of, or with grains of sand on some distant continent or planet, are largely irrelevant and external to who we are. Many things in the universe do not affect us, or do so only in utterly trivial ways. By definition, physical contemporaries are things that are causally independent of one another. As social beings, we are who we are largely because of our internal relations with past events, social structures, and the unique persons who have significantly influenced us. But many relations in space and time are external to us and irrelevant to who we are. They make no discernable difference to our personalities or good-making properties. When considering relational properties that make a difference to our worth, we should not count purely external relations. Alfred North Whitehead, who believed that we are constituted largely by our relations, suggested that we should not exaggerate the community of the universe.[20]

We are unique, embodied, spatially extended, temporally developing, conscious beings. Our extrinsic physical properties, our bodies and what we do with them, definitely belong to our totally integrated property inventories. They are essential to who we are. As Whitehead also pointed out, "Our feeling of bodily unity is a primary experience....No one ever says, Here am I, and I have brought my body with me."[21] Human bodies, brains included, are more complex and richer in properties than any other known physical objects. In addition to our brains and bodies, we are centers or subjects of conscious intentions or purposes, experiences, feelings, decisions, actions, choices, thoughts, and evaluations. These facts about us are so immensely complex that they are almost beyond comprehension or practical calculation.

Robert S. Hartman argued that we are infinitely complex within ourselves, infinitely rich in positive good-making properties; thus, we are infinitely valuable. But this is very difficult if not impossible to prove![22] Hartman's "proof" says that we can think an infinite number of thoughts (which are good-making systemic properties), and then think each of them an infinite number of times. The trouble is, we simply can't do either one. All available evidence favors our finitude, conceptual and otherwise; and most theologians emphatically contrast our finitude with God's infinitely rich actuality of good-making properties. We may be infinitely valuable indirectly or relationally because an infinite God loves us, but not so merely in and by ourselves. We are not infinitely intricate within ourselves, but with our incredibly complex brains, we have at least as much presence and physical meaning or goodness as any other extrinsic realities. In addition, we are indescribably rich in psychic unconscious or conscious properties and meanings. Thus, we (intrinsic realities) are more positively valuable or meaningful than mere things (extrinsic realities) that have no consciousness. And we are more valuable than the thoughts by which we think and know ourselves and mere things.

Consciousness, self-awareness, and psychological functions may or may not be identical with our functioning brains. Very likely, consciousness is a spatiotemporally extended field that surrounds and pervades our brains. Even if brains and consciousness were physically identical, this could not be so in a reductive materialist sense. No one can reduce the fullness of conscious experience and activity to mere matter in motion without a stupendous sacrifice of good-making properties. Reductive materialists ignore such particulars, but axiologists, real people, moral people, spiritual people cannot. Innumerable meanings belong to *consciousness* that merely physical processes, *things* (e.g., brains) understood *solely* in terms of mathematically measurable empirical properties, cannot comport or comprehend.

Reductive materialists traditionally subtracted properties from conscious persons until only the measurable and predictable properties of inert gross Newtonian/Cartesian matter remain. Today's materialists make the same reduction to quantum events, but quantum matter isn't what it used to be anymore. Non-reductive physicalists,[23] by contrast, subtract no properties. They acknowledge that we are essentially embodied beings, but our embodied reality is just as rich in properties as we actually know ourselves to be. Consciousness, conscience, moral sensitivity, perceptivity, affectivity, rationality, autonomy, and spirituality are functions of our brains and of the fields that surround and pervade them. They supervene upon and causally influence more primitive physical, chemical, and biological structures and processes. As "top down" not "bottom up" causes, they are preeminently real and efficacious.

Much more could be said to establish the validity of axiology's hierarchy of positive values;[24] but, on reflection, we should be able to see that conscious intrinsic entities are more valuable than non-conscious extrinsic entities, which, in turn, are more valuable than merely symbolic systemic entities. Expressed more simply, *things are more valuable than ideas or concepts, and people are more valuable than things.* This hierarchy of positive values is rationally based, as now demonstrated. It also has evolutionary significance if, over the very long run, evolutionary selection tends to weed out the kind of people who do not generally value according to this hierarchy and does not allow them to pass along their genes to future generations. In a very weak sense, this seems to be true, as explained in Chapter One.

As for your own self-knowledge, how would you personally rank the three items in this hierarchy of positive values—persons, things, and ideas? How much worth do you attach to yourself, relative to physical things and/or immaterial ideas? At times, do you devalue yourself, underestimate your own worth, and attach more significance to your things and ideas than to your own reality? Do your habits of evaluation infect your relations with others? How much value do you attach to other people relative to things and ideas? Do you ever underestimate their worth by overestimating the worth of things or beliefs?

Three Kinds of Evaluation

> *Valuation is no more nor less a matter of feeling than is music. It is a matter of feeling structured by laws—feeling following definite laws. The feeling of value is nothing arbitrary.*[25] Robert S. Hartman

Our essential reality and worth consists partly in our capacity to attach value or disvalue to everything we consciously experience, are aware of, think about, do, and are. So we should try to understand and enhance our evaluational capacities. We can understand and value *how* we value, as well as *what* we value; but most people do not know how they value, and there are many ways. How we value has cognitive, affective, and dynamic components. All of us can learn how to value more intelligently and skillfully. Valuation (or evaluation) is how we attach value or disvalue to everything that we experience, feel, do, think, and are. To the three basic kinds of value, extrinsic, systemic, and intrinsic, correspond three related kinds of evaluation (and disvaluation).

Extrinsic Evaluation

> *Extrinsic valuation is the model of everyday pragmatic thinking.*[26] Robert S. Hartman

> *Extrinsic valuation, in practice, is based upon relatively few properties, up to about two hundred in expert valuation of an everyday thing and upon far fewer in everyday valuation and discourse.*[27] Robert S. Hartman

Extrinsic evaluation is its most familiar and commonplace form. Extrinsic evaluation is the ordinary, everyday, practical assessment of anything's actual or potential usefulness, its instrumental significance in satisfying our everyday desires, feelings, and interests. It includes learning what causes what in the world, and it recognizes and treats things, processes, and deeds as means to ends. It is our most essential survival skill. Most of the problems that our hunter/gatherer ancestors had to solve were located in the external or public sensory and social worlds. Most of us today have fairly well developed capacities for pragmatic extrinsic evaluation by the time we reach adulthood; but we can still learn how to be better pragmatists, more effective, more practical. Cognitions, feelings, and actions are three aspects of pragmatic evaluation. We can increase our skills in all three.

Cognition and Extrinsic Evaluation

> *The knowledge relevant to extrinsic valuation is the knowledge of the world of things, of the order and classification of things which correspond to their actual variety. This is the valuation of common sense, of sound situational understanding. Here we have the capacity of comparison, of judging the present in terms of the future,...and the solid open-mindedness that used to distinguish the American mind.*[28] Robert S. Hartman

> *Whenever I judge a thing for its value, I compare the meaning of its name with the properties of the thing itself.*[29] Robert S. Hartman

Extrinsic evaluation applies cognition or concepts (thoughts or ideas) to sensory experiences, objects, processes, and actions. Thoughts can function as value standards for measuring the goodness or badness of everything that exists in our common world of sense experience—physical objects, natural or social processes, and individual and collective human roles and activities. Values involve meanings that can exist both in minds (intensions or connotative meanings) and in things or realities (extensions or denotative meanings). If spatiotemporal objects, processes, and behaviors fulfill the cognitive standards that we apply to them, they are good.

Formal axiology says that goodness is concept fulfillment. We can think "sweetness" and "strength" (intensions); and sweetness and strength (extensions) can exist in things tasted and encountered in everyday experience. Technically, predicates or mental concepts are intensional or verbal meanings, and the corresponding properties in existing things are extensional meanings. Concepts can connote or denote. Both thoughts and things are meanings, connotative versus denotative meanings.

Definitions identify the nucleus of anything's conventional meaning, but definitions are not used in extrinsic evaluation. Definitions merely tell us whether something belongs to some relevant class of comparison. Things must at least fulfill their definitions if they are to be rated as good members of their kind or class; if they do not, they just don't belong to that class. Every identifiable class has good and bad members, so additional criteria are required to distinguish between them.

Meanings or intensional elements beyond definitions are the ones actually used in extrinsic evaluation; they are called "expositions."[30] The difference between a mere orange by definition and a good orange by exposition is important. Being an orange at all means being a roughly spherical, edible, pulpy citrus fruit. Oranges are orange-colored when ripe; but some oranges are green (unripe ones). Being actually orange-colored is a good-making expositional property, not a definitional property. Green oranges are still oranges, but they are not good oranges. Since some oranges, green and unripe ones, are very sour or bitter, sweetness is also a good-making expositional property. The line between extrinsic definitions and expositions is never perfectly exact; often the difference is just between potential and actual properties. A good orange when ripe exhibits expositional properties like a bright orange color, a sweet taste, the right degree of tartness and firmness, a roughly spherical shape, and a pleasant citrusy smell. Small, green, bitter, unripe oranges are oranges, but not good ones. They normally actualize their good-making expositional properties in due time. Only then are they good oranges.

When we buy oranges, we shop for color, citrusy taste, sweetness, etc. When coaches recruit linebackers, they shop for speed, size, and strength, etc., but these are not the only good-making sensory traits that we have in mind when we try to find good oranges and good linebackers. A good orange also has a preferred texture and a blemish-free shape and size. A good linebacker combines size, strength, quickness, intelligence, aggressiveness, and team spirit with the ability to fulfill a well defined athletic role on a football team. In fact, a good anything has good-making properties that fulfill the expositional or good-making standards, criteria, or concepts that we have in mind when we measure their worth. Things usually fulfill our standards by degrees, so there are degrees of value. Something that is really good fulfills all relevant criteria; it is what it is supposed to be. Otherwise, by degrees it is only fair, so-so, poor, or no good.

All mere forms are blank. Ever since Plato, philosophers have tried unsuccessfully, but in many ingenious and deviant ways, to find "The Form of the Good." Robert S. Hartman found it, saw it, and described it, and here is its blank form.

GOOD-MAKING PREDICATES	ACTUAL PROPERTIES
1. _____	1. _____
2. _____	2. _____
3. _____	3. _____
4. _____	4. _____
5. _____	5. _____
6. Add more as needed.	6. Add more as needed.

An indefinite number of good-making features, not just five, may be present in these forms when applied. The question is, does the actuality match or correspond with the ideal? If the object being evaluated actually has all the properties in its conceptual set of good-making predicates, then it is good. "Good" itself is not an additional good-making property of a good thing. It applies only to the total set of a thing's good-making properties; it indicates the *completeness* of the normative set. Less than good things (fair, average, etc.) are less than complete.

If goodness is concept or standard fulfillment, how do we apply this rule? Determining whether extrinsic objects are good of their kind or class involves observing them and then matching or comparing their actual properties with our conceptualized expectations. Anything is truly *good* if it fulfills all our conceptualized expectations, *fair* if it fulfills most of them, *average* if it fulfills about half of them, *poor* if less than half, and *bad* or *no good* at all if it completely fails to fulfill any of our expectations.[31] The good-making properties of good things (items one through six above) stand in one to one correlation with the predicates that constitute our norms or standards for them. Less than good things correspond less and less to their norms. Good-making properties contribute to or constitute the goodness of a good thing without being identical in meaning with "good." That a good thing is good means that *all* of its good-making properties are present in it. In a truly good thing, the set of its good-making properties is complete, so goodness is a property of the total set, not of the thing itself. It is only fair, average, poor, or no-good when, by degrees, some of its good-making properties are lacking.

Thus, to be skilled at valuing extrinsically or practically, we must have clear standards in mind, inspect things carefully to discover their properties, then determine through experience whether their properties fulfill their norms and to what degree. Many of us use consumer magazines like *Consumer Reports* when we want to buy a good computer, lawn mower, camera, car, or some other consumer product or service. Without knowing it, consumer magazines have mastered the art of extrinsic evaluation. They give us standards to be fulfilled, examine products to determine their actual properties, and then tell us which ones best fulfill the standards and to what degree. Without realizing it, they practice applied axiology. Axiology is the science of values and evaluations; and consumer publications show us how to be scientific or rational about extrinsic or practical values.

Feelings and Extrinsic Evaluation

> Conceptually, extrinsic valuation is a matter of measuring a thing's properties by means of a concept, as is also the case with both systemic and intrinsic valuations. But some valuations have an affective or emotional aspect....What then of the extrinsic? On the one hand, the process of measuring the extrinsic value of a thing can be characterized, like the systemic, as objective, impartial, and dispassionate, for a set of predicates is compared with a set of properties. The evaluator need not take a "pro-attitude" toward the thing being measured. On the other hand, the

determination of the set of predicates used as a measure may involve emotion. "Extrinsic valuation is the model of everyday pragmatic thinking," writes Hartman. But such thinking involves human desires and interests. We order and classify the things that we interact with in space and time for all sorts of purposes. Our abstract concepts help us get what we want. However, this is not to say that there is no logic involved in the formulation of such concepts.[32] John W. Davis

Indirectly or directly, feelings, broadly understood, play a part in positive extrinsic evaluations. To be good at managing our practical affairs, we must understand our feelings, emotions, attitudes, and desires and the role they play in everyday practical life. All sensations, actions, and thoughts bear emotional charges, however faint. *Ordinary feelings, desires, emotions, moods, and attitudes are directly involved in setting the conceptual standards by which we measure the goodness of things, deeds, roles, and processes.* They come into play when we judge that a particular sort of thing, role, action, or process is a good instance of its kind. Seeing and appreciating anything in its full individuality and uniqueness has no place in extrinsic evaluation. Uniqueness belongs to intrinsic values and evaluations.

Often we do not know how we think or feel about things. Reading a consumer review or consulting with an expert can help us to clarify our feelings, desires, and thoughts or beliefs about useful things. Conceptual standards for measuring goodness are set by people who have positive feelings or attitudes about things like spherical balls, rough linebackers, speedy computers with lots of memory, powerful zoom and resolution in cameras, fuel efficiency, style, and comfort in automobiles, and color, texture, odor, and taste qualities in apples.

We may disagree with judgments of goodness expressed by other people, by experts, by conventions, or in consumer magazines, not because we doubt that standards are being fulfilled, but because we do not accept the standards, because do not take pro-attitudes toward some or all of the good-making traits that comprise the standards. Hartman wrote, "It is not the case that axiological judgment would differ from man to man only because one man did not know the expositional properties of the thing in question, but rather because one man does, and another does not, approve of these properties as exhibited by a phenomenon."[33]

A *direct* positive emotional, affective, or attitudinal involvement with the proclaimed good-making properties of a thing is essential for embracing fully the judgment that it is good because it fulfills the appropriate norms. We must both make that judgment *and* feel that the norms themselves are appropriate. The norms will seem appropriate to us only if we have positive feelings about the good-making properties of that which is being evaluated. Evolution and God have equipped us to approve of many ends or goals in life, especially successful means to practical ends.

Indirect or truncated extrinsic evaluation can exist without taking normal pro-attitudes toward the good-making descriptive predicates included in a given set of norms, or toward the properties of the objects measured by them. At times, extrinsic valuers may employ only the conceptual and sensory aspects of extrinsic evaluation. Apple graders or auto inspectors need little or no positive emotional involvement with the apples or autos they classify as good or less-than-good. More or less dispassionately, they can just apply the conceptual standards set by the pro-attitudes of others to the products they evaluate. At this "indirect" extreme, extrinsic evaluation affectively resembles systemic evaluation, as John W. Davis indicated in the above quote. Much if not most valuation even seems to take place on an unconscious level, where habit-formed standard-matching is done quickly and efficiently without involving conscious effort.[34]

The feelings and desires involved in direct extrinsic positive evaluation are the ordinary prosaic and pragmatic or practical feelings, desires, emotions, affections, tastes, and attitudes of everyday life and practice. They are not the extremely intense and special feelings and self-with-other-identifications that characterize intrinsic evaluation or profound spirituality. However, the ordinary shades off into the extraordinary by degrees, and where their borders come together, the dimensions of evaluation become affectively indistinguishable. When their extremes of feeling approach one another, all three dimensions merge with the next in line, but hard-core instances of each are easy enough to identify.

Dynamics and Extrinsic Evaluation

> *But the combination of things can be bad: and bad is indeed nothing but the incompatibility of things, or things in transposition....A good Buick and a good Ford transpose each other when they collide....The result is both a bad Buick and a bad Ford, or rather, a Buick disvalued in terms of a Ford and vice versa....The wreck, however, is a good wreck, fulfilling the definition of "wreck," which in turn means a combination of two bad cars. On the other hand, a good Buick and a good Ford in a showroom form a composition of values,...and this complex is a whole whose concept contains the expositions of both automobiles.*[35] Robert S. Hartman

Often, value-objects and value combinations in all dimensions are just found in or given by nature or society, but they can also be created both by circumstances and by deliberate choices and actions. We can create them by deciding to do something and then doing it. A dynamic or active feature of positive extrinsic evaluation appears whenever extrinsically good things are actively combined with other goods. Good cooks well understand this.

Extrinsic objects can be intentionally and forcefully combined with other extrinsic objects, even with systemic and intrinsic objects. They can be combined positively to create more complex positive values or *compositions*, or negatively to create complex disvalues or *transpositions*. Gifts can be given to loved ones. Blocks of marble can be shaped into ideal sculptural forms. Nets and hoops can be combined to produce basketball goals; leather and laces can be united to make baseballs; running and grabbing are complementary talents in football tackles; plastic, steel, and chrome can be merged to make sports cars; wires and computer chips can be consolidated in electronic equipment, and so on. Additional standards for judging excellence are then required by these more complex extrinsic value combinations. The goodness of a gourmet dish cannot be determined or even guessed in advance merely by knowing the goodness of its ingredients. Its goodness cannot be measured by the standards that apply to its separate ingredients. The goodness of all novel organic wholes cannot be equated with or reduced to the goodness of their parts. Their goodness is greater than the sum of their parts.

Extrinsic physical objects, processes, and actions can also be combined to produce disvalues. Crash a Ford into a Buick, and junk is created. A crashed Ford is a good junker, but not a good sports car or family sedan. Crash a tackle into a quarterback's knee and more junk (an injury) is created. Pour sawdust into a Coke and we have poor sawdust and a poor Coke. Shoot a bullet into a human body, or stick a finger into a rival player's eye, and no good comes of it. Bombing a building may destroy it and reduce it to useless rubble. To the extent that we have a use for rubble, it might be good rubble, but it is no longer a good building. Spewing pollutants into the atmosphere yields bad air to breathe but good smog as smog.

Active living consists largely of doing things that unite extrinsic value-objects with other value-objects in positive or negative ways to produce novel valuable or disvaluable combinations. We should think carefully about the consequences of our acts. Everything that we do creates values or disvalues of some kind, but we may lack concepts suitable for identifying and measuring them. Learning how to value more effectively is partly a matter of increasing or clarifying the number, range, contents, and depth of our normative concepts.

Systemic Evaluation

> *Since valuation is a matter of thinking, it is important to see what kind of valuation regular logical thinking represents.*[36] Robert S. Hartman

Systemic evaluation also involves cognition, feeling, and dynamics. Its natural home is with systemic value-objects like logic, mathematics, science, philosophy, theology, word-meanings, definitions, beliefs, doctrines, ritual forms, and behavioral rules; but it too can be extended beyond its natural limits. Non-systemic values can also be evaluated systemically in all three of the following ways: cognitively, affectively, and dynamically.

Cognition and Systemic Evaluation

> *Systemic valuation denies all degrees of value and sees things in either black or white; the thing either is or is not a member of its class, it either is* perfect *or* no good. *In a systemic organization you either belong or you don't belong. Shades and*

differences of opinion and character are not tolerated. The one value is conformity and the one disvalue non-conformity—which leads to expulsion or "liquidation."

All members of a system must be the same or else be no members....Things that are all the same are indistinguishable of one another and interchangeable....All the elements are on the lowest common denominator, namely, as elements of the system, and all their intrinsic or extrinsic differences are erased; they are, as individuals, unavailable. There is nothing but a mass of interchangeable, formless elements. Chaos numbered and indexed. The culmination of such systemic organization was Nazi Germany.[37] Robert S. Hartman

Positive systemic or conceptual evaluation measures by systemic cognitive standards, and systemic measuring can become an enduring habit or state of mind, often unconscious. Systemically, things can be regarded as perfect instances of their concepts, or they do not have any value at all. Not all systemic thinking is like this, but rigid ideological systemic evaluation neither recognizes nor appreciates *degrees* of concept fulfillment. The number "three" is always a perfect trinity, or it is not a trinity at all. It does not have to be, but systemic evaluation can be rigidly dualistic—"all or nothing," "black or white," "either/or," "absolutely for or against." It incorporates very small and definite sets of definitional properties into norms for judging value or disvalue. Rigid systemic constructs are either perfect when they are as they should be, or worthless and non-existent whenever the tiniest flaws exist. This way of thinking is how perfectionists make themselves and others miserable, and how ideologists justify eliminating people who don't conform to their systems.

Rigid systemic evaluation is most appropriate when dealing with or relating to formal systemic constructs like logic and mathematics. These are created by our own minds, exist only in our minds, and have only the formal, precise, and limited features that we choose to give to them. Purely formal systemic constructs never fail to fulfill their concepts because they are identical with those concepts. They have no other reality or reference. They are created by our minds, not abstracted from experience. They are not recollected from some prior existence in a Platonic realm of ideas. They are totally mind-dependent for their being. Experienced entities (e.g., *almost* circular objects) may resemble and approximate to them, but never perfectly.

Trouble arises when rigid systemic habits of mind are applied to less formal thoughts, or to non-systemic entities like people and things. Then it becomes ideological. People, cars, and apples are not pure conceptual constructs, but they can be valued and treated as if they were. Applied to extrinsic and intrinsic realities, rigid systemic ideological evaluation (1) focuses on very limited sets of traits and refuses to see all that is there, and (2) prejudges everything to be either perfect or utterly worthless. It is the "all-or-nothing" mind-set of prejudice, ideology, reductionism, dualism, totalitarianism, perfectionism, dogmatism, inerrancy, and fanaticism.

For rigidly systemic ideological mentalities, finite sets of traits like those defining race, sex, nationality, species, social class, or religious beliefs, formalities, and affiliations mean absolutely everything. What fits the preconceptions of the ideological system has perfect value; what does not fit is utterly worthless. For that reason, from an ideological perspective, things and people can be eliminated or exterminated without much loss of worth and without qualms of systemic ideological conscience. Pure ideologists and dogmatists have only systemic conscience and a black or white mentality to guide them; but most people keep systemic values in their proper place, supplemented by a more open mind plus extrinsic and intrinsic conscience. Existing ideologists always have some degree of extrinsic practicality and intrinsic social bonding, but these are usually dominated and overridden by their all or nothing ideologies, dogmas, dogmatism, and authoritarianism.

Feelings and Systemic Evaluation

> Systemic measurement is the abstract, formal kind of measurement used by the scientist, objective and detached.[38] Robert S. Hartman

> [The three axiological] dimensions indicate, precisely, the distance *of the valuer from the valued object*. This distance gives us the *feeling tone accompanying valuation*. That we are most involved in intrinsic and least involved in systemic value means, precisely, that in intrinsic valuation the distance of the valuer from the valued object is closest, up to identification, while in systemic valuation it is farthest.[39] Robert S. Hartman

Affectively, positive systemic evaluation as such is devoid of *distorting* feelings, emotions, moods, pro or con attitudes, and desires; but it is not void of all feelings whatsoever. It is deliberate affective detachment or "objectivity" designed to achieve the scientific, philosophical, and intellectual goals of conceptual clarity and open or fair-mindedness and freedom from bias. It is not uninterestedness but disinterestedness, which is open, impartial, fair-minded interestedness. It is the least involved kind of evaluational involvement, but it is not complete indifference. Being conscious of anything is personal valuational involvement with it, which is why we cannot escape values and evaluations. Systemic involvement tends toward complete non-involvement or indifference, but it never goes quite that far. Total indifference passes beyond systemic evaluation; it means being altogether out of sight, mind, and heart. It is off the axiological chart. A "cool mind" is not the same thing as "cold blood," even if they on the same continuum of decreasing emotional or affective involvement. Systemic evaluation may degenerate into aloofness, indifference, condescension, or hostility; but judges, intellectuals, scientists, and philosophers are quite passionate about impartiality, fair-mindedness, or disinterestedness and quite interested in their subject-matter.

When Kierkegaard decreed that subjectivity is truth, he meant being involved personally, passionately, and intrinsically with what seems to be real. However, conceptual truth often mediates between us and reality, and it must first be identified as such before we can have any passionate feelings about it or that to which it refers. For that, despite Kierkegaard, passion may stand in the way. While searching for objective truth, reasonable people, intellectuals, judges, scientists, philosophers, and even theologians eschew the subjectivity of distorting passionate affections or emotions.

This does not mean that rational inquiry is unmotivated or devoid of all feelings, emotions, interests, and desires, even if some people (e.g., a few Greek Philosophers, Kant, and Kierkegaard) may have had that misconception. William James correctly insisted that there are many "sentiments of rationality."[40] This means that many feelings, emotions, and desires are integral to the very meaning and function of reason itself. Reason is not a "faculty" that operates in complete independence of all affections, desires, and interests. It serves practical as well as theoretical purposes. Being a reasonable person does not involve eliminating *all* feelings, emotions, and desires. Rationality constrains feelings that distort, but it does not suppress all feelings. Systemic evaluation is disinterested, not uninterested.

Philosophical and scientific inquiry are powerfully motivated by curiosity, the desire to know, and wanting to seek truth in an objective, open-minded, or fair-minded way without being blinded by pre-conceptions, prejudices, uncontrolled emotions, or unconscious dispositions and processes. Authentic rational impartiality or disinterestedness should never be confused with uninterestedness, indifference, or lack of motivation. The two have often been confused. Kierkegaard consistently confused them,[41] which is why he championed the subjectivity of passionate commitment at the expense of objectivity, misunderstood as uninterestedness or indifference. Yet, subjectivity and objectivity are not incompatible.

Fair-mindedness and earnest dedication can be combined consistently by: (a) restraining *obstructive* emotions and prejudices while searching for truth, (b) being passionately committed to the search, c) experiencing totally absorbing moments of intellectual creative or revelatory insight, (d) reflecting on and gaining information from ordinary perceptual experience; (e) delighting in the contemplation of truth, once found, (f) passionately committing oneself to it, and (g) being open to further intellectual growth and change in light of new insights and information.

Aristotle astutely recognized that actualizing intellectual virtue, that is, being cognitively or rationally active, is accompanied by very high quality pleasures. Aristotle did not believe that human intellectual activity is devoid of all feeling. His intellectual bias was that cognitive, systemic, rational enjoyments are the highest and most desirable pleasures of all, even better than those of friendship, interpersonal intimacy, and virtuous moral activity. Aristotle's totally systemic and purely rational God who thinks only about thinking and nothing else is unmoved, without feelings, but Aristotle allows rational human beings to enjoy thinking and knowing.

Successful, objective, impartial, disinterested rational inquiry may culminate in affectively powerful and exhilarating intrinsic "Aha!" or "Eureka!" experiences of intrinsic intellectual creativity and enlightenment. Rationality, properly understood, functions only in conjunction with feelings, not in total separation from them. William James rightly insisted that there are sentiments of rationality. At its best, and correctly understood, intellectual activity actually *requires* affective involvement and does not exclude it. Passionate curiosity, the intense desire to be open or fair minded, the exhilaration of mental creativity and discovery, and sheer delight in rational activity, commitment, and contemplation, are all properly involved in rational cognition and the search for truth. Systemic detachment or objectivity can work in conjunction with intrinsic intellectual passion, concentration, and creativity. Systemic objectivity is *minimal* affective involvement, not *no* affective involvement.

Dynamic Systemic Evaluation

> There are even life situations where systemic valuation is necessary: all situations where no play is allowed and it is a matter of either being or not being. Thus, when meeting a deadline, when making a train, when stopping at a red light or before a railroad crossing—you either do or you don't—and when you don't you miss, and sometimes [lose] your life.[42] Robert S. Hartman

Dynamically, systemic evaluation actively combines systemic ideas or forms with other value-objects. This can occur through natural processes or through deliberate human effort and activity. It can be done positively or compositionally to enhance value and negatively or transpositionally to diminish value. Positive systemic evaluation is very important and even useful. We can combine systemic numbers and logic with extrinsic mechanical devices to make watches, clocks, airships, rockets, buildings, computers, and smart bombs. We can number our seconds, minutes, hours, days, months, and years. As citizens, we have Social Security numbers; as savers and depositors, we have bank numbers; as investors, we have account numbers, as international travelers, we have passport numbers. Athletes are identified with the numbers on their jerseys and are highly honored when their numbers are permanently retired.

Systemic value-objects have many constructive uses. Without numbers, we could not get to church on time for weddings, our own or that of others. Without numbered bracelets, a mother might take someone else's baby home from the hospital. Without geometrical and numerical patterns, no one could construct basketball courts and baseball diamonds, or distinguish winners from losers. Numbers are essential for doing the work of physical scientists, architects, engineers, builders, and statisticians.

Without moral rules, which are also systemic entities, we could not tell the difference between patterns of right and wrong. Without conceptual standards, we could not distinguish between good and bad of any kind. Without a government of laws, we would be ruled by brute force and transient whims. Without belief systems, life would be conceptually meaningless. Systemic values, properly used, enrich our lives. But they can be either overvalued or undervalued.

Systemic forms can also be actively combined with other things to decrease value. Ideologists do this to people, but so do all the rest of us at times. Convicted lawbreakers wear numbered uniforms in prisons to degrade their worth. Students in large classes or huge universities frequently complain about being reduced to mere numbers. The Nazis tattooed numbers on the Jews that they imprisoned and exterminated. They reduced them to mere numbers, ignored everything else about them, and then found it easy to torture and murder them. They organized evil very methodically, numerically, and systematically, just as Hartman claimed. Rigidly systemic-minded ideologists actually ignore or devalue everything important about unique individual human subjects of experience, action, and evaluation. They employ numbers and formal patterns to reduce people to insignificant tokens in dehumanizing systems. Dehumanizing ideological systems deprive people not only of their common humanity but also of their distinctive individuality.

Intrinsic Evaluation

Intrinsic valuation involves the valuer completely.[43] Robert S. Hartman

If identification is the ability to feel closer to one object in the environment than other, and to make the situation of the first to some extent one's own, this is a very basic ability indeed. It makes it possible to reach out mentally to others, making them an extension of the self, paying close attention to their situation so as to influence it or gain information from it. Identification underlies both empathy and imitation.[44] Frans de Waal

Intrinsic evaluation, how we value intrinsically, also has three aspects, conceptual, affective, and dynamic. We can learn to increase our capacities for intrinsic evaluation by understanding each of these. This is both the most important and the most neglected form of evaluation.

Cognition and Intrinsic Evaluation

The formal norm says that a person, like anything, ought to be good, that is to say, ought to fulfill his concept.[45] Robert S. Hartman

According to the axiom of formal axiology, we have seen, a thing has value in the degree that it fulfills the meaning, or intension, of its concept. Applied to the self-concept, "I," this means that a person has value to himself in the degree that he fulfills the intension of his [or her] self-concept. This intension, however, may vary, depending on whether a person defines himself [or herself] systemically, extrinsically, or intrinsically.[46] Robert S. Hartman

> *The first thing the intellect does with an object is to class it along with something else. But any object that is infinitely important to us and awakens our devotion feels to us also as if it must be* sui generis *and unique. Probably a crab would be filled with a sense of personal outrage if it could hear us class it without ado or apology as a crustacean, and thus dispose of it. 'I am no such thing,' it would say; 'I am MYSELF, MYSELF alone.'*[47] William James

> *Identifying with and caring about another without losing one's own identity is the crux of human sympathy. As we have seen, this requires certain cognitive abilities, the most important one being a well-developed sense of self and the ability to assume another individual's perspective.*[48] Frans de Waal

Cognitively, intrinsic evaluation involves taking the fullest possible conceptual inventory of who we and others are as unique individual subjects, agents, and valuers. Conceptually, intrinsic evaluation focuses on uniqueness, wholeness, integration, configuration, and inner personal riches and enrichment. Unlike systemic evaluation, which considers very few features of what it values, intrinsic evaluation ideally considers everything about, the integrated wholeness of, what is valued. Unlike extrinsic evaluation, which sees things only as repeatable members of useful classes, intrinsic evaluation understands, appreciates, and identifies with entities just as they are in their full irreplaceable individuality, uniqueness, completeness, and concreteness.

We unique human beings, intrinsic values proper, are temporally ordered realities. Our full property inventory includes our future potentials as well as our fully determinate present and past attributes, qualities, and relations. Our future potentials do not yet exist and count only as possible but not actual value properties; we will never actualize most of the futures that are logically possible for us. We have to choose what we will become. Intrinsically valuing ourselves as temporally ordered intrinsic goods looks to the past, present, and future. It aims to further enhance the lives of intrinsically valuable persons with intrinsic value enrichers like happiness, knowledge, love, creativity, virtue, constructive self-realization, and so on. Such things are good for us, but not good in, to, or by themselves.

Cognitively, intrinsically evaluating intrinsic value-objects concentrates on conscious subjects of experience, activity, and evaluation. It focuses on unique conscious beings that have proper names, not just general or class names. We understand that general or class names like "track," "swimming," "running," and "studying" have meanings that can be defined and explicated; but proper names also have meanings. In a trivial sense, we know who we are; we know our own names. But do we really understand the *full meaning* of our own proper names? Consider your name carefully. What is the meaning of _____ (your name)? If and only if you have an inclusive answer to that question do you know who you really are. Most of us do not know and may never know!

Only incompletely do we understanding the full meaning of our proper names, the full meaning of our individual lives, all of our properties, who we really are. We only know ourselves in part. God, who presumably knows everything, would have access to our full property inventory, at least as far as it has been developed in time, but in our finitude, we do not. Even omniscience could not know as actual the possible future free decisions that we have not yet made. Temporality is an essential part of our existential reality, and we should not allow ourselves to be conned out of it by the theological belief that for God everything is finished and settled from eternity. Process or temporalistic theology, the viable alternative, allows us to know ourselves as the genuinely unfinished and partly self-creative realities that we really are. Knowing ourselves means understanding that we exist in time and are now creating who we will become out of who we have been. Our total property inventory is always incomplete and ever increasing for as long as we survive, here and/or hereafter.

Perhaps we have never seriously tried to know ourselves, never asked "Who am I?" Memories fail; we forget who we have been. We erect conscious and unconscious barriers to knowing who we really are and were. Self-deception is easy and commonplace. Imagination and evaluational awareness often fail us, and we do not know who we want or ought to become. The full meaning of our proper name, our complete individual existence, is never available to us. Still, much self-knowledge is accessible to us here and now, especially if we concentrate intensely on ourselves in our totality, inwardness, uniqueness, and wholeness and are committed to ongoing growth in self-understanding and personal enrichment. We cannot measure the value of ourselves or others unless we have adequate concepts of who we are and who we aspire to be. What good-making properties compose your own ideal self? By what good-making properties do you judge other intrinsically valuable persons? Could you have even better self-expectations than you now have? To what degree do you fall short and are not true to yourself or to God, who also has expectations of you.

Feelings and Intrinsic Evaluation

> *Intrinsic value is the valuation of poets and artists, lovers and mystics, magicians and advertisers, chefs de cuisine and politicians, creative theologians and scientists. It is empathetic—and empathic—valuation.*[49] Robert S. Hartman

Intrinsic evaluation involves profound feelings as well as conceptual self-knowledge and self-ideals. If we approach knowing self and others only cognitively and disinterestedly, we are nowhere close to full-scale intrinsic evaluation. Systemic evaluation approximates complete non-involvement without going all the way; intrinsic evaluation is at the opposite extreme. It is complete affective concentration on, attachment to, and identification with what is being valued. Positive intrinsic evaluation also goes far beyond the "everyday interestedness" level of extrinsic evaluation. It is maximal conscious personal identification and bonding with some value-object. This may take many forms like deeply felt sympathy, empathy, compassion, love, enjoyment, delight, appreciation, concentration, conscience, creativity, and mystical/spiritual/social union.

During the experience of intrinsic identification, the distinction between self and other, subject and object, melts away and becomes evaluationally and experientially insignificant. This does not mean that our unique independent realities just disappear or that they coalesce or fuse together metaphysically or existentially. But psychologically, phenomenologically, and evaluationally, these differences no longer matter and are hardly noticed, if noticed at all. For many people, this type of evaluation is quite rare; but without it, human lives are greatly impoverished. Moments of intrinsic evaluation are the "peak experiences"[50] of human existence, and they are essential for truly abundant living.

Intrinsic evaluation has its natural home with intrinsic value-objects (animals, people, God), but anything in any value dimension can be valued intrinsically. Artistic creativity is total involvement with non-conscious objects of art. Intrinsic morality is total identification with conscious individuals who can be affected by what we do—animals, people, God. With what do you fully identify yourself? We may identify ourselves fully with our belongings, property, tools, jobs, cars, athletic teams, star athletes, rock stars, political leaders or parties, universities, home towns, nations, churches, religions, scriptures, beliefs, moral ideals, and so on. We can even identify ourselves with evil, as did the Nazis, and as do all ideologically prejudiced people everywhere. What is your identity?

Even the best of things can be abused or misused, as we all know. This is definitely true of our capacities for intrinsic evaluation. Complex (and sinful) human beings often love and identify themselves with evil doing and with wicked people. Some people identify themselves with horrendous evils like mass genocide, ethnic cleansing, racial purity and prejudice, or philosophical or religious dogmatism, intolerance, exclusivism, and persecution. Captives often come to identify themselves with their captors, the persecuted with their persecutors, the oppressed with their oppressors, doubters with dogmatic authorities, "inferiors" with "superiors." Abused wives, husbands, and children may love and thus fully identify themselves with those who abuse them. This can be so intense and complete that they become abusers themselves who perpetuate or resign to the very evils that they abhor. "Stand by my man, no matter what," and "My country right or wrong" are simply wrong; but many people defend and fully identify themselves with wicked persons, with pernicious social and political policies and regimes, and with evil powers and principalities. Yes, this happens even today, perhaps especially today. Can you think of any examples? Speaking metaphorically, some people are "devil-worshipers" without knowing it, but some know it perfectly well.

Without identifying fully with injustice, greed, exploitation, violence, abusiveness, discrimination, decadence, deceit, dogmatism, and debauchery, most of us find wickedness appealing, attractive, and even entertaining. If you do not believe this, just turn on your TV, or go to the movies, and watch what you watch! We regularly pay good money to be entertained by spectacles of sin and evil! We are not far removed from the Roman Colosseum. Self-identification with sinfulness or the dark side always lies just below the surface in most of us. The positive intrinsic evaluation of lesser goods, of evils, of disvalues, creates many if not most of the horrors of human existence. Yet, wicked people can change, repent, and learn to identify themselves with goodness. Then redemption begins.

Dynamics and Intrinsic Evaluation

> The relationship between systemic, extrinsic and intrinsic value corresponds to a process of continuous enrichment with definite leaps from one value dimension to the next. Thus, if I buy a package of cigarettes from a saleslady, I am in a legal, a systemic relationship with her. If I take her out for dinner I am in an extrinsic relationship, and if I take her to church and marry her I am in an intrinsic relationship with her: my total being is joined with hers in a common intrinsic Gestalt. This Gestalt grew through successive enrichments, out of the first tenuous bond, the original sales contract.[51] Robert S. Hartman

Dynamically, positive intrinsic evaluation is the process or activity by which intrinsic positive values or evaluations are combined with other positive intrinsic, extrinsic, or systemic value-objects. Any value-object in any dimension can be evaluated by or actively combined with any other value-objects in any dimension. Anything can be valued intrinsically (or in any dimension), even if it is not a conscious intrinsic value-object. For example, systemically, a house is merely an investment; extrinsically, it is just a shelter or dwelling; but intrinsically, a house is a home.

Positive intrinsic value-objects (persons) can be actively combined with one another into unified gestalts, as in marriage, family, deep friendships, and the communion of the saints, all of which take considerable time, effort, and personal investment. In the most profound instances of positive intrinsic relations, two or more persons become one axiologically and psychologically. Distinctions between self and other cease to matter without ceasing to exist. The subject/object distinction is overcome evaluationally. What happens to anyone happens to everyone; and what happens to everyone happens to oneself. If you have ever experienced this kind of valuational social union and identification with another person, even for a short period of time, you should consider yourself blessed. You have tasted abundant life, but you may still have a long way to go. The more you love unselfishly and comprehensively, the more abundantly you live. The paradox of abundant living is that we cannot get it by aiming at it directly or from selfish motives. If we would save our life directly and selfishly, we will lose it. Abundant living comes indirectly from valuing and promoting the well being of others and from self-less-ly identifying ourselves with them, thereby taking their well being and all their good-making properties into ourselves. To find abundant life, we must lose our selfish reasons for wanting it! Apply this to all references to abundant living in this book.

Positive intrinsic value-objects (unique conscious beings) can also be combined positively with extrinsic value-objects, as when we realize and fully appreciate the fact that we are embodied souls, or when creative artists or writers become one with their tools, instruments, artifacts, and performances, or when athletes pour their hearts and their total being into their performances, teams, and games. Intrinsic values can be fused dynamically with systemic values, as when we bet our souls on biblical inerrancy, or when we judge that our entire worth and salvation rests on passionately believing a handful of conceptually constructed philosophical or religious doctrines.

Consider what we say when we first introduce ourselves to other people. Normally, we give our proper names and mention a very small number of our extrinsic social roles like the jobs we hold, our marital status, our home towns, or the games and positions we play. Most people are better developed extrinsically than in other ways. When we first introduce ourselves to others, we almost never mention our systemic or intrinsic capacities and attributes—what and how much we know, or who and what we love. Do we at times think of ourselves (or others) as being only extrinsic selves, only exteriors without interiors? Sharing information about our systemic traits usually takes place in formal, governmental, educational or occupational contexts; and disclosing our intrinsic inner self is usually reserved for intimate interpersonal relations.

Our self-esteem depends largely on the richness of the positive ways that we think about ourselves. At times our self-esteem may be very low because we have an inordinately low opinion or knowledge of ourselves, because we keep running excessively limited, distorted, or mistaken scripts or beliefs about ourselves through our minds, or because we just do not know how to measure much less appreciate ourselves. "Love thyself" is intimately related to "Know thyself."

Systemic, Extrinsic, and Intrinsic Dimensions of Self[52]

> Man is spirit. But what is spirit? Spirit is the self. But what is the self? The self is a relation which relates itself to its own self;...the self is not the relation but [consists in the fact] that the relation relates itself to its own self.[53] Søren Kierkegaard

> Our inner or moral Self, our outer or social self, and our systemic, or thinking self, comprise our total value pattern, our Personality.[54] Robert S. Hartman

Complete self-knowledge involves understanding all value dimensions of ourselves, our "total value pattern," all the systemic, extrinsic, and distinctively intrinsic aspects of our personalities, and how they are integrated, configured, and interrelated. We are not purely immaterial, self-contained, conscious beings or spirits. We are unique, embodied, conscious subjects who think, feel, choose, and act in a common world of spacetime shared by others.

Most of what we value, are, and can be resides in the unconscious storehouses of our brains. In extrinsic physiological terms, our systemic, extrinsic, and intrinsic self-dimensions may be located in different but overlapping parts of our brains. Our evaluations depend upon which parts of our brains are working, which not, and whether they are working in harmony or at odds with one another. The same is true with respect to the spiritual distinctions between worldliness, ideology, and saintliness. The trick to becoming a holistic saint is to get *all* parts of our brains to working and in harmony with each other, including the prefrontal area of the cerebral cortex and the lymbic system where conscience and moral feelings seem to be embodied.[55] As explained in the third chapter, holistic saintliness use it all in order not to loose it all, but non-saints just aren't using all their brains!

Warren S. Brown explained that both self-knowledge and conscience, our sense of moral right and wrong, involve capacities residing in identifiable localized parts or regions of our brains. Localized in very broad brain regions are our capacities for language, perceptual recognition, emotional responsiveness to things present and imagined, long-term memory, especially episodic memories of events in our own lives that largely constitute of our sense of self-identity over time and our autobiography, and our capabilities for long-range foresight and planning.[56] Brain diseased or damaged persons lack some or all of these capabilities, depending on the locus and extent of their brain injuries or lesions. Our capacities for religious experience are also localized in definite areas of our brains. Different religions and kinds of spiritual union may be built upon very different experiences located in different brain regions. We should not find that troublesome; God made it so.

Ideologists and worldlings conspicuously under-develop and under-utilize many of their brain regions. Systemic and extrinsic evaluation are largely left-brain functions in most people, and intrinsic evaluation is largely fore-brained, right-brained, and mid-brained, though not entirely so. Most people most of the time live in their extrinsic/systemic left brains. The commonplace condition of extrinsic dominance is what the theologians call sinful "worldliness;" the sinful condition of systemic dominance is "dogmatism," "authoritarianism," or "ideology."

With today's marvelous brain-scan technology, we can actually see which parts of our brains are active and which are not when various psychological, evaluational, moral, and spiritual experiences, activities, and processes transpire. We can also see where and when various parts of our brains are unused or impaired. The main task of ethical and spiritual development is getting human beings to use their right brains, or better yet, their whole brains, and to stop being only half-brained people.

Predictably and verifiably, worldlings and ideologists regularly use only parts of their brains, but holistic saints use it all. Only holistic saints have it all and play the game of life with a full deck!

The Systemic Self-dimension

> Systemic *value applied to individual persons shows the individual as a system.*[57]
> Robert S. Hartman

Our *systemic self-dimension* is our most abstract conceptual self. It consists of our actual and potential:

a. knowledge and application of language, mathematics, logic, computer programs, authorities, rules, regulations, laws, symbols, ritual forms, the formal aspects of music and the arts, and the formal aspects of the sciences, including the natural sciences and value science or axiology;

b. knowledge of and obedience or conformity to ideal constructs, rituals, institutional regulations, laws, moral rules, and social action-guiding principles;

c. patterns of offices, memberships, social roles, and positions in institutions and organizations;

d. non-empirical, formal, theoretical, philosophical, and religious concepts, beliefs, doctrines, dogmas, ideologies, ritual forms, rules, and laws;

e. capacity for systemic evaluation, for measuring things objectively with concepts, for using "all or nothing" logic, for reducing things to minimal essentials, and for combining systemic with other values.

The Extrinsic Self-dimension

> *The application of* extrinsic *value to individual persons shows each person as a class of functions.*[58] Robert S. Hartman

Our *extrinsic self-dimension* is our public and practical self, our actual or potential:

a. perceptions or sensations of and relations with perceptual objects and processes, including our own possessions, our immediate physical environment, the world of nature, our own bodies, and the bodies of other persons and living things;

b. mastery of facts, including both knowing and actually using means/ends, cause/effect relations;

c. bodily structures, functions, and behaviors or actions;

d. physical skills, talents, abilities, habits, hobbies, exercises, and disciplines;

e. social skills, talents, abilities, habits, discipline—relating socially and practically to others;

f. actually conforming to the ideal demands or expectations of self or others such as parents, peers, and society;

g. conforming to established manners, customs, conventions, dress codes, and social morality;

h. acting out social roles such as student, teacher, rabbi, minister athlete, coach, parent, child, sibling, spouse, citizen, alien, high caste, outcast, employer, employee, producer, consumer, leader, follower, ruler, ruled, *etc.*

I. actual social status, rank, reputation, honors, roles, positions in social hierarchies;

j. managing practical affairs, career, work, ambitions, business, property or possessions, meeting physical needs, health habits, amusements, hobbies, athletics, and so on;

k. competing with others;

l. comparing ourselves with others;

m. proneness to accidents, to good or bad luck;

n. having analytic, empirical, factual information and social concepts and beliefs—the systemic aspect of the extrinsic;

o. immersion and absorption in the present moment; short range hindsight and foresight.

p. employing capacities for extrinsic evaluation, using means to ends, measuring practically with empirical class concepts and standards, manifesting ordinary human desires, emotions, interests, and actively combining extrinsic with other values.

The Intrinsic Inner Self-dimension

> Intrinsic *value applied to individual persons shows the uniqueness of each person and its fulfilling or failing to fulfill its own self.*[59] Robert S. Hartman

> *This is the important thing; you cannot fully be systemic or extrinsic unless you are fully intrinsic. In other words, the moral man will also be a better accountant, pilot, or surgeon. The value dimensions are within each other. The human contains the social, and the social the systematic. The lower value is within the higher. The systemic is within the extrinsic, and the extrinsic within the intrinsic. The more fully you are yourself, the better you will be at your job, and in your social role, and in your thinking. Out of your intrinsic being you summon the resources to be anything you want to be. Thus, the intrinsic, the development of your inner self, is not a luxury. It is a necessity for your own being yourself in all three dimensions.*[60] Robert S. Hartman

In the broadest sense of the term, our *intrinsic self-dimension* is our total self with *all* its integrated properties. It is our inner consciousness, our thinking minds, our bodies, the relationships that help to make us who and what we are, and all else about us. It is the set of the integrated totality of all our properties, all our qualities and the relations that help to make us who and what we are, down to the very last detail. As such it is our richest self because *it includes our systemic and extrinsic selves*, but to these *it adds* the inner or *primordial conscious self-dimension*, the *distinctively intrinsic* aspects of selfhood. Systemic and extrinsic self-development are immensely enhanced by intrinsic self-development. Our systemic beliefs and extrinsic behaviors express the inner intrinsic states and activities of our souls.

Our *inner or primordial conscious self-dimension* consists of our actual or potential:

a. experiential inwardness or self-awareness, paying direct attention to our internal psychological states, processes, activities, and experiences;

b. awareness and appreciation of ourselves and others as unique centers of conscious activity, experience, and evaluation;

c. capacities for attention, concentration, choice or decision, self-control, effort-making, free will, autonomy;

d. affections, emotions, feelings, desires, interests, the most intense and focused of which belong to intrinsic evaluation;

e. intense enjoyments, pleasures, delights, joys, happiness, euphoria, ecstasy;

f. empathetic identification with and compassion for others; taking the perspective of others;

g. imagination and creativity in any field of human endeavor;

h. religious experience, encounter, devotion, spiritual identification and union;

I. conscience, the most profoundly experienced ideal demands or expectations that we place upon ourselves and others, including our deepest moral sense of right and wrong, virtue and vice, good and evil;

j. authenticity, being true to ourselves;

k. moral virtues or dispositions like honesty, sincerity, truthfulness, courage, integrity, temperance, fidelity, gratitude, justice, wisdom, benevolence, harm-avoidance, harm-prevention, etc;

l. self-acceptance, self-forgiveness, self-respect, self-esteem, self-love, and delight in our own existence;

m. acceptance of and respect, esteem, love, and compassion for others, delight in their existence and well-being, and personal identification with them;

n. acute aesthetic sensitivities and creativity;

o. faith (in Kierkegaard's sense of knowing and accepting ourselves as unique individuals trusting in, being faithful to, and living out our lives before God);

p. deepest hopes for ourselves and others, our long and short range objectives and plans of life;

q. cooperation with others;

r. sense of intrinsic unity with others, or with anything and everything,

s. singular and metaphorical concepts and beliefs, including our concepts of ourselves and others as unique individuals;

t. the capacity for intrinsic evaluation, for all the foregoing forms of self and other understanding, identification, and measurement; and the capacity for combining intrinsic realities with other value-objects.

The self was portrayed positively above. Yet, our neglect and perversion of all of the above dimensions and elements of who we are also belong to the inner intrinsic total self. Our total persons cannot be separated from our evil thoughts, dispositions, actions, or bad-making properties. We cannot simply "love the person and hate his or her sinfulness" because our sinfulness is an integral part of who we are. As explained earlier, all of us have a dark side that we cannot love and affirm, though we can acknowledge its reality, forgive it, outgrow it, be reconciled to ourselves, and seek forgiveness from and reconciliation with others, including God. What we have lost or never found can be created, restored, or reborn. Spirituality says that we should not be satisfied with the dark, sinful, undesirable side of ourselves. We need to be saved from it. God's help is available!

Now, all we have to do to know ourselves is work through the details of this outline of the dimensions of selfhood, improve it where it is deficient, and apply each item to ourselves in depth!

Once we gain self-knowledge, what do we do with it? Robert S. Hartman gave this excellent advice:

> Thus, Self-development is not a luxury; it is a necessity for our being truly ourselves on all three levels....But how?
>
> First of all, I would say, you have to achieve clarity about yourself. Philosophers have tried to show you how to do it, from Socrates to Kierkegaard. What they have said can be synthesized into what I call the four Self rules.
>
> The first is Socrates': *know thyself.* You...have to find out what kind of person you are, what kind of properties you have, what kind of material has been given to you to live with.
>
> The second is Kierkegaard's: *choose thyself.* This means that once you have found out what kind of person you are, you have to accept yourself and make the best of it because this is all you have. You have to choose yourself; you are your own material. This is the material you have to develop to infinity, and there is absolutely no limit, from the bottom at which you start, to the height to which you can go. Jesus said to the thief who repented: "Today shalt thou be with me in Paradise." Mary Magdalene was a prostitute and became a saint: Matthew was a tax collector, which at that time meant a robber and collaborator with the Romans, and he became a writer of the Gospel. There is no limit to the lowness at which you may start. But no matter how despicable you may be to yourself, you must choose yourself, accept yourself as the one you are.
>
> The third rule is Pico della Mirandola's and also Kierkegaard's: *create thyself.* Make yourself into the very best person you can. You are your own creation. It's never too late, but start as early as you can, and never stop. There is more joy in heaven for one sinner who repents than for ninety-nine just persons who need no repentance.

The fourth is Jesus': *give thyself*. This means forget all limitations, be generous with your own Self. Give your Self to your fellow man and to the world. Love your neighbor as you love yourself. Throw your bread upon the water. Lack of love is the cause of our trouble. If everyone would love himself and his neighbor, fear of war and violence would fade away. This is the Gospel truth, expressed both by Jesus and the Prophets, both in the Old Testament (Leviticus 19:18) and the New (Matthew 22:37-40).[61]

Knowing and Valuing Our Uniqueness

Nobody can be exactly like me, and sometimes even I have trouble doing it.[62]
Tallulah Bankhead

The key to the kingdom [of God] is in the hands of everyone of us: it is love of our own Selves—or, in order to exclude misunderstanding as if self-love were the same as selfishness—it is liking our Selves. Unless you like yourself you cannot like anybody else. Unless you feel that you are of importance nothing can be of importance to you. You must feel that you are important. You must take yourself seriously. If you take yourself as an accident that just as well might not have happened, if you dislike your own self, then you are lost. You are a loss to the universe. You cannot enrich the world of God. God has created you for the enrichment of His world. If you yourself feel unworthy of yourself, then, of course, you cannot fulfill the mission that you are given by your birth. You must make yourself worthy of yourself in order to be worthy of God and worthy of your fellowman.[63] Robert S. Hartman

Do we really know and value ourselves and others as unique centers or subjects of conscious experience, thought, activity, feeling, and evaluation? We may think that we should love our neighbors as ourselves; but how do we, how should we, love ourselves? What about ourselves do we, should we, love? Unless we love ourselves, we cannot love others, including God. If we do not regard and respect ourselves, we cannot regard anything or everything that we have to offer to others as gifts worth giving.

Immanuel Kant said that we should respect *humanity* within ourselves as an end in itself. Surely this is only a small part of the story. Humanity is something very abstract that we have in common with other people, and there is nothing unique about it, even if it is distinctively human. If we value only our common and/or distinctive humanity (for example, our rationality or morality), we still do not value our unique individuality. When Immanuel Kant explained what he meant by valuing humanity, "respecting persons," it turns out that he had in mind valuing only the moral law within us,[64] something purely systemic, which falls very far short of both our common humanity and our distinctive personal individuality. Valuing our general capacities for rationality, morality, self-consciousness, activity, experience, or evaluation in general is not the same as valuing concretely existing, unique, self-conscious, holistic centers or subjects of such properties *in toto*.

Think of some things that you have in common with all other people. The moral demands of deepest-level conscience spring from the better parts of our common humanity or human nature. Humanity, whatever that is, is indeed an important part of who you are, but not the whole of it, so you have to go beyond that, beyond rationality, beyond universally human conscience. Next, try to think of some things that are true of you as an individual but not true of anyone else in the universe. If nothing else, consider that no one else has ever had exactly your spacetime locus, or your particular perspective on the universe, or precisely your experiences. No one else has ever made your decisions or manifested your creativity. No one else has exactly your unique integration, synthesis, and configuration of properties, your total property inventory, even though you share innumerable particular properties or qualities with other people. No one else has exactly your station in life and its duties, or your uniquely personal responsibilities and projects. No one else can enrich the universe in your own distinctive way or take your place as an intrinsically valuable reality.

Our uniqueness consists in the concrete existence of the total set of properties and relations that we are, including the ways our attributes are arranged, ordered, integrated, or configured. It includes our common morality, rationality, affections, activities, and humanity, as well as all the definite properties and relations that belong to each of us alone. If we value ourselves, and if others value us, only for characteristics we share with others, we are in principle expendable and replaceable by others without any overall loss of goodness or worth.

All of our systemic and extrinsic properties are repeatable; and if these alone have value, we can be replaced without loss of value by others who exemplify these properties. Someone else can wear the numbers on our jerseys, work at our jobs, and be paid numbered wages by the hour. If we are a quarterback, a center, or a second baseman, other players can replace us as long as we are being valued merely as extrinsic means to filling positions or winning games. If we are teachers, coaches, students, engineers, farmers, or salespersons, others can replace us in such roles without loss of value, as long as we are being valued only through the functional class properties that we share with others.

Even if we are a friend, a husband, a wife, or a child, there is an extrinsic sense in which we can be replaced. Other people in our lives can make new friends, wed again if we divorce or die, and have additional children; but can our "replacements" really take our place in truly intimate intrinsic human relationships? Not if others know and love us as unique human beings.

When Thomas Jefferson followed Benjamin Franklin as American Ambassador to France, he was asked if he was Franklin's "replacement." He replied: "No one can replace him, sir; I am only his successor."[65] So it is with all of us! If we die prematurely, our successors will also be unique persons; but, once lost, our own unique individuality (and that of other people) is gone and can never be replaced intrinsically. A new intrinsic relationship is never a replacement relationship. Even with new intrinsic gains, lost loved ones are still lost; and people with strong capacities for intrinsic evaluation are acutely sensitive to such loss. For them, there is no such thing as final "closure." Thinking that one individual person could ever replace another in an intrinsic relationship fails to understand the concept of "uniqueness" and to appreciate its value.

Knowing Our Limitations

> *The Middle Ages were not what the romantic imagination paints, but instead a rugged age much more insensitive than ours today. Tortures, burnings, hangings were public spectacles, their thrill was like today's bullfights or prizefights. The ladies of high society went to the place of execution the night before and slept in their coaches in order not to miss the entertainment....Today's moral reality is still philosophical; it is not fundamentally different from that of antiquity or the Middle Ages. We have the same fundamental values and disvalues, even though we practice them with greater refinement, including torture.*[66] Robert S. Hartman

As we gradually discover and come to know ourselves by discerning our values and evaluational capacities, we eventually realize that we are like many other people who we do not admire. Our values and evaluations are very crude in many ways. We are much more developed in some value dimensions than in others. We have natural bents or talents for some values and evaluations but not others. We put much time and effort into knowing and developing some of our evaluational capacities but neglect or misuse others. We knowingly or unknowingly impose undesirable limits on ourselves. We fainteartedly allow other people to limit us unduly and treat us disrespectfully or abusively. We are afflicted by weakness of will. We do not live up to our full potentials as unique and exceedingly complex human beings. Like St. Paul, we often do that which we ought not do, and we do not do that which we ought to do. This darker side of self-knowledge was explored earlier.

As indicated previously, we can actually use several personality and spirituality analysis instruments, the Hartman Value Profile (HVP) created by Robert S. Hartman, and the Christian Values Profile (CVP), developed by Rem B. Edwards together with David and Vera Mefford, to pinpoint our distinctive evaluational and spiritual strengths and weaknesses with some exactitude. Visit websites for these at: http://www.hartmaninstitute.org and http://www.christianvaluesprofile.com.

Information provided by these profiles can help us to know our weaknesses and limitations and to make plans for personal and spiritual growth. It can help us to know, appreciate, develop, and partly create our own personal and spiritual realities and identities, and to expand the kind and scope of our interests, concerns, efforts, values, and evaluations, thereby enriching our lives and the lives of others.

What are the present limits of your own personal capacities for systemic, extrinsic, and intrinsic values and evaluations? Concentrate for a moment on the intrinsic. Anyone's capacity for intrinsic evaluation can be distorted or warped. Some people narrowly identify themselves with, and only with, their wealth, possessions, success, job, game, or team, and will allow themselves to have no other identity. Do you do this? Some people live constantly for only one small thing, an extrinsic thing like social popularity, or status, or success, or material possessions, or for a systemic thing like some belief, dogma, or ceremonial form. The theologian Paul Tillich defined "religion" as "being grasped by an ultimate concern." Some people, worldly people, make a religion, the whole meaning and purpose of life, out of extrinsic entities like wealth, property, success, and football. Systemic ideologists find the whole meaning of life in dogmas and systems that command their total loyalty. Some people (e.g., Nazis, White Supremists, Terrorists) even identify themselves with evil and immorality.

People are idolaters when ultimately concerned about things that are not truly ultimate. Inappropriate values are loved by some people with all their hearts, souls, minds, and strengths. They sacrifice everything else for them. They make idolatrous religions out of them. They become one with them and refuse to have any other values or personal identity. Are you like this? If so, you are omitting something important, meaningful, or valuable. But what? What is missing from your own life?

By severely limiting ourselves, our loves and values, we can impoverish ourselves and others immensely. Most of us naturally love only a few kindred people, as Jonathan Edwards realized, and as modern sociobiologists emphasize. Moral and spiritual growth involves both including more and more value-objects and expanding our capacities for evaluation, especially our intrinsic values and evaluations. Spiritual development overcomes our natural but limited in-group appreciation, our provincial concern for only "our kind of people." It sees and loves everyone as our neighbors, brothers, and sisters.

Where do we get the values with which we are stuck before spiritual conversion, spiritual growth, rational reflection, informed decision-making, and the grace of God begin to transform us? Part of the answer lies in the genetic endowments we inherited from our hunter/gatherer ancestors, so heavily emphasized by today's sociobiologists and evolutionary psychologists. Evolution and God equipped us to have certain values and capacities for evaluation. Our souls are not blank slates. Many values have survival value. Survival is itself a value. Our values and evaluations are significantly affected by our attachment relations with, and the parenting styles of, our mothers or other primary caregivers during the earliest days, months, and years of our lives. As we grow up, our values and evaluations, our profound attachments, are affected by and focused upon others in wider and wider social circles. Intense attachments (intrinsic evaluations of intrinsic value-objects) are the very essence of abundant living and the communion of the saints. We can love intrinsic value-objects, and, unlike mere things and thoughts, they can love us back.

Most important of all, as we mature, we can and do choose our own values and evaluational capacities from the broad menu that life has been given to us. Although most of us are by nature dominated by genetic worldliness, our rich hereditary, social, and constitutional heritage also allows us to choose or emphasize alternative non-worldly values. Our inherited endowments for value and evaluation are exceptionally pliable and indeterminate; their absolute limits are unknown; they allow for great diversity. They permit us to modify how we prioritize our earliest natural values and evaluational capacities as we mature in grace. They allow for moral and spiritual conversions and ongoing transformations with God's help and our own cooperation with God.

This is where attachment theory psychology comes in.[67] Children blessed with secure attachment relations with affectionate primary attachment figures who are reliable sources of protection and security usually turn out to be confident, competent, loving, self-and-other-valuing adults who conceive of God in their parents' image. Children whose mothers or primary caregivers are cold, rejecting, abusive, and unreliable as providers of protection and security turn out to be avoidant types who grasp for the security they never had and may try to find it in absolutistic ideological doctrines and dogmas. They also conceive of God in their mother's or father's (faulty) image. Somewhere in between these extremes, mothers or caregivers who are partly supportive, partly not, tend to produce children who are anxious/ambivalent types. Their positive value relations with themselves and others alternate with resistance, anger, anxiety, and mistrust; and they too conceive of and relate to God in their mother's or caregiver's (faulty) image.

Natural intrinsic saints (who are few) probably got a lot of good mothering, even if given by fathers or other caretakers. Natural systemic ideologists (who are few) may have received extremely bad mothering, and most other people (extrinsic worldlings who try to find security in mindless things?) may have received ambivalent mothering. What is here called "mothering" means love, care, protection, security, and relatively constant and reliable attention, which can be given by any devoted caregiver, not just by mothers as such. The exact relation between the parenting styles of our primary childhood attachment figures or caregivers and our own present values and evaluational capacities needs much further investigation. The good news is that all presently existing values and evaluational capacities can be transcended and transformed. A more excellent way is available.

We can begin right where we are to become what we ideally ought to be, which presumably is what our deepest and best self wants to be. But what ought we to be? This is where deep-level enlightened conscience comes in, our inner capacity to give "the law" or normative ideals to ourselves or to reaffirm already existing ideals coming from others that nevertheless ring true for ourselves after serious and careful consideration. To be true to ourselves, we must know ourselves, especially our values and the limits set by our own personal historical realities, so that we can intelligently and responsibly choose what to do and who to become.

Along the path of ethico-religious development, the first and the last steps must include gaining self knowledge and intrinsic self-valuation; but our last self will not be exactly the same as our first or even our current self. Our present self is where we are now; our last self is what we will or could become along life's way. Our current self is the actual but incomplete, unfinished, and often confused and conflicted self of the present moment. Who we are now has been created by and includes the past moments of our lives and the world that came before. Our actual or given present self is largely created for us by inherited biological structures and psychological dispositions, by our own past experiences, adventures, and choices, and by the influence of those caregivers, family, friends, peers, teachers, church members, and others (including God) who have profoundly touched our lives.

Most of us do not know who we are. We do not know our given self very well, but we cannot escape from it. It must be discovered, understood, accepted, forgiven, and transformed. Our future, final, and finished self will emerge from its current base. We will develop ourselves either haphazardly, as is usually the case; or we will develop ourselves knowingly, deliberately, and by choice. We will either continue to develop out of control, or we will develop under our own self-knowledge and self-control; but we will develop. The future will either just happen to us, or we can partly decide what will happen. Our given self, who we are right now, must be found; the self we will become, the self we ought to be, must be chosen and created. Advancing spirituality recognizes that this must be done with God's help and in God's presence. Immediate self-awareness, rational reflection, responsible decision-making, affective identification, the perspectives and models of others, the communion of the saints, good fortune, and divine grace can all contribute to the final outcome. The best self we could possibly become is the one that is richest in good-making properties in all three dimensions of value and evaluation. To be so developed is to live most abundantly.

Our lives are temporally ordered, inescapably so. Our future selves exist largely as values, ideas, ideals, and possibilities to be actualized through the decisions that we make now and later. We are largely responsible for what we make of our existence. Our past and present selves comprise what we are now; our present and future choices will determine what we can and will become. What we are places broad but not exacting restraints upon what we can become; it also contains and discloses immense horizons and possibilities for self-becoming and self-creation. Knowing ourselves involves understanding what and how we value. Self-knowledge enables us to create or choose ourselves and our future values and evaluations, at least in part. Self-knowledge tells us that we are not finished products. No matter what we have been and now are, the most important question for us at this moment is: What or who will we become? This question will confront us time and again in the days ahead—every time we face an intellectual challenge, a practical impasse, a personal tragedy, a moral temptation or predicament, a spiritual crisis, an intrinsic choice. May your own answer make a significant place for intrinsic, extrinsic, and systemic moral and spiritual values and evaluations.

Notes

Preface

1. A notorious attempt to reduce theology to ethics is R. B. Braithwaite, *An Empiricist's View of the Nature of Religious Belief* (Cambridge: Cambridge University Press, 1955). As I read him, Stephen Byrum's *The Value Structure of Theology* (Washington, DC: University Press of America, 1978) attempts to reduce theology to axiology. See his Ch. 14, especially 166 and 178.
2. Robert S. Hartman, *The Structure of Value* (Carbondale and Edwardsville: Southern Illinois University Press, 1967), 294. Republished in 2012 by Wipf & Stock Publishers, Eugene, OR.
3. Rem B. Edwards, *John Wesley's Values—And Ours* (Lexington, KY: Emeth Press, 2012).
4. Michael S. Gazzaniga, *The Ethical Brain* (New York: Dana Press, 2005), 164-178.

Chapter One

1. Plato, "Alcibiades I," *The Works of Plato*, Benjamin Jowett, ed. (New York: The Macmillan Co., 1892), 2:763-764.
2. Plato, "Apology," *The Dialogues of Plato*, Benjamin Jowett, trans. (New York: The Macmillan Company, 1892), 1:413.
3. Jonathan Edwards, from sermons entitled "A Spiritual Understanding of Divine Things Denied too the Unregenerate," "Warnings of Future Punishment Don't Seem Real to the Wicked," and "The Torments of Hell are Exceeding Great," *The Works of Jonathan Edwards*, Kenneth P. Minkema, ed. (New Haven: Yale University Press, 1997), 14:87, 84-85, 206, 323.
4. Søren Kierkegaard, *Fear and Trembling and The Sickness Unto Death* (Princeton: Princeton University Press, 1954), 168.
5. John Wesley, "Wandering Thoughts," I, 2, *The Bicentennial Edition of the Works of John Wesley,* ed. Albert C. Outler. (Nashville: Abingdon Press, 1985), 2:127.
6. Henry David Thoreau, *Walden* (New York: The Modern Library, 1950), 7.
7. Jonathan Edwards, "A Treatise Concerning Religious Affections," *The Works of Jonathan Edwards*, John E. Smith, ed. (New Haven: Yale University Press, 1959), 2:122-123.
8. Kierkegaard, 166.
9. John Dewey, "Theory of Valuation," *International Encyclopaedia of Unified Science* (Chicago: University of Chicago Press, 1939), 2:4.
10. Kierkegaard, 178.
11. See Michael P. Ghiglieri, *The Dark Side of Man: Tracing the Origins of Male Violence* (Reading, Mass.: Persus Books, 1999).
12. Frans de Waals, *Good Natured: The Origins of Right and Wrong in Humans and Other Animals* (Cambridge: Harvard University Press, 1996), 28, 207.
13. David M. Buss, *The Evolution of Desire* (New York: Basic Books, 1994), Ch. 2.
14. *Ibid.*, 59.
15. *Ibid.*, 59-69.
16. Douglas T. Kenrick, Melanie R. Trost, and Virgil L. Sheets, "Power, Harassment, and Trophy Mates: The Feminist Advantages of an Evolutionary Perspective," in *Sex, Power, Conflict: Evolutionary and Feminists Perspectives*, David M. Buss and Neil M. Malamuth, eds. (New York: Oxford University Press, 1996), 29-53.

17. For good discussions of dominance and subordination in human beings and our primate cousins, see: Abraham Maslow, *The Farther Reaches of Human Nature* (New York: The Viking Press, 1971), 351-368; Dorothy L. Cheney and Robert M. Seyfarth, *How Monkeys See the World* (Chicago: University of Chicago Press, 1990), 29-44; Frans de Waal, Good Natured: *The Origins of Right and Wrong in Humans and Other Animals* (Cambridge: Harvard University Press, 1996), 97-105; Carl Sagan and Ann Druyan, *Shadows of Forgotten Ancestors* (New York: Random House, 1992), 201-218.

18. Felicia Pratto, "Sexual Politics: The Gender Gap in the Bedroom, the Cupboard, and the Cabinet," in *Sex, Power, Conflict: Evolutionary and Feminists Perspectives*, David M. Buss and Neil M. Malamuth, eds. (New York: Oxford University Press, 1996), 179-230.

19. *Ibid.*, 183-192.

20. *Ibid.*, 189, 184.

21. *Ibid.*, 184.

22. *Ibid.*, 200, 220-222. See also 232, 256, 269, 271, 306.

23. *Ibid.*, 200.

24. Buss, 221-222. See also Pratto, 217-222.

25. On the revenge system in our primate relatives, see de Waal, 157-162. See his note 24, 246-247, for further references.

26. Sagan and Druyan, 207.

27. Aldous Huxley, *Brave New World and Brave New World Revisited* (New York: Harper & Row, 1965), 40.

28. Ralph Waldo Emerson, "The Divinity School Address," *The Complete Works of Ralph Waldo Emerson*, Edward Waldo Emerson, ed. (Boston: Houghton Mifflin, 1903), 1:126.

29. Barbara Smuts, "Male Aggression Against Women: An Evolutionary Perspective," in *Sex, Power, Conflict: Evolutionary and Feminist Perspectives*, David M. Buss and Neil M. Malamuth, eds. (New York: Oxford University Press, 1996), 231-268.

30. In Buss and Malamuth, see 217-221, 245, 315. In Buss, see 42-45, 102-106, 221-222.

31. Ralph Waldo Emerson, "Ode to W. H. Channing," *The Complete Works of Ralph Waldo Emerson*, Edward Waldo Emerson, ed. (Boston: Houghton Mifflin, 1903), 9:78.

32. Albert Schweitzer, *The Philosophy of Civilization* (New York: The Macmillan Co., 1960), 86.

33. Buss, 16.

34. Repeated by Charles Gibson on NBC's *Good Morning America*, March 16, 1999.

35. On biophilia see Edward O. Wilson, *Biophilia* (Cambridge: Harvard University Press, 1984); and Stephen R. Kellert and Edward O. Wilson, eds., *The Biophilia Hypothesis* (Washington, DC: Island Press, 1993).

36. Huxley, 16.

37. Ralph Waldo Emerson, "Compensation," *The Complete Works of Ralph Waldo Emerson*, Edward Waldo Emerson, ed. (Boston : Houghton Mifflin Co., 1903), 2:110-111.

38. Gabriel Marcel, *Man Against Mass Society* (Chicago: Henry Regnery Co., 1962), 95-96. Marcel further explores analogies between people and machines on 174-184.

39. Kenneth Keniston, "'Good Children' (Our Own), 'Bad Children' (Other People's), and the Horrible Work Ethic." *Yale Alumni Magazine* 37:7 (April 1974), 6-7.

40. David M. Buss, "Sexual Conflict: Evolutionary Insights into Feminism and the 'Battle of the Sexes'," in *Sex, Power, Conflict: Evolutionary and Feminists Perspectives*, David M. Buss and Neil M. Malamuth, eds. (New York: Oxford University Press, 1996), 299.

41. St. Bonaventure, *The Mind's Road to God* (New York: The Liberal Arts Press, 1953), 28.

42. Kierkegaard, 176.
43. *Ibid.*, 159.
44. Rollo May, *Man's Search for Himself* (New York: Dell Pub. Co., 1953), 14-15.
45. Robert S. Hartman, "The Individual in Management," (Unpublished manuscript, 1962), 36.
46. For a detailed critique of behaviorism, especially as applied to medical ethics, see: Rem B. Edwards: "Behaviorism: II. Philosophical Issues," *Encyclopedia of Bioethics, Revised Edition*, Warren T. Reich, ed. (New York: Simon & Schuster Macmillan, 1995) 1:233-238.
47. Kierkegaard, 187.
48. *Ibid.*, 175-176.
49. R. D. Alexander, *The Biology of Moral Systems* (New York: Aldine, 1987), 95.
50. Ralph Waldo Emerson, "The Poet," *The Complete Works of Ralph Waldo Emerson*, Edward Waldo Emerson, ed., (Boston: Houghton Mifflin, 1903), 3:5.
51. Alfred North Whitehead, *Science and Philosophy* (Patterson, NJ: Littlefield, Adams, 1964), 136.
52. Martin Heidegger, *Poetry, Language and Thought* (New York: Harper & Row, 1971), 208.
53. Robert Penn Warren, "Who is Relevant?" *Yale Alumni Magazine*, 34:5, (February 1964), 11.
54. Quoted at http://en.wikiquote.org/wiki/Niels_Bohr
55. Kierkegaard, 245.
56. Irene M. Pepperberg, *Alex & Me* (New York: Collins, 2008).
57. DeWitt H. Parker, *The Principles of Aesthetics* (New York: Appleton Century-Crofts, 1946), 276.
58. Jonathan Edwards, "Some Thoughts Concerning the Revival of Religion in New England," *The Works of Jonathan Edwards*, C. C. Goen, ed. (New Haven: Yale University Press, 1972), 4:393.
59. John Wesley, "Sermon on the Mount, II," II, 6, *The Bicentennial Edition of the Works of John Wesley*, ed. Albert C. Outler. (Nashville: Abingdon Press, 1984), 1:498.
60. Abraham J. Heschel, *Man's Quest for God* (New York: Charles Scribner's Sons, 1954), xii.
61. The health and survival benefits of being religious are heavily, but not exclusively, emphasized by: Herbert Benson and Mark Stark, *Timeless Healing: The Power and Biology of Belief* (New York: Scribner, 1996); Larry Dossey, *Healing Words: The Power of Prayer and the Practice of Medicine* (San Francisco: Harper, 1993); and David B. Larson, James P. Swyers, and Michael E. McCullough, eds. *Scientific Research on Spirituality and Health: A Consensus Report* (Rockville, MD: National Institute for Healthcare Research, 1998); Stephen Post and Jill Neimark, *Why Good Things Happen to Good People* (New York: Broadway Books, 2007)
62. Karen Armstrong, *The Great Transformation: The Beginning of Our Religious Traditions* (New York: Alfred A. Knopf, 2006, 84.
63. St. Thomas Aquinas, *Summa Contra Gentiles*, (New York: Benziger Brothers, 1928), Third Book, Part II, Chapter CXII.
64. Andrew Lindsay, *Christianity and the Rights of Animals* (New York: Crossroads Publishing Co., 1987), Ch. 2.
65. Jonathan Edwards, "A Treatise Concerning Religious Affections," 253.
66. Maslow, 364.
67. H. Richard Niebuhr, *Christ and Culture* (New York: Harper & Brothers, 1951), 47-48.

68. Lee A. Kirkpatrick, "Fundamentalism, Christian Orthodoxy, and Intrinsic Religious Orientation as Predictors of Discriminatory Attitudes," *Journal for the Scientific Study of Religion* 32:3 (1993), 266.
69. W. Larry Ventis, "The Relationships Between Religion and Mental Health," *Journal of Social Issues*, 51:2 (1995), 43.
70. Ralph Waldo Emerson, "Poetry and Imagination," in *The Complete Works of Ralph Waldo Emerson*, Edward Waldo Emerson, ed. (Boston: Houghton Mifflin, 1903), 8:12.
71. Jonathan Edwards, "Profitable Hearers of the Word," *The Works of Jonathan Edwards*, Kenneth P. Minkema, ed. (New Haven: Yale University Press, 1997), 14:246-247.
72. Hans Frei, *Types of Christian Theology* (New Haven: Yale University Press, 1992), 14-18.
73. Carl Michalson, *Worldly Theology: The Hermeneutical Focus of an Historical Faith* (New York: Charles Scribner's Sons, 1967), 74.
74. *Ibid.*, 77.
75. James Barr, *Fundamentalism* (Philadelphia: The Westminster Press, 1978), 40-41.
76. *Ibid.*, 41.
77. *Ibid.*, 47 ff.
78. Rem B. Edwards, "The Pagan Dogma of the Absolute Unchangableness of God," *Religious Studies*, (1978), 14:305-314.
79. Jonathan Edwards, "God the Best Portion of the Christian," *The Works of President Edwards* (New York, G. & C. & H. Carvill, 1830), 6:286.
80. Milton C. Nahm, *Selections from Early Greek Philosophy* (New York: Appleton-Century-Crofts, 1964), 84.
81. Robert S. Hartman, "The Nature of Valuation,"*Forms of s of Value and Valuation: Theory and Valuation,* 34.
82. St. Augustine, "Homilies on the Gospel of John," *The Nicene and Post-Nicene Fathers*, Philip Schaff, ed. (New York: Charles Scribner's Sons, 1903), 7:154.
83. John Wesley, *Explanatory Notes Upon the Old Testament*, comments on verse 28 of Genesis 1.
84. Jonathan Edwards, "A Spiritual Understanding of Divine Things Denied too the Unregenerate," *The Works of Jonathan Edwards*, Kenneth P. Minkema, ed. (New Haven: Yale University Press, 1997), 14:87.

Chapter Two

1. Max Mark, *Modern Ideologies* (New York: St. Martin's Press, 1973), 3.
2. Felix Gross, *Ideologies, Goals, and Values* (Westport CT.: Greenwood Press, 1985), 26.
3. For more information about historical uses of the term "ideology," see David Braybroke, "Ideology," *The Encyclopedia of Philosophy* (New York: Macmillan Pub. Co., 1967), 4:124-127; John Plamenatz, *Ideology* (New York: Praeger Publishers, 1970), especially Ch. 1.
4. Robert S. Hartman, "The Revolution Against War," in *The Critique of War*, Robert Ginsberg, ed. (Chicago: Henry Regnery, 1970), 335.
5. Robert S. Hartman, *The Hartman Value Profile (HVP) Manual of Interpretation, Second Edition* (Knoxville, TN: The Robert S. Hartman Institute, 2006), 234.
6. Robert S. Hartman, *The Structure of Value* (Carbondale and Edwardsville: Southern Illinois University Press, 1967), 81. Republished in 2012 by Wipf & Stock Publishers, Eugene, OR.
7. Marcus J. Borg, *The Heart of Christianity: Rediscovering a Life of Faith* (San Francisco: Harper Collins, 2004).

8. Hartman, *The Structure of Value*, 45-47, 69-79.
9. Robert S. Hartman, *Freedom to Live: The Robert Hartman Story* (Amsterdam - Atlanta: Editions Rodopi, 1994), 94.
10. *Ibid.*, 90.
10. Robert S. Hartman, "The Individual in Management," (Unpublished manuscript, 1962), 36.
11. Dorothy Frede, *Plato's Philebus* (Indianapolis: Hackett Pub. Co., 1993), 76.
12. Hartman, *The Structure of Value*, 253.
13. G. W. F. Hegel, *The Philosophy of History* (New York: Dover Publications, 1956), 26-27.
14. Robert S. Hartman, "The Nature of Valuation," *Forms of Value and Valuation: Theory and Applications*, Rem B. Edwards and John W. Davis, eds. (Lanham, MD: University Press of America, 1991), 33, 34.
15. Hartman, *The Structure of Value*, 112-113.
16. Rem B. Edwards, "Systemic Value and Valuation," *Forms of Value and Valuation: Theory and Applications*, Rem B. Edwards and John W. Davis, eds. (Lanham, MD: University Press of America, 1991), 40-44.
17. Hartman, *The Structure of Value*, 250-251.
18. Hartman, *Freedom to Live: The Robert Hartman Story*, 98.
19. *Ibid.*, 159-160.
20. *Ibid.*, 159.
21. Robert S. Hartman, "Applications of the Science of Axiology," *Forms of Value and Valuation: Theory and Applications*, Rem B. Edwards and John W. Davis, eds. (Lanham, MD: University Press of America, 1991), 201.
22. "A Sniper's View: Sharp-shooting Marines Witness Horror of War up Close," *Knoxville News Sentinel*, (Feb. 4. 1991), A 8.
23. Alexander H. Stephens, "Cornerstone Speech," available on line in many places. Originally published in Henry Cleveland, *Alexander H. Stephens, in Public and Private, with Letters and Speeches* (Philadelphia: National Publishing Co.), 1866), 717-729.
24. See the many relevant essays in Randall M. Miller, Harry S. Stout, Charles R. Wilson, *Religion and the American Civil War* (Oxford and New York: Oxford University Press, 1998).
25. Hartman, *The Structure of Value*, 253.
26. Alfred North Whitehead, *Science in the Making* (New York: The Free Press, 1925), 55.
27. Hartman, *The Hartman Value Profile (HVP) Manual of Interpretation, Second Edition*, 172.
28. Fyodor Dostoyevsky, *The Brothers Karamazof* (New York: The New American Library, 1957), 61.
29. Kenneth Keniston, "'Good Children' (Our Own), 'Bad Children' (Other People's), And the Horrible Work Ethic," *Yale Alumni Magazine* 37:7 (April 1974), 10.
30. Peter J. Gomes, *The Good Book* (New York: HarperCollins Publisher, 1996), 46.
31. St. Augustine, *The City of God* (New York: The Modern Library, 1950), 407.
32. Anton C. Pegis, *Basic Writings of Saint Thomas Aquinas* (New York: Random House, 1945), 1:27.
33. Sidney Norton Deane, *St. Anselm* (La Salle, Il.: Open Court Publishing Co., 1954), 190.
34. *Ibid.*, 13-14.
35. *Ibid.*, 226.
36. Pegis, 252.
37. Abraham J. Heschel, *The Prophets* (New York: Harper & Row, 1962), 258.

38. Alfred North Whitehead, *Process and Reality, Corrected Edition* (New York: The Free Press, 1978), 351.
39. Warren S. Brown, "Cognitive Contributions to Soul," *Whatever Happened to Soul: Scientific and Theological Portraits of Human Nature*, Warren S. Brown, Nancey Murphey, and H. Newton Malony, eds. (Minneapolis: Fortress Press, 1998), 122-123.
40. Pegis, 1065-1066.
41. *Ibid.*, 1111-1113, 1071, 1083.
42. Hartman, *Freedom to Live*, 153.
43. James Barr, *Fundamentalism* (Philadelphia: The Westminster Press, 1977), 62.
44. *Ibid.*, 52.
45. *Ibid.*, 51.
46. *Ibid.*
47. *Ibid.*, 54.
48. *Ibid.*, 55-89, 260-303.
49. John Wesley, "The Means of Grace," I, 1, *The Bicentennial Edition of the Works of John Wesley*, ed. Albert C. Outler. (Nashville: Abingdon Press, 1984), 1:381.
50. Alymer Maude, trans., *Leo Tolstoy, Selected Essays* (New York: The Modern Library, 1964), 87.
51. Wesley, "The Means of Grace," V, 4, *Works*, 1:396-397.
52. Tony Campolo, *Speaking My Mind* (Nashville, TN: W Publishing Group, 2004), 232.
53. John Baillie, *The Idea of Revelation in Recent Thought* (New York: Columbia University Press, 1954), 85-86.
54. Pegis, 2:1060.
55. *Ibid.*, 1075-1076.
56. *Ibid.*, 1096.
57. From an episode of the television program, *All in the Family*.
58. Joel Osteen, *Your Best Life Now* (New York: Faith Worlds, 2004), 5.
59. *Ibid.*, 257.
60. Harold S. Kushner, *To Life! A Celebration of Jewish Being and Thinking* (New York: Warner Books, 1993), 100.
61. John Wesley, "On the Trinity," 1, *Works*, 2:374.
62. John Wesley, "A Farther Appeal to Men of Reason and Religion," I, 3, *The Bicentennial Edition of the Works of John Wesley*, ed. Gerald R. Cragg. (Nashville: Abingdon Press, 1989), 11:106.
63. John Wesley, "Salvation by Faith," *Works*, 1:120.
64. John Wesley, "The Way to the Kingdom," II,10, *Works*, 1:230; Wesley, "The Marks of the New Birth," I, 3, *Works*, 1:418-419.
65. John Wesley, "The Law Established Through Faith, II," II, 6, *Works*, 2:40-41.
66. Brother Lawrence, *The Practice of the Presence of God*, Second Conversation.
67. Søren Kierkegaard, *Fear and Trembling and The Sickness Unto Death* (Princeton: Princeton University Press, 1941), 213.
68. Baillie, 95.
69. *Ibid.*, 87-108.
70. Immanuel Kant, *Fundamental Principles of the Metaphysics of Morals* (New York: Liberal Arts Press, 1949), 17.
71. Jonathan Edwards, "A Treatise Concerning Religious Affections," *The Works of Jonathan Edwards*, John E. Smith, ed. (New Haven: Yale University Press, 1959), 2:272.
72. H. Richard Niebuhr, *The Purpose of the Church and Its Ministry* (New York: Harper & Brothers, 1956), 27.
73. Paul Tillich, *The Dynamics of Faith* (New York: Harper & Brothers, 1957), 1.
74. *Ibid.*, 2-3.
75. *Ibid.*, 4-8.

76. John Wesley, "Catholic Spirit," II, 1, *Works*, 2:90.
77. John Wesley, "Scriptural Christianity," 5, *Works*, 1:161.
78. John Wesley, "On the Trinity," 4, *Works*, 2:377-378.
79. *Ibid.*, 14, *Works*, 2:383.
80. *Ibid.*, II, 6, *Works*, 2:40-41.
81. Several outstanding "Dewey Lectures" have been published recently that are keenly sensitive to both the futility and the great importance of philosophical thinking. I highly recommend Alistair MacIntyre, "On Not Knowing Where You Are Going," *Proceedings and Addresses of the American Philosophical Association,* (2012), 84:2, 61-74, and Marilyn McCord Adams, "God and Evil among the Philosophers," *Proceedings and Addresses of the American Philosophical Association,* (2011), 85:2, 65-80.
82. I developed this theme more completely with respect to issues in the philosophy of mind in Rem B. Edwards, "Know Thyself, Know Thy Psychology," *Journal of Formal Axiology: Theory and Practice*, (2008),1, 81-100.
83. John Wesley, "An Earnest Appeal to Men of Reason and Religion," 29, *Works*, 11:55.
84. Lee A. Kirkpatrick and Ralph W. Hood, Jr., "Intrinsic-Extrinsic Religious Orientation: The Boon or Bane of Contemporary Psychology of Religion?" *Journal for the Scientific Study of Religion*, (1990), 29,4: 456-457; W. Larry Ventis, "The Relationships Between Religion and Mental Health," *Journal of Social Issues*, (1995), 51,2: 42; Raymond F. Paloutzian and Lee A. Kirkpatrick, "Introduction: The Scope of Religious Influences on Personal and Societal Well-Being," *Journal of Social Issues* (1995), 51,2: 9.
85. Take a look at the many essays in Joseph A. Bracken and Marjorie H. Suchocki, eds., *Trinity in Process: A Relational Theology of God* (New York: Continuum Publishing Co., 1997). See also: John B. Cobb, Jr., *Christ in a Pluralistic Age* (Philadelphia: The Westminster Press, 1975), especially Part Two.
86. Baillie, 1954.
87. Søren Kierkegaard, *Philosophical Fragments* (Princeton: Princeton University Press, 1936), 44-58.
88. Pegis, 2:1063.

Chapter Three

1. William James, *The Varieties of Religious Experience* (New York: The Modern Library, 1902), 266-267.
2. *Ibid.*, 332-333. Read his chapter on "The Value of Saintliness" for details about the flaws of historical saints.
3. Evelyn Underhill, *Mysticism: The Nature and Development of Spiritual Consciousness.* (Oxford: Oneworld Publications, 2005), 246.
4. *Ibid.*, 320.
5. *Ibid.*, 321, 332 ff.
6. Jonathan Edwards, "A Treatise Concerning Religious Affections," *The Works of Jonathan Edwards*, John Smith, ed. (New Haven: Yale University Press, 1959), 2:185, 407-411.
7. James, 21.
8. Robert S. Hartman, *The Structure of Value* (Carbondale and Edwardsville: Southern Illinois University Press, 1967), 114. Republished in 2012 by Wipf & Stock Publishers, Eugene, OR.
9. *Ibid.*, 268.

10. Robert S. Hartman, "The Nature of Valuation," *Forms of Value and Valuation: Theory and Applications*, Rem B. Edwards and John W. Davis, eds. (Lanham, MD: University Press of America), 29.
11. Robert S. Hartman, *The Hartman Value Profile (HVP) Manual of Interpretation, Second Edition* (Knoxville, TN: The Robert S. Hartman Institute, 2006), 233.
12. David Mefford, "Self Knowledge and Self Development," *Forms of Value and Valuation: Theory and Applications*, Rem B. Edwards and John W. Davis, eds. (Lanham, MD: University Press of America, 1991), 337.
13. Richard Leggett, "Essay on Value and Individuality," unpublished paper, available in the Hartman archives at the Special Collections Library at The University of Tennessee, Knoxville, TN. Used with his permission.
14. Hartman, *The Structure of Value*, 8.
15. James, 372.
16. Ralph Waldo Emerson, "The American Scholar," *The Complete Works of Ralph Waldo Emerson*, Edward Waldo Emerson, ed. (Boston: Houghton Mifflin, Co., 1903), 1:82-83.
17. William James, *Essays in Pragmatism* (New York: Hafner Publishing Co., 1954), 7.
18. *Ibid.*, 279.
19. Ola Elizabeth Winslow, *Jonathan Edwards, 1703-1758* (New York: Collier Books, 1961), 218.
20. H. Richard Niebuhr, *Christ and Culture* (New York: Harper & Brothers, 1951), 72-73.
21. *Ibid.*, 105-106.
22. Stephen Prothero, *Religious Literacy: What Every American Needs to Know—and Doesn't* (New York: Harper One, 2007), 2.
23. Robert S. Hartman, *Freedom to Live: The Robert Hartman Story* (Amsterdam - Atlanta: Editions Rodopi, 1994), 33.
24. Emil L. Fackenheim, "Man and His World in the Perspective of Judaism," *New Theology No. 5*, Martin E. Marty and Dean G. Peerman, eds. (New York: The Macmillan Co., 1967), 50.
25. Robert S. Hartman, "Formal Axiology and Its Critics," *Formal Axiology and Its Critics*, Rem B. Edwards, ed. (Amsterdam - Atlanta: Editions Rodopi, 1995), 86.
26. Jonathan Edwards, "A Treatise Concerning Religious Affections," 106-108. See also: Jonathan Edwards, "Love the Sum of All Virtue," *The Works of Jonathan Edwards*, Paul Ramsey, ed. (New Haven: Yale University Press, 1989), 8:129-148.
27. Jonathan Edwards, "The Nature of True Virtue," *The Works of Jonathan Edwards*, Paul Ramsey, ed. (New Haven: Yale University Press, 1989), 8:545.
28. St. Augustine, "Homilies on the Gospel of John," *The Nicene and Post-Nicene Fathers*, Philip Schaff, ed. (New York: Charles Scribner's Sons, 1903), 7:155.
29. Abraham J. Heschel, *The Prophets* (New York: Harper & Row, 1992), 488.
30. Søren Kierkegaard, *Concluding Unscientific Postscript* (Princeton: Princeton University Press, 1941), 38.
31. Rudolf Bultman, "The Historicity of Man and Faith," *Existence & Faith: Shorter Writings of Rudolf Bultman*, Schubert M. Ogden, ed. (New York: Meridian Books, 1960), 305, n. 19.
32. See Robert S. Hartman's discussion of this parable in *Freedom to Live: The Robert Hartman Story*, 137-138.
33. Jonathan Edwards, "The Nature of True Virtue," 8:589.
34. *Ibid.*, 606.
35. *Ibid.*, 542, 543.

36. Hartman, "Intrinsic Value and Valuation," *Forms of Value and Valuation: Theory and Applications*, Rem B. Edwards and John W. Davis, eds. (Lanham, MD: University Press of America), 23.
37. Frederich Schleiermacher, *On Religion: Speeches to its Cultured Despisers* (New York, Frederich Ungar Pub. Co., 1955), 38.
38. *Ibid.*, 47.
39. Compare H. Richard Niebuhr's analysis of the concept of love in his *The Purpose of the Church and its Ministry* (New York: Harper & Brothers, 1956), 34-35.
40. Jonathan Edwards, "A Treatise Concerning Religious Affections," 95. Italics added.
41. *Ibid.*, 102.
42. *Ibid.*, 116, 117.
43. John Wesley, "Upon Our Lord's Sermon on the Mount, III," I, 11, *The Bicentennial Edition of the Works of John Wesley,* ed. Albert C. Outler. (Nashville: Abingdon Press, 1984), 1:516-517.
44. *Ibid.*, I, 6, *Works*, 1:513-514.
45. Harold S. Kushner, *To Life! A Celebration of Jewish Being and Thinking* (New York: Warner Books, 1993), 172.
46. *Ibid.*, 49.
47. H. Richard Niebuhr, *Radical Monotheism and Western Culture* (New York: Harper & Row, 1943), 52-53.
48. James W. Fowler, *Faith Development and Pastoral Care* (Philadelphia: Fortress Press, 1987), 28-30.
49. St. Augustine, *The Confessions of St. Augustine* (New York: Pocket Books, 1952), 297.
50. Tony Campolo and Mary Albert Darling, *The God of Intimacy and Action* (San Francisco: Jossey-Bass, 2007), 110.
51. Gail A. Eisnitz, *Slaughterhouse: The Shocking Story of Greed, Neglect, and Inhumane Treatment Inside the U.S. Meat Industry* (Amherst, NY: Prometheus Books, 1997).
52. For details about St. Francis' relations with non-human animals see: Leo Sherley-Price, *St. Francis of Assisi: His Life and Writings as Recorded by His Contemporaries* (New York: Harper & Brothers, 1959), 140-148.
53. Albert Schweitzer, *The Philosophy of Civilization* (New York: The Macmillan Co., 1960), 310-311.
54. Kierkegaard, 386.
55. Irwin Edman, ed., *The Philosophy of Schopenhauer* (New York: The Modern Library, 1928), 302-335.
56. "Emptiness" is here understood in the Indian Buddhist sense of pure negation, not in the Chinese Buddhist sense of finding the sacred within ordinary contingent existence. For more information on this distinction, see: Alan M. Olson and Leroy S. Rouner, eds., *Transcendence and the Sacred* (Notre Dame: University of Notre Dame Press, 1981, 122-123.
57. Søren Kierkegaard, *Fear and Trembling and The Sickness Unto Death*, (Princeton: Princeton University Press, 1941), 59.
58. Nikos Kazantzakis, *Zorba the Greek* (New York: Ballantine Books, 1953), 213.
59. William Blake, *Collected Works* (New York: Oxford University Press, 1927), 197.
60. Kierkegaard, *Fear and Trembling and The Sickness Unto Death*, 50-51.
61. Søren Kierkegaard, *Either/Or* (Princeton: Princeton University Press, 1971), 2:181-182.
62. *Ibid.*
63. Nikos Kazantzakis, *Saint Francis* (New York: Ballantine Books, 1962), 10.

64. S. Vernon McCasland, Grace E. Cairns, David Yu, *Religions of the World* (New York: Random House, 1969), 569. See also E. A. Burtt, ed., *The Teachings of the Compassionate Buddha* (New York: Mentor Books, 1955), 174.

65. Abraham Maslow, *The Psychology of Science* (Chicago: Henry Regnery Company, 1966), 52-54, 64.

66. Charles Darwin, *The Descent of Man, and Selection in Relation to Sex* (Princeton: Princeton University Press, 1981), 93.

67. St Thomas Aquinas, *Summa Theologica*, Second Part of the Second Part, Question 26, Article: 8.

68. Jonathan Edwards, "The Nature of True Virtue," 540.

69. John Wesley, "The Way to the Kingdom," I, 8. *Works*, 1:221-222.

70. See: Frans de Waal, *Good Natured: The Origins of Right and Wrong in Humans and Other Animals* (Cambridge: Harvard University Press, 1996); Michael Ruse, "The New Evolutionary Ethics," *Evolutionary Ethics*, eds., Nitecki, Matthew H., and Nitecki, Doris V. (Albany: State University of New York Press, 1993), especially 144-148; Neil O. Weiner, *The Harmony of the Soul* (Albany, NY: State University of New York Press, 1993), especially Ch. 5.

71. de Waal, 30.

72. Jonathan Edwards, "The Nature of True Virtue," 554-555.

73. *Ibid.*, 540. Italics added.

74. *Ibid.*, 620.

75. *Ibid.*, 555-556.

76. Hans Mohr, "The Biological Roots of Morality: Ethics in Evolutionary Perspective," *Universitas*, 35:2 (1993), 95.

77. *Ibid.*, 93.

78. Jane Goodall, *The Chimpanzees of Gombe: Patterns of Behavior* (Cambridge, Mass.: The Belknap Press of Harvard University Press, 1986); *Through A Window: My Thirty Years with the Chimpanzees of Gombe* (Boston: Houghton Mifflin, Co., 1990), especially 98-111.

79. Patricia A. Williams, "Christianity and Evolutionary Ethics: Sketch Toward a Reconciliation," *Zygon*, 31:2 (June 1996), 261.

80. Hartman, *The Structure of Value*, 357, n. 24.

81. *Ibid.*, 113-114.

82. Maslow, 65.

83. William James, *The Principles of Psychology*, (New York: Dover Publications, 1980), 1:291.

84. Hartman, *The Structure of Value*, 266.

85. Aaron Katcher and Gregory Wilkins, "Dialogue with Animals: Its Nature and Culture," *The Biophilia Hypothesis*, Stephen R. Kellert and Edward O. Wilson. eds. (Washington, DC: Island Press, 1993), 189.

86. G. W. F. Hegel, *Lectures on the Philosophy of Religion* (Berkeley: University of California Press, 1988), 148.

87. Bultman, "The Historicity of Man and Faith," 99.

88. Fowler, 37.

89. Robert S. Hartman, "The Logic of Value," *The Review of Metaphysics*, (March 1961), 14,3:417.

90. Hartman, *Freedom to Live: The Robert Hartman Story*, 134.

91. Hegel, 144-154.

92. Niebuhr, 235.

93. G. W. F. Hegel, *Hegel's Philosophy of Right* (Oxford: The Clarendon Press, 1942), 11.

94. Justus Buchler, *Philosophical Writings of Peirce* (New York: Dover Publications, 1955), 356.

95. Thomas Jefferson, "To Peter Carr," *The Writings of Thomas Jefferson*, Andrew A. Lipscomb and Albert E. Bergh, eds. (Washington, DC: The Thomas Jefferson Memorial Association, 1903), 6:258-261.

96. Hartman, "The Nature of Valuation," 34.

97. Quoted in Schubert M. Ogden, *Existence and Faith: Shorter Writings of Rudolf Bultman* (New York: Meridian Books, 1960), 14.

98. Hartman, *The Structure of Value*, 116.

99. Robert S. Hartman, "The Individual in Management," pp. 91, 92.

100. John Wesley, "Upon Our Lord's Sermon on the Mount, XXIV," *Forty-Four Sermons* (London: Epworth Press, 1944), p. 326. See also p. 515.

101. John Wesley, "A Farther Appeal to Men of Reason and Religion," Part I, I, 3, *The Bicentennial Edition of the Works of John Wesley*, ed. Gerald R. Cragg. (Nashville: Abingdon Press, 1989), 11:106.

102. John Wesley, "A Plain Account of Genuine Christianity," *John Wesley*, Albert C. Outler, ed. (New York: Oxford University Press, 1964), 184.

103. Lee A. Kirkpatrick, "An Attachment-Theory Approach to the Psychology of Religion," *The International Journal for the Psychology of Religion* 2:1 (1992), 12.

104. St. Anselm, *Basic Writings* (La Salle, IL: Open Court, 1962), 7.

105. John Hick, *Philosophy of Religion* (Englewood Cliffs, NJ: Prentice-Hall, 1963), 36.

106. For a spirited and well informed critique of attempts to find some defining property that would distinguish us absolutely from the other animals see: Carl Sagan and Ann Druyan, *Shadows of Forgotten Ancestors* (New York: Random House, 1992), 363-415.

107. Wesley, "The General Deliverance," I, 5, *Works* 2:441.

108. de Waal, especially Chs. 4, 5, and 6; Stephen R. L. Clark, *The Nature of the Beast: Are Animals Moral?* (New York: Oxford University Press, 1982); S. F. Sapontzis, *Morals, Reason, and Animals* (Philadelphia: Temple University Press, 1987), 43-44, 136, 217-218; Bruce N. Waller, *The Natural Selection of Autonomy* (Albany, NY: SUNY Press, 1998); Dorothy L. Cheney and Robert M. Seyfarth, *How Monkeys See the World* (Chicago: University of Chicago Press, 1990).

109. de Waal, especially Chs. 3 and 4. See also Frans de Waal, *Our Inner Ape*, (New York: Riverhead Books, 2005).

110. *Ibid.*, 84.

111. Jonathan Edwards, "The Nature of True Virtue," 621.

112. Jonathan Edwards, "Concerning the End for Which God Created the World," *The Works of Jonathan Edwards*, Paul Ramsey, ed. (New Haven: Yale University Press, 1989), 8:455.

113. James, 361.

114. John Wesley, "On Working Out Our Own Salvation," III, 7, *The Bicentennial Edition of the Works of John Wesley*, ed. Albert C. Outler. (Nashville: Abingdon Press, 1986), 3:208.

115. John Wesley, "The Scripture Way of Salvation," I, 1, *Works*, 2:156.

116. Charles Hartshorne, *Man's Vision of God and the Logic of Theism* (Hamden, CT: Archon Books, 1964), 144-155; Charles Hartshorne, *Creative Synthesis and Philosophic Method* (La Salle, Il.: Open Court Publishing Co., 1970), xix-xx, 190-204.

Chapter Four

1. Thomas À. Kempis, *The Imitation of Christ* (New York: Grosset & Dunlap, n.d.), 21.

2. John Wesley, "Upon Our Lord's Sermon on the Mount, I," I, 10, *The Bicentennial Edition of the Works of John Wesley*, ed. Albert C. Outler. (Nashville: Abingdon Press, 1984), 1:480.

3. John Wesley, "The Way to the Kingdom," II, 1, *Works*, 1:225.
4. Jonathan Edwards, "Freedom of the Will," *The Works of Jonathan Edwards*, Paul Ramsey, ed. (New Haven, Yale University Press, 1957), 1:133.
5. Robert S. Hartman, "The Nature of Valuation," *Forms of Value and Valuation: Theory and Applications*, eds. Rem B. Edwards and John W. Davis (Lanham, MD: University Press of America, 1991), 15, 16.
6. Robert S. Hartman, "The Individual in Management," (Unpublished manuscript, 1962), 20.
7. *Ibid.*, 37-38.
8. John Wesley, "The Witness of Our Own Spirit," 5, *Works*, 1:302.
9. William James, *The Varieties of Religious Experience* (New York: The Modern Library, 1902), 498-499.
10. John Wesley, "On the Danger of Increasing Riches," I, 1-8, *The Bicentennial Edition of the Works of John Wesley,* ed. Albert C. Outler. (Nashville: Abingdon Press, 1985), 2:268-273.
11. James, 193.
12. Jonathan Edwards, "A Treatise Concerning Religious Affections," *The Works of Jonathan Edwards*, John Smith, ed. (New Haven: Yale University Press, 1959), 2:391.
13. C. C. Goen, "Editor's Introduction," *The Works of Jonathan Edwards*, C. C. Goen, ed. (New Haven: Yale University Press, 1972), 4:25-32.
14. Kenneth P. Minkema, "Preface to the Period," *The Works of Jonathan Edwards,* Kenneth P. Minkema, ed. (New Haven, Yale University Press, 1997), 14:27-30.
15. Alexander H. Stephens, *A Constitutional View of the Late War Between the States* (Philadelphia: National Publishing Co., 1870), 2:83. Rem B. Edwards grew up in Crawfordville, GA, the home town of Alexander Stephens, who was the Vice President of the Confederacy and the author of this Bible-supports-slavery quote, but of course Edwards abhors slavery and racism. It is possible to outgrow your upbringing!
16. Frederick Douglass, "An Antislavery Tocsin: An Address Delivered in Rochester, New York, on 8 September 1850," in *The Frederick Douglass Papers, 1847–54,* John W. Blassingame, ed. (New Haven: Yale University Press, 1982), 2:267.
17. Ira Gershwin, *Porgy and Bess* (New York: Gershwin Pub. Co., 1935).
18. Kurt Kaltreider, *American Indian Prophecies: Conversations with Chasing Deer*, (Carlsbad, CA: Hay House, Inc., 1998), Ch. 4. See also: Benjamin Franklin, *The Works of Benjamin Franklin* (Boston: Hilliard Gray and Co., 1840), 4:62.
19. Harold S. Kushner, *To Life! A Celebration of Jewish Being and Thinking* (New York: Warner Books, 1993), 41. Copyright 1993 by Harold S. Kushner. First appeared in TO LIFE! by Harold S. Kushner. Originally published by Little, Brown & Company.
20. One possible exception is Rousas John Rushdoony, *The Institutes of Biblical Law*, (Dallas: Craig Press, 1973). Rushdoony's ideal Christian theocracy would execute adulterers, blasphemers, homosexuals, and astrologers.
21. A good case for this is made by Peter J. Gomes, *The Good Book: Reading the Bible with Mind and Heart* (New York: William Morrow and Co., 1996), Part Two.
22. William Beardsley, *First Corinthians: A Commentary for Today* (St. Louis: Chalice Press, 1994), 139-140.
23. As well discussed by Gomes, 80-82, 142-143, 216.
24. Kristen Moulton, "Baptists Told to Win Souls: Doctrine Requires Wives to Submit," *Knoxville News Sentinel* (June 10, 1998), A 1, A 7.
25. John Wesley, "On Charity," *The Bicentennial Edition of the Works of John Wesley,* ed. Albert C. Outler. (Nashville: Abingdon Press, 1986), 3:292.
26. Hartman, "The Nature of Valuation," 12.

27. See Leon Pomeroy and Richard Bishop, "Behavioral Axiology: Cross Cultural Study of Values," in *Forms of Value and Valuation: Theory and Applications*, Rem B. Edwards and John W. Davis, eds. (Lanham, MD: University Press of America, 1991), 315-327. The most recent definitive presentation of these findings are in Leon Pomeroy, *The New Science of Axiological Psychology* (Amsterdam - New York: Editions Rodopi, 2005, Chs. 16 and 17.

28. Jonathan Edwards, "A Spiritual Understanding," *The Works of Jonathan Edwards*, Kenneth P. Minkema, ed. (New Haven: Yale University Press, 1997), 14:81.

29. Kushner, 235.

30. Rem B. Edwards, "Universals, Individuals, and Intrinsic Good," *Forms of Value and Valuation: Theory and Applications*, Rem B. Edwards and John W. Davis, eds. (Lanham, Md., University Press of America, 1991), 81-104.

31. John Wesley, *A Plain Account of Christian Perfection* (London: Epworth Press, 1952), 19.

32. *Ibid.*, 11, 13.

33. *Ibid.*, 42.

34. John Calvin, *The Institutes of Christian Religion* (Grand Rapids: Baker Book House, 1993), 156.

35. Robert S. Hartman, *The Structure of Value: Foundations of Scientific Axiology* (Carbondale and Edwardsville: Southern Illinois University Press, 268. Republished in 2012 by Wipf & Stock Publishers, Eugene, OR.

36. James, 48.

37. Recent studies of forgiveness and reconciliation are available in *Dimensions of Forgiveness: Psychological Research and Theological Perspectives*, Everett Worthington, Jr., ed. (Philadelphia: Templeton Foundation Press, 1998) and in many other books and articles.

38. Jonathan Edwards, "A Treatise Concerning Religious Affections," 119.

39. John Hick, *God Has Many Names* (Philadelphia: The Westminster Press, 1982), 34.

40. *Ibid.*, 9 and Ch. 3.

41. Paul Tillich, *Christianity and the Encounter with the World Religions* (New York: Columbia University Press, 1963), 4.

42. Rem B. Edwards, *Reason and Religion* (Lanham, MD: University Press of America, 1979), 37-38.

161. See: Rem B. Edwards, David Mefford, and Vera Mefford, *Developing your Christian Values: The Christian Values Profile* (Lexington, KY: Emeth Press, 2012).

44. Wesley, "The Spirit of Bondage and of Adoption," IV, 1-4, *Works*, 1:263-265.

Appendix

1. A much more detailed presentation of this theory is in Rem B. Edwards, *The Essentials of Formal Axiology* (Lanham, MD: University Press of America, 2010).

2. Robert S. Hartman, *The Structure of Value* (Carbondale and Edwardsville: Southern Illinois University Press, 1967), 294. Republished in 2012 by Wipf & Stock Publishers, Eugene, OR.

3. See: Rem B. Edwards, David Mefford, and Vera Mefford, *Developing your Christian Values: The Christian Values Profile* (Lexington, KY: Emeth Press, 2012).

4. Hartman, *The Structure of Value*, 154.

5. Robert S. Hartman, *The Hartman Value Profile (HVP) Manual of Interpretation, Second Edition* (Knoxville, TN: Robert S. Hartman Institute, 2006), 28.

6. *Ibid.*, 113.

7. Robert S. Hartman, "The Nature of Valuation," *Forms of Value and Valuation: Theory and Applications*, Rem B. Edwards and John W. Davis, eds. (Lanham, MD: University Press of America, 1991), 26.
8. William James, *Essays in Pragmatism* (New York: Hafner Publishing Co., 1954), 7-8.
9. Hartman, "The Nature of Valuation," 14.
10. Hartman, *The Structure of Value*, 330, n. 29.
11. *Ibid.*, 112.
12. Hartman, "The Nature of Valuation," 25.
13. Hartman, *The Structure of Value*, 195.
14. Hartman, "The Nature of Valuation," 25-26.
15. For more on ethics and animals, listen to the two audio cassette tapes authored by Rem B. Edwards and read aloud first by Robert Guillaume and later by Cliff Robertson titled *Animals and Ethics* (Nashville, TN: Knowledge Products, 1995).
16. Hartman, *The Structure of Value*, 114.
17. *Ibid.*, 267.
18. Leon Pomeroy and Arthur R. Ellis, "Psychology and Value Theory," *Forms of Value and Valuation: Theory and Applications*, Rem B. Edwards and John W. Davis, eds. (Lanham, MD: University Press of America, 1991), 298, 315-318, 325, 326; Leon Pomeroy, *The New Science of Axiological Psychology* (Amsterdam - New York: Editions Rodopi, 2005).
19. Immanuel Kant, *Foundations of the Metaphysics of Morals* (Indianapolis: The Bobbs-Merrill Co., 1959), 53.
20. Alfred North Whitehead, *Adventures of Ideas* (New York: The Free Press, 1967), 198.
21. Alfred North Whitehead, *Modes of Thought* (New York: The Free Press, 1968), 114.
22. For an attempted but unsuccessful proof see: Robert S. Hartman, "Four Axiological Proofs of the Infinite Value of Man," *Kant-Studien*, (1964),55:194-198. For a critique see: Rem B. Edwards, "The Value of Man in the Hartman Value System," *The Journal of Value Inquiry*, (1973), 7:141-147 and Edwards, *The Essentials of Formal Axiology*, 67-82.
23. Non-reductive physicalism is explained, developed, and effectively related to morality and religion by the contributors to Warren S. Brown, Nancey Murphey, and H. Newton Maloney, eds., *Whatever Happened to the Soul? Scientific and Theological Portraits of Human Nature* (Minneapolis: Fortress Press, 1998).
24. For those interested in justifying the hierarchy of value, more philosophical arguments are given in Rem B. Edwards, "Universals, Individuals, and Intrinsic Goods," *Forms of Value and Valuation: Theory and Applications*, Rem B. Edwards and John W. Davis, eds. (Lanham, MD: University Press of America, 1991), 81-104. See also Thomas M. Dicken and Rem B. Edwards, *Dialogues on Values and Centers of Value*, (New York – Amsterdam: Editions Rodopi, 2001), 139-142, 171-179 and Edwards, *The Essentials of Formal Axiology*, 45-67.
25. Hartman, *The Structure of Value*, 129.
26. *Ibid.*, 113.
27. *Ibid.*, 194.
28. Hartman, "The Nature of Valuation," 27-28.
29. Hartman, *The Structure of Value*, 109.
30. *Ibid.*, 195-197.
31. *Ibid.*, 160, 209-212.
32. John W. Davis, "Extrinsic Value and Valuation," *Forms of Value and Valuation: Theory and Applications*, Rem B. Edwards and John W. Davis, eds. (Lanham, MD: University Press of America, 1991), 72.

33. Robert S. Hartman, "Reply to Robert W. Mueller, 1969," in Rem B. Edwards, ed., *Formal Axiology and Its Critics* (Amsterdam - Atlanta: Editions Rodopi, 1995), 87.
34. John A. Bargh and Tanya L. Chartrand, "The Unbearable Automaticity of Being," *American Psychologist*, July, 1999, 462-479.
35. Hartman, *The Structure of Value*, 268.
36. Hartman, "The Nature of Valuation," 18.
37. *Ibid.*, 20.
38. Hartman, *The Structure of Value*, 250-251.
39. Hartman, *The Hartman Value Profile (HVP) Manual of Interpretation, Second Edition*, 237.
40. William James, "The Sentiment of Rationality," *Essays in Pragmatism* (New York: Hafner Publishing Co., 1948), 3-36.
41. Søren Kierkegaard, *Concluding Scientific Postscript* (Princeton: Princeton University Press, 1941), 23-24, 53, 173, 282, 302, 358, 540.
42. Robert S. Hartman, "The Nature of Valuation," 33.
43. Robert S. Hartman, *The Structure of Value*, 260.
44. Frans de Waal, *Good Natured: The Origins of Right and Wrong in Humans and Other Animals* (Cambridge: Harvard University Press, 1996), 71-72.
45. Hartman, *The Structure of Value*, 293.
46. Hartman, *The Hartman Value Profile (HVP) Manual of Interpretation, Second Edition*, 234.
47. William James, *The Varieties of Religious Experience* (New York: The Modern Library, 1902), 10.
48. de Waal, 82.
49. Hartman, *The Structure of Value*, 113-114.
50. For Maslow's discussions of "peak experiences" see: Abraham Maslow, *Religions, Values, and Peak-Experiences* (Columbus, OH: Ohio State University Press, 1970; Abraham Maslow, *The Farther Reaches of Human Nature* (New York: The Viking Press, 1971), 168-179; 343-350.
51. Hartman, *The Structure of Value*, 223-224. This example is fleshed out in much more detail in Robert S. Hartman, *Freedom to Live: The Robert Hartman Story* (Amsterdam - Atlanta: Editions Rodopi, 1994), 85-86.
52. The outline of self-dimensions given here is adapted from Edwards, "Universals, Individuals, and Intrinsic Good," 89-91.
53. Kierkegaard, *Fear and Trembling and The Sickness Unto Death* (Princeton: Princeton University Press, 1954), 146.
54. Hartman, *Freedom to Live: The Robert Hartman Story*, 61.
55. de Waal, 116-218. See also: Warren S. Brown, "Cognitive Contributions to Soul," in *Whatever Happened to the Soul? Scientific and Theological Portraits of Human Nature*, eds. Warren S. Brown, Nancey Murphey, and H. Newton Malone (Minneapolis: Fortress Press, 1998), 120-123.
56. Brown, 99-125. For studies of religious experience, morality, and brains, see: Andrew Newberg, Eugene D'Aquili and Vince Rause, *Why God Won't Go Away: Brain Science and the Biology of Belief* (New York: Ballantine Books, 2001); Michael S. Gazzaniga, *The Ethical Brain* (New York: Dana Press, 2005, 160-161. Look especially his endnotes and Ch. 10. What these authors study depends on what they take to be the essence of religious experience and spiritual values, and they may not always get that right. So far, researchers have concentrated on a rather esoteric variety of mystical experience, but no one to my knowledge has measured what is going on in the brain when people lovingly identify themselves completely with All Inclusive Personal Reality (as opposed to emptiness), or when they are engaged in doing works of love and compassion, or when they are

contemplating or adoring "that Being than whom none richer in good-making properties can be conceived" and the reality to which this refers.

57. Robert S. Hartman, *The Structure of Value*, 309.
58. *Ibid.*, 307.
59. *Ibid.*, 308.
60. Robert S. Hartman, "The Individual in Management," (Unpublished manuscript, 1962), 31).
61. Hartman, *Freedom to Live: The Robert Hartman Story*, 111-112.
62. *Words of Women*—on line.
63. Robert S. Hartman, "The Individual in Management," 68.
64. Immanuel Kant, *Fundamental Principles of the Metaphysics of Morals* (New York: Liberal Arts Press, 1949), 19, n. 3.
65. Bernard Mayo, *Jefferson Himself* (Charlottesville: University Press of Virginia, 1942), 115.
66. Hartman, *The Structure of Value*, 67, 68.
67. Lee A. Kirkpatrick, "An Attachment-Theory Approach to the Psychology of Religion," *The International Journal for the Psychology of Religion*, (1992), 2,1:12.

INDEX

abundant living, 17, 23, 34, 73, 74, 149, 184, 209, 245-247, 256
Adam and Eve, 23, 32, 57, 160, 190
animals, 28, 29, 31, 40, 51, 56, 57, 84, 95, 96, 118, 119, 134-136, 147, 148, 151, 156, 163, 176-179, 182, 183, 191, 197, 199, 203, 204, 207, 210, 220, 223, 226, 242, 245, 283
Anselm, St., 14, 65, 96-98, 174
Aquinas, St. Thomas, 14, 56, 65, 95-98, 100, 106, 107, 113, 121, 155, 157, 161, 169
Aristotle, 14, 26, 37, 97, 169, 240
Armstrong, Karen, 55
attachment, 14, 23, 36, 136, 143, 149, 173, 177, 244, 256, 257
Attachment-Theory, 173, 257
Augustine, St., 14, 20, 38, 39, 65, 70, 96, 97, 107, 136, 138, 146, 151, 180
axiological, 13, 22, 28, 34, 35, 37, 38, 43, 45, 71, 76, 79, 84, 85, 89, 108, 126, 127, 133, 134, 143, 147, 156, 162, 175, 178, 190, 191, 203, 204, 216, 217, 220, 225, 228, 230, 235, 239, 284
axiology, 8, 11, 12, 15, 32, 69, 78, 83, 88, 116, 117, 134, 143, 149, 161, 200, 202, 203, 209, 212, 214, 217-219, 225, 230, 232, 234, 235, 242, 249, 283, 284

Baillie, John, 106, 112, 120
Bankhead, Tallulah, 253
Barth, Karl, 172
behaviorism, 42, 45, 140
beliefs, 8, 12, 13, 18, 19, 24, 40, 43, 59, 60, 62, 65, 72, 75-78, 80-84, 90, 91, 93, 95, 100, 102, 105, 107-112, 114-116, 119-122, 133, 142, 144, 149, 151-153, 162, 171, 173, 179, 181, 182, 188, 190, 191, 193, 204, 205, 207, 211, 212, 221, 225, 226, 228, 231, 235, 237, 238, 245, 247, 249, 251
Blake, William, 150, 179
Bohr, Niels, 48
Bonaventure, St., 12, 44
Brainerd, David, 129
Brother Lawrence, 112
Brown, Warren S., 248, 265, 273-274
Buber, Martin, 145
Buddhism, 108, 116, 154, 212
bullying, 31, 42, 160, 203
Bultman, Rudolf, 138, 166, 169, 172
Bush, George H. W., 89
Buss, David M., 28-30, 32, 36, 39, 44

Calvin, John, 68, 209
Campolo, Tony, 105, 147
Civil War, 59, 87-90, 199
combinations, 60, 151, 152, 214, 227, 236, 237
compassion, 13, 18, 24, 26, 32, 33, 69, 73, 74, 91, 94, 96-99, 113, 114, 116, 118, 132, 134, 135, 142, 144, 147, 149, 154, 156, 157, 160, 161, 172, 174-176, 182-184, 191, 200, 201, 206-211, 245, 248, 251
compositions, 151, 227, 236
conscience, 8, 38, 43, 45, 47, 85, 88, 156, 157, 183, 185-191, 193-195, 200-204, 210, 228, 230, 239, 245, 248, 251, 254, 257
conversion, 8, 57, 74, 177, 192-195, 205-207, 209-212, 256
creation care, 57, 147, 182

Index 277

dark side, 8, 25, 32, 35, 59, 159-161, 185, 186, 189, 193-196, 204, 205, 210, 246, 252
Darwin, Charles, 41, 155-157, 160, 176
de Waal, Franz, 29, 32, 156, 157, 160, 176, 242, 243, 248
Derrida, Jacques, 170
Dewey, John, 24, 170
disinterestedness, 53, 84, 85, 97, 106, 118, 239, 240
dominance, 25-32, 34, 35, 38, 47, 53, 56, 57, 81, 113, 136, 138, 147, 159, 206, 215, 248
dominate, 21, 29, 56, 72, 81, 123, 160
dominion, 56
Dostoyevsky, Fyodor, 94
Douglass, Frederick, 196

Edwards, Jonathan, 3, 14, 15, 20-22, 45, 53, 57, 61, 63-66, 72, 82, 83, 88, 113, 114, 116, 124-126, 129, 134, 135, 141-144, 155, 157, 158, 160, 161, 177, 178, 181, 185, 186, 192, 193, 195, 196, 203, 205, 207, 210, 212, 213, 217-219, 223, 225, 230, 235, 247, 256, 283, 284
Edwards, Rem B., 15, 255, 261-268, 271-274, 283-284
Eisnitz, Gail A., 148
Emerson, Ralph Waldo, 35, 37, 40, 48, 61, 128
equal worth, 138, 139, 192
equality, 31, 32, 34, 57, 90, 139-141
equals, 30, 141, 182, 204
evolution, 14, 23, 25, 26, 28-32, 35-39, 44, 64, 96, 147, 156-160, 171, 187, 189, 190, 220, 225, 231, 235, 256
evolutionary psychology, 14, 29, 31, 35, 37, 38, 171, 189
extrinsic evaluation, 9, 18, 34, 56, 149, 220, 231-236, 243, 245, 248, 250

extrinsic faith, 8, 108
extrinsic values, 8, 13, 18, 19, 22-24, 43, 67, 71, 76, 109, 123, 130, 152, 153, 171, 182, 206, 219, 220, 223, 225, 228

figurative, 49, 64, 166, 167
Fowler, James W., 12, 146, 166
Francis, St. 54, 78, 134, 135, 147, 148, 154, 165, 192
Franklin, Benjamin, 199, 254
Freud, Sigmund, 174
fundamentalis(m)(ists), 61-62, 64-66, 70, 83, 101, 102, 107, 166, 197

Gandhi, Mahatma, 131, 135
genes, 28, 31, 32, 35, 80, 159, 231
Gershwin, Ira, 197
godlikeness, 69, 71, 99
godliness, 53, 55, 146
Goen, C. C., 53, 193
Gomes, Peter, 95, 201, 202
good religion, 99, 118, 119, 149
good works, 109, 125, 134, 142, 144, 180
Grant, Gen. Ulysses S., 88
graven images, 68, 70, 194

Hartman, Robert S., 12, 15, 20, 45, 68, 71, 76-79, 81-88, 91, 93, 100, 118, 125-127, 131, 134, 139, 141, 142, 154, 161, 163, 166, 172, 186, 187, 203, 209, 213, 217-222, 224, 225, 230-233, 235-239, 241, 242, 244, 246, 247, 249, 250, 252, 253, 255
Hartshorne, Charles, 169, 182, 283
Heidegger, Martin, 38, 48, 51, 169, 170
Heschel, Rabbi Abraham J., 14, 54, 98, 136, 138
Hick, John, 174, 175, 211, 212

hierarchy of value, 8, 19, 37, 76, 87, 99, 119, 125-127, 151, 191, 203, 204, 215, 224-226, 230
high status, 25, 28-30, 36, 49, 67, 80
Hitler, Adolf, 94, 131
holistic saints, 13, 19, 51, 60, 80, 109, 115, 129-131, 133, 135, 139, 141, 144, 150, 151, 153, 161, 165, 173, 180-184, 215, 249
human nature, 14, 25, 26, 29, 32, 34, 35, 98, 99, 102, 147, 158, 160, 161, 187-189, 225, 230, 245, 248, 254
hunter/gatherer, 14, 25-27, 31, 32, 157, 158, 160, 177, 232, 256
Huxley, Aldous, 34, 40

iconoclastic controversy, 68
iconodules, 68
identification, 35, 36, 46, 52, 69, 74, 104, 112, 113, 116, 118, 133-135, 142, 143, 161-164, 172, 175, 182, 184, 190, 239, 242, 244-246, 251, 252, 258
identification spirituality, 133, 182
identify with, 29, 36, 41, 47, 74, 84, 121, 122, 133, 134, 146, 163, 182, 186, 188, 224
ideological, 7, 50, 66, 71, 74-87, 91, 93-96, 99, 100, 103, 104, 107, 123, 130, 141, 150, 179, 206, 238, 239, 242, 257
ideological evaluation, 7, 81, 82, 84, 238
ideological religion, 7, 75, 95, 96
ideological values, 7, 77, 79
ideology, 7, 11, 13, 35, 73, 75, 76, 82, 84-87, 91, 92, 94, 148, 149, 156, 181, 194, 211, 238, 248
image of God, 7, 8, 44, 68, 69, 71, 96, 98, 111, 141, 172-177, 184, 196
impassible, 96, 98
inerrancy, 64-66, 78, 101, 238, 247

infallibility, 78, 82, 101, 102, 198
inferiors, 24, 27, 31, 54, 59, 141, 158
intrinsic evaluation, 8, 9, 14, 18, 34, 35, 37, 74, 82, 85, 104, 111, 114, 124, 127, 128, 134, 135, 142-144, 146, 148-153, 156-158, 161-165, 171, 177, 178, 182-184, 207, 209, 211, 213, 223, 236, 242-246, 248, 251, 252, 255, 256
intrinsic faith, 8, 105, 111-117, 137
intrinsic saints, 13, 19, 110, 129-131, 165, 257
intrinsic value, 24, 86, 88, 91, 95, 109, 118, 124-126, 134, 151, 152, 161, 166, 186, 209, 214, 222-225, 243-247, 250, 256
intrinsic values, 8, 13, 18, 19, 22-24, 58, 60, 69, 71, 73, 76, 77, 79, 86, 89, 92, 93, 122-124, 126, 128, 131, 133, 135, 151, 153, 154, 165, 182, 191, 206, 210, 215, 222, 223, 228, 235, 243, 247, 256
Irenaeus, St., 181, 190
Islam, 67, 69, 194

James, William, 14, 123, 124, 128, 129, 132, 162, 163, 179, 188, 192, 193, 210, 220, 240, 241, 243
Jefferson, Thomas, 168, 254
Jesus, 20, 26, 54, 55, 58, 62-64, 69, 96, 98, 100, 103-106, 108, 111, 114, 119-122, 128, 130-132, 135, 139, 146, 151, 168, 171, 174, 175, 177, 194, 197-202, 213, 252, 253
Judaism, 59, 67, 69, 98, 103, 133, 145, 193, 194, 205, 213

Kagawa, Toyohiko, 135
Kierkegaard, Søren, 12, 14, 20, 21, 23-25, 38, 39, 44, 46, 48, 49, 71, 112, 121, 137, 148-150, 153, 215, 239, 240, 247, 252

Kirkpatrick, Lee A., 60, 117, 173, 257
Kushner, Rabbi Harold S., 14, 111, 145, 199, 205

least of these, 56, 58
liberal arts, 34, 44, 51, 52, 113, 253
limitations, 9, 48, 51, 120, 213, 214, 253, 255
Lincoln, Abraham, 89, 90, 195, 200
literal, 48, 62-67, 70, 97, 101, 121, 160, 163, 164, 168, 177, 190, 197, 200, 204
literalistic, 34, 51, 52, 61, 64, 66, 68, 165, 168
Logical Positivism, 170
Logical Positivists, 62, 63
love, 11-13, 18, 19, 21-24, 26, 27, 30, 32, 33, 35-37, 39-42, 44-46, 54, 55, 59, 69, 71-74, 77, 80, 84, 94-96, 98, 99, 102-107, 109-119, 121, 122, 129, 131-135, 137-144, 146, 149, 151, 155-161, 163, 171-183, 186, 190, 191, 195, 198-202, 205-209, 211, 212, 214, 215, 223, 226, 243, 245-248, 251-254, 256, 257
low status, 28, 30, 31
Loyola, St. Ignatius, 12
Luther, Martin, 68, 135, 146

Maimonides, Moses, 98
Marcel, Gabriel, 43, 71
Mark, Max, 75, 264
Marx, Karl, 75
Maslow, Abraham, 29, 57, 154, 161, 245
materialistic, 24, 38, 42, 43, 48, 223
May, Rollo, 45, 262
metaphor(s), 8, 32, 48, 51, 62, 63, 65, 97, 102, 105, 119, 121, 154, 161-167, 169-171, 177, 182, 222
Michalson, Carl, 62
militarism, 83, 86

military, 31, 83, 86, 87
Minkema, Kenneth P., 21, 61, 72, 195, 205
Mohr, Hans, 158-160
morality, 11, 26, 33, 41, 94, 117, 147, 159, 160, 162, 176, 184, 188, 191, 192, 230, 245, 248, 250, 253, 254
Moslems, 50, 146, 197, 199, 213
Mother Teresa, 135
mystical, 67, 69, 128, 132, 133, 143, 144, 168, 245, 248
mystics, 22, 128, 132, 133, 146, 161, 166, 179, 244
myth(s), 28, 33, 48, 51, 62, 63, 97, 102, 147, 163, 165-167, 169, 171, 181

Napoleon, 75, 81
Nazis, 100, 131, 158, 242, 245, 256
new birth, 8, 106, 111, 204, 205, 208
Nietzsche, Friederich, 29
nirvana, 132, 154

objective, 38, 84, 87, 95, 118, 160, 183, 205, 234, 239, 240
objectivity, 84, 85, 240, 241
ordinary language, 22, 37, 46, 48-51, 62, 63, 127, 165, 168, 222
original sin, 69, 71, 138, 159, 160, 180, 189, 190
Osteen, Joel, 108
other worlds, 7, 66, 67
overvalue, 13, 19, 20, 76, 78, 182

Parker, DeWitt H., 52
patripassionism, 113
Patton, Gen. George, 81
Paul, St., 50, 57, 69, 71, 103, 105, 128, 134, 137, 172, 188, 191, 199, 201, 202, 205, 211, 255
Peirce, Charles S., 167
Persian Gulf War, 87-89

personality, 8, 11-14, 19, 45, 94, 114, 153, 211, 214, 215, 218, 247, 255
personality types, 8, 11, 13, 19, 45, 214
Philistines, 52
philosophical, 12, 20, 42, 43, 45, 46, 48, 49, 62, 63, 65, 78, 83, 92, 95, 97, 107, 116, 121, 154, 158, 159, 166-171, 181, 187, 196, 197, 212, 214, 220, 221, 225, 230, 239, 240, 245, 247, 249, 255, 284
philosophy, 13-15, 34, 37, 43, 48, 49, 68, 75, 78, 81, 102, 107, 112, 114, 116, 117, 139, 148, 149, 166-172, 175, 181, 237, 283, 284
Plato, 17, 20, 37, 48, 80, 97, 189, 221, 226, 233
poetry, 48, 51, 52, 63, 163, 165, 171
positivism, 42, 67, 116, 140, 170
Pratto, Felicia, 30, 32
prejudice, 50, 60, 82, 84, 238, 245
Principle of Verification, 48
Process Theology, 178
prosaic, 22, 46, 49, 51, 52, 66, 156, 163-165, 170, 182, 236
prose, 34, 37, 48, 49, 51, 52, 61, 62, 154, 164, 165
prosperity, 7, 11, 13, 22, 24, 37, 41, 48, 54, 55, 57-59, 66, 67, 71, 73, 80, 105, 109-111, 138, 141, 143, 194, 199, 206, 208
prosperity gospel, 54, 55, 110, 111
psychological, 22, 23, 25, 28, 34, 37, 43, 45, 62, 63, 69, 75, 107, 133, 143, 160, 171, 174, 175, 178, 181, 182, 186, 187, 205, 206, 210, 222, 230, 248, 251, 258
psychology, 13, 14, 29-31, 35, 37, 38, 60, 79, 107, 114, 116, 117, 154, 156, 162, 163, 171, 173, 178, 189, 192, 203, 225, 257, 284
psychology of religion, 13, 14, 60, 117, 173, 257

racism, 83, 160, 196, 201, 202
rank, 23, 25, 29, 34, 35, 57, 95, 111, 181, 202, 231, 250
ranking, 12, 25, 30, 210, 225, 228
rational(ity), 27, 39, 43, 47, 51, 56, 69, 84, 85, 97, 99, 106, 107, 111, 113, 118, 149, 150, 162, 168, 169, 173, 175-178, 181, 182, 184, 190, 191, 195, 218, 219, 225, 230, 234, 240, 241, 253, 254, 256, 258, 283
Rawls, John, 156
reason, 21, 26, 34, 44, 56, 61, 64, 88-90, 96-99, 104, 107, 111-113, 116, 117, 120, 128, 131, 132, 141, 149, 165, 168, 172, 173, 176, 178, 180, 181, 184, 201, 212, 215, 239, 240, 283
reciprocal altruism, 25, 206
religious language, 7, 61, 166, 168-171
renunciation, 148-150, 152
reproduction, 14, 23, 25, 28, 38, 54, 190
revenge, 21, 23, 25-27, 31-35, 46, 54, 59, 109, 110, 141, 159, 187, 202, 206
rituals, 8, 76, 95, 96, 103-105, 107, 115, 119, 130, 135, 151, 171, 249
rules, 8, 13, 18, 62, 64, 76, 93, 95, 96, 103-105, 119, 151, 176, 188, 191, 194-204, 207, 208, 212, 221, 225, 228, 237, 241, 249, 252

sacraments, 58, 171
salvation, 8, 55, 73, 100, 103, 106, 107, 110, 111, 114, 116, 142, 172, 180, 184, 193, 195, 208, 209, 211, 247
sanctification, 8, 137, 145, 180, 182, 193, 195, 204-209, 211
Schleiermacher, Friedrich, 142
Schopenhauer, Arthur 149

Schweitzer, Albert, 37, 134, 135, 148, 149
science, 20, 24, 31, 34, 41, 48, 49, 78, 79, 88, 93, 107, 114, 154, 192, 203, 217, 225, 234, 237, 248, 249, 284
scope, 8, 23, 33, 73, 74, 117, 155-159, 161, 171, 173-175, 177, 184, 206, 207, 226, 255
self knowledge, 258
self-development, 17, 38, 126, 134, 136, 181, 251, 252
self-knowledge, 7, 8, 11, 12, 17, 18, 37, 44, 46, 47, 79, 121, 136-138, 162, 163, 169, 174, 185-187, 189, 193-196, 204, 208, 209, 211, 217, 224, 231, 244, 247, 248, 252, 255, 258
self-realization, 8, 39, 125, 126, 149, 223, 224, 243
sex, 23-26, 28-31, 36, 44, 54, 67, 155, 199, 203, 238
sexual, 14, 23-30, 32, 34-37, 42, 54, 55, 58, 68, 80, 179, 194, 197
sexual fidelity, 35, 36, 42
slavery, 56, 59, 83, 88-90, 160, 196, 199, 201, 202, 204
slaves, 50, 51, 57, 89, 90, 197, 199, 202, 204
social animals, 156, 176
Social Darwinism, 32
social dominance, 25-30, 32, 136
social roles, 30, 40, 41, 45, 46, 49, 93, 118, 136, 137, 153, 162, 177, 188, 191, 247, 249, 250
social status, 7, 13, 23, 28, 29, 34, 40, 47, 49, 55, 58, 152, 190, 206, 207, 210, 250
sociobiology, 14, 73, 138, 156, 207
Socrates, 17, 20, 71, 94, 107, 188, 252
Spinoza, Baruch, 95, 97
spiritual strengths, 7, 13, 71, 255
spiritual weaknesses, 125

Stalin, Joseph, 131
Stephens, Alexander H., 90, 94, 196
Stoics, 71, 97, 99, 149
strengths, 7, 13, 19, 20, 71, 117, 134, 189, 194, 207, 255, 256
success, 11, 13, 22, 23, 26, 28, 29, 42, 54, 55, 58, 66, 109, 110, 140, 141, 166, 189, 191, 193, 194, 206, 208, 211, 256
systemic evaluation, 9, 19, 81-85, 100, 118, 128, 236-241, 243, 244, 249
systemic faith, 8, 73, 102, 106, 107, 112, 113, 115, 116, 142
systemic values, 8, 13, 18-20, 40, 69, 76-78, 82, 83, 91, 109, 119, 122-124, 171, 173, 182, 206, 221,223, 228, 237, 239, 242, 247

Tauler, Johann, 146
Ten Commandments, 42, 194, 227
Thoreau, Henry David, 21, 24, 46
Tillich, Paul, 114, 212, 256
transpositions, 151, 236
Tutu, Desmond, 135

Underhill, Evelyn, 124, 125
undervalue, 19, 20, 78, 82, 84, 129, 182
uniforms, 88, 242
unique, 13, 26, 44, 47, 49, 50, 68, 73, 79, 86, 88, 90, 93, 117, 118, 120, 127, 134-137, 139, 140, 142, 143, 145, 146, 161, 162, 165, 178, 183, 188, 204, 207, 212, 214, 215, 222-225, 229, 242, 243, 245, 247, 248, 251, 253-255
uniqueness, 9, 18, 22, 50, 52, 133, 139, 142, 146, 161, 165, 188, 191, 214, 215, 222, 223, 235, 243, 244, 250, 253, 254

Ventis, Larry, 60, 117

war, 33, 59, 76, 80, 85-90, 159, 160, 179, 196, 197, 199, 228, 253
Warren, Robert Penn, 48, 263
weaknesses, 7, 13, 19, 71, 72, 125, 134, 186, 189, 255
Wesley, John, 14, 20, 21, 53, 70, 103, 104, 111, 112, 115, 117, 145, 147, 155, 161, 168, 172-174, 176, 177, 180, 185-187, 191-193, 202, 208, 214
Whitehead, Alfred North, 48, 51, 93, 98, 169, 229
Williams, Patricia A., 159, 160
Wittgenstein, Ludwig, 51, 63, 170
works of love, 12, 73, 106, 109, 134, 141, 142, 183, 205, 248
worldliness, 7, 11, 13, 14, 17, 19-21, 23, 25, 31, 33, 35, 37-42, 48-50, 52, 58, 59, 61, 66, 67, 71, 73, 77, 84, 86, 123, 130, 131, 138, 140, 148, 149, 156, 180, 181, 206, 211, 248, 257
worldlings, 7, 20, 22-25, 27, 31, 33, 34, 37-40, 42-53, 55, 57-59, 61-63, 67, 69-73, 76, 80, 83, 86, 91, 93, 94, 107, 109-111, 136, 138-141, 144, 147, 150-154, 165, 166, 175, 179, 182, 184, 189, 203, 207, 215, 248, 257
worldly language, 34, 49, 66
worldly religion, 7, 17, 53-61, 66, 67, 69, 72, 74, 108, 111, 177
worldly values, 7, 20, 35, 37, 40, 42, 43, 53, 54, 147, 150, 152, 206, 219, 257

Xenophanes, 68

About the Author

REM B. EDWARDS, Ph.D., grew up in the small town of Crawfordville, GA. He attended Emory at Oxford, then graduated as a Philosophy major from Emory University with an A.B. degree in 1956. There he was elected to Phi Beta Kappa. Throughout graduate school, he was a Danforth Graduate Fellow. He received a B.D. degree from Yale University Divinity School (YDS) in 1959 and a Ph.D. in Philosophy from Emory University in 1962, where he studied under Charles Hartshorne. While at YDS, during the summer of 1958 he was the minister at the Old Brick Church Congregational in Clarendon, VT. After finishing YDS, he served for a year as the minister of Dixie Methodist Church in La Grange, GA. After completing his Ph.D. at Emory, he taught for four years at Jacksonville University in Florida, moved from there to the University of Tennessee in 1966, and retired from there partly in 1997 and partly in 1998. He kept an office on the University campus until the end of May, 2000. He was a U. T. Chancellor's Research Scholar in 1985 and a distinguished Lindsay Young Professor between 1987–1998. He continues to be professionally active.

His areas of specialization are Philosophy of Religion, American Philosophy, Medical Ethics, and Ethical Theory, with a special focus on Mental Health Care Ethics, Ethics and Animals, and Formal Axiology.

He has published twenty other books, including *Reason and Religion* (New York: Harcourt, 1972 and Lanham, MD: University Press of America, 1979); *Pleasures and Pains: A Theory of Qualitative Hedonism* (Ithaca: Cornell University Press, 1979); with Glenn Graber, *BioEthics* (San Diego: Harcourt, 1988); with John W. Davis, *Forms of Value and Valuation: Theory and Applications* (Lanham, MD: University Press of America, 1991); *Formal Axiology and Its Critics* (Amsterdam – Atlanta: Rodopi, 1995); *Violence, Neglect, and the Elderly*, co-edited with Roy Cebik, Glenn Graber, and Frank H. Marsh (Greenwich, CT: JAI Press, 1996); *New Essays on Abortion and Bioethics*, (Greenwich, CT: JAI Press, 1997); *Ethics of Psychiatry: Insanity, Rational Autonomy, and Mental Health Care*, (Buffalo, NY: Prometheus Books, 1997); *Values, Ethics, and Alcoholism*, co-edited with Wayne

Shelton, (Greenwich, CT: JAI Press, 1997); *Bioethics for Medical Education*, co-edited with Dr. Edward Bittar, (Stamford, CT: JAI Press, 1999); *Dialogues on Values and Centers of Value* (Amsterdam – New York: Rodopi, 2001), co-authored with Thomas M. Dicken; and *What Caused the Big Bang?* (Amsterdam – New York: Rodopi, 2001). *What Caused the Big Bang* received the "Best Book of 2001" award from the Editors of the Value Inquiry Book Series. His *The Essentials of Formal Axiology* was published in 2010 by the University Press of America. In 2012, Emeth Press is also publishing his *John Wesley's Values—And Ours,* and his *Developing Your Christian Values: The Christian Values Profile*, co-authored with David Mefford and Vera Mefford. Edwards has also authored over eighty five articles and reviews.

He is an Associate Editor with the Value Inquiry Book Series, published by Rodopi, where he is responsible for the Hartman Institute Axiological Studies special series. For a number of years he was co-editor of the Advances in Bioethics book series published by JAI Press. He also did significant editorial work on the following books published in Rodopi's Hartman Institute Axiological Studies: Frank G. Forrest, *Valuemetrics: The Science of Personal and Professional Ethics*, 1994; Robert S. Hartman, *Freedom to Live: The Robert Hartman Story*, 1994; Armando Molina, *Our Ways: Values and Character*, 1997; Gary Acquaviva, *Violence, Values, and Our Future*, 2000; Robert S. Hartman, *The Knowledge of Good*, 2002, co-edited with Arthur Ellis; Leon Pomeroy, *The New Science of Axiological Psychology*, 2005; Gary Gallopin, *Beyond Perestroika: Axiology and the New Russian Entrepreneurs*, 2009. In 2008, Edwards became the senior editor of the new *Journal of Formal Axiology: Theory and Practice.*

Edwards has been the President of the Tennessee Philosophical Association (1973–74), the Society for Philosophy of Religion (1981–82), and the Southern Society for Philosophy and Psychology, (1984–85). He is a Charter Member and Fellow of the Robert S. Hartman Institute for Formal and Applied Axiology and has served on its Board of Directors since 1987. In 1989 he became its Secretary/ Treasurer; after October of 2007, he continued as its Secretary until October, 2009 and is now the Contact Secretary. He is a Webmaster for the website of the Robert S. Hartman Institute at: http://www.hartmaninstitute.org. He is a lifelong Methodist.

www.ingramcontent.com/pod-product-compliance
Lightning Source LLC
Chambersburg PA
CBHW021835220426
43663CB00005B/265